Colonial American Newspapers

Colonial American Newspapers

Character and Content

David A. Copeland

DELAWARE

Newark: University of Delaware Press
London: Associated University Presses

Associated University Presses
440 Forsgate Drive
Cranbury, NJ 08512

Associated University Presses
16 Barter Street
London WC1A 2AH, England

Associated University Presses
P.O. Box 338, Port Credit
Mississauga, Ontario
Canada L5G 4L8

The paper used in this publication meets the requirements
of the American National Standard for Permanence of Paper
for Printed Library Materials Z39.48–1984.

Library of Congress Cataloging-in-Publication Data

Copeland, David A., 1951–
    Colonial American newspapers : character and content / David A.
Copeland.
      p. cm.
    Includes bibliographical references and index.
    ISBN 0-87413-591-5 (alk. paper)
    1. American newspapers—History—18th century. I. Title.
PN4861.C74   1997   96-17172
071'.3'09033—dc20   CIP

PRINTED IN THE UNITED STATES OF AMERICA

Contents

Acknowledgements

A number of people helped to make this research possible. Dr. Gary D. Gaddy of the Institute for Research in Social Science at the University of North Carolina at Chapel Hill suggested a method of researching the large number of issues of colonial newspapers that provided accurate and complete coverage of the newspapers of the period while at the same time keeping the total number of issues to be read at a manageable number.

Professors John Nelson and John Semonche of the UNC department of history suggested readings in a number of areas of American colonial history that helped in understanding and interpreting the body of information discovered in this research. Professors Cathy Packer and Ruth Walden of the UNC School of Journalism and Mass Communication read the manuscript and offered advice on how to maintain focus on such an expansive topic. Professor Margaret A. Blanchard of the UNC School of Journalism and Mass Communication helped shape this project through her insight into research and encouragement for this project. She read chapters, corrected mistakes, and suggested ways to improve the presentation of material. Without her untiring support, it is doubtful this project would have been undertaken or completed.

I wish to thank *American Journalism* and *American Periodicals* for permission to incorporate portions of articles that appeared in their pages in this book. I especially thank Professor Wallace Eberhard of the University of Georgia for his positive encouragement for my study of the colonial press. I am also indebted to those individuals who for the last two centuries have preserved the record of our colonial past as found in America's newspapers.

Finally, I thank my family—Robin, Holly, and Hunter—for putting up with my endless hours of reading newspapers and writing about them and for always asking at the supper table, "Tell us what you read about today." Their support made all the difference and to them this book is dedicated.

Colonial American
Newspapers

Introduction

Containing the freshest Advices, both Foreign and Domestic;
with a Variety of other Matter; useful and entertaining.
—Nameplate, *Pennsylvania Chronicle*

BENJAMIN Franklin, talking to his acquaintance and fellow printer George Webb in 1728, disclosed that he was certain "a good paper would scarcely fail" in Philadelphia. The city already had one newspaper, but Franklin told Webb that he planned to begin printing the city's second in the near future. Within a year, Franklin had his newspaper, and the *Pennsylvania Gazette* started a run that continued, with only a brief respite in 1777, into the nineteenth century.[1]

But what constituted "a good paper" in the eighteenth century? There was no standard by which to judge a newspaper's quality. Near the end of the century, a London printer stated that all newspapers "ought to be the Register of the times, and faithful recorder of every species of intelligence."[2] But English newspapers were in their infancy at the beginning of the century, even though the first had been printed in 1620.[3] America's first effort at a newspaper, *Publick Occurrences*, was suppressed after one printing in 1690, and only one paper, the *Boston News-Letter*, existed from the first decade of the 1700s to the last month of 1719. The idea of what constituted a good newspaper, therefore, was taking shape in America as newspapers themselves were coming into existence. Printers, as they developed a concept of what comprised a good paper, placed that notion in the nameplate. Most of the newspapers that began printing in the colonial period after the first few efforts believed a good newspaper should provide for its readers "the freshest Advices Foreign and Domestic."

"The freshest Advices Foreign and Domestic," however, was a nebulous phrase. It could be taken to represent the blandest of news, like that William Brooker proposed to print in the initial issue of the *Boston Gazette* in December 1719. Brooker promised

11

to deliver "an Account of the Prices of Merchandize," "how they govern at this Place," "the nature of a Price Currant," news "from the Publick Prints," and "Occurrences of the adjacent provinces."[4] Or, it could be much more, as William Goddard had realized fifty years later. Goddard, in the nameplate of the *Pennsylvania Chronicle,* vowed to give his readers a variety of news that was "useful, instructive and entertaining" in addition to "the freshest Advices, both Foreign and Domestic."[5] Perhaps understanding what constituted a good newspaper can be attributed to the wisdom of the individual responsible for placing the news in the papers. Franklin realized in 1729 that a "good paper" needed a variety of news, so he asked his correspondents to keep the newspaper apprised of "every remarkable Accident, Occurrence, &c. fit for public Notice."[6]

According to media history scholarship, however, the colonial newspapers were two or four page sheets of stale, clipped political news from London newspapers concerning Europe or clippings from other colonial newspapers. They contained no headlines to separate one story from the other. The news was stale, sometimes six months old or older. Their greatest moment—and perhaps only moment—occurred in 1735 during the trial of New York printer John Peter Zenger. The foundation of a free press was spawned in that trial. The colonial newspapers also helped produce the greatest citizen of the colonial period, Benjamin Franklin. Yet Franklin's fame in American history rests on his achievements as a statesman, inventor, and scientist, not as a printer and journalist. The colonial newspapers finally grew into political machines that fired a revolution of colonies against the mother country, and they remained political in the early Republic until the Penny Press in the 1830s with James Gordon Bennett and the "yellow journalism" of Joseph Pulitzer and William Randolph Hearst in the 1890s outfitted the newspapers with a more exploitational tone.

Unfortunately, most media historians have assumed that the above description aptly fits colonial newspapers. "The freshest Advices Foreign and Domestic," in this understanding, applied almost exclusively to political news from Europe, thereby leaving local news woefully lacking.[7] As a result, "a good paper"—if a good newspaper includes more than just a single type of news—could have hardly been produced, and anyone reading the sheets of colonial newspapers before the revolutionary crisis could find little outside of political news or European events. The newspapers of colonial America did contain large amounts of political news from Europe and the British colonies of North America. But the news of the colonial papers included more; news that had nothing to do with the politics of the period appeared regularly in them. The purpose of this study is to find out exactly what subjects the news of colonial newspapers discussed other than the high matters of state, European news and free press issues, topics that are considered to be the basis for eighteenth-century American journalism and have been researched by scholars.[8] After the other news topics have been identified, they will be catalogued into content areas. As a result, many of the misconceptions surrounding the news of the colonial period should be erased.

Studies of the history of news, outside of the free press or political arenas, are relatively new in media history[9] and a response to the call by James Carey for such a cultural approach to understanding media history in 1974.[10] Carey said that media historians needed to realize that news reflects the culture of those writing and reading it. According to Carey, media historians have continued to reconstruct journalism's past by joining together a series of facts that rarely relate to the milieu in which the media exist. As a result, the histories produced by these scholars relate the founding of newspapers, their editorial policies, the development of new technologies, and legislative and judicial decisions that affect the press.[11]

Carey's description of the study of media history is an accurate representation of the work that has been done in colonial journalism. The major media history textbooks, including those published during the last five years, concentrate on colonial newspapers' editorial policies and on governmental decisions that have affected the press by focusing upon individual printers and newspapers rather than on how the news serves and reflects society.[12]

In order to attempt what Carey has suggested, one must look beyond the individual printer, newspaper, and event of media history. The news as a whole must be the focus of research, not the individual entities—the printers and newspapers—that comprise or present it. The results of such a study will produce specific news on specific subjects and reveal information about individuals, but it will also demonstrate that news of the colonial period was varied in content. "The freshest Advices Foreign and Domestic" may have applied mainly to political news but not solely to the politics of the age, especially the political situation of Europe. A study of the news contained in the colonial newspapers from 1690–1776 reveals thousands of news items that dealt with topics as varied as religion and slaves, crime and comets, obituaries and animals, disease and weather, Native Americans and medicine, sensationalism and agriculture, to name a few. Knowing that such diverse types of news existed in colonial newspapers reveals their richness and in turn provides a glimpse into the times of those who read them.

CURRENT SCHOLARSHIP: THE COLONIAL NEWSPAPER

Scholars have told us that the birth of the newspaper in British colonial America occurred quietly on 25 September 1690. On that day printer Benjamin Harris issued his *Publick Occurrences Both Forreign and Domestick* in Boston. Harris's first newspaper turned out to be the last *Publick Occurrences* to be printed. This first newspaper promised to provide once a month "an account of such considerable things as have arrived unto our Notion,"[13] but political suppression ended the newspaper's chances of a second edition.[14] Harris returned to England, and the American colonies waited until 1704 when John Campbell began the *Boston News-Letter* for its next weekly printed sheet. Campbell's attempt at a newspaper succeeded. One of the main reasons for success was the fact that Campbell printed his newspaper "with authority" of the Massachusetts government. The *News-Letter* continued to print up to 1776.

From 1704 until December 1719, the *News-Letter* was the only colonial newspaper. But in that year, just days before Christmas, two more newspapers joined Campbell's two-page sheet in providing news. On 21 December, James Franklin printed the first *Boston Gazette* for William Brooker, giving Boston a pair of newspapers. A day later, Andrew Bradford initiated the *American Weekly Mercury* for the citizens of Philadelphia. Within a decade another five newspapers were initiated in the colonies. The production of mass news had begun and continued to grow throughout the colonial period, culminating in the wealth of newspapers produced because of the Stamp Act crisis of 1764–1765 and the ensuing political and armed revolution in 1775.[15]

The newspapers of colonial America were an outgrowth of London newspapers and their predecessors, the newsletters. Newsletters were exactly what their name implied—letters handwritten and sent by the post throughout the English countryside. Each newsletter contained news from London, and they went out three times a week with the mail.[16] The earliest known printed English newspaper came from Amsterdam and carried a 2 December 1620 dateline.[17] First called corantos[18] in Holland and then elsewhere, these printed newspapers rolled off presses in England the next year.[19]

John Campbell's *Boston News-Letter* followed a similar path of development as the newspapers of England. For at least a year before he began printing the *News-Letter,* Campbell, Boston's postmaster, sent handwritten newsletters to the governors of each colony.[20] Finding the practice of preparing numerous newsletters by quill too time-consuming, Campbell turned to a printing press to produce his newsletter.

The actual content of the colonial newspapers was obtained from a number of sources, but the most common sources of news in the 1720s and early 1730s were English newspapers and magazines brought to America. Ships arrived after weeks at sea, and printers sought out captains, crew members, and passengers for the latest "advices" from Europe. The port of Charleston, South Carolina, in 1738 offers an example of the length of time that news required to cross the Atlantic. By this time Charleston was the most active port in the colonies in trade with the sugar colonies of the Caribbean. For that reason most of the news reaching the colony from England or Europe came by way of ships running the sugar route from England to the Caribbean and then to the port of Charleston. News traveling this route usually took between nine and eleven weeks to make the trip from England to Jamaica.[21] If the news came from Europe, especially eastern Europe, it was already weeks old when it arrived in London. That means that sometimes the foreign news that appeared in the *South Carolina Gazette*—or any other colonial newspaper—could be six months old or older. Despite the fact that the news was old by current standards, colonial seaports—and consequently the newspapers printed in those port cities—were in "constant communication" with the mother country by the middle 1730s.[22]

Colonial newspapers also received their news in ways other than foreign publications. After Benjamin Franklin assumed control of the *Universal Instructor* from Samuel Keimer, he printed a notice in his *Pennsylvania Gazette* calling for correspondents throughout the countryside to send news of "every remarkable Accident, Occurrence, &c. fit for public Notice."[23] News obtained from correspondents as well as correspondence from other colonies and from travelers appeared in colonial newspapers. A common method of identifying this news was the introductory phrase "We hear from" followed by the location of the news.

Even though colonial printers received their news from other sources and clipped that news for republication, the inclusion of specific news within an edition of a colonial newspaper was not based purely on availability, even though availability of news did play a vital role in some of the very early newspaper printing.[24] As trade increased in the 1730s, news was more readily accessible not only from England but from other colonies as well. The development of a colonial postal system from Boston to Charleston (the South Carolina port was connected to the system in 1738)[25] also increased the dissemination of news and its availability to printers for inclusion in newspapers.

One of the primary types of news printed in the newspapers prior to 1750 was the essay, and the Southern newspapers like the *Maryland Gazette, Virginia Gazette,* and the *South-Carolina Gazette* were more literary in the nature of their essays than those in the North. Scholars have found, however, that all of the papers tended to avoid political topics that could bring charges of libel during this period, at least until after the trial of John Peter Zenger.[26] Political topics increased in the newspapers with the growing conflict with France over control of North America, and political news continued to swell as England sought tax money from America to pay debts that the British government incurred during the French and Indian War.[27] As the split with England approached, newspapers expanded their frequency and size to handle the increased amounts of political news that poured in from different colonies and the surrounding countryside.

Colonial newspapers after 1719 were usually printed on a single sheet, folded to create four pages.[28] No distinguishing headlines were used on stories, but occasionally, newspapers would separate large bodies of news by using titles such as "News from London" or "Boston News" before a section of news items from the area stated in the title. News items on different subjects were not separated except by paragraph indentations. Advertisements generally appeared on the last page of the newspaper, but the colonial newspapers did not limit their ads to a single page. The *South-Carolina Gazette* of 1734–35 sometimes ran as many as two and a half pages of ads in a four-page edition. Franklin was known to run advertisements on the front page of the *Pennsylvania Gazette,*[29] as did many other printers.

The printing process used by colonial newspaper printers was essentially the same that had been used for the two and one half centuries since the development of the printing press by Johann Gutenburg in 1455. Type was set by hand, the printer having to pick up each letter and slide it onto the "stick," a piece of metal designed to hold letters. The type was then transferred to an iron frame and placed on the press. The letters in the iron form were inked, generally by an apprentice, with a dauber made of animal skin. By pulling a lever on the press, the printer transferred the impression of letters in the iron frame to the paper, made of cloth. A press could produce up to 250 impressions an hour. Each sheet after inking had to be hung up to dry. After the printed side dried, the other side of the sheet could be printed.[30]

But who printed the papers? A printing press that produced 250 impressions an hour was not a one-person operation. Printing shops in the colonies were run by master printers, whose names are preserved by history. From the time the first press arrived in America in 1639 to 1740, thirty-eight master printers plied their trade in the colonies. The names of numerous journeymen, apprentices, and other shop help that produced the newspapers mostly remain unknown.[31] As a whole, printers before the Revolution did not command the respect that the legacy of Benjamin Franklin has produced, but newspapers were a way at least to make a printer known to the citizens of a colony and region. Three-fourths of all master printers from 1700–1765 attempted to print newspapers, and the growth of newspapers in the 1720s and 1730s led to some economic stability and prosperity for them.[32]

Attaining financial stability for printers was not easy,[33] and the task was even more difficult for the journeymen and apprentices, even though the journeyman printer was one of the best-paid craftsmen of the period.[34] The printing trade required its practitioners to work during daylight hours, since type set by candlelight rarely produced the results printers or their clientele desired. Printing colonial newspapers and other publications was further complicated by a lack of resources. Paper, which was made from rags, and type, which had to be imported, were constantly in short supply. Printers often asked for rags, although not always as cleverly as did William Parks of the *Virginia Gazette* in 1744:

> Nice Delia's Smock, which, neat and whole,
> No man durst finger for his Soul;
> Turn'd to Gazette, now all the Town,
> May take it up, or smooth it down.
> Whilst Delia may with it dispense,
> And no Affront to Innocence.[35]

The newspapers produced from "Delia's Smock" cost the citizens of the colonies on average between ten and twelve shillings a year. The average circulation of the papers in 1750 was 600 per year, but subscribers shared their newspapers with friends, and the taverns and other public places made newspapers available for general consumption.[36] Even though the circulation of newspapers may have been small in comparison to the population of the colonies—estimated to be more that 2.8 million in 1775[37]—Warren Johnson believes their influence was far greater, with the newspapers reaching "virtually all the literate persons in the colonies" and even a large part of those who were illiterate through public readings in taverns.[38] Because it can never be proved just how much newspapers were shared, the full effect of newspaper influence upon colonists can only be speculated. But, as Richard Brown has pointed out, knowledge in colonial America meant power.[39] That means that the news presented within the colonial newspaper was of value to its readers.

The success of newspapers during the colonial period supports the value of the news they contained, be that news six months old and from Europe or news six hours old of a drowning at the local wharf. It is the second type of news that is the focus of this study, the news of the colonial sheets that addressed issues other than the political situation in Europe, high matters of state in the colonies, and issues that fueled the concept of freedom of the press.

READING THE NEWS

No citizen of the current information age can deny the significance and value of news reports describing momentous political events nearly anywhere in the world, available within minutes of their occurrence. Political news was and is the staple of informational power in countries where political systems choose rulers, make policies, and set the basic standards for survival within society. Yet no citizen of the current age—nor of any age—can deny that news of floods, disastrous storms, gruesome murders, freak births, the deaths of important people, or any threats to a way of life capture the attention of people more than almost all political news. The tendency toward sensationalizing the news, as Mitchell Stephens has pointed out, is rooted in the nature of news,[40] and in all honesty, its origins lie deep within the nature of human beings as well.

The news of the colonial newspapers was often sensational in nature, and the descriptions of events supplied by the newspapers were often very graphic. The initial *South-Carolina Gazette* of 8 January, 1732, offers a prime example. Printer Thomas Whitmarsh recounted for his Charleston readers how an entire French family died in one afternoon, the father hitting a son over the head in anger and killing him. In distress the father jumped into the well; the mother, who left an infant lying on the ground while running to stop the suicide, was pulled to her death as well. To cap off the account, "a Hog came and killed the young Child [lying on the ground]; so the whole Family perished at once."[41]

Even though news of the colonial papers could fit into this graphic, sensational category, some of it did not. Accounts could be very ordinary yet carry momentous importance for all citizens, just as this terse line from the *Connecticut Gazette* did. "We hear from almost all Parts of the Province," the news item said, "that a great Drought has already entirely burnt up the Flax and Oats."[42] News of the destruction of crops was just as significant a threat to the welfare of the colony as any political action.

Other news in colonial newspapers naturally combined news of everyday occurrences and the political events of the colonies. News in the colonial period dealt with the sea and Native Americans, and because the welfare of colonists and colonies depended on security on the first and security from the second, governmental involvement in affairs dealing with both occurred. This fact, however, does not make news of pirate attacks on Philadelphia ships in the Caribbean or an Indian massacre of a settlement thirty miles west of Boston high matters of state.[43] True political issues or high matters of state, as Robert A. Gross has explained in relation to the colonial press, were concerned with issues of authority and the control of knowledge.[44] Other news items in colonial newspapers— even when there was some governmental involvement in them— concerned themselves more with survival, entertainment, and the inquisitive, rather than authoritarian issues. It may have been politically important for England to control the seas so that ships could safely trade with England and the Caribbean, but survival in the physical and economic sense precipitated that concern. Colonists wanted the government to eradicate hostile Native Americans, but survival and domination of the land for individuals was the motivating factor, not the concept that the land should be conquered for the glory of the king or to enhance the standing of a colonial governor.

Even though portions of the news discussed in this study contain elements similar or identical to those described above, discussion of individual news topics is the best way to approach the character and content of colonial news. This study is organized to do just that.

The first chapter, "There is a Vessel lately arrived from England, or Infested by those Hell-Hounds the Pirates," deals with all aspects of shipping and the sea. Trade and communication with England were vital for the colonies, therefore, news of ship arrivals, ship welfare, and ship contents played a crucial role in nearly all aspects of colonial life. Ship wrecks, pirates, privateers, and news from the custom houses of the colonies all are a part of this news.

News of "the Sculking Indian Enemy" comprises the next chapter. Native American news in the colonial papers dealt with Indians as both friend and foe, although the latter greatly outweighed the former. News of Native Americans was a regular feature of the newspapers through the French and Indian War. After 1763 news of Native Americans continued in the colonial papers, but it was not nearly as prominent as in the years before the end of the war.

Sensationalism, or news that entertained and informed in a morbid way or shocked the moral and aesthetic sensibilities or the readers, was a feature of the colonial press. The chapter, "Melancholy Accidents and Deplorable News," discusses the use of sensationalism in the newspapers. This type of news overlaps almost every other category of news, especially the crime news of the period.

"Whipt through the Streets and burnt with a hot Iron" deals specifically with the news of crime and the courts of the period. Crimes could be heinous and sensational, but they could also be mundane. The viciousness of a particular crime may have made for interesting reading, but knowing that the local authorities had apprehended a ring of £10 note counterfeiters had far-reaching effects. How the newspapers presented crime news and court cases makes up the fourth chapter.

Slavery was a regular part of life in colonial America. When Sir Francis Drake came to Roanoke Island in 1586 for England's first attempt at permanent colonization, African slaves arrived with him,[45] and slavery existed in all the British colonies in the eighteenth century. "The Proceedings of the Rebellious Negroes" describes the news involving African slaves that appeared in the newspapers. Most of the news exhibits a fear of slaves and insurrection, but a growing antislavery movement begins to make itself evident toward the end of the period.

In "Adapted to the Female World," the news content of colonial papers that deals with women, children, and the home is discussed. Women—or at least the feminine perspective—were a part of many newspapers, beginning with Franklin's pseudonymous "Silence Dogood" letters that appeared in the *New-England Courant*. The

South-Carolina Gazette ran several letters attributed to females during its first year of publication. By the end of the period, poetry was a regular feature in many colonial newspapers, and its appearance runs parallel with the growing literacy of females.

Fatal diseases had few if any cures during the colonial period, so doctors and quacks alike sought remedies. The colonial newspapers provided their readers with continual reports of cures for everything from smallpox to stomachaches. Those cure-alls are described in the chapter, "A Receipt against the Plague," along with how the papers covered the outbreaks of disease and epidemics.

Religion, as portrayed in the colonial newspapers, is the subject of "The Presence of God was much seen in the Assemblies." The most consistent news feature and the first news story of intercolonial importance during the period did not deal with any political crisis; it dealt with a preacher, George Whitefield. The papers's treatment of Whitefield and other religious news and inferences are discussed here.

While the above topics are the most consistent news topics, they are not inclusive. In "The Chief Amusement of this City," the less frequently discussed topics of news are presented. Literature, poetry, gaming, sports, animals, agriculture, oddities, natural occurrences, weather, obituaries, accidents, and social news are all included.

Appendixes are included in this study. The first deals with the methodology employed in this research. The second compares the total number of news items that are discussed in this study from major colonial newspapers from 1720–1775. Newspapers representing Boston (3), New York (3), Philadelphia (3), Annapolis, and Charleston are used. This appendix allows one to observe news changes over most of the eighteenth century. In addition, this appendix allows one to recognize the "hot topics," those items that attracted large amounts of news space and when those subjects were of most interest in colonial American newspapers. A third appendix explains the name changes in colonial newspapers. Many newspapers underwent name changes and knowing how the names of newspapers were altered or changed completely should help in following the evolution of colonial sheets.

The colonial newspaper contained a wealth of news. The topics were as varied as the imagination would allow and eighteenth-century customs would permit. The newspapers, as found by other scholars, were political; no amount of research into colonial news can erase that truism. But the news that deals with other subjects of the period may be even more valuable in helping to understand life in the eighteenth century than the political news. Understanding everyday life, though, is not the purpose of this investigation, only a logical by-product for future study.

The content of colonial newspapers—outside their European, free press, and high matters of state connections—has been overlooked by media historians. "The freshest Advices Foreign and Domestic" was as varied as a printer thought valuable for himself and his readers. The assortment could have appeared because, as Thomas Fleet said, "I had a prospect of getting a Penny by it."[46] It could have also appeared because assorted news provided readers, in the words of William Parks, with "inexhaustable Treasures, out of which may be extracted everything that is necessary for the Support of Virtue, the Suppression of Vice, the Promotion of Learning, Wit, Ingenuity, &c."[47]

Either reason is valid; both reasons are important. What has been uncovered in this study of the news of colonial American newspapers will add to our knowledge of media history and help eventually to relate the period of colonial journalism, as James Carey has called for, to the milieu in which the newspapers existed.

1

There is a Vessel Lately Arrived from England, or Infested by Those Hell-Hounds the Pirates

After a long Dearth of News, we have, by the late Ships, received English Papers to the 12th of November.
—*Pennsylvania Gazette,* 22 January 1745

In January 1745 Benjamin Franklin was no doubt worried. It had been several weeks since ships entering the Philadelphia harbor had contained any information resembling news. A winter storm now forced all ships to remain at the wharf on the Delaware River. The same storm kept other ships at sea. Further complicating the situation, England and France were at war, and French privateers constantly patrolled the waters of the Atlantic that led to American ports. Finally around January 22, several ships made their way up river to Philadelphia. A relieved Franklin reported the ships' arrival but lamented that war meant that newspapers had to go "sometimes Months without having a Syllable" of fresh news to print.[1]

Franklin's dilemma of 1745 was common among the printers of colonial America. Even though printers had a number of sources for receiving news including overland mail routes, most of the news that appeared in the newspapers reached the hands of printers via ships. When shipping was interrupted for any reason, the flow of information ceased as well. Shipping and newspapers, therefore, became mutually dependent. Merchants needed a way to inform people that they had goods lately arrived by ship. In turn, printers needed ships to bring news from Europe and other colonies. For newspapers, the situation was profitable; they received commercial news even if a ship brought no foreign newspapers or news from other American colonies.

23

While ships were newspapers' greatest link to information, the ships also provided newspapers with their largest single news topic. It would be nearly impossible to read any edition of a colonial newspaper without finding some news relating to ships, shipping, or the sea. Hundreds of news items appeared each year that dealt directly with ship news and news of the sea. In fact, America's newspapers in 1720, the *Boston News-Letter,* the *Boston Gazette,* and the *American Weekly Mercury,* printed on average 220 items of sea news during that twelve-month period. By 1755, the number of ship-related news items that appeared in colonial newspapers increased to an average of 265 per year. The average number of news items concerning the sea did not begin to decrease until American nonimportation agreements and British embargoes in the 1770s greatly limited the shipping of the American colonies, yet even with the nonimportation agreements and embargoes—in reality, as much shipping news as political news—the American newspapers in this study averaged 180 ship news items per year in 1770.[2]

News of the sea could be as exciting and sensational as a first-hand account of a ship and crew adrift at sea without provisions that included the cannibalistic way those on board remained alive, or it could describe for readers the way in which America's shipping lanes were "infested by those Hell-hounds the Pirates,"[3] those roving sea thieves who murdered, robbed, and plundered cargo ships from Newfoundland to the Caribbean. News of the sea could also be as mundane as a "Vessel lately arrived from England,"[4] a typical example of the way in which colonial newspapers informed readers that a ship had entered harbor.[5] While the first type of sea news may have entertained readers more, the second was of immense importance to the citizens throughout the colonies. Overseas commerce made colonial life both comfortable and possible. Foreign trade allowed colonists to earn money to purchase European goods, and the accessibility of these goods in turn made America attractive to emigrants from Europe.[6]

This chapter deals with all facets of the news of the sea that were presented in colonial newspapers. News of the sea often related brief but essential items that told of arrivals and departures of ships, and this news was vital to life in the ports of America.[7] But the news of the sea that appeared in colonial newspapers also possessed a sensational side. Newspapers reported on pirate activity and shipwrecks throughout the colonial period. This type of ship news was often quite extended in its length, detailed in its description of fighting or methods of survival, and could fill a page or more in a newspaper. For many colonists in America, sea travel was a necessity, and the constant reports of shipwrecks and barbarous pirates lurking in hidden coves just outside of colonial ports heightened the apprehension that accompanied this type of travel. This type of news about the sea, although not as prominent as the basic news of departures, arrivals, ship cargoes, and customhouse reports, remained a feature of colonial newspapers. The fact that both types of ship news played such vital roles in the content of colonial newspapers demonstrates the value of shipping news as both a source of critical information in the colonial period and as the topic of news. Before exploring the news of the sea in the papers, however, a brief discussion of trade routes, British trading policies, and length of time required for ships to reach ports in America may shed some light on the strong tie that existed between colonial commerce and news.

SHIPPING AND TRADE IN COLONIAL AMERICA

From the beginning of the eighteenth century to 1775, the population of the American colonies increased ninefold.[8] Although many of those new settlers joined in a westward migration away from the coast into what the colonists called the "backcountry," their sights were firmly fixed on Europe.[9] The colonists of eighteenth-century America generally perceived their future—that is their welfare both physically and financially—not to the West but back across the Atlantic Ocean. Maintaining contact with the European way of life was paramount. Sea travel, therefore, was of extreme importance.

Successful navigation of the Atlantic to America was extremely important in England, too. Within fifteen years of the settlement of Jamestown, British merchants realized that there was a great deal of money to be made off the resources of the colonies, especially through the importation of the "stinking custom" of tobacco products.[10] England saw tremendous monetary potential in her American colonies and set in place commercial legislation that gave the kingdom a monopoly on trade with the colonies. Other European countries were not precluded from enjoying the bounteous resources of British colonial America; they were, however, required to use English merchant ships for all exchanges.[11] This monopolistic practice ultimately encouraged smuggling by colonial American merchants, especially illegal trade with the French.[12] Because of the British monopoly on trade, American merchants in the seventeenth and early eighteenth century were often unable to obtain the best prices for their goods, having to settle for whatever was offered by British trading companies. Much greater profit, especially in the purchasing of goods, was available through deals with the buccaneers who sailed the Caribbean and robbed ships, principally Spanish vessels. Colonial merchants, through tacit approval by government officials, were "allowed" to trade with pirates.[13]

Growing production of American crops and the need for laborers to work in producing and harvesting them helped American trade slowly outgrow the need to deal with pirates. By the second third of the century, trade was flourishing, due in part to increased tobacco and slave trade.[14] Another reason that American merchants no longer needed to trade with pirates was based upon Europe's difficulty in providing sufficient amounts of food for its citizenry, necessitating the importation of American rice and wheat for survival at prices that greatly favored American interests.[15]

The growing economic ties with Europe furthered American concern in European activities and created a desire for increased and more quickly received European news. At the same time, most American ports developed significant trade among themselves.[16] Events from Boston, Massachusetts, to Charleston, South Carolina, and eventually from St. John's, Newfoundland, to Savannah, Georgia, therefore, would be of interest to citizens all along the Atlantic seaboard. The faster information and goods could be transported, the better informed and financially successful colonial citizens and their communities could be.[17]

But how fast could news possibly travel by sailing ship? By 1735, the average age of a London news story appearing in a Boston or Philadelphia newspaper was between eighty-five and ninety-five days.[18] By 1740, an avenue of "constant communication" existed, provided England was not at war with another European nation. Sailing time decreased to five weeks to Newfoundland and eight weeks to the Caribbean from England.[19] In addition, growing maritime commerce increased transatlantic news flow three hundred percent.[20]

The American colonies also greatly increased intercolonial trade in the second third of the eighteenth century. Ships from New England regularly put in at ports in the Middle Colonies on their way to and from the lucrative rum-slave trade in the West Indies.[21] News placed on a ship in New England could reach New York in four days, Philadelphia in five. To communicate with Annapolis from New England required a week at sea, provided no other ports of call were mandated. Ten days sailing was needed to reach Williamsburg.[22]

News traveling farther south than Williamsburg needed additional time at sea because of the distance to the next important port in the Southern Colonies—New Bern—and because of the hazardous waters and shoals around Hatteras, North Carolina. A voyage from New England to New Bern could be covered in fifteen days. Another five days were needed to reach Charleston. Ships traveling from Boston to Savannah required at least five to six weeks.[23]

No matter the age of news received by ships, it generally fell into two categories, that which might be termed news of daily necessities and sensational sea news, that which dealt with shipwrecks and pirate and privateer attacks. Both types of news provided readers with valuable information. The latter, however, added treachery and barbarity to newspapers. Both types give us an insight into the importance of ships and the sea to colonial America as a source of well-being for the colonies as a source of news.

THE SEA AND COLONIAL NEWSPAPERS

News of the Sea: Daily Necessities. The *Boston News-Letter* stated on 14 January 1706, that "a Vessel lately arrived here from England." The one-line news item said nothing about the cargo of the ship. It probably brought prints of some London newspapers and assorted commodities for purchase by the citizens of Massachusetts Bay. The transatlantic carrier could have been filled with important personages who made the trip in order to attend the wedding of Governor Jonathan Belcher and Mary Partridge, daughter of the colony's late Lieutenant Governor, William Partridge.[24] Whatever or whoever was on board, the arrival of the ship was worth noting, as was news that privateers continued to attack ships in the Caribbean.

To printers of colonial newspapers, ships first and foremost meant news, as both a source and a topic.[25] In the winter of 1730, Andrew Bradford despaired of the fact that news that he could print in his *American Weekly Mercury* was scarce. He asked a friend to help him secure any news possible to print since he was experiencing "a Time when fresh Advices from Abroad cannot be had."[26] In return, Bradford received an essay on women from his friend, and that occupied the first two pages and part of the third in the week's edition.

The arrival of a ship in port sometimes provided news that had immediate repercussions for the port, merchants, and ship crews alike. In such cases the ship was both the source and topic of news. Ships arriving in American ports often traveled to Europe, Africa, and the Caribbean before docking in the colonies and provide a good example of this dualism. At each stop, cargo was exchanged, and often the crew or cargo on board the ship became infected with some type of disease. Such an infected ship arrived in Boston in November 1730, and the *New-England Weekly Journal* gave notice that the ship had been placed in quarantine and not allowed to dock. Merchants, shippers looking to hire crews for a voyage, and the citizens of the city were all given fair warning to steer clear of the ship, its crew, and cargo.[27]

In the same manner, newspapers warned outbound ships loaded with merchandise or passengers to avoid certain ports. Ships entering Boston harbor in March and May 1735 alerted other vessels and port authorities to bypass North Carolina ports from Ocracoke Island southward because "Pestilential Distemper" was spreading among the region's citizens. In addition, it would be unwise to allow ships coming from North Carolina to enter port.[28] Similarly, the *Connecticut Journal* warned of plague in Hispaniola. Only that colony needed to be avoided in the Caribbean, however, since "the Disorder was not bro't from any infected Place, but supposed to originate there."[29]

The majority of ship news that appeared in the papers was much more "ordinary" than warnings of quarantined ships and disease-infested ports that ships needed to avoid. It told of ships arriving, loading, and departing like this *Boston Gazette* notice:

> On the 12th Capt. Hayes Ship Benjamin Arrived here from Barbadoes, and Coden from Rhode Island. Capt. Barrington [on the ship] Sheppard will sail hence for London about the 10th of January, being now half loaded and the rest ready. Coden sails this day for Rhode Island.[30]

Other regular features of colonial newspaper ship news included customhouse reports, the price current for goods at individual ports, and tides. Customhouse reports listed the names of ships entered into a port, ships cleared for departure, and ships that had departed. Many times, newspapers ran customhouse reports from several cities. In the *Boston Gazette*'s first year of publication, it regularly provided readers with reports from Boston, as well as the customhouses in New York, Philadelphia, New London, Salem, Portsmouth, Burlington, and the ports of Rhode Island.[31] As the availability of news increased during the colonial period, customhouse reports were sometimes omitted in order to place news from other colonies and Europe into newspapers.

The "Price Currant" of goods allowed merchants to know the going rate for imported or exported items from individual ports. The current price of goods included staples necessary for survival like flour, corn, and bread, and it included exported items peculiar to the region. The *South-Carolina Gazette* regularly listed the current prices for naval stores—tar, pitch, and turpentine—and rice.[32] After Charleston grew into a major shipping center, printer Peter Timothy produced a standard weekly column called "Timothy's Marine List," which included imports, exports, custom house ledgers, price current, tides, and the week's weather.[33] Because ships could better leave a port at high tide, many papers listed the high tides for the week, along with the price current just below the nameplate.[34]

At times, the "ordinary" news was mixed with news of extraordinary social cargo. When the *Sea-Horse* arrived in Boston on 11 October 1720, William Burnet, the "Governour of New York and New-Jersey"[35] was the "merchandise of note." In the midst of war news in 1775, the *Pennsylvania Gazette* informed the city that John Hancock and his bride had arrived to visit.[36] Sometimes the cargo was extraordinary but unwanted. That was the case with numerous boatloads of British convicts sent to America by order of the British government.[37]

Ships entering the ports of colonial America formed an informational network that kept each port apprised of the shipping situation throughout the Atlantic. *Publick Occurrences* provided news of a safe harbor for British ships in Tobago.[38] When a Brigantine docked in Annapolis after sailing from Barbados, the captain advised "that the West-India Fleets from England and Ireland, were safe arrived" in Barbados.[39] Ships often brought news of other ships outfitting at ports that they had just departed. Similar news was received second-hand from ships met at sea. This news let merchants and others know that ships that had been sent out earlier from particular ports had arrived safely. It also notified them that ships could be expected in the near future. If the ships did not dock at specified ports within a reasonable amount of time, it could be assumed that some harm had befallen them at sea.[40]

The informational network was especially sensitive to the conditions found on the various shipping routes that could hamper or even curtail trade ships. In February 1745, for example, the *New-York Evening-Post* forewarned shippers that storms were currently interrupting shipping to Virginia, Barbados, and St. Kitts, while at the same time French vessels were cruising all through the Caribbean making prizes of ships sailing under British colors.[41] Ships sometimes were successful at maneuvering through gales at sea; other times they were lost.[42]

Because of the precarious nature of the weather and the ocean, news of shipwrecks, lost cargo, and drownings appeared in colonial newspapers frequently. Just how perilous ventures into the ocean were both physically and financially was summed up in a *Connecticut Journal* news story in January 1770:

> The Number of Vessels, belonging to this Place, which have been lost since January, 1768, is as follows, viz. 3 Fishing Schooners in 1768, 13 Ditto in Spring, 1769; 3 Ditto last Fall. 4 Sail of Merchantmen. Total 23 Sail, & all the Men belonging to them, amounting to 160 Whites, and 2 Negroes, (besides some Strangers belonging to the Merchantmen, of whom no Account has been kept) were lost. The Number of Widows left by these Men were 70, with 155 Children. The Value of the Interest lost, amounting to £14124–8.[43]

Often, the crew was forced to "cast away," or abandon, a ship in order to save itself. A large storm hit England in November 1703, and it forced the casting away of "3 or 4 Merchant Ships" at Plymouth as well as ships from eight more ports on the island.[44] Ships arriving in Boston from Jamaica reported seeing the entire London fleet in tatters in Cuba. The unstable August weather of the Caribbean had wreaked havoc upon the British sailing vessels, and Captain Masse of the ship *Maremaid* said that he "saw the Wrecks, and the Shore covered with dead Bodies."[45]

Although many of the ships damaged at sea were English vessels, their destruction or loss of cargo affected the colonies. A snow, the name given the largest of the two-masted vessels to ply the oceans in the eighteenth century,[46] the *Maryland Gazette* informed, had recently left Virginia bound for London. Navigating into the ocean, she was "stranded on the Back of the Isle of Wight, and the whole Cargo lost, but the Crew were saved." The cargo included 314 hogsheads of tobacco grown, cured, and loaded by Virginians.[47] When ships were stranded or run ashore in storms, the crew and cargo could sometimes be saved, but the vessels themselves usually were destroyed.[48]

Even when the ocean was calm, ships were not completely safe from nature's threats. In 1755, sailors on a boat loaded with fish discovered that fact. The ship "met with a Mountain of Ice, and it being calm, she could not get clear, but was drove against it by the Current, by which the Vessel received so much Damage that she sunk directly." The six-member crew survived six days in a lifeboat before being picked up by a French ship bound for Spain.[49] And it was not only icebergs that sank ships at sea in nonstormy weather. Ships sometimes—despite the immense size of the Atlantic—could not avoid one another. The ship *America,* for one, sank to the bottom of the ocean after colliding with another boat in 1770.[50]

With all the danger that the weather and sea combined to inflict upon ships, their cargoes, and crews, it is no wonder that crews would implore God for safe sailing or offer thanks for deliverance from situations of imminent danger. The crew of the *Grafton* offered words of thanks after a narrow escape:

> TO Thee our Thanks, O great JEHOVAH's due,
> Accept it then from all the Grafton's Crew;
> Who for thy great Assistance did implore,
> To help us off a dang'rous rocky Shore.
> Thou heard'st our Cries, it did thy Favour gain,
> Expell'd our Fears, and bid us live again.
> While GOD's our Friend, and he the Helm doth steer,
> No Rocks, no Shoals, no Dangers need we fear.[51]

The dangers of sea travel were no less for the fishing fleets that plied the waters from New England to Greenland searching for fish and whales. Whalers often "were lost among the Ice" as they followed schools of the migrating animals toward Greenland and further north.[52] Whales, especially, were a valuable commodity in America. The oil made from their blubber was used to light lamps, and whalers from Nantucket alone provided three thousand barrels of oil in 1730, thirty thousand in 1775.[53] But whaling was a dangerous occupation. A Nantucket sloop ventured out in May 1720 and quickly "fell in with a Scool [sic] of Sperma Cetæ Whales,"[54] the richest of all whale species in their yield of oil.[55] One sperm whale that had already been taken by the sloop produced a dozen barrels of oil and a large amount of ivory from the teeth, but successfully landing an animal that reached lengths of sixty feet with only iron harpoons was difficult. When the harpoon sank into the whale, it dove toward the bottom pulling the small rowboat containing the whalers with it. The whalers were left "a sprawling and swiming [sic] for life." They were saved, but the whale eluded capture.[56]

Fishing as an industry was important in both America and Europe. When the price of fish dropped in Europe, it was news in

America. The *American Weekly Mercury* learned through private letters "that Fish bears nothing of a Price in any of the Ports in the Mediterranean" and from a ship captain "that the Price for Fish is exceeding low in Foreign Markets."[57] But the price of ocean produce did not remain low, and a *Pennsylvania Gazette* essay from London intimated that the rich fishing grounds that stretched from New England to Newfoundland were a prime cause for the French and Indian War. The cod fisheries, the essay declared, meant so much to England that "his gracious Majesty, our Sovereign, drew the Sword" to protect England's interest in them from the French.[58]

Even after America revolted against English rule, the politics of fishing found a place in American papers. The *North Carolina Gazette* of New Bern filled all of page one and part of page two on 16 June 1775 with Parliament's discussion of a fishing bill. Every other piece of information in the paper—with the exception of a short poem on beauty—dealt with the war and the provincial politics surrounding it.

Because of the necessity of sea travel, inventors and scientists of the colonial period continually attempted to improve ships and the instruments used to navigate the oceans. The *Boston Evening-Post,* for example, announced that an experiment was being conducted in London on a new design of ship that could not be sunk, even when it filled with water.[59] Another London inventor claimed to have developed a new set of instruments that would continue to point out directions in all types of weather.[60] And doctors and scientists continually professed to have perfected a treatment for the boards used to build ships that would keep worms and rot out of the wood. In 1740, one Searl Knowles "found a wonderful Expedient to hinder the Worms penetrating into Ship Plank."[61] Yet a decade later, the *Boston Evening-Post* proclaimed that "Mr. George Bridges, the famous Bug-Doctor . . . tried his Experiment in Deptford Yard, on six different Sorts of Timber, in order to prevent the Worms from boring Holes in Ships Bottoms." The news item claimed that if Bridges was successful, it would be "the first of its Kind ever discovered in Europe."[62]

All of the claims for improvements in ships and navigation, however, proved to be only claims. Ships continued to sink, rot, and become lost on transatlantic voyages. Shipping was a daily necessity in colonial America, and the large amount of "ordinary" news concerning the sea affirms the importance of ship trade and the goods that they procured for the colonies. Shipping was so important that Massachusetts issued a proclamation to protect it from the marauding French in 1755.[63] And it is no coincidence that more shipping news appeared in colonial newspapers in 1755 than in any other year studied (See appendix 2). Even with all this emphasis on ship arrivals, departures, and the like, all of the news of the sea that appeared in colonial newspapers was not presented for such bland but vital informational purposes. Much of the news of the sea was filled with gruesome brutality and stark realism. That news of the sea was anything but "ordinary"; a very different type of news from the waters of the Atlantic also emerged from the pages the colonial newspapers.

News of the Sea: Disaster, Treachery and Sensationalism. In the last edition of the *Boston News-Letter* printed in 1720, one of John Campbell's news items lamented the fact that "those Hell-hounds the Pirates" had returned to torment ships trading in the Caribbean.[64] Pirates, the self-declared enemies of the whole world, had been a threat to shipping and the lives of ship crews in the West Indies for a century.[65] Since around 1692, pirate activity had increased greatly in the region, and the buccaneers, who originally attacked Spanish vessels almost exclusively, now waged war on any merchant vessel so unlucky to be discovered entering the region.[66]

News of pirate activity made quick and interesting reading in the colonial newspapers. And Ian Steele postulates that the colonial newspapers helped to stifle piracy after 1720 through their detailed printing of the names of pirate vessels and descriptions of the executions of pirates.[67] Pirate news was valuable information for the readers of colonial newspapers, but it was anything but ordinary.

Several works, including John Esquemeling's *The Buccaneers of America* and *The General History of Pyrates,* had been sold in England and America since 1684.[68] These works painted a graphic picture of the way pirates dealt with those they captured. Typical torture of a prisoner was described by Esquemeling:

[T]hey soon after hung him up, giving him infinite blows and stripes, while he was under that intolerable pain and posture of body. After-wards they cut off his nose and ears, and singed his face with burning straw, till he could speak nor lament his misery no longer. Then losing all hopes of hearing any confession from his mouth, they commanded a negro to run him through with a lance. . . . After this execrable manner did many others of those miserable prisoners finish their days, the common sport and recreation of these Pirates being these and other tragedies not inferior.[69]

Newspaper readers, therefore, already knew of the horrors that could be expected if a ship's crew was captured by pirates. The most horrible news of pirate barbarity could rarely find its way into the newspapers because very few lived to report it.

Three types of pirate news appeared, and all three played upon the vivid descriptions of pirate brutality offered by the histories of pirates. The first reported pirate activity. This news offered few graphic descriptions of pirate activity; it merely warned ships to be alert. Around 1740, however, this type of news gradually changed more into news of French and Spanish privateers who raided ships flying the English flag, and the descriptions in this news were often quite graphic in their portrayal of fighting and brutality. A second type of pirate news mentioned by Steele related the accounts of trials and executions of pirates. The third type described pirate activity and the treatment of prisoners whenever captives were fortunate enough to live to report it.

By the eighteenth century, pirate activity was not confined to the West Indies. Pirates roamed the Atlantic in search of booty and places to trade. Reports of their activity as far north as Newfoundland turned up in the newspapers as a warning for ships. "Our Coast is again infested with those Common Enemy of Mankind the Pirates," a *Boston News-Letter* notice from Canada proclaimed. Ships arriving in Boston noted that one pirate sloop "had taken Thirteen Sail of French and English Fishing Ships in One day, and has us'd the Men very Barbarously."[70] Because American shipping activity encompassed the whole Atlantic, notices of pirate activity anywhere were valuable. A Jamaican letter warned ships involved in the African slave trade to avoid the Gamboa River in Gambia because "nine Vessels have been lately taken in by the said Pyrates" that currently infested that area of the West African coast.[71]

By 1740 and the War of Jenkins Ear between Spain and England, news of privateer activity began to capture large amounts of the ship news in the colonial papers. News of privateer activity had always been reported in the newspapers beginning with an account of the French taking an American ship and killing the crew in *Publick Occurrences* in 1690. But by 1740, privateers increased their activity along the American coast, largely due to the increased interest in the resources of North America. Privateers differed from pirates in only one respect; their vessels were generally outfitted by nations or merchants of a nation to go out and rob other countries' vessels, the money made on the resale of the booty going to the privateer and sponsor.[72] Ships started to sail in convoys to better avoid harassment and capture, and American colonies and merchants launched privateers as well to raid Spanish and French ships working the waters of North America and the Caribbean.[73] At times, the confrontations between privateers and the ships they attacked led to bloody battles, like the one described in the *Boston Weekly News-Letter* between sailors from New Providence and Spain off Havana:

> I was forward, cutting the Anchor, and no-body on the Deck but myself with 3 great He-dogs of Spaniards. And hearing a great Noise in the Cabbin, I ran aft, and found one of the Spaniards there killing Mr. Bow. . . . I came to the Lieutenant's Assistance with a fine Broad-Ax, and made several Strokes at the Spaniard to no Purpose; but by good Luck, the Dog looking about, at last I was up with him, for I cut off his Chin, and all lower Jaw; yet he, knowing what they said when we crav'd quarter, never flinch'd at all; Then one of his Legs slipping out on the Blood, I got another fair Stroke at him, and cut his right Foot off. Then the Dog cry'd out for Quarter, which was granted for a few Hours, that he might make his Peace with God, and then we shot him through the body.[74]

Newspaper accounts of the activities of pirates and the bloody revenge inflicted upon privateers may have helped to diminish their numbers, but these news reports did not eradicate them. Pirates and privateers continued to operate in the Atlantic throughout the colonial period, and newspapers related their activity. In 1745, a report of a ship turning pirate proved to be false,[75] but a 1765 news item related how the *Nancy* had turned to piracy. The captain and loyal members of the crew were set adrift, fortunately surviving for six weeks at sea.[76] Another captain was not so fortunate. The mutinying crew tossed the captain and mate overboard and proceeded to Cuba to plunder ships and towns.[77]

Trials and executions of pirates by governments, the second type of pirate news, were common in colonial newspapers, and the concerted effort by the colonies to try and execute pirates, as newspapers reported, may well have played a role in the reduction of piracy, along with America's growing European trade. Two dozen pirates, for example, were condemned to death in the Caribbean in 1730. The *New-England Weekly Journal* reported:

> Twelve of them, who were all Frenchmen, were Executed in one Day, their hands were first cut off at the place of Execution, and then nine of them were wrack'd to Death, and Three of them Hang'd; the next Day the other Twelve, who were all Switz's, were Executed, and these likewise having their hands cut off at the place of Execution, were some wrack'd, some saw'd asunder, and the rest hang'd.[78]

At other times, the description of the trial and execution of the pirates was minimized. Pirates were taken, executed, and hung in chains in Virginia, but the fact that the colony collected £2,000 sterling in silver and gold for the capture—the colony kept the booty that the pirates had taken from a ship off Brazil—may have been more important to the welfare of the Virginia than the eradication of some high seas criminals.[79]

Because pirates often forced sailors to either take up the life of piracy or die, it was important for the names of as many pirates as possible to appear in the newspapers whenever Americans were suspected of piracy. News articles often implicated or exonerated individuals. One Simon Vanvorst of New York was implicated along with several European pirates in one article.[80] The *Pennsylvania Gazette* exonerated several officers accused of turning pirate in St. Kitts, saying an earlier report "proves a Mistake."[81] When pirate ships proved to be especially troublesome to shipping, the name of the captured ship and its buccaneer captain were printed to allow shippers to know of their removal from the shipping lanes.[82]

Pirates' treatment of those on a boarded vessel evoked all the horrors of sea travel. Indian, Negro, and Spanish pirates overtook a ship out of Boston in late 1729. They used the flints of their guns as thumbscrews[83] on many members of the crew. All of the crew and passengers were then striped naked, the captain and two others thrown overboard. The rest were whipped with the flat side of cutlasses and set adrift.[84]

The most gruesome of all descriptions of the treatment of sailors by pirates in the newspapers occurred at the end of the colonial period. Ships sailing around North Africa in both the Atlantic Ocean and Mediterranean Sea were under constant threat from Barbary Coast pirates who then sold crews into slavery in Algiers. A Rhode Island sailor, John Owens, miraculously escaped and brought back a description of the crew's torture:

> Two men belonging to Newport, Rhode-Island . . . were sentenced to have their tongues cut out, which was done by first suspending them by the hair of their heads, then seizing their tongues by pincers, drawing them out, and with a hooked knife cutting them off near the root. Capt. Glitz was condemned to die by an instrument called the maid. . . . A wooden figure curiously dressed, like a woman, was introduced and approached him, seemingly as if going to kiss him, immediately pressed in her arms till the blood gushed out of his mouth, nose, ears, &c. &c. . . . I was hung up by a hook thrust through the fleshy part of my right arm, above the elbow, and a spike driven through the

thick part of the thumb. Thus I expected to hang in torture, till death should relieve me, but after hanging 37 minutes, the flesh and ligaments in my arm gave way. . . . I was then seized and fastened to a machine called a rack, where I underwent excruciating tortures, had my collar bone and all my ribs broken except two. After this, I was cruelly dismembered and then delivered into the hands of the surgeons.[85]

The prospects of completing sea travel without falling victim to pirates and all the other dangers possible on the ocean must have played upon the minds of many who either made a living on the sea or traveled on it out of necessity. Perhaps worse even than the horrors inflicted upon sea travelers by pirates were the revulsions that accompanied staying alive when lost or adrift at sea or when a crew mutinied. Colonial newspapers were quite graphic in their descriptions of how these people remained alive.

The ships that sailed the Atlantic could carry only a certain amount of provisions for the crew, and if a boat somehow blew off course or miscalculated, the results were often deadly. Crews were forced to eat whatever they could find, often turning to cannibalism.[86] Survivors on one cruise were able to live by "God's good providence." It seems that "two Boobies [sea birds] . . . alighted down between them, whose blood they suck'd and flesh they eat." The blood and bird flesh kept them alive until rescue.[87] On another ship blown off course by a strong gale, the crew was reduced to drinking "their own Urine" before casting lots to see which member of the crew would be slaughtered first for food.[88]

Cannibalism seemed to be the option that many of those shipwrecked and adrift resorted to. A rescued ship captain died ten hours after being brought in. "It was a very melancholy prospect, to see him," the newspaper report said, "and to find five of the peoples fingers in his pocket as a store." On the same ship were found, nailed to the ship's mast, five skeletons of crew members who served as food.[89]

Cannibalism was the survival method of last resort, and crews often agreed to choose one crew member to die to serve as food for the rest of the crew. Newspaper accounts could be very explicit when describing these events:

> . . . It was agreed, that one should die to support the rest; and accordingly they cast lots. The first fell upon Patrick Lidane, the only son of a poor widow in this town; who requested that, for their immediate subsistence, they would dispense with the calves of his legs and that perhaps before they should be necessitated to have further recourse to him, Providence might do more for them than they expected. His

request was granted, and after cutting away the flesh of his legs, which they eat raw, and whereof he begged a morsel himself, but was refused, he was permitted to live 30 hours. . . . On these . . . without any kind of drink, but what rain water they could catch in the skulls of the killed, did the rest subsist.[90]

Not all newspaper descriptions of shipwrecks were so gruesome. Sometimes they played upon emotions, as the story of a mother and infant trapped in the cabin of an overturned ship did. Those who had escaped the vessel when a squall overset it tried furiously to cut a hole in the hull of the ship with an axe. The woman inside was, "held all the while by a small hook, and was up to the chin in the water." She remained this way with her infant for three and one half hours, with the child drowning only moments before rescue.[91] Later, in a first-person account, the woman, a Mrs. Temple, recounted what happened for the *New-York Evening-Post:*

The Vessel overset about eleven o'Clock on Tuesday, I was in the Cabbin with the Door shut, one of the Men on board attempted to open the Door when a Sea or Wave coming shut it too again: The Vessel then sunk so low that the Door was under Water and the Cabbin almost full of Water, I sustained myself by my Hand so as to keep me out of the Water, but from the first, the Water was to my Breast, sometimes to my Chin, and sometimes quite overwhelmed me, while I held by a Hook to keep from sinking, I kept my Senses 'till almost the last, but have no Remembrance of my being taken out which was about half after One, when I had just lost my Hold and was sinking, and my Child had expired in my Arms.[92]

One final hazard of ship travel was possible. Passengers could face a crew or crewman out for personal gain. A woman on board a man of war bound for London was the victim of one such cabin boy, who

stuffed her mouth full of oakem and chips, gave her several blows, then left her weltering in her gore, and went to the gunner her husband, knocked him down with a carpenter's mallet, and gave him so many blows, that he left him for dead; then broke open his chest took his watch, money, several shirts and shifts, and other wearing apparel . . . then went to his wife, took her gold rings and ear rings; one being hard to come out, he cut it out of her ear, and left them both in that deplorable condition.[93]

CONCLUSION

Ships and colonial newspapers formed the most basic of informational relationships. Ships provided newspapers with the majority of their news items. In addition, ships and their cargoes were important news in colonial America, and the newspapers continually published information about the arrival and departure of vessels, their cargo, sailing conditions, and any bit of intelligence that could be perceived to be valuable to ships, the merchants that filled them and the citizens of the port.

While thousands of articles appeared in colonial papers concerning ships, most of them contained only basic and mundane news. Even though this news was not exciting, its value would be difficult to measure, given the tremendous amount of intercontinental and intercolonial trade that transpired from the ports of eighteenth-century colonial America.

Shipping and news flow increased simultaneously in eighteenth-century America. Colonists had looked to Europe for politial and economic direction during this period, but increasingly, the colonies discovered a way to attain independence through a growing European trade that provided the colonies with much-needed revenue and through intercolonial trade that helped colonists in each region attain the goods needed to live. This fostered political independence as well. By 1775, it was England that needed American goods imported not vice versa, as a report from Bristol, England, in the *Essex Journal* proves. During a one-year period, from August 1773 to August 1774, England imported 102,388 bushels of wheat, 31,682 bushels of Indian corn, 22,646 bushels of barley, 15,432 bushels of oats, 14,720 barrels of flour, and 2,000 bushels of beans through the port of Bristol alone.[94]

Even though shipping news as it related to the economic welfare of America dominated the news of the sea, the penchant for graphic, sensational news by colonial newspapers was not omitted from the newspapers. Numerous reports concerning pirates and shipwrecks illustrated the dangers of sea travel in gruesome, bloody detail. Although this type of sea news was much more entertaining than the more ordinary types of news from the sea, its informational value was not completely lost in the shock value that these stories possessed. These graphic accounts disclosed the location of pirates and privateers and gave the names of survivors rescued from ships assumed lost. Despite these facts, the bloody episodes of ship news describing cannibalism and murderous pirates probably enhanced the fear of sea travel more than anything else.

Improvements in ships were not made during the period, so the time that it took for news to reach American ports from either England or from another American colony remained relatively constant. What changed was the amount of shipping. The great increase in trade expanded the base of news received by printers, who in turn were afforded greater options in the news they chose to disseminate to their readers. Many news stories appear in only one or two newspapers because printers in other regions opted to print different news that was of more interest to the people of that area even though the same news printed by other newspapers was available to them.[95] Even though the amount of news received in ports increased because of expanded trade and printers could exercise greater selection of news that they placed in their newspapers, it should be pointed out that printers continued to print news on very similar topics throughout the colonies during the colonial period and continued to copy from each other's newspapers. This meant that colonial newspapers continued to be very similar in appearance and news content.

Ships, then, provided the bulk of the news that colonial newspapers printed, and news on and about the sea remained a primary type of news during the colonial period. From 1720–1770, newspapers never averaged fewer than 155 news items on the sea per year, and sea news never comprised less than 37 percent of the total items in selected colonial newspapers that were not news of the European events and high matters of state in America. (See appendix 2.) The growth of American trade may be seen in the numbers as well. By 1760, the last year of this study before America and England became embroiled in political turmoil concerning taxes on goods shipped into America and nonimportation became the practice of America's colonies, the selected newspapers averaged just under three hundred news items, meaning more than 46 percent of the news topics of this study dealt with the sea. And despite the fact that England and America did not see eye to eye politically in 1765 and 1770 and trade suffered because of it, colonial newspapers still printed large amounts of ship news, nearly 240 items in 1765 and more than 180 in 1770. Ship news represented 40 percent of the news studied in 1765 and 37.4 percent in 1770. Only when war became the focus of American news in 1775 did ship news move from its place of prominence in newspapers. No other news that was not purely political in its orientation ever approached the total numbers of news items like that which ran yearly about the sea.[96]

The news of the sea that appeared in colonial newspapers also tells the story of piracy in the eighteenth century. Pirates plagued the coastal waters of North America and the Caribbean during the first three decades of the century, but news of pirate activity in these waters almost entirely disappeared from newspapers after 1730. The news of the sea in newspapers, however, made it very evident that piracy merely changed its political stripes around this time because of the rise in privateering, and from 1735–1760, privateers sailing under French and Spanish colors continually interrupted American trade and captured ships sailing under the British flag. According to colonial newspaper reports, the successful campaigns against France and Spain in both America and in Europe evidently put an end to most of the privateering activities in American and Caribbean waters after 1765 because newspaper news of privateering—although it did not disappear completely—decreased significantly in the last decade of the colonial period.

Pirates and privateers may have been slowly eradicated, but the Atlantic and the storms encountered upon it were not. British American colonists were, however, able to conquer another natural enemy that threatened their existence in North America. That enemy was the original inhabitants of New England, the Middle, and the Southern Colonies, the Native Americans, and colonial newspapers approached Indian news with a voracity unparalleled in nearly every other type of news of the colonial period.

2

The Sculking Indian Enemy

3 Souldiers going to the place of Publick Worship, passing over
a Fence through a Field of Corn, some of the Sculking Indian
Enemy being hid in the Field, shot at them, kill'd two and Captivated the third.

—Boston News-Letter, 29 July 1706

Not long after Benjamin Franklin began printing the *Pennsylvania Gazette,* the following news item appeared in the paper:

They made the Prisoner Sing and Dance for some Time, while six Gun
Barrels were heating red hot in the Fire; after which they began to
burn the Soals of the poor Wretches Feet until the Bones appeared,
and continued burning him by slow Degrees up to his Privites, where
they took much Pains. . . . This Barbarity they continued about six
Hours, and then, notwithstanding his Feet were in such a Condition,
they drove him to a Stake . . . and stuck Splinters of Pine all over his
Body, and put Fire to them. . . . In the next Place they scalp'd him
and threw hot Embers on his Head. . . . At last they ran two Gun
Barrels, one after the other, red hot up his Fundament, upon which
expired. . . . P.S. They cut off his Thumbs and offer'd them him to eat
and pluck'd off all of his Nails.[1]

The brutality and savagery exhibited in the way the "Shawnese" Indians treated their prisoner—whether reported accurately or embellished by the trader who witnessed it—only intensified the fear many white colonists felt for Native Americans.

The Indians of the Eastern Seaboard of North America, from the beginning of British colonization, "became enemies in the eyes of Pilgrim fathers, who believed that the New World was the promised land which was theirs to possess even if every one of the Canaanites perished at the point of the sword."[2] More than a century after John Smith wrote those words, Native Americans still represented a threat to the expanding white population along the Atlantic coastline. From Boston to Savannah newspapers reported atrocities inflicted upon innocent white settlers by "the Sculking Indian Enemy," a phrase John Campbell repeatedly used in the *Boston News-Letter* to describe Native Americans.[3]

This chapter discusses colonial newspapers' treatment of news of Native Americans. From the issuance of *Publick Occurrences* in 1690 through 1765, the year the Stamp Act crisis and growing revolutionary fervor captured the attention of the presses of America, the colonial press's treatment of Native Americans was extensive. Following the Stamp Act, newspapers did not ignore Indians, but the threat posed to the colonies along the Eastern Seaboard changed. Indians, except in several very isolated events, no longer posed a serious danger to white colonists east of the Appalachian Mountains. Native Americans now threatened westward expansion into the Ohio River Valley and along the fertile Gulf of Mexico frontier that reached from Georgia to the Mississippi River. For that reason, Indian news diminished somewhat in its total amount, but it never completely disappeared. When hostilities erupted between the colonies and England in 1775, one of the big questions posed in colonial newspapers was the role Native Americans would play in the confrontation. The American colonists had neither forgotten that Native Americans still lived among them nor that the Indians could be a fierce and persistent adversary.

The Indian population of the colonies during the colonial period shrank continually, primarily because of disease[4] but also through Indian migration and through war. Despite the reduction in Indian population,[5] the colonial newspapers continued to report on Native American activities because Indians remained a threat to colonization throughout the eighteenth century. In fact, Native Americans threatened American settlement throughout the nineteenth century as the ever-growing white population pushed westward across the Mississippi River and Great Plains, and newly implanted English-speaking whites reached eastward from California in an effort to connect with their Atlantic compatriots.[6]

Before looking at Indians as reported by the colonial press, a brief overview of Native Americans' representation in English prints prior to *Publick Occurrences* and in pamphlets of the period should help in understanding the white colonists' later perceptions of Native Americans.

NATIVE AMERICANS IN PRINT OUTSIDE COLONIAL NEWSPAPERS

The English concept of the inhabitants of the New World originated before any Englishman stepped foot in North America. Sir Thomas More, in his 1517 work *Utopia,* described some of the inhabitants of his imagined country as "no less savage, wild, and noisome than the very beasts themselves."[7] Two years later, More's brother-in-law, John Rastell, stated that the Indians "nother knowe God nor the diuill, nor never harde tell of wrytynge nor other scripture." He went on to say that Europeans would be performing "a great meritoryouse dede" by exposing Native Americans to European ways of life.[8] By the middle of the sixteenth century, English writers such as Richard Eden were positing that Christian nations had a right and an obligation to occupy lands not in the possession of any other Christian people.[9]

With these preconceived notions of Native American characteristics and the belief in *vacuum domicilium,* or the duty of civilized nations to seize underused lands from barbarians, the English began their colonization attempts in North America. Indian troubles for the British settlers started almost immediately,[10] and the first long account of those woes appeared in a London newspaper, *Mercurius Civicus,* in 1645 when the paper reported on an Indian massacre in Virginia that claimed four hundred colonists.[11]

In America the written attacks on Native Americans started in 1682.[12] In *A True HISTORY of the Captivity & Restoration of Mrs. Mary Rowlandson,* all the horrors imaginable concerning Indians were recorded for colonists to read. Rowlandson, a minister's wife, was abducted 1 February 1675, and her narrative inflamed the fears of being captured by Indians. "I had often before this said," Rowlandson wrote, "that if Indians should come, I should chuse rather to be killed by them, than taken alive."[13] Rowlandson described how the Indians took one man and "stripped him naked, and split open his Bowels" and took a woman and "knockt her on the head, and the child in her arms with her: when they had done that they made a fire and put them both into it."[14]

Even after the appearance of *Publick Occurrences,* the narratives of Indian captivities continued. Cotton Mather wrote in his *Humiliations follow'd with Deliverance* how Indians, after taking English captives, "dash'd out the Brains of the Infants, against a Tree, and several of the other captives . . . were soon sent unto their long House, but the Salvages would presently bury their

Hatchets in their Brains, and leave the carcasses on the ground."[15] Oral reports of this kind had caused Mather's father, Increase, sixty years earlier to tell his congregation to offer thanks to God because "we have sent six hundred heathen souls to hell."[16]

This anti–Indian captivity literature continued throughout the colonial period with recommendations from outstanding ministers on its validity and value in understanding the danger that Native Americans posed to white colonists.[17] One entire volume was devoted to French and Indian cruelty during the Seven Years War.[18] With such literature circulating through the colonies, colonial printers needed only to mention the taking of captives within their weekly newspapers to spur the imaginations of their readers. Newspapers, then, fostered the fear and hatred of Native Americans that had already been built into other literature of the period. Along with various other types of reporting concerning Indians, colonial newspapers created a sizable body of news dealing with Native Americans.

NATIVE AMERICANS AND COLONIAL NEWSPAPERS

Publick Occurrences offers the perfect prototype for news coverage of Native Americans by colonial newspapers. Three categories of Indian news appeared in Benjamin Harris's lone edition. Those three types of news dealt with the "barbarous" or "Sculking Indian Enemy," the Native American and French alliance, and the peaceful relations between the English and Native Americans. The first type of news constitutes the majority of Native American news stories in *Publick Occurrences,* as well as in the other colonial newspapers. Hundreds of news items appeared that discussed Indian atrocities and wars against colonists. The second type of Native American news in *Publick Occurrences* dealt with the Indians' alliance with England's long-time nemesis, France. This news culminated in the Seven Years or French and Indian War that lasted from 1754–1763. The third type of Indian news often discussed activities carried on by Indians that provided services or were advantageous to the colonists. *Publick Occurrences* referred to Indians that functioned in this way as "Christianized Indians."

A fourth type of Indian news that did not appear in *Publick Occurrences* dealt with the political dialogue between colonial leaders and the Indians. Indian treaties were serious business for colonial governments, and Indian conferences were attended by the most influential of colonial leaders, often at sites many hundreds of miles away from colonial capitals in the backcountry.[19] While treaties between the English colonists and Native Americans may have been the most important exchange between the two groups, news of the horrors of "the Sculking Indian Enemy" dominated the Indian news in colonial newspapers. The discussion of Native Americans and the newspapers of colonial America begins there.

The Sculking Indian Enemy. News of Indian attacks and atrocities committed upon English colonists appeared with regularity throughout the colonial period. The number of Native American news items rose whenever there was a large Indian war with the settlers. Various Native American tribes declared war on the colonists along the Eastern Seaboard in 1711, 1715, 1760, and 1764[20] and on whites beyond the Appalachians in 1763 and 1767.[21] In addition, individual colonies declared war upon Indian tribes. Massachusetts encouraged its inhabitants to kill all male Indians over the age of twelve and capture women and children under the age of twelve for rewards in 1706.[22] The colony of South Carolina declared war against the Tuscaroras in 1735 when Lieutenant Governor Thomas Broughton issued a proclamation offering "Fifty Pounds Current Money, and Sixty Pounds like Current Money for every Tuscoraw Indian who shall be taken alive."[23] Massachusetts declared war against the "Penobscot and Norridgewack tribes, and other Eastern Indians" in 1745. The colony promised £100 to anyone or any group that would "go out and kill a Male Indian of the Age of twelve Years or upwards." To collect, all one had to do was "produce the Scalp in Evidence of his Death." Women and children under the age of twelve were worth £50 if the scalp was produced.[24] Farther north, the *Boston Evening-Post* reported that £50 sterling awaited "any Person, who shall take any Indian Prisoner, and for every Head or Scalp of an Indian killed as aforesaid" in Nova Scotia.[25]

The proclamations of war that were issued by individual colonies followed acts of violence committed by the Indians. Before the South Carolina proclamation, the *South-Carolina Gazette* described for its readers the wounds that took the life of a Carolina Indian trader named George Stevens: "Three cuts on the Head, one on the back & sculp'd, his left hand was split to the wrist, his left shoulder jointed, his Stomach cut open to his Belly, and prick'd all over the Body."[26]

In Boston, the reporting of Indian activity was much more frequent than in other areas of America, probably because colonists and Native Americans shared a smaller geographical area. The number of whites in New England increased, and as a result more fighting for control of land took place. Attacks by Indians, in such a case, would be more likely. The *Boston News-Letter* of 1 May 1704, devoted nearly half of its news coverage to Indian trouble in South Carolina and then told how a local farmer, burning brush around one of his fields, was attacked by Indians "who shot him through the thigh and leggs, then took, Scalpt, kill'd, and stript him Naked." The next day, according to the *News-Letter*, a local sawmill operator was killed by Indians and his wife and son taken captive.[27]

"The Sculking Indian Enemy" continually attacked the colonists of New England during the first two decades of the eighteenth century, and John Campbell regularly reported those attacks in the *News-Letter*. In fact, Campbell did not let news of Native American activities throughout the colonies go unnoticed; he provided his readers with reports from up and down the Atlantic seaboard. The *News-Letter*, for example, gave the citizens of Boston extensive coverage of the Tuscarora War in the Carolinas.[28] The first report arrived via letter from South Carolina in November 1711. The letter related how the "Cape Fair Indians" had cut off twenty families in North Carolina and "Men, Women & Children scalpt them" all.[29] The reports continued throughout 1712 with the last stories on the Tuscaroras appearing from May–July 1713. In May, Campbell presented his readers with an 16 April report from Charleston that said "the heart of the Tuskeraro war is broken."[30] Two months later, news from Philadelphia revealed the fact that the Tuscaroras were still killing English families,[31] but the earlier report was accurate. The Tuscaroras had been defeated, and no more activity by them appeared in the *News-Letter*.

The Indians of South Carolina declared war on the white settlers of the colony in 1715,[32] but that war was the last proclaimed by Native Americans against the colonists until the 1760 Cherokee War. News of Indian attacks upon the colonists continued because the Indians continued to harass and attack the colonists and vice versa. Even if there was no proof that Native Americans had inflicted horrors upon the colonists, they were often blamed for them, as a *New-England Courant* article aptly demonstrates:

They write from Stratford in Connecticut, that a Woman of that Place having lately left a young Child for a little Tiwe [*sic*], miss'd it when she came home; and hearing nothing of it, concluded it was drown'd. About a Week after the Child was found two Miles from the House, above high-Water Mark, with the Hands, Head and Private Parts cut off, and a Hole under each Arm, suppos'd to be stabb'd with a Knife. Some Indians being suspected of the Murdre [*sic*], a Council was held at Stratford, and the Indians were summon'd to appear.[33]

Reports like this only affirmed the Indian captivity literature that was available to colonists.

The way in which news surrounding Indians was reported also varied from region to region. In August 1735, a trader was found dead three hundred miles north of Philadelphia. The *American Weekly Mercury* reported a man was found murdered who "was out on a Trading Journey with the Indians."[34] The same day Franklin's *Pennsylvania Gazette* said, "We have an Account that our Indian Traders lately found an Englishman murther'd and scalp'd. . . . [H]is Name was James Dowthel. . . . The Murther is suppos'd to have been done by some of the Southern Indians."[35] The *Boston Evening-Post,* however, carried a much more thorough report of the murder than either of the Pennsylvania papers:

We have an Account by a Person, who about 3 Weeks since with another Man, was out on a Trading Journey with the Indians, That when they were about 300 Miles to the Northward, and 150 (as near as they could Guess) from any Inhabitants, they found a parcel of Skins, and began to suspect that Murder had been committed there-abouts, and presently after finding another parcel of Skins, this greatly increas'd their suspicion; upon which they made search, and found the Body of one James Dowthell lying very near the Path, and they sup-pos'd him to have lain there about two Days; he was shot thro' the Body, and hack'd very much on one of his Shoulders, and his Scalp was taken off. This Dowthell had been out a Hunting with one William Balden, whom (it is fear'd) is also Murder'd. . . . Both their Dogs re-turned to their dwellings soon after the Murder was committed. Upon the Discovery of the murder'd Body, they [the dogs] made the best of their way home again; fearing (if they should proceed) that they should be serv'd in the same Manner.[36]

While ventures into a backcountry inhabited by Native Ameri-cans were risky business, attempts at everyday life in New En-gland were no less risky, even in the 1730s and 1740s. This may help to explain the extended report of the death of James Dowthell in the *Boston Evening-Post* versus the more sanitized versions that appeared in the Philadelphia papers. In 1745, the Indians in the Massachusetts colony began attacks upon the white settlements. In July, settlers were forced into their garrison on the George's River because of continuing Indian attacks. *Evening-Post* printer

Thomas Fleet reported the gruesome results of one of those attacks:

> The Enemies had 2 kill'd and as many wounded in the Engagement, which being over, the Indians cut open Capt. Donahew's Breast, and suck'd his Blood, and hack'd and mangled his Body in a most inhuman and barbarous Manner, and then eat a great part of his Flesh. They also suck'd the Blood and mangled the Bodies of the other Slain.[37]

The attacks continued, culminating in a declaration of war by Massachusetts upon the "Eastern Indians," and the *Evening-Post* continued to provide coverage.

Inhabitants of other colonies worried at increased Indian activity as well during the middle of the century. A writer to the *Maryland Gazette* exemplified the fear that many settlers possessed of Native Americans when he berated his fellow colonists:

> Are we asleep! Are we stupified or benumbed! by some Charm or magical Power, that we seem to sleep and eat from Day to Day in Security, while Murder and Massacre, and all the horrid Consequences of a barbarous Foe's getting Footing among us, hang over [us].[38]

Two weeks later the *Gazette* reported the murder and scalping of two men,[39] and the 18 December paper carried a description of how a home, once considered a haven of safety, could be invaded by Indians:

> [A] Lad rose from the Table and opened the Door, and immediately an Indian fired into the House, which lightly grazed along the Lad's Chin, and killed one of the Persons at the Table, whereupon a most sad and lamentable Cry was heard all over the House: One Woman ran out of Doors, and they forced her back; some attempted to run up Stairs, but were torn down again: in short they killed five in the House, who were all burnt and consumed in the Flames. One Man that got out of the House was shot in the Back, and had also three of four Blows in his Body by a Tomahawk, him they also scalped. The Lad that first opened the Door got up Stairs to the second Story, and as he was looking out of the Window an Indian fired at him, which grazed along the Side of his Face, but did not do him much Damage; as soon as the Lad perceived that the Indians were gone to another Part of the House he jumped out of the Window, and saved himself, by Flight.[40]

The conflicts between the "Sculking Indian Enemy" and the white colonists remained a staple of the colonial newspaper. The *Virginia Gazette,* during a one-month period in 1755, carried local

Indian news, as well as news of Indian activities in Maine, New York, Nova Scotia, New Hampshire, North Carolina, Boston, Annapolis, and South Carolina.[41] The *Boston Evening-Post,* in its 23 June 1760 edition, gave its readers several pieces of Indian news from the South Carolina Cherokee War along with Indian news from Annapolis, New York, Quebec, and New Hampshire. By 1765, Indian activities against white settlers in the Detroit area found their way into the colonial newspapers.[42] Most of the Indians of the Eastern seaboard had become victims of the white men, just as John Smith had predicted, and "perished at the point of the sword" or from some English-inflicted malady.

The largest single concerted effort by Native Americans against the white colonists of America during the eighteenth century occurred in 1760. That is when the once friendly Cherokee Indians in South Carolina mounted an offensive against the colonists. The Cherokees could be found from Georgia through Virginia, and any uprising by them could prove costly to all of British colonial America. The Cherokees had, however, been considered allies of the colonists. A 1755 South Carolina meeting of colonial and Cherokee leaders produced an eloquent soliloquy by a Cherokee chief intended for the ears not only of those in attendance but also of King George:

> We are now Brothers with the People of Carolina, and one House covers us all: The Great King is our common Father. We, our Wives, and all our Children, are the Children of the Great King George, and his Subjects . . . and we will obey him as such. I bring this litle [sic] Child, that, when he grows up, he may remember what is now agreed to, and that he may tell it to the next Generation, that so it may be handed down from one Generation to another for ever.[43]

When this Cherokee policy changed, it was news from Charleston to Boston, and the colonial newspapers followed the activity in South Carolina very carefully.

The "policy" of the Cherokees toward the white inhabitants of South Carolina changed within five years of the above speech. The *South-Carolina Gazette* reported in February 1760 that the "whole Province is now is Arms, or arming, to repress the Invasion of the persidious Cherokees."[44] The same announcement appeared in the *Maryland Gazette* on 3 April. The news reached Boston much sooner, though, through letters, and the *Boston Evening-Post* related how the Cherokees, who had at least three thousand warriors not counting any Indian allies,[45] had started the killings "by cruelly murdering every white man they could lay hands on . . . and followed the bloody stroke, by massacring numbers of families in the remote parts of the province."[46] Notices of Cherokee activity throughout the Southern Colonies found their way into Boston. The *Evening-Post* recounted how "the Cherokees have made incursions into Augusta County in Virginia." There, regiments of Virginia militia "repulsed the enemy and kept the field, tho' with great loss of men."[47]

In South Carolina, hostilities escalated. At Ninety-Six, the garrison further inflamed Cherokee hatred by taking a brave "who was killed and scalped, and whose Body was given to the Dogs, and his Scalp hoisted along-side of the Colours to provoke the Enemy to come nearer." The *Gazette* stated that "the Bodies of the Savages were cut to Pieces and given to the Dogs" as a means of solace for grieving colonists.[48] The Indian situation in South Carolina, aggravated by an outbreak of smallpox, became so tenuous that Lieutenant Governor William Bull ordered a day of "FASTING, HUMILIATION, and PRAYER to ALMIGHTY GOD, for averting the Evils which at present threaten us" on April 12.[49]

The war was at full force by summer, and the atrocities inflicted upon the settlers matched those that the settlers had perpetrated on the Cherokees. A lengthy *South-Carolina Gazette* war report told of rotten meat and a bit of corn being the sole food supplies of the people held in siege at several forts. A ransom was paid by white settlers at one of the forts for a woman and three children, "but the Woman had been so cruelly used that she died soon after." In addition, the report stated that "the Indians burn all their Men Prisoners; they had lately burnt Six at Conasatchee . . . amongst them John Downing, whose Arms and Legs they first cut off."[50]

By the end of August, the colonists held captive in Fort Loudoun had surrendered the fort and its artillery to the Cherokees in agreement for safe passage northward.[51] But one thing that the South Carolina settlers did not realize was that the Cherokees were divided into several groups, and the surrender to one group at Fort Loudoun did not ensure that Cherokees farther north would not attack soldiers or settlers on the march. That is exactly what happened to the men who left the fort under articles of capitulation. The attack left the colonists in "utmost confusion." The Cherokees, according to the *South-Carolina Gazette*'s report, tortured all of their captives:

Capt. Demeré received two wounds the first volley, was directly scalped, and the Indians made him dance about for their diversion some time, after which they chopped off one hand or arm, than the other, and so his legs, &c. using the most shocking barbarities on the bodies of others of our people.[52]

Coverage of the war continued throughout 1760, but the Cherokees, tired of the fighting, agreed to articles of surrender in late 1761,[53] although reports of fighting could be found in the newspapers into December.[54]

The Cherokees may have tired from fighting with the colonists, but the Native Americans living beyond the Appalachians had not. No sooner had the Cherokee war (1760) and French and Indian War (1754–1763)[55] ended than the Indians of the Great Lakes region, led by the Ottawa chief, "Pondiac,"[56] declared war on the British Americans.

Known as Pondiac's War, Indians from Western Pennsylvania to Detroit joined together in the spring of 1763 to battle British-speaking whites who flowed into the Ohio River Valley and Great Lakes regions in the anticipation of France's capitulation to England and subsequent removal of French settlers from much of North America. The Indian war effort lasted into 1765. An extended but unsuccessful siege of the British outposts at Fort Detroit and Fort Pitt, British attacks on Ohio Valley Indian towns, and the intentional spread of smallpox among the Indians through infected blankets by the officers at Fort Pitt broke the Indians' resolve and ended the war.[57]

Colonial newspapers in Georgia, New England, and all points between closely monitored the events in Pittsburgh and Detroit. By 1765, the colonials' tactics had swung the balance in the war toward the whites. The first reports to appear in the colonial newspapers in January 1765 concerning the fighting were very optimistic that peace was at hand. In an address printed by the *Boston Gazette, and Country Journal,* Governor Francis Bernard announced to Massachusetts citizens:

> The happy Termination of the Indian War, in which so many of our Fellow subjects have been massacred, and so extensive a Frontier desolated must give sincere Joy to every Breast susceptible of the Feelings of Humanity; at least to every one, that bears any affection for British America.[58]

Governor Bernard's joyous proclamation proved erroneous because the fighting in the Ohio Valley continued. In April, news that scalping knives and ammunition intended for the warring Indians had been intercepted before they could reach the Pittsburgh area was reported.[59] The war goods, evidently, were shipped by an en-

terprising ship captain from Philadelphia who was more intent on
making money than sparing the lives of colonists.[60] In addition,
the *Georgia Gazette* related that supplies for "the enemy Indians
at Detroit" were being sent up the Mississippi River; the source
of the goods was the French who remained in the area around
New Orleans.[61]

News reaching New England in June said "that Pondiac had
seized 6 Englishmen" and several of their Indian allies. The Ottawa
chief, the extract of a 19 May letter said, had burned at the stake
all but two of the prisoners, which Pondiac intended as presents
for another tribe. The letter left no doubt that the two survivors
would face similar, violent deaths.[62]

The news arriving from the Ohio Valley, however, continued to
provide the colonists living along the Atlantic seaboard with conflicting accounts of Pondiac's War, no doubt because of the large
number of tribes living in the area, the success that the British
troops had had in retaliating against the Indians, and the autonomy
each Native American nation enjoyed. One week newspapers
would ease fears of hostilities by printing reports that stated that
recently reported stories of war were groundless. In July, this belief
was based on the fact that traders around Lake Erie were treated
"with great Love and Friendship" by some Indians.[63] Yet in August, the *Newport Mercury* stated that Pondiac had cut off a large
contingent of troops in Illinois and then printed that the chief had
ordered the preparation of a large kettle, "in which he was determined to boil [English prisoners] and all other Englishmen that
came that way."[64]

A *Boston Post-Boy* article captured fully the confusion surrounding the war news of the Ohio saying in one sentence that the
reports concerning Pondiac cutting off British troops were not true
and in the next sentence correcting the earlier correspondence
by noting Pondiac had done just that—cut off the troops under
Lieutenant Fraser and killed several of the soldiers.[65] The conflicting reports may be blamed upon the length of time it took to bring
news back from the region and the sources. Traders, who were
less interested in being correspondents than in earning a living
through barter, told what they knew, but often they spent months
in the backcountry before returning to a city with a newspaper. By
the time of their return, traders' news and that brought back by
soldiers or missionaries could easily provide conflicting stories because the events had occurred months apart and in different regions. Hostilities also ended during 1765, but one should not
assume that a multilateral cease-fire occurred when communica-

tion was so sporadic. Fighting, therefore, continued in isolated places while peaceful relations resumed in others. These facts help explain the conflicting news items.

By December 1765, though, it may be assumed that the Indians had capitulated. Pondiac was even alleged now to be an ally of the English. Weyman's *New-York Gazette* happily reported:

> We have the Pleasure of assuring our Readers, that [Colonel Croghan] has, beyond the most sanguine Expectations, not only attached PON-DIAC, and the Chiefs of many other very numerous Nations . . . to the British Interest . . . but he has also obtained their Consent to our Troops taking quiet Possession of Fort Charters, and of all the other French Posts in the Illinois Country.[66]

Pondiac's War had ended, but the activity of "the Sculking Indian Enemy" and their equally vicious white counterparts had not. Before the colonial newspapers turned their attention almost exclusively toward the fight for independence, more massacres by both sides took place.

The tenuous coexistence of Native Americans and colonists was placed in jeopardy—at least from the British perspective—in 1770 when the Shawnee and Delaware tribes of the Great Lakes and Illinois area entered into a peace pact with their longtime southern enemies, the Cherokees and Creeks. The tribes agreed to share hunting grounds in Kentucky, lands that the Six Nations had already ceded to the British for settlement, and the British saw a general peace among Native Americans of the two regions as an open invitation among Indians for another war upon the whites.[67]

The likelihood of such a war spread throughout the colonies in the summer of 1770. The *Boston Evening-Post* carried a letter from Wilmington, North Carolina, sent to Philadelphia that contained dispatches from the colonial governments of both South Carolina and Virginia. The letter reported that twenty or thirty families in "the back parts of Virginia" had been murdered by Indians. Prospects of another war with "the Sculking Indian Enemy" was dreaded more than a war with the major powers of Europe. The letter stated concerning another Indian war, "It would have given us more pleasure to have heard of a war with France and Spain, than with those Savages."[68]

The peace between colonists and Native Americans was so fragile that any hostility committed by either side led newspaper accounts to assume war would erupt. "A Creek Indian was found murdered at one Andrew Burney's Door in Augusta," the *South-*

Carolina and American General Advertiser advised. "He was stabbed in two or three Places, scalped, his Throat cut, and one of his Arms broken. This occasioned a great Alarm in that Part of the Country."[69] When traders in the Detroit area retaliated against an alleged Indian attack, war was deemed imminent:

> By Letters of the 14th ult. from Detroit, we are informed that a French Trader having been stabbed by some Indians on an Island within 6 Miles of Michimackmac, 30 of the principal Traders at that Post, both English and French, went in Canoes, landed on the Island, surrounded the Huts, fired upon the Indians, shot one of them in several Parts of his Body, and then tomahawk'd him till dead. This Affair, it is expected, will occasion great Disturbances in those Parts.[70]

Even into 1775, the relationship between American colonists and Native Americans remained on unstable footing. The colonists wanted trade with the Indians, but they did not want the Indians living anywhere near the rapidly expanding white settlements.[71] The Americans would soon ask for Native Americans' help in fighting the British, but a letter in the *Maryland Gazette* printed a decade earlier best summed up the feelings of most British colonists in America when the writer recounted his dream for Annapolis readers:

> His Majesty's Agent in order effectually to prevent all farther Ravages by those barbarous Savages, had summoned all the Indians in America to meet him at a grand Congress, at which every individual adult Indian in America attended; the whole Number amounting to Three Million Five Thousand Seven Hundred and Thirty-four. At this Congress the Agent informed them . . . that they were a People whose Promises could not be relied on; and that from the immense Increase of the Whites the Country would soon be too narrow for both. . . . Upon which the whole Audience who all heard him very distinctly and easily took the Hint, unanimously rose up and immediately went and hanged themselves.—It is thought that the Subject of Ways and Means how to dispose of their Wives and Children to prevent the tragical Consequences of the Repopulation of america by such Savages, will be one of the first that will engage the Deliberation of the Parliament at their next Sitting.[72]

Not all white men from Europe, however, proved to be the Indians' enemies. Many Native Americans discovered an affinity for the French and allied themselves with these trappers and missionaries. The French were a formidable foe for the English settlers in America, and their confederation with Native Americans ultimately resulted in a war against the English colonists. When the Indians allied themselves with England's old nemesis France, considerable news appeared in the colonial newspapers, and the nature of that information was very similar to news of "the Sculking Indian Enemy."

Native American and French Alliance. Unlike the Spanish who came before them and the English who arrived at roughly the same time, the French settlers in North America realized that the only way to peaceably exist with the Native Americans was to accept them exactly as they were. The French in America learned the differences in the various Indian cultures and did not try to force their language or religion upon the Native Americans.[73] As a result, by the time of *Publick Occurrences,* the French and many Indian tribes were political allies and friends, and Benjamin Harris's onetime offering related to Boston's citizens the following:

> Two English Captives escaped from the Hands of Indians and French at Pascadamodquady, came into Portsmouth on the sixteenth Instant & say, That when Capt. Mason was at Fort Real, he cut the faces, and ript the bellies of two Indians, and threw a third Over board in the sight of the French, who informing the other Indians of it, they have in revenge barbarously Butcher'd forty Captives of our that were in their hands.[74]

Publick Occurrence's story demonstrates that by 1690, the French and some Indians were at war with the English colonists of Massachusetts Bay. In fact, certain groups of Native Americans initiated a war against the settlers in 1688, according to Cotton Mather, that lasted for a decade.[75] The French success with the Native Americans, coupled with the "bad blood" that existed between England and France helped many Indian tribes lose any autonomy that the tribe may have gained from the English settlers. Once Native Americans allied themselves with the French, they became known in the English colonies and in the colonial press as French Indians.[76]

The "French Indians" joined the French in a number of raids on English settlements early in the eighteenth century, according to the *Boston News-Letter.* One letter reprinted by John Campbell said that in order for a new English settlement to survive, "God must work Miracles, to preserve it" from attacks by the French and Indians.[77] Another time, four hundred French and Indians attacked six English garrisons following an English raid on an empty Indian village, where forty houses were destroyed.[78] The French and Indians also used "Sloops and Canoo's" in their raids on English settlements along the coast.[79] Because the French and Indians took to the water for their raids, not even English ships were safe from attack. The *News-Letter* related how

> in a narrow Passage of the River about 60 or 70 Panabicot Indians mixt with French as 'tis thought about 1150 in all . . . kill'd the whale Boats Crew, wounded Fort-Major William Elliot, & afterwards Barbarously Murdered him. . . . 34 Men were carried Captive to Menis & so to La Bay Verte to be Transported to Cannada.[80]

The raids by the French and Indians on English settlements occurred with regularity in the first half of the eighteenth century, according to newspaper accounts. At times the raids produced gruesome results such as one the *American Weekly Mercury* reported in 1725. Two New England boys, abducted and carried back to Canada, were not discovered, at least not until the decapitated and mangled body of one was found.[81] The French and Indian alliance even staged attacks on Indians who aligned themselves with the English. The *New-England Weekly Journal* informed its readers in February 1740, that "700 French Indians had made an Inroad into Mohawks Country," forcing the Mohawks into English forts in northern New York.[82]

The French and Indian assault upon the English settlements in North America culminated in the French and Indian War. Officially listed as a war that lasted from 1754–1763, the conflict between the English and the Native American and French alliance produced an escalation in hostilities much earlier. A New England garrison was attacked by "an Army of French and Indians" late in 1745,[83] and the New York village of "Soraghtoga" had been cut off by "a great Body of French and Indians,"[84] leaving ninety either dead or taken captive.[85] The *Maryland Gazette,* reporting on Indian activity from the Boston area, pointed out that "it is credibly reported, that the Indians are paid and subsisted as French troops."[86] And the *Pennsylvania Gazette,* in passing on information contained in a letter received in Philadelphia from someone Boston, recounted how the Penobscot Indians had been on board a French sloop loaded with Indians preparing to attack English settlements.[87]

By 1755 the French and Indian hostilities—along with French privateering activities in the shipping lanes—captured most of the space in colonial newspapers. Even though England had yet to declare war upon France, there was a war being waged in British colonial America. "Indians, with French Officers among them, have been hovering about our Settlements for several Days," a notice received in Boston from the English north of that city stated.[88] Along the coast, the French were setting up blockades of the colonial ports,[89] while "the French, and their Indians" were cutting off the supply routes for the English in the backcountry[90] and trying to make the Appalachian Mountains the border of Great Britain in America.[91] As the fall of 1755 arrived, Indian hostilities, spurred on by the French, were on the rise in all colonies. From Boston to Charleston, fresh Indian atrocities appeared each week in the colonial newspapers. The French were doing all they could to stir hostilities between the Indians and English surfaced when a French prize was brought to harbor containing a large cache of scalping knives sent from France to be distributed among the Native Americans.[92]

The content of several colonial newspapers during a typical five-day period in 1755[93] demonstrates the extent of French and Indian war news at this time. The *Boston Evening-Post*[94] printed three accounts that dealt with Indians and war, three others that reported fighting with the French, and three that dealt with the direct war situation between England and France in Europe. The *New-York Gazette: or the Weekly Post-Boy*[95] ran six news items on hostilities with Indians and two more on fighting that took place in the waters off New York with the French. In Philadelphia, the *Pennsylvania Journal*[96] printed five stories about fighting between colonials and Indians, four on hostilities between England and France, and twelve on confrontations among French and ships trading with American ports. The *Maryland Gazette*[97] reported four different accounts of war with Native Americans and eight others on war with the French. The *Virginia Gazette*[98] contained only news of the war with the French and Indians in three long stories along with a letter on growing indigo and a notice of the proroguing of the House of Burgesses. The *South-Carolina Gazette*[99] ran one account that dealt with Indians and war and nine more that addressed war with the French and Indians.

Although the French and Indian War officially continued until the signing of the Peace of Paris in 1763, French and Indian War news in the colonial newspapers decreased by 1760. In its wake came reports of the Cherokee War in the Southern colonies. Yet even there, the French were blamed for inflaming hostilities, as a letter sent from Charleston to New York that found its way into the *Maryland Gazette* demonstrates. The Upper Tribe of Creeks joined in the hostilities as Cherokee allies, leaving the letter writer to speculate, "Thus it appears the French and their Agents have not been inactive."[100]

With the conclusion of the French and Indian War, the French alliance with Native Americans was greatly curtailed, but it did not disappear completely. Although the French were officially expelled from North America with the Peace of Paris and the lands east of the Mississippi River were considered a part of England, the Indians received some support from the French who ignored the treaty and remained in America. Their assistance, however, was minute compared with the French aid that had greatly benefited the Indians in the century and a half prior to the conclusion of the French and Indian War.

French traders sent boats loaded with supplies up the Mississippi River from New Orleans to aid in Pondiac's siege of Fort Detroit.[101] And for that reason, continued economic exchanges between the French and the Illinois Indians presented a major impediment to peace in that region, according to a letter in the *Georgia Gazette*.[102] Illegal French assistance to the Native Americans in the Ohio valley continued into 1770, and newspaper accounts stated that colonists were "alarmed with the apprehensions of France's making attempts to excise the Indians to take up the hatchet against their new masters." British intelligence reports speculated that "the French would carry on their schemes clandestinely by the river Missisippi; while a few have imagined that they would send a strong fleet up St. Lawrence, and try openly to regain their old possessions" with the assistance of their old allies, the Indians.[103]

The news of a new French and Indian offensive was only speculation. The French presence in North America east of the Mississippi River had diminished greatly from 1763–1770, and this in turn ensured the failure of Native American war efforts to stop British colonial expansion. With most of the Indian trouble now in the West, the Indians who remained east of the Appalachian Mountains generally received different treatment from white colonists. In many places Native Americans were assimilated into the white culture. This fact, and the fact that white colonists found certain alliances with Native Americans profitable led to a series of peaceful encounters between the two cultures throughout the period. While the news of "the Sculking Indian Enemy" dominated Native American news in the colonial newspapers, news of more cordial relations appeared as well.

Peaceful relations, English and Native Americans. When *Publick Occurrences* told Boston's citizens about the happenings of the "Christianized Indians in some parts of Plimouth," Benjamin Harris was reporting on more than a peaceful group of Native Americans. He was reporting on one of the English settlers' objectives for the New World, converting the Indians to Christianity. Unfortunately for the Native Americans living in the vicinity of English immigrants, Christianity, as presented in New England, did not fit into the Indians' lifestyle very successfully. Approximately twenty percent of the Native Americans had been converted by 1670, and the colonists had begun to realize that mass conversion of the Indians was not likely. If the Indians could not be converted, they needed to be destroyed.[104] Considering this fact, it is amazing that friendly relations with the Native Americans occurred at all. But they did, and evidence of those relationships appeared in the colonial newspapers.

One of the most consistent presentations of friendly Indians in the colonial press related how the Indians helped colonists search out their enemies, be that enemy other Indians or the French. "One Englishman and four Indians" were "sent out upon discovery of the Enemy" in 1704 and destroyed the enemy, a group of Native Americans.[105] When the Tuscaroras instituted hostilities in North Carolina in 1711, a large military force, comprised mostly of Indians from South Carolina, marched northward to the assistance of the North Carolinians. "Just now arrived here Mr. Edward Foster our Agent from South Carolina," the *News-Letter* printed, "with Advice that 1200 Indians and 50 or 60 English under the Command of Col. Moor are upon their march for this place [North Carolina] to our Assistance against the Indian Enemy."[106] Three months later, "none of the Tuscarorowes [were] to be seen" because "the South Carolina Indians were there and were Masters of the Country."[107]

Native Americans continued to serve in the military for the English. When hostilities erupted between Spain and England in 1739, Southern Indians were quick to volunteer to defend the provincial interests of South Carolina and Georgia. They even joined James Oglethorpe in an English assault upon St. Augustine in Spanish Florida. Several nations of Indians—the Uchees, Chickasaws, Talapoosies, Creeks, and Cherokees—met Oglethorpe in Savannah and proceeded "immediately for the Spanish Frontiers."[108] Even during the French and Indian War, some Native Americans allied themselves with the English. When a French and Indian force of seven thousand assaulted the forts around Albany, New York, Indians fought "with great Intrepidity" against them. Later the Indian allies of the English, or "the Indians in the English Interest" as the newspapers often referred to them, came into Albany with approximately eighty enemy scalps each on war poles, which helped to bolster the English morale.[109] A force of sixteen hundred Cherokees marched from North Carolina to fight the French and

Indians in 1755.[110] When the Cherokees declared war on the colonists in 1760, the Catawbas fought against them and brought Cherokee scalps into Charleston to claim the bounty that had been placed on the Cherokees.[111]

In addition to fighting for the English colonies, the Native Americans helped the white settlers in reducing the Indian population by continuing tribal hostilities.[112] In 1716, the Cherokees in South Carolina assisted the white settlers by declaring war against "our Enemy Indians." The colonial leaders were so thrilled that they sent the Cherokees ammunition.[113] Other wars took place between Indian nations in 1730 and 1745, and the colonial newspapers reported on them.[114]

Unless Native Americans were involved in fighting for the colonists, positive news items about them were rare. Equitable and humanitarian efforts toward the Indians were even rarer. The *Boston Evening-Post* reported on a Pennsylvania treaty to send food to Indians,[115] and a bill was introduced into Parliament in 1765 to protect the free Indians in the colonies.[116] Usually, positive news on Native Americans was the result of their misfortune. "We hear from Albany that 6 Indians in a bark canoe, attempting to cross the ferry at Green Bush, were overset," the *Boston Evening-Post* printed, "& four of them *happily* drowned."[117] Rarely was justice served on Native Americans—or at least rarely was it reported in the first half of the eighteenth century. One account of justice that did make the colonial newspapers came from Boston. Six white men, the *Pennsylvania Gazette* related, discovered three Indians camped and asleep in the woods. They shot at them, killing two. The squaw of one of the deceased obtained a warrant for murder, and five of the six "were taken and committed to goal."[118] Cruelty to Native Americans closer to Philadelphia during the same period, however, did not make it into the local newspapers,[119] nor into other colonial sheets. By 1760 though, Pennsylvania offered £100 to anyone providing information leading to arrests for the murders of an entire Indian family in Cumberland County.[120]

In the years following the French and Indian War, newspaper reports that dealt with peaceful relations with Native Americans along the Atlantic seaboard reflected the assimilation of some Indians into the white culture. In August 1770, the *Essex Gazette* provided a short crime notice of the arrest of a murderer. The accused, one "Tim. Metaukus, an Indian" had stabbed another Indian who later died.[121] Metaukus's arrest under Massachusetts law demonstrates how some Native Americans had become a part of the British culture of the colonies. Similarly, the deaths of important

Native Americans began to appear in the newspapers. When the sachem of a tribe living "In the North Part of New-London" died, the Connecticut city paid its respects through "a numerous Concourse of white People who attended the Funeral."[122]

In the Southern colonies, provincial governments passed laws specifically designed to protect the rights of Native American tribes that had sworn loyalty to the British crown. Settlers in Georgia, South Carolina, and North Carolina were concerned over white trappers who were violating a North Carolina treaty with the Cherokees that prohibited the trapping of beaver in lands deeded to the Indian nation.[123] South Carolina passed "An Act for the Preservation of Deer" that specifically forbade any white colonist "to interrupt or hinder the said Catawba Indians, or any Indians in Amity with this Government, in their Deer-Hunting, for the Future."[124]

The news in colonial newspapers dealing with the positive aspects of Native Americans never approached the quantity of news that dealt with Indians as the colonials' enemies. One type of closely related news—that dealing with treaties between the colonists and Indians—demonstrates that the colonists understood the significant role Native Americans played in the success of English settlements in America. The two groups' political confrontations, as they appeared in the colonial newspapers, were crucial to the success of the colonies.

Political relations, English and Native Americans. Although no political meeting between Native Americans and the English appeared in *Publick Occurrences,* the nature of some of its news on Indian-white relationships proves that such alliances were important. One item stated that the "Albanians, New-Yorkers and the five Nations of Indians" had long attempted to get Massachusetts to launch a naval attack on Canada while they mounted a land assault.[125] At numerous times during the colonial period, individual colonies entered into political agreements with various Native American tribes. Not unexpectedly, these political agreements were weighed heavily toward the colonial interest.

In 1712, in the midst of the Tuscarora War in North Carolina, a group of Indians on the Eastern Shore of Maryland put on their war paint in what appeared to be preparation for hostilities against the white colonists. Immediately, the Maryland government sent a messenger to uncover exactly what was happening. The Indians, the messengers discovered, were not preparing to wage war on the white settlers.[126] Usually when delegations of colonists met with Native Americans, the most important of political leaders from a colony were sent. In November 1734, for example, South Carolina's governor met with a group of seventy Cherokees in Charleston for peace talks.[127] In 1735, Massachusetts Governor Jonathan Belcher traveled to the frontier "to preserve and perpetuate the happy Peace with the Indians."[128] Later that same year the "Governour, being attended by a Number of his Majesty's Council and House of Representatives, and divers other Gentlemen, set out for Deerfield, to have an Interview with the Western Indians."[129] That "interview" led to a series of treaties with several tribes.[130] On very special occasions, Native American chiefs even boarded ships and sailed to England for meetings with the king.[131]

As the relationship between Native Americans and the English deteriorated with the growing French activity among the Indians in the 1740s and 1750s, colonial governments sought treaties of peace and friendship with Indian nations. In 1740 and 1745, treaties of alliance were signed with the Six Nations at Albany.[132] By 1755, the governments of New York and the New England colonies realized that Native Americans as adversaries rather than as allies would, in all likelihood, doom the colonials to defeat in the war with the French. A New York letter predicted, "If the Indians are neglected, and nothing more done to secure them in our Interest than has been, Time will show the great Disparity between us . . . and the Indians of the Woods."[133]

The British colonists proved, however, that they had learned something from the Indians concerning "sculking" or guerilla warfare in the century and a half of colonization efforts and proved the *Boston Gazette*'s prediction wrong. By defeating the French and Indian allies and by overcoming the efforts of the Cherokees in the Southern Colonies in 1760, the colonists now held the upper hand in all Indian-colonial negotiations.

Native Americans still posed threats to the colonists despite the growing white domination of the eastern fourth of the North American continent. For that reason, the colonies continually sought and reached accords with the Indians in the Ohio River Valley and in the Southeast. These pacts, from 1765 on, provided the colonists moving west of the Appalachians and west toward the Ozarks through West Florida, Alabama, Mississippi, and Louisiana a more peaceful migration than had taken place from 1760–1765.

That period was marred by wars with the Cherokees and other Southern tribes and by the Ohio Valley wars with the Ottawa chief, Pondiac. After 1765, a tenuous peace existed between the whites and most of the Native Americans, and Parliament used the respite to secure British rights in the western territories for trade and settlement.[134] Indian agents in America worked to arrange treaties with the Shawnee and Delaware Indians in the area around Fort Pittsburgh.[135] New York's governor, William Johnson, invited approximately one thousand Indians to his plantation to negotiate treaties "to the good of his Majestie's subjects."[136] In the South, the superintendent of Indian affairs met with Chickasaw and Choctaw headmen to secure peaceful relations at a meeting in Mobile. A similar meeting was held in Pensacola for the same purpose with the Creek Indians,[137] both ultimately leading to peace treaties "with all the Indian nations upon the River Missisippi, as high as fort Natchee" except for the "Arkansas's."[138] The diplomatic meetings between colonists and Indians at Mobile, Pensacola, Pittsburgh, and upstate New York were covered extensively by newspapers in all regions of the colonies.

By 1775 and the time of armed rebellion by the colonies against English rule, one of the most important political actions taken by the colonies—at least according to the numerous newspaper accounts—was to enlist Native American tribes to the colonial cause. If an alliance could not be obtained, the united colonies sought an agreement of neutrality from Indian tribes. Native American tribes, according to newspaper accounts, were treated as independent nations, and the colonies vied for their services against England before the British could obtain similar assurances from tribes.[139]

A month after shots were fired at Lexington and Concord, the *Massachusetts Gazette* informed citizens of Boston that the Stockbridge Indians, with "500 Men in Readiness," awaited the word for American colonial leaders to do battle with "the King's Troops" if they were needed.[140] Throughout 1775, the Native Americans of New England assisted the colonials around Boston by attacking British troops as an independent fighting unit[141] or by enlisting as regulars in the Continental Army.[142] The colonies regularly sent ambassadors to the various tribes,[143] and whenever an important tribe like the Shawnee declared in favor of the Americans in the conflict, it was important news.[144]

Newspaper reports reflected the hazards that an English-Indian alliance against the colonies could pose. The *Pennsylvania Evening Post*'s good news of the Shawnee alliance was overshadowed by the fact "that many more western and south western tribes seem determined to take up the hatchet against us."[145] A news item out of Williamsburg reported that a Philadelphia man had been "intrusted by Lord North with the sum of forty thousand pounds to see the Indians cut our throats." The news, however, was deemed to be a tory ploy to create worry and dissention among patriots.[146]

According to the news of 1775, very few Native American tribes sided against the colonies. As the *New-York Gazette and Weekly Mercury* reported:

> We can't yet learn that a single Tribe of Savages on this continent have been persuaded to take up the Hatchet against the Colonies, notwithstanding the great Pains made use of by the vile Emissaries of a savage Ministry for that Purpose.[147]

The neutrality of the Native Americans included those living in Canada.[148]

Although some Native Americans sided with the colonies and others eventually fought for the British, the Indians were more content to allow white to kill white. For two centuries, Native Americans had incurred the wrath of the white men's weapons, diseases, and disputes over land and food, and they had made treaties with the whites that generally worked against the autonomy of Native American tribes. In a poignant statement that appeared in the *New Hampshire Gazette,* the "Anderscoggin" tribe presented its own "Declaration of Independence" from the white men to Colonel Samuel Thompson. The tribe asserted that neither the Indians nor the whites had any right to interfere in the politics or daily life of the other's sovereign nation. The Americans and British could, the declaration intimated, fight each other to the death, but they needed to leave the Native Americans alone. The tribe declared:

> WE allow that passive Obedience, and Non-resistance, is only due to the Laws of God, and our own Tribe. . . . We allow that every Indian's Wigwam, is his own Citadel of Defence, in which he has a Right to defend himself, his Squaw & Papposs. We allow that every one's Person and Property ought to be protected by the Laws of his own Tribe.
>
> We allow that if any Tribe or even white People with their great Canoes should attempt to stop our little Canoes from going to catch Fish, get Clams, sell our Furs and Skins, or to buy Rum, their great Canoes ought to be set on fire, as ever they come into our River Anderscoggen. . . .
>
> We allow that no other Tribe of black or white Folks ought to come and build Forts on any of our Land without the Leave of the Heads of our Tribe, or buying the Land first of us.
>
> We allow that every Tribe on this our Land ought to make their own Sagamors, Sachems and Captains, to learn & instruct their young Men

in the Use of the Bow, the Tomahawke, and Scalping-Knife, & to muster them together often for that Purpose.[149]

The white Americans of British North America would make a similar declaration slightly more than a year later, but for the Anderscoggin Indians, at least, the time for independence from the white domination came in 1775, and the Indian declaration no doubt was realized as the colonies turned their attention toward fighting the British and temporarily away from further expansion into Native American territory. Indians, except for efforts at alliance against Britain then, became secondary in America and in colonial newspapers.

Yet even though Native American news lost its importance as news of war erupted upon the pages of colonial newspapers, newspapers had continually reported on the political relationships between the colonists and Native Americans throughout the eighteenth century because those meetings never ceased nor diminished in importance. The significance of the treaties waned somewhat after the French and Indian War period because the basic confrontations between Indians and whites moved west of the Appalachians, and the majority of Americans were more concerned with taxation and other political issues that had arisen with England. Nonetheless, the political relationships between Native Americans and the colonists continued to be a regular feature of the colonial newspaper, culminating in the desire of the colonies to have Indian tribes either fight for the American cause or remain neutral in the American Revolution. But after seventy-five years of eighteenth-century treaties, Native Americans learned, as the declaration by the Anderscoggins demonstrates, that neutrality and a complete separation from the doings of the white men was the only way for Indians to survive. Attaining that goal, however, was only an illusion for the Indians.

CONCLUSION

News of Native Americans occupied a significant position in colonial newspapers. In fact, in 1750, 1755, and 1760, news of Native Americans rose significantly in colonial newspapers. During those war years, colonial newspapers averaged sixty-seven news stories per year on Native Americans, and in 1760 when the Cherokee war was being waged in South Carolina and other Southern colonies, colonial newspapers average ninety news stories per year on Indian affairs, many of those news stories occupying one or more pages in colonial newspapers. Native American news in 1760 captured more than 30 percent of the news content applicable to this study found in the *South-Carolina Gazette.*[150] News of Indians declined greatly between 1760 and 1765, but more information about Native Americans appeared in colonial newspapers in 1765—when westward migration was hampered by Indian wars in the Ohio and Mississippi River valleys—than appeared in most newspapers from 1720–1745.

News of Native American activity in one colony was important to the inhabitants of other colonies, and for that reason, Indian war news run in South Carolina newspapers in 1760, for example, was picked up by almost all of the newspapers in America. The Indian news was clipped by the other newspapers from one of the South Carolina weeklies, and it served as the official war report. The great increase in Native American news from 1750–1760, in turn, caused a decrease in other types of news in newspapers. In the *Pennsylvania Gazette,* for instance, Native American news represented only 6.4 percent of the total news under consideration in this study found in the Philadelphia newspaper in 1750, while crime and court news accounted for approximately 15.3 percent of its content. In 1755, the figures reversed. Indian news captured slightly less than 17 percent of the news space in the *Gazette,* and crime news represented only 5 percent of the content. It is safe to assume that the crime news available to the printers of the *Gazette* did not decrease proportionally with the amount of crime news that the newspaper printed. It is, however, likely that the great amount of news of Native American activity in New England and the Middle colonies in 1755 was more timely and of more importance to readers of the *Pennsylvania Gazette.* Native Americans represented an immediate threat to Pennsylvania, and for that reason, the newspaper kept its readers apprised of hostile Indian activity throughout the colonies.

Because Native Americans were seen as a barbarous group that threatened the life and success of the English colonists, most of the news dealing with Native Americans that appeared in colonial newspapers presented Indians as "the Sculking Indian Enemy." Colonial news often described the horrors of Indian attacks upon the colonists with graphic descriptions of how settlers were murdered. In doing this, colonial news followed a practice already established in the colonies by captivity literature, which described the way in which Indians treated their prisoners. Colonial newspapers gave graphic accounts of the treatment of captives by Native Americans when it was available, but because the captivity literature had already described the treatment of Indian captives—especially women and children—newspapers needed only mention that prisoners were taken to set the minds of colonial readers to work imagining the horrors that were taking place.

Throughout the colonial period, the relationship between white settlers and Native Americans remained tenuous at best. Periods of peace, as demonstrated by colonial newspapers, usually ended with either whites or Indians declaring war upon the other because of some hostility perpetrated upon one group by the other. Colonists, according to the news of colonial newspapers, generally feared Native Americans, and this fear of Indians usually disappeared only with the removal of the Indians. Fear of Native Americans led to a certain amount of respect of them, too. Colonial governments dealt with Indian tribes as nations, and numerous treaties were reached between colonies and Native American tribes.

Colonial newspapers' characterization of Indian news is an accurate reflection of the perceptions of Native Americans in the colonies, one that many historians have ignored.[151] According to the colonial newspapers, Native Americans were "the Sculking Indian Enemy," and as such they needed to be removed from America as English colonists assumed control of the land. For the Native Americans, the question posed to the white English settlers was, "Shew me where I an Indian can retire. 'Tis thou that chasest me; shew me where thou wilt that I take refuge."[152] According to the news of the colonial newspapers, the answer was nowhere, so the Indians had to fight for survival. America was to be England's, and the Indian news of colonial America's newspapers demonstrates the hatred and fear of Native Americans, a hatred and fear that could only be satiated by the removal of the Indians.

Within the hatred and fear that characterized the news of Native Americans that appeared in colonial newspapers was a great amount of graphic detail. The gruesomeness of this news was representative of a larger theme present in the news of colonial America. News that could shock the moral sensibilities of readers penetrated nearly every news topic making sensationalism, the topic of the next chapter, one of the most important types of news to appear colonial newspapers.

3

Melancholy Accidents and Deplorable News

Yesterday morning was found in a Pond . . . a sack, in which
was the Body of a Man, with his Head cut off and not to be
found, his Belly ript open and his Bowels taken out, and one
Leg and one Arm cut off and gone; In this condition the mangled Corpse was carried . . . and expos'd to publick View.
—*Boston Weekly Post-Boy,* 13 October 1735

ELLIS Huske's *Boston Weekly Post-Boy* was not quite a year old
when the newly appointed Boston postmaster printed the above
graphic description of a man's mutilated body that had been discovered in a pond outside of London.[1] No other information concerning the incident accompanied the reporting of the man's
dismemberment. The murder had taken place in London, therefore,
the news of the crime could not help locate any missing person in
New England, if a person were known to be missing. The heinous
crime's perpetrator was not on the loose in the New England countryside ready to commit another savage slaying. The murderer was
not even in America. The brief news item had no real value to the
readers of the *Post-Boy*—except for the shock and entertainment
value that it provided. As such, it represents a body of news that
appeared in colonial newspapers that was sensational in nature.

This type of news has come to be known as sensationalism, a
type of news that Warren Francke said "exploits sensation, the
experience of the senses and even life itself."[2] Sensationalism was
standard fare for colonial newspapers and colonial printers often
prefaced this news with a word of introduction referring to it as a
"Melancholy Accident" or as "Deplorable News." This exploitational news was more prevalent prior to the Stamp Act crisis of
1765 than after. Despite this fact, colonial printers knew the value
of a shocking and brutal story in terms of reader interest and ran
these stories even after Revolution had broken out between the
colonies and England.

69

Sensational news permeated the content of colonial newspapers. Huske's relating of the gruesome London dismemberment in the *Boston Weekly Post-Boy* represents the most prevalent type of sensationalism found in colonial newspapers, that which deals with a brutal murder graphically described. But as has already been seen in the chapters on the sea and Native Americans, sensational news and its shock value could capture the interest of readers no matter what the topic of discussion. The graphic description of sailors "suspended by the hair of their heads" and then having their tongues grabbed, pulled out "and with a hooked knife cutting them off near the root" by Barbary coast pirates[3] was every bit as appalling as a dismemberment. And the *Pennsylvania Gazette*'s explicit account of the "Shawnese" Indians' torture of a prisoner to whom they offered his severed thumbs for food and finally killed by running "two Gun Barrels, one after the other, red hot up his Fundament,"[4] may have served a purpose to warn readers of the dangers of Indians in western Pennsylvania, but it certainly evoked horror and fear more than anything else.

This chapter deals with the sensationalism found in colonial newspapers. Sensational news could be based on almost any subject such as news of the sea, Native Americans, or other topics, and in this study this fact has already been observed. But much of the sensationalism of colonial newspapers has its roots in crime and accident news. The majority of the sensationalism of colonial newspapers might also be considered crime news or news of accidents because most sensationalism has the roots of its story lodged in these areas. There is a difference, however, in the sensationalism and most accident reports in colonial newspapers. In most cases, crime news and news of accidents that is not sensational focuses upon specifics of an incident such as who murdered whom and why if known. The graphic details of a murder, execution, or accidental death are generally omitted or are not the prime focus of the story. Sensational news builds its story on these graphic items and is more intent on providing explicit details that will shock rather than relate a certain event.

Even though this chapter describes the sensational character of some news items in colonial newspapers, it also serves another purpose. This chapter seeks to refute the standard perception of media historians who have portrayed sensationalism as a feature of nineteenth-century journalism or as part of the sixteenth-or seventeenth-century English broadsides and newsbooks while overlooking colonial newspapers' sensational nature. The very fact that so much sensationalism can be found in colonial papers proves this omission is an error. Before looking at the assorted sensationalism of colonial newspapers, however, a working definition of sensationalism needs to be established, and media historians' portrayal and understanding of sensationalism's role in journalism must be discussed.

SENSATIONALISM AND THE NEWS

Sensationalism, as the term is known and used in American media history, is closely tied to a certain type of news associated with the nineteenth century. With the development of the Penny Press in 1833 and more specifically with the start of the *New York Herald* in 1835 under the guiding hand of James Gordon Bennett, news took on an exploitational tone. No better example exists than Bennett's series of news features on the Ellen Jewett murder.[5] Similar reporting and exploitation appeared in the "yellow journalism" wars precipitated by William Randolph Hearst and Joseph Pulitzer in the 1890s.[6]

Sensationalism was not invented by Bennett, Hearst, or Pulitzer. In fact, the roots of sensationalism run to the very beginning of humankind's retelling of events.[7] According to Frank Luther Mott, the origins of America's sensationalism can be traced to printing in England.[8] There, broadsides and newsbooks of the sixteenth and seventeenth centuries were replete with stories with titles such as *A Horrible Cruel and bloudy Murther . . . upon the body of Edward Hall a Miller . . . Done by the hands of . . . his servants . . . each of them giving him a deadly blow (as he lay sleeping) with a Pickax*[9] and "Mrs. Dier brought forth her horned-foure-talented [taloned]-monster" as a London publication characterized the story of the stillborn, deformed baby of Ann Dyer.[10]

These examples of news stories reinforce the idea that sensationalism existed before its nineteenth-century incarnation. But if sensationalism existed in the sixteenth and seventeenth centuries and was raised to a fevered pitch by the end of the nineteenth century, how did sensationalism, as most media historians suggest, miss the eighteenth century? The answer is simple: it did not. Scholars, however, have tended to overlook the fact that the colonial press presented sensationalism.[11]

One reason for the omission has been suggested by David Paul Nord whose study of teleology and the news points out that often seventeenth-century and early eighteenth-century news items, which would be considered sensational, were reported to elicit an

"Oh, my God" response because, in some way, divine intervention was a part of the event's news value.[12] This moral aspect of reporting was a carryover from the English broadsides and newsbooks.[13] As a result, such reporting appears to have a religious purpose rather than sensational tone. Yet Nord's research goes only through 1730. Even if God's providence played a part in the news reported, a good sensational account shocked readers and no doubt created discussion among them about the horrors of the story. This, probably more than anything else, was the printer's purpose for including such a news item. But either way, readers talked about the news accounts, creating interest in the papers.

Another reason for the omission of colonial papers from media history studies of sensationalism rests in the fact that colonial journalism lacked the flair of the Penny Press and the yellow journals of the nineteenth century. There were no bold headlines to invite the reader to the newspaper, nor were there the striking poems and titles found on the seventeenth-century broadsides of England. Many of the news stories appearing in colonial newspapers were "clipped" from other newspapers or taken from letters from distant places. The clipping of news items, however, should not detract from the sensational nature of news or the purpose of printers who selected pieces of news. Regardless of the age of a bit of information, its inclusion was intentional. When Benjamin Franklin took over the *Philadelphia Gazette* in 1729, he asked for correspondents who could supply news of "every remarkable Accident, Occurrence, &c. fit for public Notice."[14] That was more than a request for political and social news from Philadelphia and the surrounding area. Franklin asked for the "remarkable."

Knowing that sensationalism existed in the colonial press and defining it, however, are two different issues. Most media scholars turn to Mott for the foundations of sensationalism's definition. Following his lead, they cite the basis of sensationalism as "the detailed newspaper treatment of crimes, disasters, sex scandals, and monstrosities."[15] Another study says that sensationalism "provides thrills, is fascinating in a morbid way . . . shocking to our moral and aesthetic sensibilities. It arouses unwholesome emotional responses. It appeals to man's unsatiable appetite to hear of horrors, crimes, disasters, sex scandals, etc."[16]

Sensationalism, according to Donald Shaw, also dealt with jilted brides and cows with two heads.[17] Michael and Edwin Emery describe sensationalism as "emotion for its own sake . . . [that can] be seen in the periods when the most noteworthy developments in popular journalism were apparent." For the Emerys, these periods included 1620, 1833, the 1890s, and the 1920s.[18]

In the most recent study of sensationalism, John D. Stevens' *Sensationalism and the New York Press* (1991), sensationalism seems restricted to crime news. Stevens says that "no other type of news is of such universal interest."[19] But Stevens relies upon the definition of sensationalism provided by George Juergens in *Joseph Pulitzer and the New York World.* That definition includes three parts: 1) emphasis on personalities, 2) preference for trivial over significant news, and 3) use of colloquial, personal language.[20]

The treatment of news by the colonial press that might be considered sensational includes all of the above and more. As Mitchell Stephens said in describing sensationalism, "Heinousness helps qualify it, and it helps to have a woman or a child involved, a high-born or well-known victim [and] some doubt in murders about guilt."[21]

In this chapter, sensationalism includes news that provides thrills, entertains, fascinates in a morbid way, and shocks the moral and aesthetic sensibilities. It includes crimes, disasters, sex scandals, and monstrosities. It may elicit an "Oh, my God" response—for either the religious implications that the event might hold or for the reaction reading such news produces in the reader. The latter reason may well have been the more important to the colonial printer because readership meant livelihood, and colonial readers evidently possessed a desire to read material that shocked and thrilled in a morbid way as witnessed by the amount of sensational news that appeared in colonial newspapers.

The sensationalism of colonial newspapers provides a glimpse into the brutality that often accompanied eighteenth-century life. Although humankind's inclination toward violence may not have been greater in the 1700s than at any time in history either before or after, newspapers' detailed descriptions of the brutality of the period often makes it seem to be a more violent time. In fact, James Gordon Bennett's description of the prostitute Ellen Jewett's demise pales in comparison with most sensational accounts of murder in colonial newspapers. Bennett described the murder of Jewett as follows: "He then drew from beneath his cloak the hatchet, and inflicted upon her head three blows, either of which must have proved fatal, as the bone was cleft to the extent of three inches in each place."[22] Witness how a similar hatchet slaying in 1730 was described in the *Boston News-Letter:*

She was barbarously Murdered by the hands of her Husband Joseph Fuller, in his House by her Brains being beaten out, she being knock'd on the head with an Ax which was found there bloody, and the head of the Ax fitting a dent made in her head . . . and some of her Brains (as we suppose) sticking on said Ax.[23]

Colonial sensationalism has never been acknowledged or given the attention that the sensational news of the Penny Press and "yellow journalism" periods of the nineteeth century have. But as will be seen, the omission of the colonial period's wealth of sensationalism is a mistake that close inspection of the content of colonial newspapers rectifies.

SENSATIONALISM AND COLONIAL NEWSPAPERS

Brains, bowels, blood, and puddings[24]—each was splashed across the pages of colonial newspapers. Sometimes the stories evoked sympathy for the victim; at other times the horrible incidents described were the just desserts imparted upon the receiver of them. Regardless, the sensational content of colonial papers rarely left a graphic description uncovered, if the precise details that could paint an explicit word picture were available.

Publick Occurrences employed both of these methods of presenting sensational news. Benjamin Harris's sole edition contained a graphic account of Indians having their bellies ripped open and passed it along. He let Boston readers' minds imagine the adulterous liaison between the king of France and his son's wife.[25] The first news item provided a graphic picture of a violent act; the second played more upon moral sensibilites. Many colonial newspaper sensational stories did both, but the latter was not always included in the sensational stories of colonial newspapers, although emotionally charging an event with moral overtones certainly made the graphic description of an event seem more sensational.

The helpless victim and women as sensational news. The helpless victim was a prime feature of colonial sensationalism, and those stories brought together some of the best examples of graphic violence and moral indignation found in the sensationalism of colonial newspapers, items that made *Publick Occurrences*'s sensationalism appear tame. Those stories generally revolved around women and children, with women serving as both victim and perpetrator of violence. The more graphic the depiction of the injustice done, the greater the moral indignation that would be registered with readers.

The accounts of the murder or accidental deaths were especially shocking, and the penchant for detail only enhanced the passions of readers. Helpless children were central to this type of news story. A London man and woman, for example, were observed dropping something into the Thames River early in the morning. Upon closer inspection, a basket sewn closed was discovered and in it was

> a female Child, thought by the Bigness of the Limbs to be about four Years old, her head being off and not there, one Arm off, and both the Legs, with the Belly ript open and Bowels taken out. . . . No discovery has as yet been made of the Authors of this barbarous Murder, the Head being taken away that the Child may not be known.[26]

Whenever the parents harmed children, the emotional aspect of the sensationalism was further enhanced. That was exactly the way in which a story in the *New-York Mercury* read. A young girl, wanting only to please her father despite her poor physical condition, was instead clubbed to death by her ogre-father when she informed him that she could work no more. Instead of exhibiting compassion, the father

> dragg'd her to the Field, kicking and beating her all the Way . . . though his Daughter was unable to stand, he fetch'd a great stick out of a Hedge and beat her till one of her Rib-Bones towards her Back stuck into her Lungs, which kill'd her immediately; she bled much at the Mouth, one Shoulder was out, her Head was broke in several Places, and her whole Body was a perfect Jelly.[27]

Usually, children did nothing to provoke parents to inflict these cruelties upon them. It did not matter where in the world such actions occurred; colonial newspapers picked up the stories to allow their readers to imagine what it would be like to experience the event and the gut-wrenching emotions reading it would cause. That is exactly what a story from Bristol, England, did in 1740. A young boy adopted by his aunt and uncle met a hideous fate at the hands of his aunt. The *Boston News-Letter* reported:

> The Boy appeared inhumanely used: For round its Neck was a black Lift, as if it had been hang'd; and in several Parts of it were divers long Blisters, the Effect of Poison; but what is most shocking, the barbarous Wretch attempted to burn it; for its Nose was quite burnt off, his Eyes burnt out. . . . The Body appear'd so barbarously used, that it was difficult to tell whether it was human or not.[28]

Central to the moral issue of the sensational news that dealt with children was trust. Parents were entrusted with the care of their offspring. So, too, were the other important people of the community like physicians. The disgust and distrust that a story in the *American Weekly Mercury* in 1730 must have produced can be imagined after reading of the actions of one doctor. The physician, requesting a neighbor to cook for him a pie of immense proportions said to be filled with pears, was revealed to be not only a murderer but a cannibal as well. When the pastry covering the pie ripped during baking, the juice inside ran out and filled the kitchen with an odor "so excessively strong, that they could hardly remain in the Bakehouse." The cook then examined the doctor's pie "and found a Child of about 3 Years old in full Proportion, the hand and Arm of a grown person, and several Parts of Human Flesh and Bones."[29]

Other stories reached deep into parents and captured their feelings for their own children. In these sensational stories the emotions triggered by the tragedies that the parents in the news account faced were superimposed upon the emotions of the parents reading the story. The sensational story was relived in a "what if that happened to me" way for the reader. In "one of the most melancholy Accidents" that had happened in recent memory, the *Pennsylvania Gazette* related, fourteen young boys out playing near a cave were caught in a rock slide that "crush'd them to pieces." Not only had the parents lost their children but in death, "Parents could not distinguish the Corpses of their own Children.—the Parts of some who were close together when the Rock fell, are so mixed, that there is no Distinction [of body parts]."[30] The "extraordinary Grief" that the parents experienced in the tragic accident could be transferred to the readers who might imagine how they would react in such an unresolved situation.

Sometimes the sensationalism that dealt with children and women served no purpose other than the shock value that it could produce. One story told of a woman who had been out earning money by recaning a chair. Upon returning home, her husband demanded the money. When she did not hand it over, he beat her skull in with a hammer. While the news story up to this point may have been ample for describing a murder, its shock value was slight, unlike the remainder of the story. After killing his wife, the man

stript her naked, and carried her up Stairs, and put her into Bed [with] her two Children, one of whom was near four Years old, and to keep the Child from crying, he gave him a Piece of Bread to eat; and some of the Neighbours going accidentally into the Room, found the poor Baby eating the Bread sopp'd in his Mother's Blood.[31]

Although the readers of this story could well have felt sympathy for the "poor Baby" that was in the bed eating the bloody bread, the story's focus was more on the shock of the action, not on the child's situation.

In another account, sympathy for an expectant mother was lacking. In its place was a story of unbelievable disgust. When a woman failed to deliver after nine months, she waited another nine months before seeing a doctor. The resulting story did little to evoke emotional sympathy for the woman, but it did no doubt elicit disgust among readers. The report stated:

> The Child was come to its full Time and Growth; the Flesh was turned into a black Jelly, and had tinged the Bones all black. She never felt the Child stir after she came to the end of her Reckoning, nor felt any Pain, until about six Weeks ago, when a Tumour gathered in her Groin, and she sent for a Surgeon, who . . . extracted first the head, and after all the other Bones at different Times, the Ligaments being so rotten, that it could not be brought away at once.[32]

Sensational stories that dealt with women, children, and families that lacked any emotional aspects were uncommon. The most ordinary of events could take on sensational qualities, providing the right set of circumstances were involved. That is exactly what happened in the summer of 1765 when two boys pretended to be butchers like their father. The graphic descriptions in the news item were outweighed by the heart-rending emotion that must have been felt by the mother in the story. The story built with each succeeding event and culminated with a cruel twist that must have disturbed every mother that read the account:

> Two boys belonging to a country butcher being at play together, the oldest brother told the youngest he would shew him how his father killed sheep, and immediately seizing him the head, thrust a knife into his throat. The boy shrieking, the mother, who was rocking the cradle with another young one in it, ran out hastily to see what was the matter. The boy seeing his mother concious [sic] of his guilt, ran away with all speed, and a jumping the mill-dam, tumbled in, and was forced down the water under the mill-wheel, where he was crushed to pieces. And to compleat the catastrophe, the poor mother returning home found the cradle overturned, and the poor infant smothered.[33]

The sensational stories of colonial papers also played upon the love that existed—or should have existed—between husbands and wives and mothers and children. The graphic descriptions of murder in these stories were further enhanced by this love that characterized most similar relationships. In one of the most graphic of these types of sensational stories received from Vienna, a husband, in the presence of his mother-in-law

> stripped his wife, and having fastened her to the wall with wooden pegs, he cut off her ears, nose, and two breasts, and drove a stake into her belly. He then cut open her side with a knife, and not finding her heart, which he wanted, he opened the other side, from which he took it out.[34]

A mother who refused a request for money from her soldier son also received brutal treatment from a supposed loved one. The young man proceeded to beat his mother with his sword "and then shot her thro' the Head, so that her Brains flew about the Room."[35]

Mothers could be equally cruel, and these types of sensational stories were especially emotion-packed. Cases dealing with infanticide filled court dockets in England and America,[36] and the descriptions of the deaths of these children ran in the papers. A prime example appeared in the *New-England Courant* in 1725. A woman birthed twins, "whose Backs she broke, and then thrust them into a Pitcher [chamber pot]."[37] These sensational stories garnered no sympathy for the perpetrator of the cruel action but used love as a catalyst to provide pity for the innocent children.

Women played a vital role in the sensationalism of colonial newspapers outside of their dual role as wife and mother and outside of the home, as well. Women were the "innocent victims" of the heinous of crimes. An "infamous villian" in London, for no reason but pure evil, assaulted a woman and "forced a stick up her body with nails [sticking] transversely [out of it]; so that by extracting the stick the nails tore out part of the body of the womb."[38] Another innocent victim "was stab'd in the Belly so her Bowels came out." Unbelievably, the attack was performed by the woman's minister in the midst of a group of people.[39]

Sex, oddities, animals, and the supernatural as sensational news. The topic of sex was never very far away from sensational news items that dealt with women in colonial newspapers. News stories that shocked the moral sensibilities of most of their readers and dealt with sexual issues at the same time were popular. These stories could be filled with humor for readers, but the more odd the event described, the better the story's sensational value. The *South-Carolina Gazette* ran an excellent example of this kind of sensational story in 1735, relating how the "Daughter of a famous Attorney" in Paris, reaching the age of sixteen, "chang'd her Sex." After that the "young man" "made Application to the Parliament to be confirm'd in the Priviledges of Manhood." The court, upon examining "the said Person heretofore a Girl, [decreed he] shall be henceforward deem'd a Man." If the sex change were not enough, the female-become-male now became her-his father's oldest son, and the court ruled that "she shall take Place in the Inheritance of her Father's Estates," but her younger brother appealed to the court declaring that he was still the elder son.[40]

Odd events and occurrences like the Parisian sex change were standard sensational fare for colonial newspapers, but most stories involving oddities lacked the humor of a girl becoming a son and being awarded the family inheritance. Oddities often evoked imagery that harkened back to a more medieval time when anything that varied from what was considered normal must be considered evil. Colonial newspapers included these stories on a fairly regular basis throughout the period. Whether they created an "Oh, my God" response among readers for any religious implications or not is open to speculation since the news stories contained no religious quotes.[41] Still, the subjects of many of these sensational stories with their monstrous births, supernatural activities, and witches left ample room for readers to infuse them with any religious beliefs or moral conundrums they might possess.

Many of the sensational accounts of oddities dealt with deformities among babies. A child born with a nose "exactly like a Hog's Snout" was put on display in London in 1730.[42] A New Hampshire woman, the *New-London Summary* reported, recently gave birth to a child with five fingers and a thumb on each hand and six toes on each foot. The child was the fourth that the woman had delivered with extra digits.[43] Naturally, the more animal-like the deformed births were, the more speculation they caused among readers. The *New-York Mercury* told of a child with "four Legs, four Arms, and four Eyes" that was born in London,[44] while the *Georgia Gazette* referred to a similar account as a "monstrous birth." The stillborn child in the *Gazette*'s story possessed "two faces parted assunder by a small partition of skin, four eyes, two noses, and two mouths, two external noses. . . . It was rough, covered over like an hare-skin, and its forehead was dented in."[45]

The sensational news concerned with deformities in colonial newspapers never speculated that any supernatural forces may have caused these births, but supernatural events were a part of eighteenth-century sensationalism. While these news items were never gruesome in the way that crime and accident sensational news pieces were, they were sensational nonetheless because they provided thrills and entertained as they brought into question moral issues. Despite David Nord's contention that such news items lost their religious implications early in the colonial period,[46] the supernatural events that were described in the colonial newspapers rarely offered any rational explanation for the occurrence. If Enlightenment thinking could not offer a rationale for the happenings, then religion—even if the news items did not always mention God or the spiritual realm—probably did.[47]

A *Pennsylvania Gazette* report from London in the first week of 1730 credited an unnatural sighting to "some Evil," "which struck with Terror all the Beholders."[48] In a similar story from just outside of Boston, the house of Richard Davenport became "a surprizing Scene of Preter-naturals" in 1745 when stones began to fly through the sitting room even though the doors and windows were shut tightly. The flying stones were reckoned to be the work of some evil spirit that found its way "into the haunted-Room."[49] Ghosts also appeared in colonial newspaper stories.[50]

The supernatural's sensationalism in colonial newspapers also included stories concerning witchcraft trials. Rarely were the trials reported on conducted in America. Before the Enlightenment, most western European nations—including their American colonies—accepted the concept that demonic powers were at work in the world. These beliefs in America culminated in the Salem Witch Trials of 1692 where twenty people were put to death and countless others tortured to obtain confessions.[51] Although Massachusetts Bay eventually admitted most of those put to death were probably not witches, most residents of the region truly believed supernatural evil had been at work in Salem.[52]

Enlightenment thought had found its way into America at around the same time as the Salem Witch Trials, but the idea that all theology was inaccurate unless it could be explained in a rational manner never completely supplanted the belief in supernatural activities or divine intervention in America, as many of the revivalists in midcentury demonstrated.[53] Most newspaper stories in the colonial newspapers concerning witches were written in a way that questioned highly whether the supernatural events had occurred, even though other supernatural stories in the papers seemed to acknowledge that evil forces beyond the physical realm existed. The witchcraft stories may have been printed for entertainment or to provide a shock to the reader concerning evil in the world, or to do both.

In 1720, for instance, the *Boston News-Letter* added a sentence of editorial comment concerning a man beheaded and then burned in Strasbourg. The paper said that proof of witchcraft, which was accepted as fact in that city on the Rhine River, would not be so easily believed in other places. The man, in this case, had transformed himself into a wolf and eaten peasants' sheep, according to witnesses.[54] The comment intimated that no rational explanation existed for the metamorphosis. The story probably carried some credibility for some readers and sensational value for others who would be shocked that a man would be put to death on such superstitious charges.

Benjamin Franklin obviously found nothing but ignorance and folly in accusations of witchcraft. He turned what could have been a sensational story of evil triumphing over good at one trial into a tongue-in-cheek denunciation of such beliefs. The resulting news report, after Franklin added his interpretation of it, was anything but shocking, unless the fact that "englightened" citizens of the eighteenth century could carry on in such a manner was shocking. On trial for "making their Neighbours Sheep dance in a uncommon manner" and for "causing Hogs to speak and sing Psalms," the "witches" were first weighed against the Bible, "but to the great Surprize of the Spectators, Flesh and Bone came down plump, and outweighed that great good Book by Abundance." Next, the accused were thrown into the water with their accusers, all bound hand and foot. According to belief, only those on the side of God would swim, but to the amazement of all present, the evil-doers swam while the righteous sank. This led to a declaration by one of the accusers that the accused had bewitched him and caused one of the accused to declare, "*If I am a Witch, it is more than I know.*" The crowd, not being convinced of anyone's innocence, decided to reconvene in warm weather and to retry the witches in the water, this time all being naked.[55]

Allegations of witchcraft likely reached the point of absurdity for Franklin and other colonial printers; therefore, news of witchcraft was more of a humorous diversion than a shocking account. Even though these stories were not sensational in the sense of colonial newspaper stories that dealt with monstrous births and supernatural occurrences, all of the witchcraft news stories fit Franklin's call for the "remarkable." Animals figured into the remarkable, as well, and sensational news items that involved animals both shocked and grabbed at the emotions of colonial readers.

Mostly shock and disgust, not emotion, played upon readers when Franklin informed his readers that a Mr. Aldsworth of the Jerseys had washed up on shore with "His Privities" eaten off.[56] A very similar story in the *New-England Weekly Journal,* however, contained both the shock and emotion that made colonial sensationalism so powerful. A nursemaid left her home to take her husband food. To console one of the children, she placed a puppy in the cradle with it, "but when she came home she found her Child as black as the Chimney & the Puppy very busy in sucking the Privy Parts."[57]

Animals of the sea played a role in sensational news, too. Travelers on the oceans were already concerned with storms, pirates, and privateers, but they also needed to be worried about sharks and sea monsters, whose destructive nature added to the fears of ship travel. For example, one good swimmer who fell overboard could not be rescued before a sea serpent "gnawed almost through his heart."[58] Another, the captain of a ship, was not seen again after going to ship's bow until sharks were spotted tossing his body up out of the water.[59]

Executions, accidents, and crime as sensational news. The sensationalism of colonial newspapers, although it may have dealt with animals and accidents and supernatural occurrences, usually based its potency upon a combination of emotion and violence, as the vast amount of sensationalism that focused upon women and children demonstrates. Not all of the sensational news of colonial newspapers combined these two features. In the sensational news of executions, hideousness for its sake alone was sufficient. Moral outrage replaced the emotional aspect of the sensational story. The sentences were justified by the biblical teaching of "an eye for an eye."

As a result, executions became especially powerful forms of sensationalism. Not only could a story provide precise descriptions of the carrying out of a sentence, but the readers could also feel that a valid moral decree had been upheld. Anyone who could kill another person did not deserve either human or divine pity according to the "an eye for an eye" system of punishment. While moral and religious reasons for an execution may have been acceptable to those who read of an execution, many executions that were presented in colonial newspapers merely demonstrated how cruel humans could be to one another, even when law was being enforced. And true to the definition of sensationalism of the colonial period, the sensational news of executions often used women as its focal point.

A woman who was convicted of poisoning her father and mother was tied to a post and pinched with red hot tongs before she was burned alive. As a way to ease the pain of the fire, a bag of gunpowder was tied around her neck, which exploded when exposed to the flame and no doubt ended her torture.[60] No such favors were done for a woman convicted of poisoning her husband or for a midwife condemned to die for murdering newborns.

The woman who murdered her husband was coated with tar and fastened to the stake with iron bands before fire was set to the bundles of kindling and wood below her. What followed next in the story could not have been more graphic:

> There being a great Quantity of Tar, and the Wood in the Pile being quite dry, the Fire burnt with amazing Fury; notwithstanding which, a great Part of her could be discovered for near Half an Hour. Nothing could be more shocking than to behold, after her Bowels fell out, the Fire flaming between her Ribs, and issueing out at her Ears, Mouth, Eye-holes, &c. In short, it was so terrible a Sight, that great Numbers turned their Backs and screamed, not being able to look at it.[61]

The woman coated with tar died much quicker than her French counterpart. "The murderous Midwife" faced a ghastly death suspended from a gibbet in a cage filled with sixteen wild cats after being convicted for the murder of sixty-two children. The cage with murderer and cats was suspended over a large fire. What happened next vividly demonstrates the cruelty of humans in carrying out the biblical injunction of "an eye for an eye":

> When the heat of the fire became too great to be endured with patience, the cats flew upon the woman, as the cause of the intense pain they felt.—In about fifteen minutes they had pulled out her intrails, though she continued yet alive, and sensible, imploring, as the greatest favour, an immediate death from the hands of the charitable spectators. No one however dared to afford her the least assistance; and she continued in this wretched situation for the space of thirty-five minutes, and then expired in unspeakable torture.[62]

The article justified the method of death and said, "However cruel this execution may appear with regard to the poor animals, it certainly cannot be thought too severe a punishment for such a monster of iniquity." It also suggested that England adopt similar methods of dealing with murderers of the same ilk throughout the empire, saying if it were done, "perhaps the horrid crime of murder might not so frequently disgrace the annals of the present times."[63]

At other times, no motive for a crime was given, and the newspaper accounts intimated that there was none for the violent acts of some individuals. The evidence presented in a trial stated that a man swore he would kill another. The murder occurred, but the news stories did not stop the story with notice of the homicide; it described the murder in exact detail. The murderer hit the victim over the head and then "cut his Throat, ripp'd his Belly and turn'd out his Puddings, and cut of[f] his private Parts."[64]

For each of the extended sensational accounts in colonial newspapers, there were at least twice as many stories that presented short, biting statements that were tacked onto murder and accident reports for the "Oh, my God" shock value they could produce. In fact, these statements were so common that the brains, bowels, and body parts that they splashed about the pages may have meant that readers were growing immune to such grotesque descriptions. That cannot be ascertained from the papers, however, but the following barrage of sensational snippets could have easily been left out of the newspaper accounts that contained them. They demonstrate how easily parts of the body flew across the pages of the papers in murder and accident reports.

One story tells that while cutting down a tree, a man died when the tree fell the wrong way and "scatter'd his brains on the ground."[65] Another man died when his house caught on fire. The house subsequently blew up, and the man's "bowels were blown out of his Body."[66] A man unloading a ship had his "brains beat out" and "other Parts of his Body so mangled that he was the most frightful Spectacle, perhaps, ever seen" when a wheel slipped.[67] A woman was killed by her husband, who was found "with her Liver, which he tore out of her Body, fast held in his Teeth."[68] A Philadelphia child was left too close to a fire. The little one died from its parents' carelessness but not before the fire "burnt its Brains out."[69] A New York man, trying to fix the flint on his pistol, had the horrid experience of having the gun accidentally discharge and kill the man next to him "in such a Manner that some of his Brains came out."[70] And a young servant woman near Albany who wanted to consummate her nuptials left her master's home for the night. When found the next day, she immediately agreed to return. Not satisfied, her master bound her by her hands to his horse's tail, but the horse took flight "and tore the poor Creature Limb from Limb; nothing being found hanging to his Tail but her two Hands, and Part of her Arms."[71]

It was not the tragedy of these stories that made them valuable to the newspapers. Tragedy was, unfortunately, a part of everyday life in the eighteenth century, just as it is today. What made these short stories interesting reading was the sensationalism, the unexpected and explicit grotesqueness. The brains and bowels were necessary to capture the interest of readers. Colonial newspapers sought to provide information, and they sought to entertain. Most of the sensationalism of colonial newspapers did both with shocking statements and descriptions that elicited some emotional response by the reader.

Most of the sensational stories lacked humor, for there is very little humor in rapes, murders, fires, or other accidents. In rare cases news stories managed to insert humor in a sensational account, the way the *South-Carolina Gazette* did with the story of sex change by the young French woman and the way the *Pennsylvania Gazette* did as it poked fun at the medieval practices of a witch trial. Neither of these stories, however, managed to insert humor into a story that provided an explicit description of something repugnant to all sensibilities like one piece of news in the *American Weekly Mercury* did.

A man, according to the *Mercury*'s story, checked into an inn with a cask of wine. The innkeeper, not approving of this obvious smuggling violation, sent for the constable who had a hole poked into the keg and "having tasted some of the liquid matter in it, declar'd 'Twas fine Mum." Having thought that a smuggler had been apprehended, the keg was opened all the way. The story then provided its twist for humor and odiousness. The cask was found not to contain a "fine Wine" but "the Bowels of a Gentleman who died the Day before, his Body being embalm'd."[72] Readers could be thoroughly disgusted and laugh at the foolishness of the supposed wine-tasting expert.

No matter what the purpose of the sensationalism of colonial newspapers, the amount of it appearing declined following 1765. The *Boston Evening-Post,* for example, ran nine sensational accounts up to October 1765, but none after that. The ever-growing political uneasiness of the colonies that affected the livelihoods of so many people through the Stamp Act, assorted other taxes, and questions of political representation and trade practices captured much of the *Evening-Post*'s and the rest of the colonial newspapers' attention from October 1765 onward.

Readers had not completely outgrown sensationalism in the 1770s, though, because printers still found a place for sensational news stories in their papers. Assuming readers had outgrown sensationalism must be discounted. Sensational stories just appeared much more infrequently. Printers still realized a well-told shocking story attracted reader interest, but so many more subjects were now of vital concern for American newspaper readers that sensational news items, no doubt, were crowded out of the papers to make room for political news. When sensational stories did appear, they were intense, often capturing all facets of what made sensationalism such entertaining news.

The *Essex Gazette* in 1770, for example, ran a sensational story about a woman and her infant that was filled with blood and intimated strongly at supernatural possession. The report told of a woman from Waterbury

who in the fourth or fifth Month of her Pregnancy, was taken with a most violent Longing, to eat the flesh from her Husband's Arms—he indulged her in making several Attempts; but her Teeth were not sufficient for her Purpose;—and her unaccountable Longing continued, until her Delivery, which was about three Weeks ago. The Infant refusing the Breast, or any other Sustenance usually given to Infants, it was offered the raw Flesh of a Fowl, cut fine, and dipt in the Fowl's Blood; on which it has fed heartily every Day since its Birth, and is the only Food the Child has taken, till a few Days since, when it eat a little Milk, mixt with Blood.[73]

The horrors of what faced a British ship's crew at New Zealand, according to a 1775 news report, covered any aspect of sensationalism that the *Essex Gazette*'s story might have missed. With the *Adventure*'s crew missing, a rescue team was sent out to discover what might have happened. The team found out when it got to an Aborigine village:

We had not advanced far from the water side before we beheld the most horrible sight that ever was seen by an European; the heads, hearts, livers, and lights, of three or four of our people, broiling on the fire, and their bowels lying at the distance of about six yards from the fire, with several of their hands and limbs in a mangled condition, some broiled, and some raw; but no other parts of their bodies, which gave cause to suspect that the cannibals had feasted and eaten all the rest.[74]

Colonial newspapers may have curtailed the amount of sensational news that they presented in the 1770s, but as can be seen, sensationalism still flourished to a certain degree in all of its shocking glory even as American newspapers turned their attention to revolution and war.

CONCLUSION

Sensationalism was a vital part of the information presented by colonial newspapers. The content of the papers used sensationalism as a tool to shock, inform, and entertain. Almost any subject could be sensational, but most of the sensational news dealt either with crime or accident reports. The large amount of sensationalism presented during the colonial period in newspapers from Georgia to New Hampshire amply demonstrates that sensational news flourished in the eighteenth century, something that media scholars have tended to overlook. Most newspapers prior to the Stamp Act crisis averaged five to ten articles per year that dealt purely with shocking murders, executions, or other types of sensational news included in this chapter. When the sensational nature of many of the accounts concerning Native Americans, shipwrecks, pirates, slave insurrections, animals, and the treatment of disease are figured in, newspaper sensationalism's total yearly content grows considerably. And as will be discovered in the next chapter dealing with crime, court, and legal punishments, even news stories that lacked shock as their prime focus and instead aimed at deterring crime were not always stripped completely of sensational aspects, adding further to the sensationalism of colonial newspapers.

Most sensationalism originated from areas outside the immediate area of the paper that ran the news. The origin of sensational news, obviously, was less important than the shock value the story possessed. But just because much of the sensationalism in colonial papers came from other regions did not preclude the inclusion of local sensationalism. The *Boston Gazette,* for example, spoke of a young man whose head was "jammed to pieces" between a ship and timber at the wharf in Boston.[75] Local sensationalism, as this news item and numerous other ones prove, was a regular part of the news of colonial papers. But most sensational news originated in locations other than those printing newspapers because areas such as Boston and Philadelphia, for example, did not have enough citizens to provide newspapers with a continual source of sensational topics. By using news from all the colonies, Canada, the Caribbean, Europe, or any other location from which news could be obtained, colonial newspapers opened their readers to a world full of shocking and gruesome incidents. If local newspapers had depended solely on local sensational news, they could not have run nearly as much sensationalism as they did.

The *Pennsylvania Gazette* offers a perfect example. In 1735,

Benjamin Franklin ran eighteen sensational news stories that dealt with murders, executions, and accidents. Only one, which described the graphic murder of an infant by its mother, originated in Philadelphia.[76] Fourteen of the sensational items were reprints from newspapers in either London or Edinburgh. One story came from Barbados; another, from Jamaica. The final two accounts arrived in Philadelphia via Boston, the actions in one taking place there and the other in New York. Sensationalism was clearly a popular type of news with readers, and it did not matter the origin of the stories. The amount of sensational news that appeared in the colonial papers affirms this.

Timeliness was also of less value with sensational news than with other types of news in colonial newspapers. It did not matter when the *Boston Evening-Post* reported the execution of "the Murderous Midwife" in relation to the actual event. What mattered was the shock value of actions in killing sixty-plus children and the equally disgusting report of her painful demise at the claws of sixteen terrified wild cats.

Colonial sensationalism appeared more often before the Stamp Act crisis of 1765 than after, despite its popularity with the eighteenth-century newspaper reader and regardless of the fact that its appearance in papers was not contingent upon any time factor. As the colonies became absorbed in topics of political or economic interests or embroiled in war, sensational news often decreased. During the French and Indian War, for example, sensational news of crimes and accidents may have diminished, but news of Indian atrocities increased dramatically. Generally, if news was sensational during this period, it dealt with Indian atrocities or with the treatment of those on board ships that were attacked by the French. The *South-Carolina Gazette,* for example, ran 154 separate news items on Native Americans in 1760, many of them ran for more than one page and contained graphic descriptions of Indian barbarities as well as reciprocating actions by colonists.[77]

In the 1770s, sensationalism and many other types of news that served more as entertainment than as valuable and timely pieces of information lost their places in the papers. They were crowded out by news of nonimportation agreements from up and down the Atlantic seaboard and by news of armed insurrection. If Americans required a shock to the senses in the 1770s, they did not necessarily need sensationalism that dealt solely with crime and accidents to deliver it. Colonists needed only to consider the actions of British troops. The Boston Massacre of 5 March 1770, provided all the shocking news many newspapers needed for months following. In

1775, the fighting at Lexington and Concord offered the opportunity for the same. One thing, however, was very different in these newspaper accounts. News of impending revolution contained very little blood; rarely did brains and bowels spill out of victims and onto the pages of the newspapers. The omission of these graphic descriptions may have been lacking because the subjects—brave American patriots—were too close to the hearts of the readers, or the exclusions may have occurred because colonial newspapers and readers in general had outgrown the need to be shocked and morally outraged by news accounts.

As shocking entertainment, sensationalism was present in the papers to entertain readers. Timeliness was becoming important to readers; therefore, other types of news continued to flourish including news of Native Americans and news of medical breakthroughs and disease outbreaks. These two subjects were presented to provide readers with information vital to their welfare and in some cases the welfare of the colonies rather than as pieces of entertainment. Still, as the colonies matured from subservient English colonies into a unified confederation of individual states able to hold off attacks by the strongest nation in the Western world, newspaper printers still found some room for news that could thrill, fascinate, and entertain as it shocked the reader's sensibilities.

The diminution of sensationalism that proceeded the Stamp Act crisis, however, represents only a part of a greater overall process that was occurring in America. Of prime importance to the colonists during this period was making sure that an increasingly independent group of colonies could survive as a nation and succeed in war with the Mother Country. While diversion from the woes of war was important, news of war and the politics of an emerging nation replaced most sensationalism in colonial newspapers.

Even though more timely news and news of war in the post-Stamp Act period combined to reduce the sensational nature of colonial news, sensationalism has been the most prominent type of news in American media history. It helped the Penny Press to flourish and built the yellow journalism papers of the 1890s into giant, competing organs vying for readership with the most sensational news that could be found or imagined. As Warren Francke pointed out, sensationalism allowed nineteenth-century newspapers to attract a larger audience.[78] Sensational news served no less a function for the papers of the eighteenth century, the newspapers that initiated sensationalism in American journalism. When "a shocking and melancholy affair happened,"[79] people wanted to read about it. American newspapers provided those readers with shocking news regularly during the colonial period, until news of more pressing matters like war and the birth of a nation slowed sensationlism's inclusion.

The sensationalism of colonial newspapers provided nineteenth-century newspapers with a strong foundation for presenting sensational news. Even though the sensationalism of the nineteenth century overshadows that of the eighteenth as far as scholarship has been concerned, the sensationalism of the eighteenth century—as has been seen—cannot be surpassed as far as gruesome, shocking, and emotionally disturbing news is concerned.

Sensationalism may have been the most dramatic news that dealt with crime and punishments in eighteenth-century American newspapers, but it was not the only type. An even larger body of crime and court reports—from which most sensationalism was based—appeared weekly in colonial papers. This type of news, discussed next, worked to help maintain peace and civil order in the colonies. And as will be seen, even though crime and court reporting in colonial newspapers differed from sensationalism in purpose and language, it never completely eradicated all of the sensational flavor employed by its more flamboyant relative.

4

Whipt Through the Streets and Burnt with a Hot Iron

On Monday last the following criminals were brought to the bar of the General Court to receive sentence, viz. Jeff Townsend from Augusta, for murder: Guilty. Death. Samuel Butts, from Augusta, for gouging; Burnt in the hand. James Shawness, from Loudoun, for rape: Pardoned. Joseph Mair, from Chesterfield, for murder: Acquitted. William Watkins, from Henrico, for felony: Acquitted.

—*Virginia Gazette,* 8 November 1770

WHEN court convened in Williamsburg, the capital of Virginia in the first week of November, 1770, the verdicts and punishments followed swiftly for the criminals found guilty at the bar. Jeff Townsend was sent to the gallows for murder, and Samuel Butts was burned on the hand for digging out another man's eye in a fight.[1] Retribution for crimes, as reported in Virginia's newspapers and in other colonial newspapers as well, had long been made in America with quick, reciprocating actions that matched crime and punishment. As one reader of William Park's *Virginia Gazette* pointed out in 1745:

Having perused some occasional Lawyer Debates in your Paper, with Regard to County Courts . . . Law is a dead Letter, and lives only in the due Administration thereof. . . . The Laws of England are our best Inheritance, the Ties of harmonious Society, and Defense of Life, Liberty, and Property, against arbitrary Power, Tyranny, and Oppression.[2]

The American colonies, the writer said, had a solid foundation for law based upon the English judicial system, but unless the law was put into constant action, it was of no value.[3] That is why colonial newspapers continually reported the administration of punishments that convicted criminals received.

America of the eighteenth century was still largely an untamed land. Estimates made from official British records in 1755 listed the English population of the colonies at 1,051,000,[4] and in 1775, no American city had a population exceeding 25,000.[5] The punishments employed to handle the various criminal offenses matched the nation's untamed nature. Prisons were not the answer; strict physical punishment administered in public was. And because punishments were usually corporal in nature, it was not uncommon to read that a felon was "Whipt through the Streets and burnt with a hot Iron"[6] or administered some similar type of immediate and public punishment that could be observed by citizens, either first-hand or through an explicit, third-person recreation in the newspaper.

This chapter discusses colonial newspapers' presentation of crime and court news that deals with criminal proceedings. The legal news of the colonial era was not confined solely to the criminal sphere, obviously.[7] Some of the greatest issues of the period were legal in nature and involved the press, the trial of John Peter Zenger over press freedom and the right to criticize the government[8] and the legal questions that permeated the Stamp Act taxation crisis[9] being perhaps the two best examples. But these two issues have been the subject of numerous scholarly reviews.[10]

The crime and court news of colonial newspapers differs in many respects from the sensationalism of the period, even though much of the sensational news of colonial newspapers dealt with crimes. Crime and court news' first priority was not purely to shock the moral sensibilities of the readers as sensationalism did; its purpose was to demonstrate how citizens' moral and legal standards were protected. Punishment may have been cruel and unusual by current standards, but the corporal punishment used by courts from New Hampshire to Georgia was standard practice for English courts in the eighteenth century.[11] It followed the philosophy of Thomas Hobbes who stated that "it is the nature of punishment to have for an end, the disposing of men to obey the law."[12] When colonial citizens witnessed a punishment that created a great deal of suffering in the wrongdoer, it reinforced the concept of obeying the law. If the punishment could be witnessed in person, it became, naturally, a better deterrent. If, however, this was impossible, a very graphic account in a colonial newspaper might serve the purpose sufficiently. In this way, crime and court reporting in colonial newspapers was very much akin to its sensationalism cousin; it was to shock the reader. Readers would then realize that violation of the laws of a colony would mean a painful end, perhaps even death.

While media historians have failed to study the crime and court news of the colonial era, legal historians have delved into the colonial records to study crime and punishment in the period. Their findings do not always agree with the crime and court news of colonial newspapers. This may be true for two reasons. First, although the colonial legal system was based upon the English legal system, each colony established its laws and judicial system based on the population, social arrangement, ideologies, institutions, and economics of the colony.[13] Second, many colonial statutes exist only in ancient editions and many have been lost. These laws generally follow the written laws of England, and American regional traditions concerning the law were rarely committed to parchment. In addition, the reports of American court cases did not become easily accessible until after the Declaration of Independence.[14]

Legal historians, however, have provided us with a basic picture of the judicial system of the colonial period. Understanding that system will help in understanding the presentation of crime and court news in colonial newspapers. It will also help to point out the differences in what the existing court records and newspaper accounts reveal about crime and court news of the period.

THE COLONIAL LEGAL SYSTEM

One fact stands out concerning the colonial legal system: there was no general uniformity in law from New Hampshire to Georgia.[15] As each colony was settled, the conditions of settlement, that is, the geographical conditions and the date of settlement of each colony, coupled with the absence of outside supervision or control from England ultimately led to the evolution of thirteen separate legal systems.[16] Necessity, therefore, was the supreme lawmaker in America.[17]

Closely tied to the development of these legal systems was the homogeneity of the colonists within an individual colony. The closer the ethnic and cultural origins and religious preference of colonists, the easier it became to establish a legal system that met the approval of colonists. The homogeneous New England colonies are a prime example. They possessed the most effective criminal justice system in America.[18] Because most New Englanders were in general agreement religiously and morally, their laws could easily be made to adapt to their colonial environment. As a result, there was less crime in these colonies.[19] These facts applied much more to seventeenth-century New England than to the eighteenth-century situation. The *Book of the General Lawes and Libertyes* of Massachusetts Bay of 1648 demonstrates the homogeneity of the colony's seventeenth-century law. The Puritans injected their own biblical understanding into each law. Their approach to crime and punishment, therefore, reflected their understanding of God, man, and society. Crime equaled sin.[20]

But the Puritans' understanding of law in relation to the Bible and sin did not necessarily correspond to the interpretation of law in other colonies. In addition, as immigration continued in the late seventeenth century and into the eighteenth, homogeneity of population even within the New England colonies could not be maintained.

Although the colonial legal system varied from colony to colony and was based to varying degrees upon morals, certain aspects of the system were similar, regardless the colony. Similarities could always be found in the punishments imposed upon those found guilty of a crime. Punishment was almost always corporal and included whipping, branding, public caging, symbol wearing, and ear cropping. For the most serious offenses, criminals were put to death while lesser offenses often required that guilty parties be placed in public stocks or pillories.[21] As the Massachusetts Bay *Book of the General Lawes and Libertyes* stated:

> No Man shall be forced by Torture to confess any Crime against himselfe nor any other unless it be in some Capitall case where he is first fullie convicted by cleare and suffitient evidence to be guilty. . . . Then he may be tortured, yet not with such Tortures as be Barbarous and inhumane.[22]

None of the punishments listed were considered "Barbarous" or "inhumane" in the colonial period. Noncorporal punishments included fines and imprisonment, but the latter was rarely used since prisons were little more than houses—or a room in a house—during the period making prison breaks an easy proposition.[23] In addition, most of the accused who appeared for trial in the seventeenth century pleaded guilty. They knew that a not-guilty plea followed by a conviction would produce a harsher penalty. Between 70–80 percent of all who pleaded not guilty were convicted in the seventeenth century.[24]

But, what constituted a crime and what was its punishment? Of course, murder, rape, robbery, larceny, burglary, and counterfeiting were crimes, but so, too, were adultery, blasphemy, witchcraft, and idolatry in many colonies in the colonial period.[25] When the Quakers of Pennsylvania drafted a legal code in 1700, a man could be castrated for rape, and an adulterer could have an "A" branded on the forehead.[26] In 1718, Pennsylvania passed "An Act for the advancement of justice and the more certain Administration thereof." This act made a dozen crimes punishable by death. They included high treason, counterfeiting, murder, sodomy, rape, highway robbery that included threats, premeditated mayhem, witchcraft, burglary, and arson.[27] Very few moral issues were capital offenses in Pennsylvania by the eighteenth century, nor were they in many places in the Middle and Southern colonies. In New England, adultery, idolatry, blasphemy, and cursing parents remained capital crimes until 1692. After that, they remained on the books as crimes not punishable by death.[28]

In the eighteenth century, colonial legal systems became more standardized. This was due to the fact that proprietory governments were introduced into all of the colonies, which consequently made America's legal system more "English" in nature.[29] Courts and the law began to focus more upon offenses like theft and violence than upon those that involved immoral acts, and from 1760 into the nineteenth century, law's basic function shifted to the protection of property.[30] The American legal system applied William Blackstone's understanding of law, which said:

All crimes ought therefore to be established merely according to the mischiefs which they produce in civil society: and, of consequence, private vices, or the breach of mere absolute duties, which man is bound to perform considered only as an individual, ar not, cannot be, the object of municipal law.[31]

The morals of Americans, John Adams noted in 1778, "must be laid in private families," and the concept of not regulating morality with state law began to emerge.[32]

For any kind of legal system to function, some sort of law enforcement organization had to exist in a colony. Sheriffs served that purpose in the counties and parishes of colonial America, but sheriffs' methods of operation were reactionary rather than preventative. Sheriffs responded to lawbreakers only after violations had been committed or after formal complaints or information pertaining to a specific violation of the law had been reported. There was no effort at first in America to patrol streets to halt potential illegal activities. In addition, any kind of policing that might take place in the colonies was generally limited to the settlements.[33] Villages and cities gradually added other law-enforcement agents to help maintain order as the population of the town dictated it. In New York, for example, "the mayor, Common Council, high constable, police justices, constables, marshalls and the night watch all bore some responsibility for the protection of the city."[34]

In the backcountry of the colonies, courts were held and some sheriffs were employed, but punishments tended to follow the rule of *lex talonis,* the rule of retaliation, and individuals viewed themselves as law enforcement officers upon their own property.[35] "Every man should be sheriff of his own hearth" was a commonly-heard declaration among North Carolinians of the backcountry.[36] If a criminal was tried in the courts of the backcountry, a sentence of death was much more likely—and for lesser crimes—than was the case for criminals tried in the courts of the colonial towns of the Eastern seaboard.[37]

Going to trial for the average citizen of colonial America generally meant that the defendant appeared alone in court. If a lawyer represented the defendant, that lawyer was likely to be a part-time barrister with either little or no training or some on-the-job experience much like that received by a printer's apprentice.[38] Representing a client also carried a different connotation in the eighteenth century than in succeeding centuries. Lawyers "set the machinery of the court in motion" for their clients.[39] Once in court, felony defendants had the option of a jury or bench trial, where defendants could request that their cases be tried by a judge alone without a jury, something not possible in England where juries alone heard all felony offenses. Bench trials may have functioned as a plea bargain arrangement for the defendant.[40] As the eighteenth century progressed and Americans became disillusioned with British rule, the jury trial grew in favor. An appointed judge, who kept his position through a proprietory appointment, would not likely rule in favor of a lawbreaker against the crown.[41] Juries, in contrast, would often hand down sentences based on jury "lawlessness," that is, based upon their dislike of a law more than upon the guilt or innocence of the defendant. Although jury decisions of this kind were often entwined with political issues, they were also applied to felony issues such as larceny.[42]

Once a sentence was handed down, a defendant had two closely related options to reduce his sentence. The felon could fully acknowledge guilt and swear full intent of reform. If this repentance was acknowledged by the court, a full pardon for a crime could be granted.[43] More universal to the colonies, however, was the application for "benefit of the clergy" by convicted felons. Benefit of the clergy was a holdover from the Middle Ages that exempted clergy from many crimes. It was gradually applied to laypeople who could prove their religious sincerity by either reading or reciting the "neck verse" from Psalm 51.[44] In colonial America, any one sentenced to death could claim "benefit of the clergy" and have their punishment reduced to a less severe form of punishment such as branding.[45] Benefit of the clergy applied to women, slaves, and Indians, but it was denied to slaves who murdered white people or who broke into whites' houses and stole more than five shillings.[46] Benefit of the clergy was also disallowed for extremely "heinous" offenses, whatever those offenses might be deemed by a colony. Maryland law, for example, stated that benefit of the clergy would not be available to anyone who was found guilty of robbing a tobacco house.[47]

As American society developed and became more heterogenous, so, too, did its legal system.[48] In this process of development, newspapers were also developing, and they played a vital role in disseminating news of crimes and punishments.

CRIME, COURT NEWS, AND COLONIAL NEWSPAPERS

If sensational news was splashed across the pages of colonial newspapers, crime and court news—sensationalism's less shocking counterpart—was added to colonial newspapers in large, carefully measured doses. Crime, according to the court records of colonial America, dealt with either morals crimes like adultery, blasphemy, and idolatry or felony crimes like robbery, arson, and murder. Colonial newspapers dealt with both as well, but there were very few morals offenses in the papers, except in the most heinous of crimes like sodomy because many morals crimes had lost their significance in the eighteenth century. Instead, the crime and court news of eighteenth-century American newspapers was concerned almost exclusively with crimes of property, personal injury, and murder.

Crime and court news in colonial newspapers also furthered the fear of overland travel with a large amount of news dealing with highway robberies in much the way ship news evoked fear of traveling at sea through pirate, storm, and privateer reports.[49] News of highway robberies, because of the fear it generated, was sensational, but it also served the purpose of warning newspaper readers of the potential for danger if certain roads were traveled. Women were central characters in a large portion of crime and court news in colonial papers, in much the same way that they were central to sensational news. Women were often the victims of rape or some other crime, but by far the largest amount of crime and court news concerning women portrayed females as criminals, especially as murderers of bastard children. Although these murders had moral overtones, newspaper accounts left the moral speculation on the murder of bastards to the reader.

Morals Crimes. Only one morals crime consistently found its way into the papers. That crime was sodomy. Fornication, polygamy, prostitution, and adultery were reported as crimes as well. In addition, suicide was treated as an immoral act in colonial America, according to colonial newspapers' crime stories. Crimes such as breach of the Sabbath rarely appeared in colonial newspapers.[50]

"The detestable Sin of Sodomy"[51] was perhaps the most unforgivable crime found in colonial newspapers. This was probably due to the biblical injunctions against the practice combined with the disapproval that same-sex sexual relations between men and sexual relations with animals evoked. Murder could be forgiven along with every other type of crime but not sodomy. The *South-Carolina Gazette* summed up what happened to violators of this morals crime succinctly: "John Perrins for Beastiality; Death."[52]

Reports of sodomy appeared regularly through 1755 in colonial newspapers, but a 1730 trial and execution of sodomists in the Netherlands may have been the most sensational and largest in terms of individuals involved. This crime had all the facets necessary to capture the attention of readers. Not only was there a crime committed that insulted the moral sensibilities of readers, but the offenders were citizens "of great note and Substance,"[53] including many of the religious and political leaders of Amsterdam. The *Pennsylvania Gazette* told of one minister guilty of sodomy being burned alive.[54] When the minister went to court, "'tis said he was so harden'd in his Iniquity, that he has attempted to prove from Passages of Scripture, that it was not only not a Sin, but a Practice more acceptable to the Deity than the Love of Women."[55] The Netherlands sodomy trials proved that sodomy convictions would not be pardoned regardless the social standing of the guilty party. "If Money could have been of any use to them," the *Weekly Mercury* reported, "none would have been wanting to cummute the Punishment: But to the immortal Honour of the Court of Justice in these Provinces, there is no Respect of Persons in such Cases."[56]

Sodomy was always viewed as a "filthy Crime,"[57] and in the colonies, concrete proof of it was necessary in order to obtain a conviction.[58] In 1755, a wealthy Banbury, Connecticut, resident was arrested for "sodimical practices" after one Obadiah Baker swore in a letter that the gentleman had used him in way "not proper to be mentioned." The Connecticut letter relating this event was sent to the *Boston Evening-Post,* and the letter writer claimed that these homosexual activities had been taking place for twenty years. But because the accused was "a man of considerable fortune and fond of the law," he had been able to avoid prosecution because no eyewitness could be found. The letter intimated that Baker's bravery had put an end to a sinful and illegal activity.[59] Even in the 1750s, sodomy was considered a crime that violated civil law and "brought down immediate Vengeance of Heaven" on the transgressors.[60]

Another morals crime considered to be an offense against the state was adultery. A charge of adultery was grounds for more than divorce, according to crime reports in colonial newspapers. In one case, a merchant brought suit against a cane chair maker for £10,000 because the chair maker had had "Criminal Conversation" with the merchant's wife. In addition, no charges were brought against the merchant after he "broke the Head" of the chair maker when he found his wife and her paramour in bed together.[61]

Morality played a large role in making fornication and prostitution crimes, although prostitution offenses were not considered too serious during the eighteenth century.[62] As one Boston resident stated, "She keeps a house of pleasure and has done so for a good many years past in a more decent and reputable manner than common, and is Spoke of by every body in Town in a favourable manner for one of her Profession."[63] Prostitution charges were rarely if ever brought according to colonial newspaper reports. Because prostitution was an accepted if not publically condoned practice in the colonies, fornication, according to crime and court reports, was seldom prosecuted either. Four women from Portsmouth, New Hampshire, were fined fifty shillings each and given ten stripes on their bare backs in 1765.[64] Five years later, four Boston women were hauled in front of a judge for fornication, according to the *Boston Evening-Post*. This time, however, the newspaper report was more concerned with the entertainment value of the court case than any crime. No mention of conviction or punishment was mentioned, only that the four appeared "with 8 young Children, each having been delivered of Twins."[65]

Sexual activity, when it was heterosexual in nature, was not a big concern of Americans in the eighteenth century, according to colonial newspapers. Sexual mores had yet to pass through the Victorian era, so sex was not a taboo subject or activity. But sex could lead to serious crimes. Polygamy was one of those crimes, but charges of polygamy did not appear frequently in colonial newspapers. When, however, a polygamist was a woman, the news value of the crime rose. One Sarah Lane, Merchant, Errington, Flint, Morgan, or Steadman—depending upon which husband she was with—was finally caught in 1765.[66] As with the fornicators with the twins, this story was more of an entertainment piece than a deterrent to any crime since no punishment was prescribed in the account. A male bigamist in Philadelphia, however, received thirty-nine lashes at the public whipping post and was ordered to spend the rest of his life at hard labor.[67]

Immorality could cause one to be more than a polygamist, however, and when murder sprang from immoral acts, the connections between sin and crime were pointed out by colonial newspapers. In Connecticut, a man separated from his wife, considering her an unconverted Christian. Immediately, he "took his Maid as a Concubine, and called her his covenanted Wife." But in 1750s Connecticut, leaving one's wife and living unmarried with a maid was considered too great a sin to be accepted, so the man's friends convinced him to return to his lawful wife. Shorty thereafter, the man bought some ratsbane and gave it to his former lover who continued as maid for the family. Sin and murder quickly became entwined as the maid

> mix'd part of [the ratsbane] in Pancakes, and gave some of them to two Children in the Neighbourhood to try the experiment first, who died presently after:-And then returning to the Man's House, ask'd the Wife to eat some pancakes, which she took out of one of her Pockets; the Woman accepted and eat, the maid also eating some herself which she took out of another Pocket.—The Woman when eating them complain'd that they tasted very oddly, she told her she had put some Ginger in them; But insisting on it, said, you have poisoned me, and I pray God to forgive you.[68]

God may have forgiven the maid, but the people of Banbury did not. They exhumed the woman shortly after burial and discovered fifteen grains of ratsbane in her digestive system. Interestingly, only the maid was arrested according to the initial news item. Two weeks later the paper ran a follow-up story. In this account, the physical evidence connecting the maid to the children's murders was included, and the husband was implicated as well. "Respecting the Servant Maid's poisoning her Master's Wife at his Instigation," the *Boston News-Letter* reported, "both of them are now in Windham Goal."[69]

The sinful nature of crime was not of primary importance to news stories in most cases. The significance of sinful acts may have been understood, but the thoughts of readers concerning the ties between sin and criminal activity can only be speculated upon. Sodomy was the greatest exception to the application of sin to crime reports in colonial newspapers, but it was not the only crime considered a sin. Suicide was often presented as an unpardonable sin because it was caused by the failure to control passion and because colonial citizens saw no way for the self-murderer to obtain forgiveness for the act committed. *Publick Occurrences* placed the blame for suicide upon "Melancholy" caused by "The Devil" after a Water-Town man was found hanging by a rope in his "Cowhouse."[70] A Philadelphia woman, apparently rejected in some sort of love relationship, sought to end her life by jumping from one of the city's drawbridges. She was saved but not before she pleaded with her rescuers to let her drown, which they refused to do. The news story closed with this comment: "She was then hindered from perpetrating the worst of Crimes, it's hop'd she will for the future keep a strict watch over her Passions."[71] Suicides in New York led to a comment in *Parker's New-York Gazette* about the unforgivable nature of suicide:

> It must give a reasonable man no small concern to see his fellow creatures such wild desperadoes, as for a few trifling vexations and dissappointments [*sic*], to become their own butchers. Not to brand with infamy the memory of a wretch who takes away his own life, is madly to applaud the most cruel actions occasioned by melancholy and ferocity. . . . The crime is inexcusable.[72]

The true crimes of immorality in colonial newspapers that were inexusable were sodomy and suicide, but morals crimes never appeared in great numbers in the papers. Crime was a problem in America though. Crimes against property and individuals, according to colonial newspapers, happened often and everywhere in the colonies.

Felony crimes. Robbery, rape, murder, arson, and counterfeiting compounded the hardships that many colonists faced as they attempted to forge lives in America. In many cases, crime seemed to be epidemic in the colonies. The *American Weekly Mercury* of Philadelphia, for example, averaged seventy crime and court accounts per year from 1725–1735. All of these reports dealt with crimes against persons, property, or the state with the exception of the sodomy reports of 1730, and most crime stories originated in the colonies, not in Europe. It was with these felony accounts that the swift, corporal punishment that was meted out by the colonial criminal justice system played such a vital role in protecting people and property.

Robbery seemed to affect everyone in colonial America. Even printers were not immune. Andrew Bradford reported in February 1720, that his own servants had stolen between £20–30 from him along with a watch and silver spoons.[73] Every town seemed to have its own crime spree involving breaking and entering of homes and shops, as well as shoplifting and horse stealing. In 1765, crime reports coming out of Philadelphia warned that "The Inhabitants of this City are requested to be very careful in keeping their Doors shut after Night, as at present there is in, and about this Place, one of the most dangerous Gangs that has been known, who make a Practice of going about in the Dusk of the Evening, and entering where they can carry off what they first meet with."[74]

Punishments for robbery varied as well, but whenever a felon was convicted of robbery, the sentence was acted upon quickly. A New York man convicted of burglary the first week of May 1770, was to hang May 18.[75] A Philadelphia woman was sentenced to be whipped publicly on the next three market days for robbing stores.[76] Shoplifting generally brought a whipping for the guilty party,[77] while horse thieves were sentenced to death[78] or whipped.[79] Robbers often received a large number of lashes as punishment for their crimes, with fifty-five handed out to one Boston robber.[80]

Robbery accounts, just like almost every other type of news in colonial newspapers, could serve as entertainment as it related a serious and possibly life-threatening event. In one account, a barking dog saved a young woman from being robbed and probably from being killed by a housebreaker:

> A young woman . . . being in bed . . . and the rest of the family out of town, she was waked by the barking of the dog in the yard; she arose, and not seeing any body, let the dog into the house, and went to sleep again; soon after she was a second time wakened by the barking of the dog, getting up, saw a tall fellow with an axe in one hand, and a hammer in the other, and a dark lanthorn at his girdle endeavouring to break into a room, as soon as he saw her, he made a stroke at her with the axe, then threw that and the hammer at her, and run off; she happened to escape unhurt, and after he was gone found in the passage two bundles of cloths, which had been taken out of the very room where

she had been in bed. It is supposed the villain stole in and conceal'd himself in the house, in the evening.[81]

Even though this news story was entertaining for readers, it offered an admonition for newspaper readers to be on guard in their homes for possible encroachment.

Another crime, rape, could take place in a home, but usually rapes occurred on the streets of colonial towns. Understanding colonial America's legal response to rape is not easy. Although rape was a criminal offense, it carried with it moral overtones but was not as heinous as sodomy to eighteenth-century citizens. In fact, it was not even as evil a crime, according to colonial newspaper reports, as burglary. Rarely did anyone receive a death sentence for rape, although a Maryland man was executed for rape in 1760.[82] Usually, prosecutions for rape involved time in the pillory and whippings. A Boston man raped a ten-year-old and received one hour in the pillory and thirty lashes.[83] In Pennsylvania, the *Boston Evening-Post* related, a Quaker named Daniel King sexually assaulted a four-year-old. His punishment included a month's imprisonment, a fine of £10, and a day in the pillory.[84] When a slave sexually attacked a Philadelphia girl, his punishment called for him "to be whipt throu [the] Streets of the City."[85]

Reports of ravishing females—colonial newspapers' favorite way of referring to rape—were often descriptive and included names of victims. Elizabeth Rogers was raped in Philadelphia in 1730. The *American Weekly Mercury* printed her name in the story but never mentioned the name of her assailant.[86] Dublin thugs, the *New-York Weekly Post-Boy* said, raped Dorothy Jones, a 105-year-old widow. The three rapists "dragged her into a waste House near the Red Cow on Finglass Road, where each of them had carnal knowledge of her. They broke one of her Arms, and abused her in so barbarous a Manner, that she died."[87] The *Maryland Gazette* provided its readers with the transcript of a London rape trial that only omitted the details of the carnal act. A young woman, Hannah Deponent, was hired by Colonel Frances Chartre to clean house, but this was only a front for what the colonel really had in mind for the young woman:

About the middle of the fourth Night, the Prisoner called Hannah to come to Bed to him. . . . *Come hither, Nanny, you Bitch, come to Bed to me, that I may lie in State.* That upon her refusing to comply, he seemed in a great Passion, and curs'd and swore bitterly. . . . On the Tenth of November last, the fatal Day specify'd in the Indictment . . . the Prisoner at the Bar bid her start the Fire, and in the mean Time he lock'd the Door, and suddenly catching her up in his Arms, forcibly threw her on a Couch, which stood by the Fire-side, when by the Violence which he then and there us'd, he had Carnal Knowledge of her. . . . Then the Court ask'd the Prosecution after what manner did he effect it? She said, when she was laid on the Couch, the Prisoner pull'd up her Clothes; then said the Court, Did he not pull down his Breech? to which she reply'd, He did.

Being ask'd, what follow'd thereupon? she stood silent; but the Question being repeated, she made such a Reply as Modesty forbids us to repeat.

Then she was ask'd, Whether she made any Resistance, and whether she cry'd out for Help? she said, she resisted as long as she was able, and that she cry'd out till the Prisoner stop'd her Mouth with his Night-Cap. . . . The Evidence being summ'd up by the Judge, the Jury withdrew, and after a short Stay, brought in their Verdict, that he was guilty of the Indictment.[88]

Because rape was a violent crime, victims of it, like Hannah Deponent, were fortunate to escape. Some like Dorothy Jones, the 105-year-old Dublin widow, were not so lucky. Rape sometimes ended with a murder. Although not as common a crime as burglary or counterfeiting, homicide posed a serious problem in the colonies, and colonial newspapers' presentation of murder and trials for murder gives some indication of that fact. Murder stories often bordered upon the sensational, sometimes were quite entertaining, but almost always let colonial newspaper readers know that the taking of another life, unless in self-defense, was not acceptable and would necessitate a quick judicial response.

The very nature of America's settlement led to murder. As the culture of Europe collided with that of Native Americans, irreconcilable differences between the two in land ownership and almost every other facet of living led to hostilities, warfare, and death. The murder of whites by Indians and vice versa became, at times, the predominant feature of colonial newspapers.[89] The precarious nature of ocean travel also added to the homicide logs of colonial America because of pirate activity. The *Boston News-Letter* in its first edition of 24 April 1704, told of twenty men killed or wounded by pirates as the men tried to sail back to America. The violence and murder perpetrated upon colonists by Native Americans and pirates, however, was not the same as that which found its way into the legal systems of American colonies.

The violence associated with rape, as has been seen, often led to murder. The two crimes combined into one story lent a sensational nature to accounts. The crime story could serve as notice that a murderer and rapist was now off the streets, that justice was being served, and that a member of the community had lost a loved one. That is precisely what a *New-London Gazette* news item did in 1770. The newspaper reported that "a Dutch boy, about 16 years of age, servant to Mr. Lippincott . . . enticed his master's daughter (a little girl about 9 years old) from home, under pretence of gathering grapes, when he ravished and murdered her, and then buried her in a swamp where she was found."[90]

Murder occurred in almost every location in the colonies, but the home was the location of most murders, according to crime stories in colonial newspapers. Colonial newspapers' flare for the sensational may help to explain this, but it is also probable that domestic violence was just as common a problem in eighteenth-century America as it is in America today. Domestic violence was reported from up and down the Atlantic seaboard and from England. A man in Edenton, North Carolina, the *Boston Evening-Post* said, "was so inhuman as to kill his own Wife."[91] A Boston husband, in a fit of rage, accosted his wife with the butt of his rifle and then slit her throat.[92] A New York father, apparently tired of living and tired of his young son, killed the child and then sat, holding the slain child in his lap, waiting to be arrested. He hoped, the news account said, that the civil authorities would sentence him to death because "he had been long tired of his Life."[93]

Domestic violence at times revolved around love trysts. A seventeen-year-old in London, with the help of her lover, poisoned her husband. The lover, in turn, stabbed his own wife in the throat, "as a butcher does a sheep." The two had planned to spend their lives together, but their plan was foiled. Both were sentenced to death.[94] And a barber's wife, "enraged with Jealously," sought the demise of her husband by "bit[ing] him in the Testicles."[95]

Sometimes, news of domestic violence in one part of the colonies was run in a newspaper of another area in an effort to curb known, similar local violence. A soldier in New York, the basic report of the incident stated, beat "his Wife (who was very very big with Child) so unmercifully that she died immediately."[96] When the *New-England Courant* related the same crime to Boston readers, it offered an additional comment for a local resident who many felt might become a murderer, too, unless his actions were curbed. The account stated:

We hear from New-York . . . a Soldier . . . beat his Wife so Unmercifully, that she dy'd in a few Hours after.
This Article is partly inserted for the Admonition of a certain barba-

rous Fellow in Boston, who one Night this Week, and very often before, beat his Maid so unmercifully, that his Neighbours with good Reason think he will one time or other be the death of her; and unless he discovers more Humanity for the Future, he may expect a particular Description of his Body and Mind, even to his very LAST.

Remember Tom thy Father's Fate, And curb thy Wrath e'er 'tis too late.[97]

The events that newspapers described that aggravated murder were not solely domestic in nature. Homicides were often the result of everyday life encounters, as one in Beaufort, South Carolina, where a shoemaker stabbed another man over money owed.[98] In another instance, two men argued over an alleged stolen pig, and the argument ended with one man dead from a hoe to the head and the other in jail.[99] In other instances, liquor led to murder. Two friends drinking began to argue, and the argument ended with one killing the other with the cribbage board on which they had earlier been enjoying a friendly game.[100]

Unlike most of the other crime and court reports in colonial newspapers, murder stories usually ended with the murderer being sent to jail to await trial. Rarely were trials about "everyday" or domestic homicides included in the papers. This may be because most murders occurred between individuals who knew each other and therefore murderers posed no general threat to citizens. Many trials concerning murderers might have also been omitted because the verdicts were much like that in the *Virginia Gazette* that merely stated that Jeff Townsend would die for murder.[101] "Wilful murder," as many of the coroner's inquests described first-degree murder, meant death if the accused was convicted.[102] Colonial newspaper accounts of executions often informed readers that contrite murderers asked forgiveness from all those who were present to witness the execution. In Annapolis, the *Maryland Gazette* reported, one James Barrett was executed for murder. As he faced death, Barrett "admonish'd the Spectators to avoid Drunkenness and Passion," which had led him to commit his crime, and he confessed all of "his past Sins."[103]

The fact that colonial citizens wanted their convicted felons to be repentent when facing death speaks to the undercurrents of religion that ran through society. While religion and colonial newspapers is the topic of a later chapter, it is important to note religion's role in the administration of capital punishment. Murder, more than any other felony, carried religious implications in the taking of life by both murderer and executioners, and a penitent criminal helped satisfy the need for eighteenth-century citizens to die in some harmony with God. When a murderer went to the gallows demonstrating "little Sensibility of Guilt," as one did in New York in 1760,[104] life was left out of balance.

Arson, unlike murder, carried no religious implications. In addition, arson was not as common a problem in colonial America as crimes of burglary, rape, or murder, but it was still a serious threat to families and business people. The loss of homes to fire often meant the loss of most or all personal property, and furniture was difficult to replace in colonial America.[105] "Evil minded Persons" perpetrated acts of arson[106] since arson posed a serious threat to the livelihoods of people. When arson destroyed several barns in Massachusetts, it cut off the owner's supply of feed for his livestock putting his farming operation in jeopardy.[107]

Arson may not have affected many colonial citizens, but counterfeiting did. Counterfeiting, according to newspaper accounts, was the most serious criminal activity in America. All types of specie from several countries were accepted in the colonies as payment for goods and services. This fact made the possibilities for counterfeiting great. For example, in 1770, according to the *Connecticut Journal,* a New Haven man was apprehended for making Spanish milled dollars that could be spent in the colony.[108] Colonies also issued paper currency in the eighteenth century, and counterfeiters could easily replicate paper money and bills of credit if they had access to a press.[109] Counterfeiters even attempted to copy coins in an effort to obtain goods for nothing. The *Boston New-Letter* related the arrest of a man outside of Philadelphia in 1730 who had in his possession Pistoles and pieces of eight that he had made from a cheap form of metal that were then colored gold. He also had unfinished pieces of currency issued in Virginia and fake Pennsylvania £10 notes.[110]

In 1730, the *Boston Gazette* reported, a Staten Island schoolmaster was apprehended for producing fake "30 *s.* and 3 *l.* Bills of New-Jersey." The teacher "did the whole with his Pencil, and so exact that the Difference was not easily discovered."[111] Because counterfeit money was so easily produced, newspapers often printed warnings about the fake money. These warnings not only discussed the fact that bogus bills were being circulated within a colony, they also described the bills whenever possible. By doing this, citizens could carefully check any bills of credit, coins, or foreign currency that came into their possession to guard against receiving counterfeit money. The *Pennsylvania Gazette* issued just such an admonition in 1750. The paper's warning stated:

The Publick are caution'd to beware of new Counterfeit Half-Crown Bills. They are of the Year 1744, and may be distinguish'd, by observing that they are struck from a Copper Plate, whereas the true Bills are done with common Printing Letters. In the Motto of the Coat of Arms the Word JUSTICE is spelt JNSRICE. And in the Word Province, the r stands close under the Bow of the P. They are supposed to be brought from Germany.[112]

Counterfeit money had the ability to ruin the economy of a colony, and this fact made it such a dangerous crime. The colony of South Carolina, for example, called in all £10 notes issued by the colony with a proclamation printed in the *South-Carolina Gazette* in July 1735 because phony notes of that value had been discovered circulating in the colony. Rather than assume that citizens would be able to recognize the bogus money, the colony declared all £10 notes valueless.[113] Counterfeiting brought on the severest punishments and was a capital offense in some colonies including Pennsylvania.[114]

Despite the mandated death penalty for counterfeiters and the fact that many such criminals were executed, some escaped this punishment. Yet even if counterfeiters escaped the legal system with their lives, they generally were given much more severe forms of punishment or more punishment than either rapists or robbers. Ear cropping was a common proscription for counterfeiters.[115] And the cutting off of a counterfeiter's ears was often just part of the punishment. One Samuel Wilson of Rhode Island "was sentenced to stand in the Pillory, be branded on both Cheeks, have both Ears cropped, and pay a Fine of Six Hundred Pounds Lawful Money" for his part in a Providence counterfeiting scheme. Three other counterfeiters on trial with Wilson received similar punishments, and a fourth was sentenced to death.[116]

When the ease of counterfeiting was combined with the greed of individuals, newspapers had ready-made stories that readers no doubt enjoyed. These news stories sometimes allowed printers to insert editorial comments. The *Massachusetts Gazette* told of a Newport counterfeiter's efforts to produce imitation gold and silver coins. "A more horrid and extensive combination to defraud the public," the paper commented, "has never been heard of in New-England."[117] When another group of New England counterfeiters were punished, they turned out to be "three Men of some Distinction" in Providence whose greed exceeded the legal ability of obtaining funds. The *Maryland Gazette* paid special attention to the reference to "Men of some Distinction" by adding in brackets at the end of the story: *"Men of DISTINCTION indeed! Pillory'd, Cropp'd, and Branded!"*[118]

The ultimate story of counterfeiting and greed appeared in the *American Weekly Mercury* in 1735. A counterfeiter hit upon a scheme that played upon the greed and superstitious nature of a New England landowner called "M. G—" in the news report. The counterfeiter manufactured a large number of brass pistoles, or Spanish coins, and carried them to the plantation of the greedy and superstitious New England man where the coins were buried. The counterfeiter then informed the landowner that a large amount of Spanish currency had been buried nearby. The counterfeiter revealed to "Mr. G—" that a conjurer had passed on this reliable information, and the swindler proceeded to lead the gullible landowner to "inchanted Ground" where the money was buried. The counterfeiter then began to dig for the money and

> soon came to the Box, open'd it, and show'd Mr. G the Pistoles as he then took 'em to be. I think it was above 1000. He told Mr. G— that he must not touch 'em for about 9 or 10 Months, for they were inchanted; but if he would lend him his Key he would put them into his Chest. . . . This done, he tells Mr. G— that there was more hid in his Plantation, which he would dig up for him in case he would give him 2000*l.* for his share of the whole, which Mr. G— agreed to and paid him down 6 or 700*l.*[119]

The story of the counterfeited pistoles ended with a twist. The swindler was discovered as he waited to collect the remainder of the £2,000 that Mr. G— had agreed to pay him, instead of leaving with the large amount of money already received. The counterfeiter quickly sought advice from a lawyer, who after he had been paid by the counterfeiter in the good money obtained from Mr. G—, "advis'd him by all means to Run for it." The counterfeiter took the lawyer's advice and escaped.[120]

The story of the "conjuring counterfeiter" may have made light of the colonies' most often practiced crime, but two other crimes—highway robbery and infanticide—were not subjects of levity in colonial newspapers. Roadside attacks hampered overland travel, and the murder of infants, specifically bastards, elicited strong reactions from colonial citizens, and any sentence for a bastard murderer other than execution was extremely unlikely. Neither highway robbery nor infanticide crimes directly affected colonials in the way counterfeiting did, but both were serious crimes, according to colonial newspapers.

Highway robbers had the potential to disrupt land travel in much the same way pirates could hamper and stop sea traffic. Colonial newspapers described the precarious nature of overland travel in both the colonies and in England, probably in an attempt to reinforce the dangers of travel and in an attempt to capture reader interest. At times, mail robberies took place on the highway.[121] But most reports of highway robbery concerned thefts commited against citizens traveling the roads of the countryside. Highway robbery occurred often enough, at least in Pennsylvania, for it to be made a capital offense punishable by death.[122]

Overland travel was dangerous throughout the colonial period, according to colonial newspaper reports. A Philadelphia man was not only stopped and robbed in January 1775, he was also shot and left to die, which he did.[123] After highway robberies occurred, newspapers would sometimes run descriptions of the footpads who commited the crimes, if descriptions were available.[124] And it was good news to read whenever highway robbers were foiled in their attempts. The *Boston Post-Boy* passed on to its readers the story of how a girl thwarted a robbery attempt by a handicapped highway robber who attempted to steal her money. "She took the Opportunity of snatching one of his Crutches," the news story said, "with which she struck him so violently, that he fell down dead."[125]

There was, however, no chance of retaliation by the victims in another common colonial crime as reported in colonial newspapers. Infants, specifically bastards, were often killed or abandoned to die by their mothers, and colonial newspapers denounced the crime and criminal regularly.

The reason for infanticide in colonial America may be traced to the laws of bastardy in England that were initiated during the reign of Elizabeth. Religious and social implications went into the creation of the law. The church saw the birth of infants to a mother out of wedlock as a sin and sought to end the activities of such immoral women. The state realized that poor people were having children in order to defraud local charities, especially the church. These two reasons were combined in the creation of a "personal control" law. In addition, some poor people were having children for begging purposes. These children were then disfigured or mutilated in some way in order to further sympathy and increase alms for the poor mother.[126]

Bastardy laws were transferred to the colonies and became a part of the legal system in colonial America.[127] But the actual crime of birthing a bastard, which David Flaherty claims was "the most important single group of cases" involving sex and morals crimes in at least the colony of Virginia,[128] was not the topic of crime or court news in colonial newspapers. The murder of the children and the way in which their "Murdering Mothers"[129] carried out the crime was.

Because of bastardy laws, unwed, pregnant woman denied that they were pregnant, no doubt in an effort to avoid prosecution under bastardy laws. The hiding of the pregnancy was almost always included as a part of the account of bastard murders in colonial newspapers, and this inclusion heightened the interest of readers. A prime example of the infanticide news story appeared in the *American Weekly Mercury* of Philadelphia in 1735. Andrew Bradford informed his readers:

> We hear from Providence in this County, that a young Woman about 19 Years of Age, is now under Confinement, for concealing the birth of her Bastard Child; and burying it in the Orchard. It seems her Master & Mistress had suspected her being with Child, but she constantly deny'd it; and they being from Home on the 4th Instant, she was Delivered by herself, and bury'd the Child about 9 Inches under Ground: After this, her Mistress observing her to appear smaller put it close to her that she had be deliver'd of a Child, but she would own nothing, 'til ten Days after, when Milk being found in her Breasts, and a Constable threatned [*sic*] to be sent for, she confess'd the whole.[130]

Trials for bastard murderers were held as soon as the mothers were able to be moved and stand trial.[131] Coroners' inquests into the deaths of bastards almost always brought back a charge of "wilful Murder,"[132] and courts almost always found the defendants guilty and sentenced them to death, as a Portsmouth, New Hampshire, court did in 1740 with Sarah Simpson and Penelope Kenny.[133] It was a rarity, according to newspaper reports, for infanticide charges to be dismissed against a woman.[134] In addition, charges of murder for infanticide could be brought against any person within the legal jurisdiction of a colony. Massachusetts, for example, charged a Native American with infanticide in 1735 and subsequently executed her.[135]

Felony crimes and court reports in colonial newspapers described hundreds of different crimes. In addition to giving a glimpse into the violence of colonial society and the crimes committed, these newspaper accounts also reveal something about how the judicial system in the colonies worked and how the system was perceived by citizens who observed it and corresponded with the newspapers.

Newspaper observations on the colonial legal system. Colonial newspapers made one thing obvious about the legal system of the colonies of America: Imprisonment was an unsatisfactory method to punish criminals because there were no adequate jails in the colonies and because there was a need to reinforce the wrongness of breaking the law with quick, corporal punishments that might have a lasting impression on felon and observer.

Some courts did hand down prison terms as parts of sentences, but the likelihood of a prisoner remaining in jail was not high, at least according to colonial newspapers. Numerous reports of prison breaks appeared in newspapers, reinforcing the idea that imprisonment was not the best way to punish criminals. Because prisons were generally nothing more than houses, it was hard to guard prisoners adequately. It evidently was also difficult to keep prisoners from obtaining tools that could be used to engineer a prison break. In order to keep breaks from occurring, law enforcement officials often initiated searches of prisoners' quarters. What they sometimes found demonstrates the difficulty of keeping felons in prison. In Boston, the *New-England Courant* reported:

> the Prison being search'd upon some Suspicion that the Prisoners intended to escape at Night, an Iron Crow a Steel Saw, and some other Tools were found, by the Help of which a Prisoner had got off his Irons, and such Preparations were made, as that they would in all probability have escap'd if they had not been timely discover'd.[136]

Part of the difficulty in keeping prisoners in jails stemmed from the fact that colonies did not have an adequate supply of law enforcement officials. Jail breaks took place with relative ease because of this fact. Men on horseback, for example, arrived in Newbury, Massachusetts, with crowbars and pried the doors off the facility used to house prisoners. No one was present to stop the escape.[137] A jail break in Philadelphia was thwarted only after citizens of the city responded to the fire set in order to free prisoners awaiting execution who had been left unguarded for the night. The *Virginia Gazette* described the situation:

> ON Wednesday evening, between the hours of 9 and 10 o'clock, a number of men in disguise (supposed about 25) assembled together, and made a most daring attempt upon the public gaol of this city, with intention, as it is said, to rescue from their confinement two criminals under sentence of death. . . . They broke a hole in the cellar door, though not large enough for their purpose of entering that way, and finding all their endeavours to break open the prison door unsuccessful, they attempted to set it on fire; but before the fire took effect, the city was alarmed, and the magistrates, with a vigour that does honour to

civil society, repaired to the prison, where a number of the inhabitants (as well those who have been learning the use of arms as others) were assembled. . . . In a few minutes the rioters were dispersed, several of them taken and put into the workhouse and gaol; a strong guard was then placed at the prison for the remainder of the night, which prevented further damage.[138]

This lack of sheriffs and other peacekeepers was blamed for prison breaking woes as well as for the ease of crime on the streets of towns. Samuel Parker added his own frustration concerning the lack of these kinds of authorities in New York at the end of one story about crime in the city. In noting that robberies had taken place every night for nearly two weeks, Parker lamented, "BUT ALAS! THE WATCH,—IS VAIN."[139] The lack of adequate law enforcement officials, and therefore, the inability to keep prisoners in jails made corporal punishment an even more attractive method of dealing with crime.

Keeping law breakers in jail was not the only problem concerning the legal system of colonial America that newspapers commented upon. Inequalities in the court system were the topic of several newspaper correspondents. The inequalities were the result of wealth according to these correspondents. The *Boston-News Letter,* for example, presented an account of a woman, who with some assistance from her daughter, beat her maid until "she run with Blood" and died. The paper doubted that the death sentence handed down against the mother and daughter would stand because of the wealth and influence of the family. "'Tis generally believ'd she will be pardon'd," the story surmised.[140] Another Boston paper reported two months later, however, that the mother and daughter had indeed received no pardon and were hanged. Again, a comment at the end of the news story gave the feeling that the execution had to take place in order to keep large numbers of the poor happy. The execution of the wealthy mother and daughter gave "a universal Satisfaction to all the Country," the account said.[141]

Any doubts that inequalities existed in the colonial legal system were quelled by a letter in the *New-York Gazette.* Inflamed over the preferential treatment that wealthy citizens of the colony received in comparison to poorer ones, an angry letter writer declared:

It is a very melancholly Reflection, to think, how different Punishments are inflicted for the same Crime; and that for no other Reason, but because the Quality of the Offender, and not the Heiniousness of the Offence, is what the Magistrate considers. If a poor Fellow not worth a Groat, gets Drunk, rambles about Town, and meeting with a Man's Daughter, should offer any Violence to her; upon a Complaint made, he is immediately taken up, and put in the Stocks till he is sober; if then, he can't get Security for his good Behaviour, he is whipt, and sent out of Town; The Magistrate is extolled for his Justice in the Case, and we all say, If such Crimes are not punished, how can a Man's Daughter be safe in walking the Streets. On the other Hand; If a rich Man happens to be guilty of the same Offence, occasioned by drinking too much, upon Complaint being made, the Magistrate advises the Party complaining, to make it up; adding, that if the Gentleman had not been drunk, he would not have offered any Violence to you Daughter; and I am sure, says the Magistrate, I will answer for him, he shall ask your Pardon. Thus the Magistrate becomes an Advocate for the Gentleman, instead of a Judge; the Consequence of which is, that the Gentleman goes on in the same Course of Wickedness; full well knowing, that the Magistrate dare not punish him; and he sounds his Argument upon this Reason, the Magistrate is elective; if he dares punish me, for abusing my Neighbour, he shall not be chosen the next Year. . . . Now, why the rich Man should be acquitted, and the poor Man put to Death, for the same Crime, I leave to the Learned in the Law to determine: I confess, I can't reconcile it to the Notions I have of Right and Justice. I believe your Divines will tell you, That no Wealth, tho' ever so considerable, will acquit a Criminal before a Tribunal, whose Justice is immutable.[142]

While wealth and preferential treatment by judges for those landowners who could keep them on the bench was a part of the colonial judicial system presented in colonial newspapers, the papers also demonstrated that at times the system sought and achieved egalitarian standards. When a Boston landowner brought two of his slaves to court and charged them with arson of his house, the superior court of the colony treated the slaves in a manner not unlike its English citizens. The trial took place; the jury listened and ruled that sufficient evidence had not been presented to convict the slaves. Both Africans were acquitted.[143]

Another aspect of the inequalities of the colonial judicial system, at least according to the research of legal historians into colonial court records, involved pardons granted after sentencing had taken place.[144] When colonial newspapers are consulted, however, one finds very few reported pardons. If, as Daniel Greenberg maintains, more than 50 percent of those sentenced to die in the colony of New York were pardoned,[145] newspapers failed to acknowledge the fact. If a pardon was mentioned in a colonial newspaper, the pardon was noted either in the briefest of notices[146] or treated as entertainment or moral exhortation. A story from the *Pennsylvania*

Gazette, for example, combined the two, making the pardon appear to be a religious experience for those whose sentences were commuted:

> They were both bid to stand up, and the ropes were order'd to be thrown over the Beam; when the Sheriff took a Paper out of his Pocket and began to read. The poor Wretches, whose Souls were at that Time fill'd with the immediate Terrors of approaching Death, having nothing else before their Eyes, and being without the least Apprenhension or Hope of a Reprieve . . . 'till they heard the Words PITY and MERCY. . . . Immediately Mitchel fell into the most violent Agony; and having only said, God bless the Governor . . . he added; I have been a great Sinner; I have been guilty of almost every Crime; Sabbath-breaking in particular, which led me into ill Company; but Theft I never was guilty of. God bless the Governor, and God Almighty's Name be praised.[147]

While the *Gazette*'s report of a pardon was entertaining and demonstrated the life-altering experience that one of the criminals experienced, the news report served a third function. Philadelphia had lately been overrun with what the *Gazette* referred to as "vagrants and idle Persons"[148] who had arrived from Europe. The death sentence for the two thieves was as much a warning for the immigrants to live under the law as it was anything else. Court news, therefore, may have also been used in colonial newspapers to warn the large number of convicts sent to America by the English judicial system to obey the laws of the colonies or face stiff penalties.[149]

The crime and court news of colonial papers touched upon nearly every facet of legal life in the colonies. From 1770 on, economic, political, and legal news often revolved around questions of nonimportation, and every colonial newspaper carried news items on this subject. Other crime and court news addressed crimes much different from the felony crimes of robbery, rape, arson, murder, and counterfeiting. A Portsmouth, New Hampshire man, for example, was convicted for cutting down a white pine tree that was less than six inches in diameter because he did not have a royal license to do so according to the *Boston Gazette*.[150] In another case, a New York man was fined £60 for selling bread that was not the proper weight. The man was, according to the *New-York Weekly Post-Boy,* not the only merchant to be arrested for swindling the people.[151]

Other crime and court stories touched upon odd cases and pieces purely presented for the social or entertainment value they contained. When a nobleman was led from the Tower in London to the scaffold to be hanged, the execution of a member of nobility gave the whole scene a party atmosphere. An "innumerable multitude" lined the streets to watch this person of note being led to the gallows, and more people surrounded the place of execution. Even the Reverend George Whitefield waited there in his coach to observe the execution, newspapers reported.[152] Philadelphia readers were treated to a bizarre account of a man attempting to spay his wife in much the same manner as he did his pigs. Holding her down with the weight of his body, he made an incision in her side and searched in vain for her female organs. The man received only a two-year prison term for his actions.[153] And in a crime that probably pleased all colonists who found the members of dissenting churches disagreeable, the *Maryland Gazette* related how a robber, waiting outside of a Methodist meetinghouse, entered the door when he heard the minister mention that it was time to take up the offering. The thief passed his hat from row-to-row, had it filled, and thanked the good people for their generosity as he left the meeting house to the protests of the minister.[154]

CONCLUSION

Crime and court news was one of the more important types of news disseminated during the colonial period. Because crime could affect everyone in a community in one way or another, crime and court news kept towns apprised of illegal activities. Newspapers also ran large amounts of crime and court news from colonies other than the ones in which a newspaper might be printed. When newspapers did this, they were helping to develop a more cohesive set of colonies. Not only could Massachusetts, for example, know what crimes were being committed in Pennsylvania and the punishments meted out for them, but the citizens of Massachusetts could also feel a certain amount of empathy with Pennsylvania victims and outrage for crimes committed there that were similar to the same actions in Massachusetts. Papers from New Hampshire to Georgia, therefore, shared news on criminal activities and court sessions, and local newspapers passed on news about Georgia to residents of New Hampshire and vice versa. They could share in each other's hardships and empathize with each other. It seems logical that crime news and other types of news that demonstrated how each region was experiencing the same tribulations or joyous occasions would help solidify thirteen separate colonies into a unified America.

The most important role of crime news was as a deterrent to crime. The large number of stories that related the punishments of criminals supports the contention that the colonies needed to punish citizens quickly, publicly, and harshly in order to deter criminal activity. Newspapers provided vivid, third-hand accounts of executions and other types of punishment in an effort to serve this purpose. By doing this, crime and court news exhibited some of characteristics of sensational news. Crime and court news, unlike sensationalism, was more concerned with demonstrating what happened to violators of the law than in shocking the moral sensibilities of readers. But crime news wanted to shock citizens into not committing crimes, and if they did commit crimes, they would have to face the possibility of having their ears cut off, their faces branded, their backs whipped, or their necks broken at the end of a rope.

By printing the vivid details of corporal punishments, newspapers sought to deter crime, which affirms the conclusions reached by legal historians who have studied the court records of the colonial period. Harsh punishments were as much to prevent crime as to punish current lawbreakers. But scholars in studying the court records of the colonies have also concluded that a great deal of leniency was exhibited by the colonial judicial system. Colonial newspaper reports of punishments, however, reveal little in the way of leniency. If a large number of criminals were pardoned, as Daniel Greenberg maintains, those pardons were not a regular part of the news in colonial newspapers. Few accounts exist like that in the 20 January 1730, *Pennsylvania Gazette* telling of the pardon for the two thieves when they reached the gallows, nor were there many listings of criminals, their crimes and their punishments like that in the *Virginia Gazette* that listed "Pardoned" beside the name of a criminal. In fact, of the sixty-nine crime and court reports in the 1735 *Pennsylvania Gazette,* for example, none mentioned pardons for any criminals, and this statistic is not an aberration for the colonial period. Details of pardons for any crimes committed in the American colonies were very rare in colonial newspapers.

The least punished major crime according to reports in colonial newspapers was rape. Punishment for ravishing children or even adults might be considered lenient, if whippings of from four to thirty-nine lashes plus time in the stocks and pillories is mild punishment. When compared to the punishments of counterfeiting, for example, rape punishments were lax. Counterfeiters were regularly whipped, cropped, branded, and fined for a single infraction. Although the death penalty was at times handed down for all felony crimes, rapists were the least likely to be sentenced to death, while first degree murderers and counterfeiters faced a strong possibility of being given a death sentence. Counterfeiting was a heinous crime because of the ease in which bogus money could be produced in the colonies and because of the damage that fake money could do to the newly established and quickly growing colonial economies.

"Wilful murder," the colonial term for first degree murder, meant death for most offenders, especially mothers who murdered their bastard infants. This capital offense bridged the gap between morals crimes and felonies against individual and property in the eighteenth-century crime and court news in colonial newspapers. Because bastard laws, which grew out of sixteenth-century English ecclesiastical legislation, remained on the books in America during the colonial period, unwed, pregnant females attempted to hide their pregnancies and then would often kill the babies rather than break this law. Colonial newspapers almost never mention an individual being arrested for a bastard law violation, but the moral stigma that having bastards must have placed on women had to have been great, considering the number of bastard murders discussed in colonial newspapers.

While bastard murders have not been considered morals crimes in this chapter, morals crimes were a part of crime and court news in the papers. Their numbers were small in comparison to crimes against individuals and property, however. Of the sixty-nine crime and court stories in the 1735 *Pennsylvania Gazette,* only two involved morals violations. Morals laws infractions diminished in the eighteenth century because colonies began to take on a more pluralistic nature. No longer were colonies such as Massachusetts able to limit their populations to rather homogeneous religious groups. Because the populations of the colonies started to include a more diverse set of people, agreeing upon morals offenses became more difficult. The relatively small number of morals crimes reported in the colonial newspapers affirms this.

Even though morals crimes played a diminishing role in the crime and court news of the eighteenth century, assuming that religious beliefs and moral standards in relation to crime disappeared completely is a mistake. As late as 1775, the *Virginia Gazette* laid the blame for a group of young men who had gone on a crime spree squarely on a lack of morals and proper religious and parental instruction. "The true causes," for the young men's criminal activity the *Gazette* postulated, "are a total ignorance of religion, mistaken education, habits of luxury and expense, and the evil examples in parents and masters; so that their minds are corrupted and prepared for the reception of every species of vice."[155]

If colonial newspapers ran crime and court news that dealt with morals crimes along with large amounts of crime and court news dealing with felonies against persons and property, the question must be asked, did this news reduce colonial crime? The answer appears to be no. Criminals were still attempting jail breaks in the summer of 1775 after America had entered into war with England.[156] Crime and court reporting no doubt helped to deter crime, but with the large influx of immigrants, including groups of English criminals, illegal activity continued. As late as 1765, newspapers were warning citizens to be on the lookout because "the most dangerous Gang that has been known" was robbing houses each night in Philadelphia.[157] Knowing just how much crime took place in America in the post-Stamp Act period based on colonial newspaper reports, however, is difficult. Crime and court news did not disappear, but just like sensationalism, crime and court news was relegated to a lesser role as news of taxation, representation, and disharmony with England grew. Crime news now focused more on nonimportation violations and assaults on stamp sellers and British importation officers. News of felons still appeared alongside these politically oriented reports.

Crime and court news served a vital function in colonial newspapers. That function was comparable to the news of ships and Native Americans that appeared in newspapers. Eliminating crime from American society would eradicate another obstacle in the path of success for the colonies, in much the way that knowing as much as possible about ships entering and departing the colonies and knowing what Indians were doing both furthered British colonial interests. The fact that the harsh corporal punishments and news of them did not eradicate crime does not mean that this news did not achieve at least some of its intended goal of reducing crime. By continually informing readers that criminals were "Whipt through the Streets and burnt with a hot Iron," newspapers at least let colonists know that American governments meant business when dealing with criminals. Newspapers, therefore, served their function in attempting to deter crime. The continuance of crime cannot be blamed on the effort of newspapers to report and thereby reduce crime. Perhaps the *Virginia Gazette* was correct; "a total ignorance of religion, mistaken education, habits of luxury and expense, and the evil examples in parents and masters" made crime inevitable. Whatever the reason, crime flourished during the colonial period, and colonial newspapers presented that crime to their readers in continual weekly doses.

Crime news, as presented in this chapter, may have dealt mainly with murder, rape, arson, robbery, and counterfeiting, but the English citizens of colonial America considered many of the activities of another group of inhabitants of British colonial America criminal as well. That group, the Africans imported as chattel to work all manner of menial occupations for affluent whites, needed to be controlled perhaps even more than white criminals. Slave crimes against whites and slave insurrections played upon the minds and fears of whites throughout the eighteenth century. Colonial newspapers did not let this news go unprinted, and as will be seen, news of slaves was news wrapped in fear that gradually for some colonial newspapers grew into news of manumission.

5

The Proceedings of the Rebellious Negroes

If one or more . . . Slaves . . . shall, in the Time of Alarm or Invasion, be found at the Distance of one Mile or more from the Habitation or Plantation of their Respective Owners . . . it shall be adjudged Felony without Benefit of Clergy in such Slave or Slaves; and it shall and may be lawful for the Person or Persons finding such Slave or Slaves . . . to shoot or otherwise destroy such Slave or Slaves, without being impeached, censured or prosecuted for the same.
—*Boston Evening-Post,* 10 March 1755

IN 1755, the colony of Massachusetts was waging a war against the French and Indians who inhabited Canada and many backcountry areas of New England. The Native American-French alliance had proven itself a formidable enemy, one the English colonists had been fighting intermittently since the seventeenth century. While the colony turned its attention toward stopping the enemy coalition, the Massachusetts General Assembly focused its legislative attention on another potential enemy of the colony. That enemy was an internal enemy, the slaves of the colony. Evidently, the Massachusetts legislators believed that if slaves and hostile Indians came into contact, the slaves would join with the Indians and turn upon the white settlers. The government, therefore, gave Massachusetts citizens the right to kill slaves on the spot under certain circumstances and not face any repercussions for doing it.[1]

Why would Massachusetts pass such a law? Were some of the slaves in Massachusetts already in league with the French and Indians? Had the colony's slaves previously rebelled against their white masters? The *Boston Evening-Post*'s report of the act passed by the General Assembly gave no reason for its passage, but the citizens of Massachusetts Bay and every other British colony along the Atlantic seaboard knew the reason such an act might be necessary. Weekly newspapers for years had been supplying readers with

121

news of "the Proceedings of the Rebellious Negroes,"[2] accounts that related insurrections by African slaves throughout the New World and even in Africa. If white colonists were forced to focus their attention upon an invader like the French and Indians, the slaves might seize the opportunity to rebel, join with the enemy, or wage war themselves upon white colonists. It had happened before in the colonies, in 1740 when invading Spaniards from Florida incited Georgia slaves to revolt,[3] and Massachusetts leaders evidently were not willing to give the French and Indians the opportunity to do the same. The colony, therefore, declared that at certain times all slaves more than a mile from their home were enemies of the colonies.

This chapter deals with "the Proceedings of the Rebellious Negroes" and the other types of news about slaves that appeared in colonial newspapers. The slave news in colonial newspapers concentrates upon two principal topics: slave insurrections and slave crimes. In addition, colonial newspapers carried numerous stories that reflected the attitudes of white colonists toward African slaves. In these news stories, the inferior nature of blacks, when compared to Europeans, is evident. But these news stories reveal another aspect of the relationship between blacks and whites in colonial America; white colonists were afraid of slaves, and that fear is apparent in many items in colonial newspapers. Fear of slaves is also reflected in the silence some colonial newspapers maintained concerning slave rebellions within their own colony or in their failure to mention revolts in other colonies, insurrections that found their way into the reports of many other colonial newspapers.

Another type of slave news also appeared in colonial newspapers, but this type of slave news was neither a universal feature of colonial newspapers nor did it appear throughout the colonial period as did news of "the Rebellious Negroes." This other type of slave news consisted of antislavery commentaries that began to appear in colonial newspapers of New England and Pennsylvania in 1770.[4] The earliest antislavery piece to appear in the papers of colonial America, however, was printed in 1740.[5] The antislavery literature of colonial newspapers, regardless of its limited appearance in the newspapers, was significant and offers a strong contrast to the news of slaves in rebellion.

Slavery was big business throughout the colonial period. Although beyond the parameters of this study, the advertisements of colonial newspapers reveal the booming slave trade that existed in the colonies and the problems that slave owners had with runaway slaves.[6] Slaves were, in the eyes of most white colonials, very much property. But as Darold D. Wax pointed out in his study of slaves and the *Maryland Gazette,* slaves were seen as more than merely property. The human qualities that slaves possessed, even if deemed to be inferior to whites, made the transplanted Africans a viable source of news.[7] The study of all colonial newspapers confirms this fact, and it also points out that the humanity of slaves led directly to their desire to be free, something they attempted to obtain through insurrection and crime.[8] Because freedom for slaves meant a loss of property and perhaps life for white colonists, news surrounding slaves was steeped in fear, derogation, and an insensitivity for Africans. The antislavery literature of colonial newspapers affirms these feelings while further enhancing the humanness of slaves.

Many readers of colonial newspapers no doubt felt that slave news provided life-or-death information. Although news in Boston of an attempted slave insurrection in South Carolina appeared in the Massachusetts city's newspapers weeks after the fact,[9] the news kept Bostonians on guard. It reminded them that similar revolts had occurred in Boston[10] and that the potential for similar rebellions still existed in their city just as much as on the plantations of the Tidewater region of South Carolina. This fact helps also to explain Massachusetts' harsh law passed against slaves in 1755 and announced in the *Boston Evening-Post.* Understanding attitudes toward slavery in America as represented in colonial newspapers, however, requires understanding the origins of slavery and some of its economic repercussions. The following brief discussion of slavery in America should help in that understanding.

SLAVERY IN AMERICA

Slavery for Africans in the British colonies of America began with the arrival of twenty Africans via Dutch ship to Jamestown, Virginia, in 1619. Although those twenty Africans were not considered to be slaves by the Jamestown residents and they worked as indentured servants in the tobacco fields of the growing English colony, the concept of perpetual slavery of blacks grew, about as quickly as the populating of the Atlantic seaboard by whites.[11] Blacks from Africa were not the only ones to serve as slaves either. Europeans attempted to force Native Americans into servitude as well, but this practice was not successful because Indians lacked experience with any intensified agricultural methods such as those used in Europe and West Africa.[12]

The whites who arrived from Europe were not establishing a new practice when they used African slaves to assist with the difficult manual labor needed to survive in America. As early as 1300, Europeans forced Africans into slavery in order to work the sugar plantations of the Mediterranean Sea region of the continent.[13] The use of Africans by the English followed, and during the ill-fated attempts at English colonization on Roanoke Island in the 1580s, blacks, in some capacity of servitude, were left with the colony in 1586.[14]

The restriction of slavery to blacks rested, ultimately, upon the principle that racially inferior beings belonged in servitude to their superiors. Carried further, this concept made the servitude of Negroes in American inheritable.[15] The boom period for tobacco during the 1620s fostered this kind of thinking. As the colony of Virginia achieved more and more financial success through the exportation of tobacco, the greater the need became for a large, inexpensive labor supply. Imported Africans filled that need, and this system of labor developed into a system that treated humans as things.[16]

The tobacco plantations of Virginia, however, were not the only places in colonial America where slavery existed. Boston was only eight years old when slaves were brought into the town of fifteen hundred citizens, and by 1690, slaves were just as numerous in northern urban centers as they were in the tobacco-growing regions of the Southern colonies.[17] Slaves comprised just over 13 percent of the total population of the colonies in that year with slaves present in all twelve colonies.[18]

During the seventeenth century, the slave trade in America was a monopoly run by the Royal African Trading Company, but the company was inefficient and unable to meet the growing demand for African slaves to work in the New World. For that reason in 1698, Parliament opened the African slave traffic to independent merchants and traders.[19] With the slave trade opened to a free-enterprise market, ship captains and merchants in America quickly discovered just how profitable slave trade could be. The main traders for slaves, however, were not merchants and shippers from the Southern colonies but shippers and traders from New England, specifically Rhode Island and Massachusetts. Their ships ran the rum triangle leaving America loaded with rum and sailing to Africa where they purchased slaves with it. With their ships loaded with slaves, the New England captains sailed to the West Indies or

Southern colonies and sold the cargoes of slaves for molasses. The molasses was used to produce more rum, thereby continuing the cycle.[20] Slaves sold in the rum triangle generally brought £21 for males, £18 for women, and £14 for children in the Caribbean.[21] Slaves sold in the Southern colonies averaged higher prices, around £30 in 1730 to as much as £60 by 1750.[22] This slave-rum trade triangle was so profitable for New England merchants and shippers that two-thirds of Rhode Island's ships and sailors directly participated in the trade.[23] In fact, from the first decade of the eighteenth century to 1740, the yearly value of the slaves imported into America grew from £28,000 to £118,000.[24]

The growing profits made by those dealing in the slave trade— in conjunction with the desire for cheap labor—helped to increase the number of slaves being brought into the colonies in the eighteenth century, estimated at 1,000 per year from 1700–1720, 2,500 per year from 1720–1740, and 5,000 per year from 1740–1760.[25] By 1770, more than 450,000 slaves resided in the thirteen colonies,[26] with one quarter of a million of dislocated Africans being taken from their homeland and sold into American slavery during the century.[27] More than 35 percent of the immigrants entering New York City in the middle third of the eighteenth century were African slaves,[28] and the Massachusetts slave population doubled from 1700 to 1750, blacks accounting for 8 percent of Boston's total population in 1755.[29] By 1720, more than half of South Carolina's total population was comprised of Africans, and blacks outnumbered whites in the colony for the rest of the century.[30] Slavery and slave trading were, by the eighteenth century, a regular part of American life with slaves in every colony.[31]

The manner in which Africans worked in the system of perpetual servitude that developed in America varied from region to region in the eighteenth century. Southern slaves were naturally used on plantations to work crops of tobacco and rice. Southern planters discovered that slave labor was so vital to the success of their farming that planters invested all their spare capital in the purchasing of more slaves.[32] The slave's work on Southern plantations was much harsher than the work of slaves in the urban centers of the Middle and New England colonies. There, slaves worked for artisans, mariners, and small manufacturers. Slaves learned a trade and were better clothed, housed, and fed than their southern counterparts, but harsh treatment still accompanied bondage for slaves, North or South.[33]

For slaves, the types of physical punishment were virtually unlimited. White owners, according to slave laws passed as early as

1669 in America, could do with and to their slaves as they pleased to correct wrongdoing.[34] The Virginia legal system in 1705 and the South Carolina code of 1740 termed slaves real estate. The South Carolina code stated that slaves were "chattel personal, in the hands of their owners and possessors and their executors, administrators and assigns, to all intents, constructions and purposes whatsoever" to be done with as the owners so deemed appropriate.[35] Colonial law was especially harsh upon runaway slaves, who could be automatically put to death if they harmed a white while running away. The slaves could also be whipped, branded, castrated, or have their ears cut off when caught under South Carolina law.[36]

Slavery, ultimately, became more than a labor system in colonial America. As Gary Nash pointed out, slavery was part an evolving attitude in America that saw labor as something to be imported, exported, bought, bartered, and sold.[37] But slavery was not universally accepted by all white colonists. As early as 1688, some Germantown, Pennsylvania, Quakers went on record opposing the enslavement of Africans.[38] The Pennsylvania Society of Friends were the first and most vocal opponents of slavery in eighteenth-century America.[39] As early as 1700, Quakers were publishing anti-slavery tracts including Samuel Sewall's *Selling of Joseph* (1700) and Ralph Sandiford's *A Brief Examination of the Practice of the Times* (1729) in attempts to halt the possession of slaves by Quakers and other colonial citizens.[40] Large audiences of slave owners could be found for these works since about half of the citizens of Philadelphia owned slaves,[41] a number that corresponded equally to slave ownership in the Virginia plantation region.[42] Others followed in the effort to halt slavery, but the practice was too entrenched into the economic fabric of American life. Another century would pass before slavery would officially end.

The success of the slave trade for New England merchants and the necessity of it for crop production on Southern plantations firmly entrenched slavery in eighteenth-century American society. Success and necessity helped produce a domestic slave trade in addition to the overseas ventures. The major expositor of this trade became the colonial newspapers, which provided a wider and more readily available market by helping to bring buyer and seller together.[43] Newspaper printers realized, too, that slavery was a means to a profit for them as well, yet the content of colonial newspapers, other than advertisements that presented the economic aspects of slavery, reveals few feelings about slaves other than fear and inferiority of Africans in their relationship with white colonists. For these reasons, news of slave revolts and slave crimes occupied the bulk of colonial news about slaves. It is with news of insurrections that this discussion of slaves and colonial newspapers begins.

SLAVES AND COLONIAL NEWSPAPERS

Slave insurrections. On 21 April 1712, the *Boston News-Letter* announced to the citizens of Boston that seventy Negroes were in custody in New York following their "late Conspiracy to Murder the Christians" in that region. A wholesale extermination of rebellious slaves followed in New York as the colony initiated a string of executions that burned, broke on the wheel, and hung up alive to be left to die those slaves who had assumed an active role in the insurrection. Many of the slaves arrested hanged themselves or slit their own throats rather than face such torturous deaths.[44] No doubt harsher treatment for slaves not involved in the revolt followed as well. The *News-Letter*'s account of the New York slave revolt was one in the long list of slave rebellion reports to appear in colonial newspapers, and according to the papers, slave revolts occurred with great frequency and throughout the New World.

When colonial newspapers reported "the Proceedings of the Rebellious Negroes," they could have been talking about slave revolts in Boston, Charleston, Kingston, or almost any other locale that had a slave population and contact with the British colonies of North America. In fact, in the years of this study, slave revolts were reported by newspapers to have taken place or have been planned at the following locations: New York (1712, 1765, 1775); Williamsburg (1730, 1770, 1775); Jamaica (1730, 1735, 1745, 1750, 1760 [two], 1765, 1770), Antigua (1740, 1765); Indies (1750); Georgia (1740); Charleston (1740, 1745); Surinam (1750, 1765); Curaçao (1750); Kingston (1750, 1760); Boston (1720); South Carolina (1730, 1740, 1745, 1760, 1775); St. Jago (1760); South America (1750); St. Kitts (1750, 1770); Santa Croix (1760); Saint Marys (1760); Honduras (1765); Annapolis (1740, 1770); Saint Eustatia (1770); New Bern (1770); Malta (1750); Saint Thomas (1760); Cayenne (1750); James River, Virginia (1730) and Esopus (1775).

The frequency of slave rebellions and the amount of news they generated attests to the concern white colonists up and down the Atlantic seaboard shared about the potential danger that slave insurrections represented for whites in the towns and regions containing relatively large concentrations of slaves, the areas not ironically where newspapers were published. News of slave revolts and slave crimes was no doubt very closely connected in the minds of the readership of colonial newspapers. Both slave revolts and lawlessness were acts of defiance by those in subjugation against those in authority. The murder of a white citizen by a black slave—especially if the slave's master was the victim—was in reality no different from an insurrection by a group of slaves. In each case freedom was generally the sole goal of the slave or slaves and whatever means necessary to obtain that goal was legitimate to its perpetrator.

Reports of slave insurrections were not confined to the colonies of the New World either. Colonial newspapers carried accounts of slave rebellions onboard ships that were bringing Africans to the colonies for servitude. Outnumbered whites had to be constantly on guard for their lives because of the great number of blacks being transported, even though the Africans were generally in irons and kept below deck most of the time. A London letter concerning an uprising upon a ship was printed by John Holt in the *New-York Journal:*

> On Sunday last, about three in the morning; we were all (who lay in the cabbin) alarmed with a most horrid noise of the negroes, which was succeeded by several dreadful shrieks from Mr. Howard and several of the people upon deck. Surprised at such an uncommon uproar, I Strove to awake Capt. Millroy, but before I could make him sensible of what had happened I received a stroke over my shoulders with a billet of wood, as also a cut with a cutlass on the back of my neck. The cries of Mr. Howard, who was murdered under the windlass, as also those of several of the people, whom the villains were butchering on the main deck, had thrown me into such a state of stupidity, that I did not in the least feel the wound I had received.[45]

Reports of slave revolts on land or sea no doubt stirred the imaginations of readers and provoked thoughts of fear by describing the activities of slaves or by just mentioning that a revolt had taken place. Both types of rebellion news stories found their way into colonial newspapers. When slaves revolted in the middle of the night and killed families in their beds in Surinam,[46] Boston readers had a clear picture of the potential danger they might face from the sizeable slave population in their city should enough slaves become discontent. When the *Boston Weekly Post-Boy,* however, announced to its readers that "a new Negro Plot is just discovered" in South Carolina in 1740,[47] nothing else was said. Readers could supply the details of what might have happened had the revolt taken place. South Carolina had suffered through the worst slave revolt to have occurred in the colonies just months before, the Stono Rebellion,[48] and the vast differences in the white and black populations of the colony were well known, at least to Boston readers, who as early as 1730 were informed of the population disparity between slaves and whites in South Carolina. In a letter from Charleston that was printed in the *Boston News-Letter,* a South Carolina resident noted, "For take the whole Province we have about 28 thousand Negros to 3 thousand Whites."[49] When the Stono Rebellion and the disparity in white and black population were taken into account by Boston newspaper readers, no real details of a revolt were needed to reach a conclusion about what might happen if an uprising were to occur.

Because of the threat large numbers of slaves presented for the white population, any activity by slaves that had the potential to lead to an insurrection was closely scrutinized.[50] This ever-watchful eye that was applied to slaves was not unlike the close examination that Native American activities received from white colonists. In the same manner that colonial newspapers repeated the news of the Cherokee War of 1760 from newspaper to newspaper,[51] colonial newspapers recounted slave revolts for their readers. Almost every report of a slave rebellion ran in multiple colonial newspapers, but two of the most repeated accounts of slave insurrections appeared in the colonial newspapers in 1745 and 1750 and discussed massive rebellions by slaves in the Caribbean.

In 1745, slaves on Jamaica prepared to stage a large insurrection on the island. This attempt was not the first by Jamaican slaves nor would it be the last. Jamaican slaves attempted approximately two hundred fifty rebellions during the period that slavery existed on the island, and those rebellions were never small. The average number of slaves taking part in Jamaican revolts averaged between three and four hundred in the eighteenth century, and six years before the 1745 revolt, thousands of Jamaican slaves had rebelled against servitude in what Jamaicans called the first Maroon war. The ratio of ten slaves to one white on the island further exacerbated relationships between whites and their black slaves.[52]

In January 1745, a plot where the slaves planned to "destroy all the Whites" on the island was "very near accomplished." The rebellion was thwarted just as the slaves planned to attack, however, and the whole affair was made known to American colonists by a letter received in Boston dated 2 February 1745, and printed in the *Boston Evening-Post* on 1 April. Within a week, the letter was reprinted in newspapers in New York,[53] and it ran twelve days later in Philadelphia.[54] The *Virginia Gazette* presented the letter in May.[55] The letter provided readers with an entertaining account of what had nearly happened on Jamaica, explaining the slaves' proposed plan to kill the whites and how the plot was sabotaged. Slaves on plantations were to murder their masters and mistresses and then proceed to the near-by town, where they would set fire to both ends of the town and shoot or stab whites as they ran in fear from the smoke and flames. The plot was revealed by a sympathetic slave who did not want to see her mistress killed. The white woman then sent news of the planned rebellion to her husband, away for several days of card playing. He ignored the note from his wife until the last minute, so the wife got help from a neighbor, who gathered the local militia and surprised the slaves in their hideout.

The letter from Jamaica, which appeared in all cities with newspapers except Charleston, reminded white citizens of the deviousness of slaves and the potential for harm if one let one's guard down as did the card-playing husband. The story also provided an ironic twist—the sympathetic house slave who warned the whites of the impending disaster. As newspaper accounts reminded readers of the inferiority of blacks to whites, they also demonstrated the humanness of slaves. The incompatibleness of these two themes would eventually lead to the divisions concerning manumission for slaves that were raised by the antislavery rhetoric found in the newspapers in the 1770s.

When a newly arrived lot of slaves in Curaçao revolted in 1750, whites reacted quickly. A 25 July letter from the Dutch settlement in the Antilles told that the settlers "had done nothing in our island but racking and executing a parcel of new Negroes, who had plotted to destroy all the whites." After being racked, the letter stated and newspapers related, the rebellious slaves had "their hearts taken out and dash'd in their faces."[56] The letter ran in newspapers north and south of New York. In Boston it appeared in two papers,[57] and it ran in both Philadelphia publications.[58] The identical letter with a New York dateline appeared in the *Maryland Gazette* the first week of September.[59] And just as the card playing account of insurrection in Jamaica failed to appear in the *South-Carolina Gazette*,[60] so, too, was the news from Curaçao concerning the slave revolt absent.[61] Interestingly, another letter from Curaçao dated 27 July concerning the slave revolt that ran in the *New-York Evening-Post*[62] was not picked up by any of the other colonial newspapers. In the *Evening-Post*'s expanded version of the insurrection, colonists and free Negroes were killed by the slaves. The killing of whites by the rebellious slaves may have been the reason that other newspapers picked up the *New-York Gazette* version as opposed to the *Evening-Post* account. Other factors may have entered into the decision, too, including availability of the two papers in other towns and the quality of writing. The *Gazette*'s report was much more succinct. Whatever the reason for the omission of the *Evening-Post*'s version, the inclusion of the *New-York Gazette* letter again points out the danger that many whites felt from slaves, be they newly imported as in Curaçao or lifetime chattel.

The same repetition of slave rebellion stories took place continually in the colonial period. When Spanish soldiers from Florida invaded Georgia during the War of Jenkin's Ear late in 1739, for example, slaves seized upon the opportunity to revolt in the newly organized English colony, and newspapers related the news up and down the Atlantic seaboard.[63] And as has been seen, these stories usually came from one source that was received by one newspaper and copied by others. This method of obtaining news items created a problem for colonial newspapers. Accuracy was sometimes lost; innuendo was acceptable for news; and verification of a news story often came weeks or months later. This problem could be applied to all news in colonial newspapers, but it appeared to be especially true of news of slave revolts. Verification was important for a news story, but confirmation could wait when an item of interest to the welfare of colonists had reached the hands of a printer. Newspapers had no way to verify the accuracy of a news story of a slave rebellion in Jamaica, Curaçao or Georgia, unless a second account from a different source was available. Newspapers generally assumed that a news item was true, but the large number of slave rebellion stories from many different locations made verification nearly impossible.

One of the best examples of the printing of inaccurate information concerning slave revolts occurred in 1760. Slaves in Jamaica, at least twelve hundred of them, had revolted, and news about the rebellion made its way to America. A letter from Saint Mary's on Jamaica addressed the issue of misinformation: "I am informed you have received several erroneous and contradictory Accounts of the Proceedings of the Rebellious Negroes; which I am not surprized at, as the Truth is difficult to come at here on the Spot. The following is the best Information I can give you thereof."[64] Whether the letter writer provided accurate information is doubtful, since it contained numerous comments about the actions and thoughts of the rebelling slaves, including the revealing way in which the slaves persuaded one of their leaders to continue the revolt even after he was wounded.[65] The letter did, however, provide newspaper readers an interesting account of the way in which whites sought "to reduce the Blackymores to obedience."[66]

Colonial newspapers printed numerous reports from Jamaica that dealt with the insurrection for the remainder of 1760, one often contradicting the other. In July, for instance, newspapers reported that the rebellion had been entirely quelled with "no Apprehension of their [the slaves] coming to any Head again"[67] and that "a second Insurrection of the Negroes had been attempted."[68] The sons of printer Thomas Fleet, who continud to print the *Boston Evening-Post* after their father's death, no doubt felt they had finally received accurate information on the activities in Jamaica in November because the pair prefaced the *Evening-Post*'s latest news from Jamaica with "we have prints to the 4th of October,"[69] referring to copies of the newspapers of Jamaica, the *Jamaica Gazette,* the *Kingston Journal,* and the *St. Jago Intelligencer.* The Fleets were relying upon printed, public news rather than letters from citizens or the hearsay of a ship's captain and probably felt this information was more accurate for that reason, despite the fact that the Jamaican newspapers may have received their news from letters and hearsay as well.

The news of the Jamaican slave revolt played continuously to the readers of newspapers from Annapolis to Boston in 1760, but in South Carolina, news about the Jamaican slave revolt—or any slave revolt for that matter—was a rarity. The omission in 1760 by the *South-Carolina Gazette* may be blamed on the fact that the colony was in the midst of a fierce war against both the Cherokees and smallpox, but after 1739, the *Gazette* carefully avoided mention of most slave revolts, especially those that were reported to have taken place in South Carolina. When the *Maryland Gazette* stated "that an Insurrection was apprehended in the Providence [*sic*] of South-Carolina" in 1760,[70] it was printing a piece of news that would never appear in a South Carolina newspaper. In South Carolina, news of slave revolts was seldom printed, and the reasons for the omissions stemmed directly from fear of a concerted effort by the colony's large slave population.

From 1720 onward, African slaves outnumbered whites in South Carolina. By 1730 there were approximately two slaves for every white inhabitant of the colony, and the ratio did not dip below that average for the remainder of the century.[71] In 1730, colonial newspapers in Boston, New York, and Philadelphia reported that a large slave revolt in the province had been uncovered and stopped. The slaves, according to the account in the *New-York Gazette,* failed because the slaves could not decide whether they "should destroy their own Masters" or "Ris[e] up in a Body, and giv[e] the Blow once in Surprize."[72] No newspaper existed in South Carolina in 1730 to print the news of the revolt, but when similar rebellions occurred in 1739 and 1740, the *South-Carolina Gazette* printed no information "that a new Negro Plot is just discover'd" in the colony.[73]

Besides the obvious fear of slaves because of the overwhelming odds they possessed in numbers versus whites, news of slave rebellion activity in South Carolina was omitted by the colony's only newspaper because of the Stono Rebellion of 1739.[74] In September 1739, slaves broke into a store, robbing it of guns and ammunition. In the process they murdered the shop owner, severed his head, and left it on the steps of the store. The slaves, who had started the revolt twenty miles from Charleston, began moving southward toward Florida picking up rebellious slaves and killing whites along the way. The slaves soon numbered between sixty and one hundred and were met by a group of white planters of approximately the same size. A battle ensued that successfully halted the main thrust of the rebelling slaves. Small groups of slaves continued their revolt, but the insurrection was doomed. The death toll for the rebellion was estimated at twenty-one whites and forty-four slaves, and the legislature granted total immunity to all persons who aided in the suppression of the rebellion.

Because of the Stono Rebellion, South Carolina enacted a strict slave code in 1740 that decreed that "the extent of . . . power over . . . slaves ought to be settled and limited by positive laws, so that the slave may be kept in due subjection and obedience." Slaves were required "to submit . . . or undergo the examination of any white person," and if the slave dared to react with violence, the slave code stated that "such slave may be lawfully killed."[75] The *South-Carolina Gazette* never mentioned the slave code during the year.

The *South-Carolina Gazette* may have ignored slave revolts, but the newspaper did not ignore slaves. In direct reaction to the activities of slaves in the colony, the colony passed strict laws banning slaves from congregating for any purpose. The *Gazette,* under the guidance of Elizabeth Timothy, printed this news. The colony made it illegal for slaves to gather in Charleston to play "Dice and other Games," and it prohibited "gathering together such great Numbers of Negroes, both in Town and Country, at their Burials and on the Sabbath Day."[76] The law was an obvious attempt to keep slaves from congregating in large enough numbers that a revolt could occur.

The South Carolina law as reported in the *South-Carolina Gazette* was just one of the numerous efforts during the colonial period to control African slaves. Increasingly, colonial laws recognized slaves as chattel or property, and newspapers printed these laws and correspondence that revealed how white colonists looked upon the black slaves. Because of the growing number of slaves in America, the slave laws that colonial governments enacted, the many reports of slave revolts, and the omission of slave rebellion news in South Carolina, many white colonists developed a fear of slaves. Reinforcing this increasing fear was the white perception that people of color, specifically blacks, were inferior and incapable of obtaining a high moral or intelligence level. This understanding led to a particular depiction of slaves that appeared in colonial newspapers.

Attitudes toward and perceptions of African slaves. The fear of slaves and the concept that people of color were inferior to whites manifested itself in a number of ways in colonial newspapers. Laws continually restricted the activities of slaves, and letters written to newspapers concerning slaves often advocated keeping Africans in the lowest positions of society. Both of these practices developed as a result of slave rebellions, slave crimes, and the feelings of superiority that white colonists possessed, and often there was no masking the fear that whites had of those whom they held in servitude. As a result, the laws of colonial legislatures and the correspondence sent to newspapers concerning slaves often advocated harsh treatment to slaves.

In 1740, for instance, a writer to the *Boston Evening-Post* criticized slave owners for their lack of control of slaves, something that created an untenable situation in Boston. "The great Disorders committed by Negroes, who are permitted by their imprudent Masters, &c. to be out late at Night," the letter writer complained, "has determined several sober and substantial Housekeepers to walk about the Town in the sore part of the Night . . . and it is hoped that all lovers of Peace and good Order will join their endeavours for preventing the like Disorders for the future."[77] Freedom and leniency were items writers to newspapers felt were evils for both slaves and their white owners. Being less than severe in a relationship with slaves was dangerous for whites as a letter from Williamsburg explained:

> Some time about Christmas last, a tragical affair happened at a plantation . . . the particulars of which . . . are as follows, viz. The Negroes

belonging to the plantation having long been treated with too much lenienty and indulgence, were grown extremely insolent and unruly. . . . The Steward's deputy . . . had ordered one of the slaves to make a fire every morning very early; the fellow did not appear till sunrise; on being examined why he came not sooner, he gave most insolent and provoking answers, upon which . . . the fellow made a stroke at him with an ax.[78]

Slaves on the plantation had been given some leeway earlier, and because a less than severe approach had been taken with them, an overseer had been axed. After the axing, a revolt broke out between the slaves and whites on the plantation that resulted in numerous deaths on both sides.

Because leniency could lead to danger from slaves, colonial governments, according to reports in colonial newspapers, passed numerous laws to suppress any kind of leisure activities for slaves. These laws, as Leon Higginbotham pointed out, were a concerted effort on the part of colonies to halt conspiratory actions by slaves, something that was very likely if slaves were given any free time.[79] Again, fear of slaves was the underlying motive behind these laws. Wherever governments felt that the potential for slave problems existed, stringent laws to inhibit slave activity were enacted. In 1730, for example, the governor of Virginia placed the militia on active duty and ordered that the quarters of slaves in the region surrounding Norfolk be inspected each night.[80] In Boston, the city passed laws that prohibited any slave from leaving the home of his master after nine o'clock at night, and if slaves were caught on the street after that hour, they were to be publicly whipped.[81] In New York, slaves were not allowed to congregate in groups larger than three because slaves with free time had been on the streets of the city uttering "very insolent Expressions, and otherways misbehaved themselves."[82]

Repressive laws were only one way that whites attempted to suppress slaves. Newspapers echoed the views of colonial society that African blood produced inferior beings in numerous ways. This fact, according to some newspaper reports, was very obvious if one observed mulattos. Even though mulattos were the product of one white parent, they were still considered inferior because of their mixed racial ancestry. The company of mulattos was to be avoided by all whites, and one writer to the *South-Carolina Gazette* remarked, "none appear to me so monstrously ridiculous as the Molatto Gentleman."[83] Slaves were thought of as inferior to whites. By reaffirming this concept, colonial newspapers helped colonial society keep order. If whites could continually reaffirm their dominance over blacks in both physical and emotional ways, they could hold on to their tenuous position as masters over another, and sometimes more populous group.

A poem, *On a Negro girl making her Court to a fair Youth,* spoke of the impossibility of white and black existing together. In the poetry, the slave girl desired a physical relationship with a white boy, but the reply by the young man addressed the fact that such an action would cost the whites their property as black would overshadow white. In putting down the slave as foolish for such a request as a relationship on par with whites, the underlying fear of black dominance of whites was being addressed. The importance of white over black may also be detected in the poem through its capitalization, white being capitalized while black remains in lower case. The poem stated:

> Negro, complain not, that I fly;
> When Fate commands Antipathy.
> Prodigious might that Union prove,
> When Day and Night together move.
> And the Communion of our Lips,
> Not Kisses make, but an Eclipse;
> In which the mixed black and White,
> Portends more Horror than Delight.
> Yet, if thou wild my shadow be,
> Enjoy thy dearest Wish, but see
> You take my shadows Property;
> Which always flys when I draw near
> And don't so much as drop a Tear,
> And nothing shew of Love or Fear.[84]

The view of the inferiority of blacks in colonial society was greatly enhanced by the white belief that slaves, specifically black slaves, were property. As early as 1706, that concept was appearing in news stories. In 1705, forty-four African slaves died in Massachusetts, and the *Boston News-Letter* reported that those deaths amounted to a loss "to the Sum of One Thousand three hundred and Twenty Pounds."[85] Parliament reported England's earnings on the importation and exportation of slaves in the nation's economic report.[86] Drownings in North Carolina of four slaves were not lamented as a loss of life but as the loss of "most Valuable Slaves," whose monetary significance was the only true forfeiture.[87] Slaves were property, and as such they could be put on display as a mulatto slave was in Boston because "a White Negro was such a

Novelty in America that one was exhibited Night by Night at the Sign of the White House."[88]

All of the efforts of the colonies to suppress slaves through laws and all newspaper accounts of the inferiority of African slaves were of little value, however, when slaves actually decided to revolt against whites. African slaves, who had been free before being sold into captivity, sought freedom. This desire for freedom manifested itself in the form of slave insurrections, but slaves sought freedom in another way as well, through acts of violence in crime.

Slave crimes. As long as whites maintained physical superiority over slaves, control belonged to them. When the balance of power swung to the slaves, criminal violence was often the result, which is exactly what happened to a Maryland overseer who walked alone into the woods with a group of slaves to chastise them. The overseer never returned alive.[89] Such actions by slaves were acts of defiance against whites and created yet another fear of slaves that colonial newspapers reported with great regularity.

Not all slave crimes were overt attempts at self-manumission. Some of the slave crimes reported in colonial newspapers were simply criminal activity. Psychological analysis might reveal that all violent attacks by slaves were still caused by their forced bondage, but rapes and burglaries do not fit into the pattern of reactionary violence like rebellions and murders of slave owners, acts that offered slaves at least temporary freedom from those in direct control of them. Regardless the reasoning for the crimes, criminal activity by slaves produced news for colonial newspapers, and slaves, with few exceptions, received harsher punishments than whites for the same crimes.

Slaves, despite colonial efforts to keep them from communicating with one another as witnessed in many of the laws already discussed, evidently were able to overcome such decrees against them. In South Carolina in 1735, a crime ring operated by slaves was uncovered. Apparently, slaves had successfully robbed stores and storehouses of more than £2,000 in goods and had funneled the goods through an underground network for months before authorities were able to discern the robbers' identities or even that they were slaves.[90] In 1775, a similar group of slaves in Virginia known as "Dunmore's banditti," worked the region around Norfolk, robbing homes and taking away slaves.[91]

The rape of a white female by a slave was a heinous crime according to colonial newspaper reports. Although slaves were sometimes whipped and shipped out of a colony for such acts,[92] execution was the usual fate for slaves who committed a rape. A

New Jersey slave, the *Pennsylvania Gazette* reported, was executed for the attempted rape of a white girl.[93] Whites who committed similar acts of violence against comparable victims usually received much more lenient sentences. An attempted rape by a Quaker against a four-year-old near Philadelphia, as reported in the *Boston Evening-Post,* earned the Quaker only "a Month's Imprisonment," "a fine of 10*l*.," and a short stint "in the Pillory." The sentence came down after testimony that the Quaker "had torn open the poor Creature with his Fingers and most vilely used her."[94]

The same types of strict punishments that were handed out for rape were also meted out to slaves convicted of burglary or attempted burglary, according to colonial newspapers. Slaves were hanged in Annapolis and Charleston for house breaking and horse stealing.[95] Whipping was the general mode of punishment for white robbers.[96]

While rapes and burglaries were serious offenses, slaves seeking freedom from whites through murder and arson posed much more danger to the whites of colonial America. Newspapers reported these crimes and trials closely. Arson by slaves was a continual source of danger for whites. The diversion created by the fire also allowed slaves time to escape. Slaves, according to colonial newspapers, had discovered arson as a means of getting even with or for eliminating their owners by the early 1720s,[97] and a rash of New York fires in 1712 and more in Boston in 1723 were attributed to slaves.[98] In 1730, a Massachusetts slave used fire as a means of retribution for his being sold and as a screen for his attempted flight to freedom. The report, as presented in Philadelphia, stated:

> We are inform'd, that on the last Lord's Day a House was burnt at Malden, we are further told, that the Owner of the said House lately Sold a Negro Man to a Person in Salem, which the Fellow not liking, to be reveng'd on his Master at Malden, came on the said Day from Salem to the said House, and finding the Family were at meeting went up into the Chamber thereof, and stole 50*l*. in Money, and then set the Chamber on Fire, and ran away . . . and accordingly was pursu'd after, and was taken up in or about Lyn.[99]

Fire remained an effective means of retribution for slaves throughout the colonial period, as one female slave admitted in 1760 was her intent after she was taken into custody for burning her master's barn and house.[100]

Outright attempts at murder, however, offered a much greater chance for retaliation against white owners than arson did. Long

Island slaves murdered their owners in 1712 to achieve freedom of movement on Sundays, something the slaves' owners had recently taken away from the slaves.[101] The avenues for murdering either master or master and family were wide for slaves, and the most popular means of removing white slave-owning families by slaves, according to colonial newspapers, was through poisoning. Slaves were in charge of the cooking and daily maintenance of households. Slaves entering the local apothecary and purchasing ratsbane in order to remove rodents from homes was no doubt a common practice. The rat poison—or some other lethal substance—could be easily placed in the food of the whites by the slaves to eliminate them.

Chocolate was the means to the end for one Boston family in 1735. The family of Humphrey Scarlet was treated to chocolate for breakfast, but the chocolate had been laced with "Arsenick, or Rats-bane" and fed to Mrs. Scarlet and her children. In telling of this act by the Scarlets' slaves, the news report called for all poisons to be available only to whites. "If this Method had been observed," the report concluded, "Mr. Scarlet's Negroes would not have had such a Stock of Arsenick by them."[102] Poisonings by slaves, according to the *Boston Evening-Post* in the summer of 1755, made life dangerous for all whites who owned slaves. Just across the Charles River from Boston, a man, whose "lower Parts turned as black as a Coal," died after ingesting "calcined Lead, such as Potters use in glazing their Ware."[103] When the murdered man's slaves were put on trial, it was discovered that the murder was a conspiracy, and his servants, who committed the crime because they discovered that their master's will called for their manumission at his death, were either burned at the stake or hanged.[104] In addition to the Massachusetts poisoning, the *Evening-Post* reported that a woman slave, with the assistance of a black doctor and a white man, poisoned the slave woman's master in Annapolis.[105]

Slaves also murdered their owners with guns,[106] axes,[107] butcher knives, or bare hands.[108] One of the most graphic of these kinds of stories appeared in 1755 when a Kittery slave realized the best way to obtain retribution against his owner was to extract revenge through his master's children. The report spread quickly in America as newspapers from Boston to Annapolis published the report, which stated:

A Negro Fellow . . . having behaved ill to his Master, he had corrected him, which the Fellow resented so highly, that he resolved to take away his Master's Life; but judging him not fit to die, he got up in the Night, took a Child [of the Master] about 6 or 7 Years old out of its Bed, and threw it into the Well, where it perished.[109]

A "wilful murder" conviction in colonial America carried with it the death sentence.[110] When slaves were convicted of murder, the execution was often carried out in an effort to deliver a strong statement that would inhibit similar acts by other slaves. A Virginia slave found guilty of murder, the Pennsylvania newspapers reported, was hanged, and then as a warning to other slaves, the convicted slave was drawn and quartered and left on exhibition.[111] The Maryland slave convicted of poisoning her master with the assistance of a black doctor and a white man was hanged in chains along with her accomplices for all passers-by—especially slaves— to see as their bodies decomposed in the July heat.[112] In 1750, after a pair of New Jersey slaves shot their mistress to death, the court sentenced them to be burned to death.[113]

The harsh punishments handed out to convicted slaves as described in colonial newspapers might lead one to the conclusion that a court date for a slave in colonial America was little more than a formality and that a guilty conviction was a foregone conclusion. Punishments may have been harsher and guilty pleas more common for slaves than for white citizens, but according to colonial newspapers, neither took place as a matter of fact. A day in court was, in colonial America, a serious affair, and evidently free men and slaves approached it in that manner.[114] As a result, slaves were not always found guilty.

In February 1735, for instance, two slaves were acquitted on charges of burglary and arson in Boston. The acquittals at the Superior Court trial were handed down because "the Evidences on the part of the King not being strong enough to convict them in the apprehension of the Jury."[115] And even though the legal codes of most colonies in the eighteenth century categorized slaves as property to be corrected by owners as deemed necessary,[116] slave owners, according to court reports in colonial newspapers, might occasionally inflict too severe a punishment upon a slave.[117] One Matthias Auble, a New York slave owner, found this out after mortally beating his slave. Newspapers reported that the Auble's man

died suddenly. . . . And a Jury being called, and his Body opened by the Physicians, it was judged his Death was occasioned by the Cruelty of his master a few Days before in chastising him for some Misdemeanor; and Auble was immediately taken up and secured in the County Goal in order to be brought to a Trial for the same.[118]

The concept that killing a slave could be a felony slowly found its way into the laws of some colonies during the colonial period, North Carolina, for example, adopting the principle in 1774.[119] Acceptance of this idea was, as colonial newspapers demonstrate, neither universally approved nor even foremost in the minds of legislators when they created laws for a colony. Massachusetts lawmakers evidently felt that under certain circumstances it was better to shoot a slave rather than find out if a slave was dangerous, and the law guaranteed that the person killing the slave could do so "without being impeached, censured or prosecuted."[120] Yet the concept that perhaps slaves should not be beaten or even owned by other humans began to appear in colonial newspapers. By 1770, a body of antislavery literature was running somewhat infrequently in newspapers studied. In 1770 and 1775, only eleven of these antislavery notices appeared, but they were almost always long, well-thought-out refutations of all of justifications for slavery that were expounded during the century.

Antislavery news. Antislavery literature was a feature of the newspapers of New England and Pennsylvania. Boston's newspapers, according to the newspapers studied, were the exception.[121] The newspapers of Connecticut and Rhode Island contained the largest amount of antislavery proclamations. This antislavery literature forms the basis of the last type of slave news in colonial newspapers as the arguments of the eighteenth-century abolitionists foreshadowed the cries that would arise in America in the nineteenth century.

Although the antislavery literature of colonial newspapers was mostly a feature of the 1770s, a letter chastising Southern colonists for their practice of permanently indenturing humans ran in Philadelphia in 1740. The Reverend George Whitefield, after completing the first leg of his preaching tour in late 1739 and early 1740 that took him to all of the Southern colonies, addressed the slaveholders in those colonies with an open letter. His letter "to the Inhabitants of Maryland, Virginia, North and South Carolina" did not question the legality of slavery but the morality of it. Whitefield declared:

I think God has a Quarrel with you for you Abuse and Cruelty to the poor Negroes. Whether it be lawful for Christians to buy Slaves, and thereby encourage the Nations from whence they are brought, to be at perpetual War with each other, I shall not take upon me to determine; sure I am, it is sinful. . . . I have wondered, that we have not more Instances of Self-Murder among the Negroes, or that they have not more frequently rose up in Arms against their Owners. . . . For God is the same to Day as he was Yesterday, and will continue the same forever. He does not reject the Prayer of the poor and destitute, nor disregard the Cry of the meanest Negroes! The Blood of them spilt for these many Years in your respective Provinces, will ascend up to Heaven against you. [122]

Whitefield's open letter, although it may have been reprinted in pamphlet form in the colonies, was found only in the *Pennsylvania Gazette*. The *Gazette*'s printer, Benjamin Franklin, may have run the letter in the *Gazette* because of the antislavery feelings of many of the Quakers of the colony, [123] because of Franklin's relationship with Whitefield, [124] because of Franklin's own conviction that slavery was both wrong and an economic disadvantage, [125] or because Franklin knew the letter would generate considerable conversation among those reading it in his paper. All may have played a part in Franklin's reasoning, but the voice of manumission was not heard in colonial newspapers again, except for in one more brief affair involving Whitefield in 1740, for nearly thirty years.

In conjunction with his denunciation of slavery, Whitefield also called for the building of a school for Negroes near Philadelphia. Schools could educate free blacks and prepare slaves for their manumission. The school was to occupy five thousand acres of Pennsylvania land. [126] Evidently, schooling of Africans was already taking place in Philadelphia because the *South-Carolina Gazette* derogatorily referred to those attending a school as "53 Black Scholars" after the school was temporarily closed because it violated the "Negro Law" of Pennsylvania. [127]

Limiting the rights of slaves to an education or almost any other facet of life deemed a right of free men was not a problem to most Americans in the colonial period, but the concept of enslavement as presented in newspapers, was abhorrent to Europeans whenever the practice might be applied to free-born whites. Even Roman Catholics, the *New-York Evening-Post* noted, refused to stoop to such a practice after a ship "offered to sell the Men [captured whites] as Slaves to the Portuguese; who not finding it agreeable to their, (even Papist) Religion to make Merchandize of Free-born Subjects, rejected the Proposal." [128] The same concept of enslavement as an abominable practice for free-born men was used by Americans to fight oppression by England concerning taxes, representation, and eventually all political control. [129] This concept did not apply, however, to free-born Africans, and an antislavery poem, printed as Americans brought their rhetoric of freedom versus oppression by Great Britain to a climax in early 1775, pointed out this contradiction in thinking:

> SEE the poor native quit the Lybian shores,
>   Ah? not in love's delightful fetters bound?
> No radiant smile his dying peace restores,
>   Nor love, nor fame, nor friendship heals his wound.
> On the wild beach in mournful guise he stood,
>   E'er the shrill boatswain gave the hated sign;
> He dropped a tear, unseen in the flood;
>   He stole one secret moment to repine———
> "Why am I ravish'd from my native strand?
>   What savage race protects this impious gain? . . .
> Where rove the brutal nation's wild desires;
>   Our limbs are purchas'd, and our life is sold!
> Yet, shores there are, blest shores for us remain,
>   And favour'd isles with golden fruitage crown'd,
> Where tufted flow'rets paint the verdant plain,
>   Where ev'ry breeze shall med'cine ev'ry wound.
> There the stern tyrant that embitters life,
>   Shall, vainly, suppliant, spread his asking hand;
> There, shall we view the billows raging strife,
>   Aid the kind breast, and waft his boat to land."[130]

The African, free-born in peace, was removed according to the poem from his peaceful country by a brutal nation and all freedom was taken away. The play on the concept of freedom for slaves in contrast to the freedom advocated for Americans from English intolerance, would not likely have been missed, even if most Americans did not agree with freedom for African slaves.

The poem, "To the Dealers of SLAVES," appeared in newspapers in Philadelphia and Providence. Other antislavery rhetoric found in colonial newspapers was unique to the newspaper in which it appeared, although the arguments may have been very similar from newspaper to newspaper. The antislavery literature was no doubt the work of assorted eighteenth-century abolitionists or groups operating in different towns and colonies. As Patricia Bradley discovered, most of the antislavery literature premised its arguments against slavery on morality, philosophy, and the biblical injunction of the Golden Rule.[131] In June 1770, the *Essex Gazette* printed a letter from "a FREE AMERICAN," who approached the argument in the same philosophical manner that Americans arguing for freedom from England had espoused:

We have said,—we repeat it,—that our liberty——our rights as Men and as Englishmen——are dearer to us than our lives——The Africans also are Men:——but men, I confess, debased——miserably debased. . . . They who regard liberty, merely as it procures freedom of thinking and acting, for themselves, are no better than the veriest Tyrants: for these also are extravagantly fond of liberty——for themselves——that they may have it in their power to make slaves of others. . . . Who . . . can, with heart and hand, impose slavery on his fellow men, the miserable Africans,——himself deserves,—richly deserves,—to wear the galling chain for life.[132]

Morality was the tool used in a letter in the *New-London Gazette* in 1770 to condemn slavery. Speaking of the "shameful, shocking Slave-Trade," the letter decried the participation in slavery by any nation "that calls herself Protestant and Christian." Death caused by the inhuman treatment of slave traders, the *Gazette*'s letter explained, was the probable end for more than a third of the Africans taken in the slave trade. With approximately one hundred thousand slaves imported into America each year, the letter writer said that "no less than 10,000 of these unhappy human creatures die in the voyage, and one fourth of an hundred thousand, in, what is called, the seasoning."[133]

Sarcasm was a common tool of the antislavery writer, also. Writers would appear to agree with the arguments of those supporting slavery and present their statement of support for slavery. The result was either a letter that subtly made the proslavery position appear ridiculous or correspondence that used those very proslavery arguments to refute the basis on which slavery was supported. In the *Connecticut Journal,* a regular essay feature entitled "the Correspondent" used the first of these methods in his eighth entry. Knowing that Americans were using their rights as Englishmen to proclaim their freedom, "the Correspondent" declared that Americans had the right to enslave black Africans because doing so was an "inestimable privilege, which had been handed down inviolable from our ancestors." Taking his position one step further, "the Correspondent" took up proslavery's Old Testament argument that slavery was God's punishment upon Africans. "The Africans are the children of Ham, which is plain from their being servants of servants to their brethren; the controversy is brought to a point, and there needs nothing further to be said on the subject." The letter then noted with some authority that if the Bible allowed Englishmen to make slaves of Africans, then no doubt "there are many other nations in the world, whom we have equal right to enslave." "The Correspondent" offered to help in this enslaving, especially of Catholic whites in Europe. The entire letter, although written without directly refuting the proslavery argument, enabled readers to observe the lack of logic that undergirded a large section of the proslavery argument.[134]

By 1775, the antislavery dialogue in colonial newspapers was using direct sarcasm to set up and refute the concept that slavery was a valid practice. A writer to Timothy Green at the *Connecticut Gazette* slyly noted that he had been an enemy to enslaving Africans until he met with a champion of that cause who presented him with "weighty suggestions and reasons" for making Africans slaves. The letter writer then said, "Now instead of opposing him, I am become the most enthusiastic abetter of his sentiments." The three reasons used to support enslavement of Africans were "That the Africans were purchased with Rum—That they were descendants of Hamm, and therefore by divine decree ought to be reduced to a state of servitude—That bringing them to a land of civilization and religion contributed to moralize and christianize them."[135]

After agreeing that the proslavery arguments were valid, the letter writer began to sarcastically refute each point. On the point of moralizing and christianizing slaves, the letter stated:

The Africans are brought here to be christianized.—Let us here pause and admire! . . . No person short of a sceptic can doubt, but it is from motives of kindness and disinterested benevolence that these poor pagans are brought into this land of learning and religion. . . . Over and above the common moral virtue, how are the negroes taught to be patient in affliction to endure hardships without being suffered to repine, to be mocked, persecuted, scoured and undergo every extraordinary christian trial, in which, nothing but the vigilance of their masters, or a peculiar degree of fortitude, could embolden them to persevere? . . . You talk of your christianity, but I have heard you say nothing of their baptism, of their instructions in the ordinances of religion, of their learning the catechism, or reading the bible. . . . But when people are impelled to practice all these duties without, it would be needless to puzzle their heads with study. It is extremely happy for servants, that since they are incapable of discovering duty by speculation, their masters are so kind as to explain it in all its various branches, and constrain them to the most strict practice of it.[136]

The issue of manumission for slaves was apparently a much discussed item in colonial America by 1775,[137] and when hostilities erupted between England and America, some slaves and abolitionists saw the fighting as an opportunity for the freeing of slaves. In Charleston, a Dutchman and "another white Man" worked hard to free slaves in July.[138] And before shots were fired at Lexington, assorted abolitionists in Boston were "enticing divers Servants to desert the Service of their Masters."[139] Even after the colonies were at war with England, at least one colony, Rhode Island, approached the issue of slavery head-on and passed "An ACT for prohibiting the Importation of Negroes into this Colony, and asserting the Right of Freedom of all those hereafter born or manumitted within the same."[140]

The struggle for independence, however, took precedence over the effort to free slaves during 1775. No antislavery literature ran in colonial newspapers studied in 1775, excepting the Rhode Island prohibition and manumission act, any later than January. American newspapers turned their attention to the War for Independence. The fledgling nation focused its attention upon manumission from England, and the manumission of Africans—and the newspaper dialogue concerning it—would have to wait.

CONCLUSION

Slave news provided readers of colonial newspapers with information about a commodity that many European colonists deemed absolutely necessary to their survival. This attitude was firmly entrenched in colonial America by the eighteenth century. As Edward Downing wrote to Governor John Winthrop concerning the colony of Massachusetts Bay in 1645, "The colony will never thrive untill we gett . . . a stock of slaves sufficient to doe all our business."[141] Even though colonists viewed slaves as indispensable for the success of the colonies, that fact was not discussed in the colonial newspapers studied. The news of colonial newspapers painted a much different portrait of slaves. African slaves revolted against their owners. Slaves murdered, robbed, raped, and burned out whites. Slaves were an inferior necessity that required stringent legislation to control. As inferior beings, slaves became the object of ridicule and ultimately were considered to be property by those who owned them and by the legal systems of the colonies.

Colonial newspapers rarely printed a positive word about slaves, except for the few charitable acts by slaves who warned their owners of impending slave revolts. Even the antislavery literature of the 1770s usually viewed Africans as inferior to whites, and argued that even if slaves were manumitted, without the continued guidance of whites, they would become a "manifest hazard to the province . . . if suffered to live at their own hand."[142] The antislavery dialogue of the 1770s, despite its references to black inferiority, did, however, elevate slaves from chattel to human status and often fought the battle for slave freedom on the same polemic plane that the war for America's independence was being waged.

The news of slaves in colonial newspapers did not occupy a position of prominence as far as volume is concerned. Ship news, court and crime news, social news, accident reports, and Native American news all appeared in colonial newspapers more often than slave news.[143] But basing conclusions purely upon numbers when dealing with colonial newspapers is neither fair nor accurate. Slave news was one of the most important types of news to run in colonial newspapers because slaves, despite the fact that they were considered an irreplaceable labor source, ironically also represented a potential danger to the very survival of colonists. This dual nature of colonists' view of slaves made information concerning slaves mandatory for Americans in the eighteenth century. The fact that news of slaves was reprinted by newspapers throughout the colonies affirms this. When a Kittery slave threw his owner's child down the well as retribution, for example, eight colonial newspapers representing all cities printing newspapers from Boston to Annapolis ran the news.[144] And the citizens of Charleston, Williamsburg, Philadelphia, New York, and Boston—every colonial city with a newspaper in 1740—read of the slave insurrection in Georgia during that year.[145] Newspaper news of slave rebellions and of slave crimes was some of the most often repeated news in all colonial newspapers. Repetition, just as much as total numbers of items, speaks to the importance of news to colonists. In fact, only news of the Cherokee War of 1760 and the activities of itinerant preacher George Whitefield received similar, consistent coverage by colonial newspapers.

But just as much as the repetition of slave news speaks to its importance, the omission of slave news does the same thing. In America's thirteen colonies, the slave population outnumbered that of whites only in South Carolina, and only in South Carolina—where news of slave activity should have been most prevalent based on the black-to-white ratio of inhabitants—was there a noticeable lack of news of slaves. Following the Stono Rebellion of 1739, news of slave activity in South Carolina or almost any other place in the New World disappeared with only a few exceptions from the *South-Carolina Gazette*'s pages. Was this omission of slave insurrection news in the *Gazette* a case of self-censorship or was it imposed upon the *Gazette*'s printers, Elizabeth Timothy followed by her son Peter, by the government of South Carolina?

The government did imprison Elizabeth briefly in 1741 for printing a letter attacking the Anglican clergy of the colony.[146] The question is probably moot because the omission, whether self-imposed or politically mandated, speaks to the fear whites felt concerning blacks.

Most of the news of slave rebellions and slave crimes that appeared in colonial newspapers took place in locales other than that in which the news was being printed, in much the same way that sensational news originated from regions outside that served by a newspaper. Unlike sensationalism that was presented more for shock value than for information value, the varied slave news allowed colonists up and down the Atlantic seaboard to stay abreast of potential threats being faced by others in America. And with the exception of South Carolina, colonial newspapers presented news of slave revolts and slave crimes that happened in their own region as well.

The insertion of this news into the local newspaper served two vital functions: it allowed the sharing of news in all the major towns of America, and it made the news of an event "official." A ship leaving Boston, for example, heading for Philadelphia with a print of the latest Boston newspaper carried information unknown to Philadelphians, and these papers from other parts of the colony were greatly desired by printers. News of a slave crime or revolt in Boston would have been, as Richard D. Brown maintains, common knowledge among the city's residents through a network of oral communication that included taverns and peer groups,[147] but its presentation in the newspaper of the city somehow made it official, in much the same way that the *Boston Evening-Post*'s printers John and Thomas Fleet considered news of slave insurrections in Jamaica authoritative once they received notice of them from the Jamaican newspapers.[148] These two priniciples applied to all local news in colonial newspapers that served the function of informing readers of important acts. The fact that the local news may have already been known did not diminish its value in colonial newspapers; the reports were no doubt still "news" to some readers of the newspapers, just as news in community newspapers today is often known to a sizable portion of its readership before the paper is ever printed. The readers of the newspapers desired as much information as possible on a subject, and the newspapers offered a chance to read what the printer considered "the freshest Advices" on a subject.

Slave news, like many other types of news in colonial newspapers, was affected by news of immediate concern. Slave news was three times more plentiful in the *Pennsylvania Gazette,* for example, in 1760 than it was in 1765 when distress over the Stamp Act weighed upon nearly every colonist. Conversely, slave news from 1730–1760 was much more prominent in newspapers. During this period, the rapid influx of slaves into America no doubt created some alarm for white colonists. The slave population of America grew from less than 100,000 in 1730 to more than 325,000 in 1760, an increase to 20 percent of America's total population from 14 percent,[149] and twenty-nine different slave revolts took place during this period according to the newspapers studied.

When colonial newspapers picked up the antislavery dialogue in the 1770s, they were echoing discussions that had been occurring within parts of colonial society for decades. And even though the total number of antislavery essays that appeared in the newspapers studied was small, their size was not. Often they covered one or more pages of a weekly edition, and no doubt, the newspaper essays reflected a similar debate that was being waged in pamphlets and taverns in many colonies.[150] The amount of antislavery literature in colonial newspapers was never great nor did it appear in many newspapers outside of New England or Pennsylvania, but it no doubt fueled the fire to abolish slavery, something that all of the states that made up New England and the Middle colonies did by or in 1800.[151] In addition, the arguments used by the colonial abolitionists would appear again after the Revolution, but like most other types of news, war pushed the antislavery dialogue out of colonial newspapers, replacing it with news of war and the struggle for independence from England at least in the issues studied. The colonial newspaper or antislavery correspondence, however, presented the same arguments against slavery that would appear in the newspapers of the last decade of the eighteenth century[152] and in the abolitionist newspapers of the 1820s and 1830s.[153]

Slave news in colonial newspapers, with the exception of the antislavery dialogue, was almost always wrapped in fear, fear that the slave population would rise up and destroy—or at least hinder greatly—the success of the colonies. In this way slave news was very similar to news of Native Americans. Both groups represented potential danger to the Europeans who now inhabited the Atlantic seaboard of North America. Native Americans, as colonial newspaper news revealed, could be eradicated, but slaves could not. Unlike the Indians who were here when the white colonists arrived, African slaves were imported, seen as a necessity for survival in this new environment. Any difficulties that slaves created were, in reality, self-inflicted upon the whites who bought former free Africans and turned them into chattel. Colonial newspapers, of course, did not view slave rebellion and criminal activity from the point of view of any self-deserving or self-inflicted position, but that is no doubt why slaves rebelled, just as white Americans rebelled against oppression from England.

Standing in contrast to the violence of slave news in colonial newspapers was the news of the hearth, the dominion of women. Colonial newspapers may have aimed a majority of their news toward a male audience, but news about and directed toward women and their sphere of influence the home, as shall be seen, was a part of the content of colonial newspapers. Newspapers praised; newspapers belittled; but eighteenth-century journalism did not overlook females.

6

Adapted to the Female World

She who makes her husband and her children happy, who re-
claims the one from vice, or trains the others to virtue, is a
much greater character than the finest lady that ever existed in
poetry, or romance, whose whole occupation it has been to
murder mankind with the shafts from her quiver, or her eyes.
—*Parker's New-York Gazette,* 4 December 1760

In 1760, a letter writer to the *New-York Gazette* was worried. He
saw a breakdown occurring within society; he believed that the
lines of demarcation between the roles of men and women were
being destroyed by brazen women who "have left the duties of
their own sex in order to invade the privileges of our's." The "prudent wife, or the careful mother," the writer felt, was being supplanted by "petticoated philosophers" and "virago Queens."
Woman was, according to the *Gazette*'s correspondent, to serve
her husband, train her children, and point the way to virtue for all
those within her sphere of influence—that is, the home—rather
than strive for education, glamor, and any aspect of eighteenth-
century life considered the domain of males. A woman's life was,
the letter writer noted, one of "duty"; a man's life was one of
"privileges." The writer saw woman's purpose as subservient to
the privileged desires of her husband. He said, "Women, it has been
observed, are not naturally formed for great cares themselves, but
to soften our's."[1] Because women were created according to the
letter writer to make the life of men easier, females played a significant role in colonial society, but that role obligated them to
service in a male-dominated culture.

Women also played a significant role in the content of colonial
newspapers. They were the primary characters in sensational news
stories. Crimes involving women were often more graphically described than news stories involving men only. News of Native
Americans or African slave activity often revolved around what

151

either might do to females. Women were sometimes prime movers in matters of religion, while much of the literature, poetry, and social news of colonial newspapers centered on the activities and interests of women.[2] But these types of news placed women within a larger scene. Crime, Indians, and slaves often shared the stage with women. When colonial newspapers dealt with issues specifically related to women, a dual portrayal of women, much as the writer to *Parker's New-York Gazette* who saw women as either "prudent wife" or "virago Queens," surfaced. Or, as an essay that ran in New York and Philadelphia newspapers put it, "There are some virtuous and some vicious"[3] among females.

This understanding of women as both virtuous and vicious was a reflection of society's understanding of women. The "virtuous woman" knew the way of piety to God and how to protect and preserve the sanctity of husband and home. The "virtuous woman" sought first the well-being of all who entered her sphere of influence. In this respect, colonial society as reflected in colonial newspapers did not deny education, social standing, or community prominence to women, but all needed to be "adapted to the Female World,"[4] a world that was subservient to the male world of the eighteenth century. In contrast to the "virtuous woman" stood the "vicious woman." She was lazy, ignored her family's needs, and often was absorbed in evil. She might steal, commit adultery, or even murder.

This Jekyll-and-Hyde understanding of women was a basic part of the mindset of the colonial period, and both views of women were the product of religious thought and social hierarchy. The religious basis for the dichotomy was plainly presented by Cotton Mather in his widely read and published 1692 book, *Ornaments for the Daughters of Zion:*

> As a woman had the Disgrace to go first in that horrid and woful Transgression of our first Parents, which has been the Parent of all our Misery; so a Woman had the Glory of bringing into the World that Second Adam, who is the Father of all our Happiness. A Woman had the Saviour of Mankind in the Circumstances of an Infant Miraculously Conceiv'd within her.[5]

And one of Protestantism's greatest sixteenth-century theologians, John Calvin, stated concerning women, "Let the women be satisfied with her state of subjection, and not take it amiss that she is made inferior to the more distinguished sex."[6] This concept of the subjugation of women to men within the social hierarchy led to the view that women were the chief source of disorder within society, unless they were kept in subordination to men.[7]

This chapter deals with the female world as presented in colonial newspapers. The female world of the eighteenth century included children, education, and the relationship between husband and wife, but generally, when colonial newspapers focused upon the female world, they concentrated upon the dualistic understanding of women as the instigator of the fall of humankind and the bringer of its savior. Women became the scapegoats for evil activities[8] and the bearers of salvation.[9] As both virtuous and vicious creatures, women were objects of interest as they attempted to encroach upon a male-dominated world in any manner and as they worked in silence to promote the welfare of society by service in the home.

Colonial news discussed the role of women in society, but women also played a part in producing the news during the colonial period. Women such as Elizabeth Timothy, Mary Crouch, Ann Franklin, Sarah Goddard, and Anna Zenger printed newspapers in the colonial period. It would be unlikely that during their tenures as newspaper printers that they never wrote anything that appeared in their newspapers nor established an agenda for news in their respective newspapers. Interestingly, when Elizabeth Timothy took over production of the *South-Carolina Gazette* from her husband, Louis, the newspaper averaged twelve news items per year about women and the home. In 1740 and 1745, when Elizabeth printed the newspaper, only one news story about women appeared during those two years. In addition, correspondence from women appeared in many newspapers, and many men, including Benjamin Franklin, who wrote to colonial newspapers assumed a female persona.

Colonial American women never fit into one homogeneous group. The lives of indentured servants, planters' wives, widows, backcountry women, and women of the cities varied in a number of ways, based upon their environments. Yet the gender roles of the women in each of these groups remained fairly constant, despite the varied circumstances of life, and newspapers reaffirm that consistency in their presentation of news of women. Knowing the role of women will help in understanding the information in colonial newspapers concerning women and their world. A synthesis of women and their role in eighteenth-century America follows.

THE ROLE AND SPHERE OF WOMEN IN COLONIAL AMERICA

The sphere of women in colonial America was the family dwelling and the yard surrounding it, no matter if women lived in a city or upon a farm or plantation.[10] Within the home, woman was to be the chief worker, administrator, educator, minister, and anything else that was needed. But even as administrators, women were still subordinates. Women were expected, even though the home was their domain, to defer to their husbands in all situations.[11] Ethnic and cultural backgrounds such as Scottish, Dutch, German, Quaker, and Moravian might produce family norms that varied from those of English Anglicans or Puritans, but the family was still to be headed by a father and served by a mother.[12]

Service was the key to understanding the role of women. By the end of the colonial period, a consensus of what encompassed the ideal woman had developed, and it had been produced, in part, by decades of sermons calling on women to be virtuous in their service to husband and home.[13] The resulting woman was a nurturant, patriotic mother who raised her children, especially her sons, to be good Christians, active citizens, and successful competitors in all aspects of life.[14]

No matter how important sermons and other types of literature may have made the role of women sound, their lives were shaped by hard work and the cycles of birth and pregnancy. Women in North Carolina, for example, spent up to two-thirds of their adult lives—which usually ended by age forty—pregnant.[15] The reproductive cycle had to occur so often because of the difficulty in producing a family. Infant mortality rates were ten to twenty-five times higher than current standards.[16] Approximately one-quarter of all children born during the colonial period never reached their first birthday, and 40 to 55 percent did not reach age twenty.[17]

Because of the difficulty in keeping children alive in colonial America, the care and instruction of children were naturally important. These vital tasks rested squarely in the sphere of women,[18] but in many situations, children were viewed more as economic necessities than as anything else.[19] This fact seems logical when one realizes that approximately one-half of society throughout the colonial period was under the age of sixteen.[20]

Even though young people comprised a large percentage of the work force in colonial America by laboring at home or as apprentices, the realization that the future of the colonies rested with them was not overlooked. This meant that children needed some sort of education. An apprenticeship was a way to learn a trade, but children needed other instruction, too. They needed to know how to read, and they needed to understand their Christian faith and the culture from which they came. These tasks were gradually adapted to the female world of colonial America. Although schools existed in many towns and well-to-do parents could send their children away to schools, the principal unit for educating children was the home.[21]

In the seventeenth century, home education had been entrusted to men, who were to teach their children to read, but men failed in this effort.[22] As a result women had to assume the task. Children needed to be able to read in order to follow their religious catechisms, which included lessons in mathematics and other disciplines in addition to religious instruction. By the beginning of the eighteenth century, women were practically the sole providers of religious and moral instruction,[23] a job that women continued to handle into the nineteenth century.[24] In order to teach reading, women had to be able to read themselves, and the majority of American women could by the end of the eighteenth century.[25]

As the eighteenth century progressed, women began to play a more active role in colonial society, even though their primary sphere of influence remained the home. As America's population balanced itself between men and women, not all women married. Unmarried women retained more rights than women who married and for all practical purposes became extensions of their husbands.[26] Single women discovered that they could make a living in America's cities by entering domestic service, becoming nurses, seamstresses and teachers, or by running inns. Widows often continued in the trades of their deceased husbands.[27]

By the second half of the eighteenth century, women's work in running farms and in artisan's shops in towns was deemed essential to family survival as well as to the stabilization and growth of society.[28] Women began to take part in some of the political affairs of the colonies, too, by the 1770s. In 1774, for example, fifty-one women in the North Carolina port of Edenton, joined the non-importation resistance in America by signing a pact refusing to purchase or use tea imported by Britain.[29] As women's political activity grew, so, too, did the notion of the "republican woman." As America sought its independence from England, it became woman's patriotic duty to educate her sons and be a moral and virtuous citizen.[30] Even though women were sometimes taking these activities to the streets in the form of public boycotts and pledges, the home was still where men assumed these activities should take place. [31] As a visitor in the late eighteenth century observed, women's life in America, despite the growth of jobs for women in cities, was still one of domesticity centered in the family home, just as it had been in the seventeenth century and as it would be in the nineteenth. The foreign observer noted:

The women every where possess, in the highest degree, the domestic virtues, and all others. . . . Good wives, and good mothers, their husbands and their children engage their whole attention; and their household affairs occupy all their time and all their cares; destined by the manners of their country to this domestic life.[32]

Women in colonial America played a vital part in its development, but their role was always viewed in a subordinate capacity, in service to husband, children, home, and colony. Service necessitated a virtuous woman, and colonial newspapers advocated the virtuous woman. It is with the virtuous woman, who stood in contrast to the vicious woman, that this look at women in colonial newspapers begins.

WOMEN, THE HOME, AND COLONIAL NEWSPAPERS

Exactly how much of the news in colonial newspapers was designed for female readers or even read by them may never be ascertained. From Benjamin Franklin's "Silence Dogood" letters that ran anonymously in the *New-England Courant* in 1722 to a conduct letter that ran in *Dunlap's Maryland Gazette* late in 1775,[33] however, colonial citizens possessed a certain fascination with the thoughts and actions of women. Why Franklin assumed the persona of a female is not known, although it may have been a way to strike out at those in power by a member of a group obviously not in control of affairs.[34] But women obviously read colonial newspapers and corresponded with them,[35] as Deborah Sherman's letters to *Boston Evening-Post* printer Thomas Fleet concerning George Whitefield,[36] poems credited to women authors and comments like "to notify your Female readers"[37] attest.[38] Many of the pieces in newspapers, including poetry, birth announcements, obituaries, and religious news were no doubt of interest to women as much or even more than to male readers.[39]

The news of virtuous women also had to be directed toward them. If its purpose was to bolster women's function as selfless servers of society, the content of these news items had to be passed along to their target audience. Women could be told what the article said, or more likely, they read it themselves in a weekly newspaper. The fact that so much of the dialogue about virtuous women was presented in poetry, rather than in long prose essays may be an indicator that women were the intended audience of these efforts to shape conduct. News of virtuous women praised selfless acts and warned women of the types of activities to avoid. All of it, as will be seen, was couched in terms of woman's obligation or duty in a society constructed upon male dominance.

Virtuous women. The entire concept of the role of women in colonial society was based upon the premise that women were inferior to men, the superior creation. "The man is superior to the woman, and the woman inferior to the man," is the straightforward way in which "The Husband's CREED," printed in the *Boston Chronicle,* explained woman's relation to man.[40] Acknowledgement of this notion of male superiority naturally led to statements in newspapers about what constituted the ideal wife, mother, or woman in general. "The GOOD WIFE," according to one 1770 piece, always put her husband's needs first because that was her duty and what he was due as the superior of the two. "His welfare, happiness, and ease," the poem said, "She mediates in all her ways."[41]

Finding a wife who possessed virtuous ideals was the goal of men seeking wives, and the characteristics of virtuous women were often outlined in newspapers. The *American Weekly Mercury* described "the Batchelor's Choice" in a wife, and she needed in her possession many qualities, each premised in the dominance of her husband:

> If Marriage gives a Happiness to life,
> Such be the Woman who shall be my Wife:
> Beauteous as the height of fancy can express,
> Meek her Nature cleanly in her dress;
> Wife without pride, and Pleasing without Art,
> With chearful Aspect and with honest Heart.
> To sooth my Cares, most high, most sweet her Song,
> To blame my Faults most low, most kind her Tongue:
> In looser Hours, in Hours more dull, still dear,
> A gay Companion, and a Friend sincere:
> Fond without folly, spirit'ous without rage,
> and as in youth shall seem the same in Age.
> Ye pow'rs above, if such a Woman be,
> (Such cou'd y make) that such a Woman give to me:
> She as a Wife must please, and she alone.
> O! give me such a Wife or give me none.[42]

Virtuous women, according to the advice given them in newspapers, were to always to be submissive to males, whether the women were married, single, or widowed. "Avoid, both before and after Marriage, all Thoughts of managing your Husband," an essay on "promoting Matrimonial Happiness" counseled in 1730.[43] Matrimonial happiness rested upon submissiveness of the wife. "Read frequently with due attention," a male writer to the *Providence Gazette* suggested to women, "the matrimonial service; and take care in doing so not to overlook the word OBEY."[44] The writer added, "Be assured a woman's power, as well as happiness, has no other foundation but her husband's esteem and love, which consequently it is her undoubted interest, by all means possible, to preserve and increase."[45] And a New England woman used every possible means to obey her husband in a bizarre story in the *Boston Evening-Post.* The editorial comment following the report may have been added for humor, but there was probably some underlying feeling that wives should react this way to the commands of their husbands. The news report said

> that last Week one of the Inhabitants [of Westchester] receiving a Curtain Lecture from his Wife, he wish'd her Tongue was cut out; whereupon the good obedient Woman snatched up a Razor, and immediately cut off great Part of that unruly Member, and had not the great Effusion of Blood put her Life a little in Danger, doubtless it would hereafter be found grateful, as well as unprecedented Sacrifice. [Happy Man! How rare a Thing is it to find a Wife so good natured and obliging, in these Parts!][46]

Virtue for women, according to the correspondence in colonial newspapers, was based not only in the superiority of man but in woman's role as the one decreed to be subservient in order meet those needs. If a woman served her husband selflessly, then she would find happiness. A virtuous woman recognized these facts, and consequently, all other aspects of her life fell positively into place. If she heeded this advice, for instance, her husband would always love her, even "when Beauty frail decays," because throughout her life she had been adorned in virtue. Virtue, not any physical attractiveness, was what made a woman beautiful to a man, as an Annapolis poet stated:

> Then ye Fair, let Virtue be your aim,
> since she with never fading Ornaments
> Embellish can your Charms; since she can feed
> Love's lambent Flame, when Beauty frail decays,
> And yields her Trophies to relentless Time.
> By Decency and Virtue still adorn'd,
> Tho' Age brings Wrinkles, and impairs the Bloom
> Of Youth, your pristine Beauties shall survive

Still in the Lover's Eye, and still command
The first Affection, and sincere Esteem.[47]

And virtue meant that women did not seek fame for themselves, excessive elegance, or education. These were best left for men, as a poem, "ADVICE to a LADY," suggested:

Virtue is amiable, 'tis mild, serene. . . .
Seek to be good, but aim not to be great,
A woman's noblest station is retreat;
Her fairest virtues fly from public sight,
Domestick worth, that shuns too strong a light.
To this great point direct you constant aim,
This makes your happiness and your fame.[48]

Virtuous women had to meet the needs of their husbands and society. This obligation was satisfied in a number of ways. Perhaps the most important of those responsibilities for women was having children. Colonial newspapers noted "the prolific Constitutions"[49] of women with respect and praise. A remarkable New Jersey woman in only seventeen years of marriage bore "her husband 18 sons and two daughters, and is now to appearance in the very bloom of life."[50] Newspapers called the attention of their readers to "fruitful Dames"[51] who delivered twins and triplets to help populate the colonies.[52] When Anne Pollard died in 1725 outside of Boston, all that was noted about her were her husband's name, her remarkable age of 105, and the fact that she left behind 130 children, grandchildren, and great-grandchildren.[53]

Another way that virtuous women met their obligation to husband and society, according to colonial newspapers, was through education. Women were not to obtain too much education, but learning for women was necessary in order for them to teach children and to be stimulating mates for their husbands. "Women of Quality, should apply themselves to Letters," the *New-York Journal* advised, "because their Husbands are generally Strangers to them."[54] The meaning of this letter was two-fold. First, women needed to obtain a certain amount of education so that they could understand the lofty topics of the conversation and correspondence of their husbands. Second, women may have needed to apply themselves to letters written to their husbands who were away on business. In either case, women would never be able to fully understand men's conversations because women "have no attention but to trifles." Women's education for the sake of conversation and mental stimulation of men would simply allow them to listen and perhaps ask questions that would allow the husband to speak with his wife. This education would not put women on an equal plane with men because women were incapable of grasping the more difficult topics and needed "to avoid all abstract learning, all difficult researches."[55] When it came to the instruction of children, women were urged to acquire "some degree of Learning" in order to be "profitable mothers to your children."[56]

If women accomplished these virtuous goals during life, they were often honored for doing so by eulogies to them printed in colonial newspapers. When the virtuous Elizabeth Prentis died in Nansemond, Virginia, the *Virginia Gazette* remarked that she left her mark upon the world by selflessly "imparting happiness to others" and printed the epitaph found upon her gravestone that said:

> If love for worth of ev'ry kind,
> Which all can with and few can find,
> E'er claim'd the tribute of a tear:
> (Here lies a maid whom virtue warm'd,
> With every pleasing grace adorn'd)
> Stop, traveller, and drop it here.[57]

When Rebeccah Fisk died, the *Boston Evening-Post*'s obituary paid her a great compliment by saying that all "should carefully imitate the Vertues of her Life."[58]

Virtue was the great attribute of colonial women. Virtuous women were a gift from "indulgent heaven," but one that men expected.[59] Standing in opposition to them were vicious women, and sometimes the news of both the virtuous and vicious could be found side-by-side in a newspaper.[60] The vicious woman was rarely a thoroughly evil or hardened individual. She was, instead, the woman who refused to submit fully to the will of a male-dominated society. In this way, the vicious woman was demonstrating her ability to be independent, at least in some ways, of men and stood in contrast with the virtuous ideal.

Vicious women. A vicious woman according to colonial newspapers did not have to be a cold-blooded killer or commit any other horrendous crime—although women certainly did commit numerous crimes.[61] All she had to do was breach the concept of the virtuous woman held by society. The vicious woman, according to colonial thought, was the evil half of the dualism of women. The vicious woman was as Cotton Mather described, the "first in that horrid and woful Transgression" of committing sin.[62] A writer to a Boston newspaper, playing upon that original transgression of humankind in sin, compared the evil of women to serpents. Getting a good wife, the writer mused, was much like picking an eel from a bag filled with snakes. "Put Nineteen Snakes and one Eel into a Bag," the writer said, "shake them well together, then put in your Hand, and by CHANCE you may pull out the Eel."[63] The inference was that getting a good wife was almost impossible, and besides, what really was the difference in an eel and a snake? They both had to crawl upon their bellies, God's punishment to the serpent for its part in the sinful act in the Garden of Eden.[64]

Although colonial newspaper correspondents repeatedly lifted up the virtuous woman, reports of vicious women, especially when criminal activity is included, greatly outweighed the notion of the virtuous woman.[65] This fact again goes back to the concept of women as inherently inferior and evil creatures when compared to men. Women naturally needed to submit to service of men and could rise above their low estate only through that submission and "polite Education." Education, however, only masked what women really were, according to one essay copied from the *Spectator:*

> *In the beginning God made the Souls of Womankind out of different Materials, and in a separate State from their Bodies. The Souls of one Kind of Women were formed out of those Ingredients which compose a Swine. A Woman of this Make is a Slut in her House, and a Glutton at her Table. She is uncleanly in her Person, a Slattern in her Dress, and her Family no better than a Dunghil.*[66]

And woman had no alternative, according to one letter written to Benjamin Franklin, to being vicious. "The best of the sex are no better than Plagues," the writer said.[67]

Women, of course, were no more inherently evil than men, but in a male-dominated society whenever women rebelled against the system of service and the concept of the virtuous woman that had been taught and espoused for years, a vicious woman was uncovered. The "Modern Lady," the *American Weekly Mercury* explained in 1730, was a woman who had forsaken her daily duties in the home for the pleasures of gaming and idle chatter with other women. In an essay covering three pages, the modern woman was described as one who rises late in the afternoon, drinks, gambles, and plays cards all night and then crawls into bed next to her hard-working husband just before sunrise.[68] Women who could afford this kind of activity were no doubt from the more affluent parts of society, but lack of wealth did not preclude women from being vicious according to colonial standards.

One man writing to the *Boston Weekly Post-Boy* could not understand why women were no longer behaving as virtuous creatures. Women did not have to partake in vices and idle time, but somehow virtuous women, "the most amiable of all Mortals at once metamorphos'd into the most hateful, most wretched and most despicable" of God's creatures, causing the man to remark, "scarce Lucifer's change from Heaven to Hell was greater."[69] Idle time was no doubt a by-product of continuing growth and affluence in colonial America, especially in the cities with newspapers. Letters to newspapers often complained that a woman had lost sight of her virtuous tasks because "she has nothing to do," at home, began thinking of herself as important, and ultimately became lost in her own vanity.[70]

Because some women were discovering that they had "idle time," they turned that time to certain leisure activities. Playing cards evidently became a very popular way with some women to fill idle time. "The Growth of so vicious a Habit, as our Womens Attachment to Cards . . . shews us the prevalent Power of Custom," one letter writer stated. Playing cards was taking women away from one of their most important duties, the care of children. "Our Youth are in the Hands of those Mothers," the writer warned,[71] and a woman who spent all her time in idle conversation and card playing had little time to properly instruct children.

Stories about the abuse and misuse of children by vicious women was especially effective in pointing out the need of women to be virtuous. In most cases, the women used as examples in the abuse of children were on the opposite end of the social spectrum from the virtuous women who were dutiful wives and daughters generally from the middle or upper parts of society. That really did not matter, however, to the moral lesson that news of these women provided. These women had failed to encompass the virtuous ideals; therefore, they were destroyers of society and all that the virtuous woman was obligated to uphold. In most instances, the cases of abuse involved women who apparently were living without husbands. Children left on the ice to die,[72] left in boxes on highways,[73] and locked naked in small rooms[74] were all done by "inhuman mothers."[75] These actions, newspaper articles intimated, would likely not have happened had these women somewhere in their lives submitted to the instruction of men and practiced virtue.

Women who forsook the virtuous way often ended up, newspapers reported, abusing the trust that their husbands placed in them. In one instance, a hard working husband left for a business trip into the country. Before he could return, his wife, pretending he was dead, filed his will and absconded with all of his wealth.[76] Similar stories were common throughout the period.[77] The worst examples of the betrayal of men involved adultery and murder. One husband suspected his wife was having a liaison with another man while he was at work. His hunch proved true, and the woman, ungrateful for all he had provided for her, was caught in the act.[78] Another man, not realizing his wife lacked virtue, was poisoned by his evil wife, the *New-York Evening-Post* reported in 1750.[79]

The news concerning evil women varied greatly. There was a vast difference between a woman who spent all of her spare time playing cards and involving herself in idle conversation and one who abused her children, stole from her husband, or committed adultery. Yet both types of vicious women, according to colonial newspaper accounts, were evil and perverted society. While the second type of vicious woman—the abuser, robber, and adulterer—may have never have been considered virtuous, those guilty of playing cards and taking up leisure time to fill idle hours were. But now, these women were beginning to exhibit some independence from men, something that was anathema to all that society and the concept of virtuous women upheld. As Mary Beth Norton rightly observed, by the mid-1700s, women remained in submission to their husbands and fathers, but the props that held this structure in place in colonial society, in all except the Southern colonies were crumbling.[80] This new-found independence was the source of considerable newspaper discussion, including women's petitions for divorce.

The move toward independence. Just as Africans in servitude naturally sought freedom, many women in the colonial period looked for ways to escape the narrow confines of the female world and gain some control over their own lives. One way to escape— although it probably took a very special woman to do so—was to assume the role of a male in society. Colonial newspapers related stories of women who posed as men for years without getting caught and even told of women having sex-change operations in order to become men.[81] Although these news items no doubt were entertaining, they also reveal that if women wanted to be free of the burdens of the virtuous women, they had to cease being women.

When women sought to escape totally from the confines of the woman's world during the colonial period, enlisting in the army or the navy was the quickest way to escape. England was involved in numerous wars and insurrections during the period in Europe,

America, and the East Indies, and troops and tars were regularly needed. A woman who chose this method of independence had to be extremely careful—and a bit lucky—not to be discovered. Newspapers reported several instances of women who successfully enlisted during the War of Jenkins Ear with Spain in 1740.[82] But the most famous woman to pose as a man during the period was probably Hannah Snell.

Snell served seven years as a Marine in His Majesty's service under the name James Gray, fighting in the East Indies, before petitioning the government to be released from service.[83] Snell was a decorated soldier and in one battle "received twelve Wounds, six in her right Arm, and five in her Left, and the other in her Groin, from the last of which she extracted the Ball, and herself perfected the Cure, in order to prevent her Sex being discovered."[84] When the King acted on Snell's petition to leave the service, she was granted a pension of £30 per year for life.[85] No one ever suspected that Snell was a female, not even when she was publicly whipped, naked from the waist up. According to the *Boston Weekly News-Letter,* Snell prevented the

discovery of her sex, by tying an handerchief round her neck, and spreading it over her breasts. When she was whipped at Carlisle, she was not so full, and her arms being drawn up, the protuberance of the breasts was inconsiderable, and they were hid by her standing close to the gate.[86]

Another woman did not pretend to be a man; she "chang'd her Sex" and "made Application to the Parliament to be confirm'd in the Priviledges of Manhood." After undergoing careful examination, it was decreed "the said person heretofore a Girl, shall be henceforward deem'd a Man." The sex-change was a true liberation for the young lady from the sphere of womanhood. Not only was she no longer a woman, but the court also ruled that since she was the oldest child of a wealthy father she rightfully should inherit his estate.[87]

Undergoing sex change operations or spending a life disguised as a man were extraordinary and difficult ways for women to gain some modicum of independence. Women, however, began gaining some independence while retaining their sexuality during the first third of the eighteenth century. A weekly assembly of women met regularly in 1725 in Philadelphia,[88] and a decade later, an assembly of women successfully placed an abusive husband on trial. The women's tribunal found the husband guilty, dunked him three times in a near-by pond, and shaved off half of his beard and hair.[89] And a letter "By a LADY" that ran in Boston in 1740 suggested that not only could women compete successfully with men if only given a chance, but women, if trained as men, would surpass their brothers in trade and industry:

> There are few Trades in which Women cannot weigh and measure as well as men. . . . If Women were train'd up to Business from their early Years 'tis highly probable they would in general be more industrious, and get more Money, than Men; and if so, what Woman of Spirit would submit to be a Slave, and fling herself away.[90]

The fact that newspapers ran articles about the growing autonomy of some women is an anomaly in the continued call for the virtuous woman and the attacks upon the evils perpetrated by women that occupied much of the news concerning women in the eighteenth-century newspapers. Printers may have been more sensitive to the abilities of women than many other tradesmen because printing was often a family business with wives and daughters working alongside husbands, sons, and apprentices.[91] Women also successfully published newspapers during the colonial period.[92] In addition, the calls for virtuous women were almost always sent to newspapers by correspondents, and the same is true for most accounts of the evils of women except crimes, which could come from local sources, other newspapers, or correspondence. Newspapers may have also been simply mirroring the times. Society, at least in this instance, was undergoing changes, and it would be an error to think that these changes would not be reflected in newspapers.

But independent actions like those by the women in Philadelphia who placed an abusive husband on trial and bold statements calling for equality in education and business like the one issued in Boston did not go unanswered by men. Even if some women were attempting to assert certain amounts of control over their own lives, the male-dominated hierarchy of eighteenth-century America was not ready to collapse into equality of the sexes, and many men reacted to the situation through newspaper correspondence. Women who gain too much independence will try "to convince you of the Inferiority of your Understanding," a writer in Philadelphia warned.[93] A man writing to the *Massachusetts Spy,* in commenting upon the actions of women in New England, blamed women's desire for some independence upon an "epidemical distemper," "a cruel disease [which] has robbed the dear creatures of their charms, and me of the designs of my life."[94] Women had evidently begun to speak publicly on certain topics, something a letter writer Philadelphia thought could be immediately quashed if women were treated like the women of China:

> The things that make matrimony void in China are, if the woman be talkative, and given to prating; for this alone is sufficient to turn her out of doors, and dissolve the matrimony. . . . If this was allowed in other countries . . . it would be a great curb to restrain women from being too free with their tongues.[95]

The question of turning out spouses—or petitioning the court for a divorce—was evidently a growing phenomenon in the 1760s and 1770s in America, and women's desire to gain some autonomy no doubt affected the divorce rate. Divorces initiated in Massachusetts, for example, grew from six requests from 1705–1714 to forty-six between 1765–1774.[96] Newspapers commented on divorce, noting that it had become a common occurrence,[97] and women were filing for many of the divorces.

Men may not have liked the fact that women were finding increased freedom in parts of colonial American society, but according to newspapers, a move to egalitarian status for women was being sought within marriages, something that was not only fair but long overdue. "A New Favourite Song for the Ladies," which appeared in the "Poet's Corner"[98] of at least two newspapers, outlined this equality that the author of the poetry felt should naturally occur within the marital relationships of a civilized country. The song poked some fun at women's quest for independence, but it also recognized that women had a legitimate complaint about the way they had been mistreated for years and had the right to a divorce under such conditions. It said:

> THO' man has long boasted an absolute sway,
> While women's hard fate was, love, honor, obey;
> At length over Wedlock fair Liberty dawns,
> And the Lords of Creation must pull in their horns;
> For Hymen among ye proclaims his decree,
> When husbands are tyrants, their wives may be free. . . .
> Nor more shall the wife, all as meek as a lamb,
> Be subject to "Zounds do you know who I am."
> Domestic politeness shall flourish again,
> When women take courage to govern the men;
> Then stand to your charter, and let the world see,
> Tho' husbands are tyrants, their wives will be free.[99]

There can be no doubt from the news about women in colonial newspapers that women were seeking a certain amount of control over their own lives. The conduct and advice literature that newspapers printed telling women that being virtuous wives and dutiful workers in the home would not have been necessary if women were remaining complacently within the domestic sphere nor would there have been so much literature belittling women for having left "the duties of their own sex in order to invade the privileges of our's."[100] Women's efforts at attaining a certain amount of independence and equality in society may not have met with men's approval when those actions threatened the male position of security within society, but many independent acts by women were approved by the male-dominated eighteenth-century American culture. Not ironically, many of these independent actions coincided with America's own moves toward independence from England. Other independent acts by women had nothing to do with efforts to obtain independence, but they were seen as beneficial steps for America.

The independent activities of women were noted in various ways in colonial newspapers. One way was through obituaries. When Elizabeth Marriot died in Annapolis in 1755, for example, the *Maryland Gazette* reported that the owner of the Ship Tavern had died leaving an estate of £3000. News of the death of Sarah Goddard in Philadelphia reached Rhode Island in January 1770, and when it did, *Providence Gazette* printer John Carter did not let the occasion pass without praising Goddard for ensuring that the *Gazette* would be a successful and prosperous newspaper. Sarah, the mother of William Goddard, the *Gazette*'s founder, ran the newspaper for three years after her son's death and established its financial success for the future.[101] Carter's eulogy of his predecessor at the newspaper spoke of her "management and direction" of it. "The credit of the paper," Carter concluded, "was greatly promoted by her virtue, ingenuity and abilities."[102] These notices demonstrate that women functioned independently within society. Newspaper obituaries also noted the success of women by listing the large estates they left behind,[103] and newspapers informed citizens when women of great importance to communities were deathly ill.[104]

When the American colonies began a united effort against English taxation and trade tariff practices, the colonies agreed multilaterally not to import or receive goods from English ships. A magazine article concerning American women and nonimportation found its way into the *Connecticut Courant* in 1770. The letter praised the independent efforts of American women for their support of the agreement. At the same time, the article spoke of the way American women had been treated. The article stated:

> From conceiving of their country to have been ill-treated, they voluntarily enter into the public measures, and dispising the caprices which the sex stand chargeable, nay nobly obviating the charge, advance with their protest against importation of an article, calculated for their own peculiar purposes.[105]

In 1775, American women furthered the cause of fighting for independence. The *Virginia Gazette* informed its readers that women in New York were working to assist in the war effort and reported:

> The Ladies in Bristol township have evidenced a laudable regard to the interest of their country. At their own expense, they have furnished the regiment of that county with a suit of colours and drums, and are now making a collection to supply muskets to such of the men as are not able to supply themselves.[106]

Women also carried on correspondence with newspapers. Deborah Sherman could not understand why Thomas Fleet would not print news that supported itinerant preacher George Whitefield in 1745 and wrote to the Boston printer questioning his biased reporting.[107] A writer named Sylvia in 1725 wrote to warn Boston women of a parlor game men in which men were attempting to trick women into very compromising situations.[108] A woman named Eliza responded in 1775 to accusations of her sexual indiscretions by attacking the character of her accuser in a Philadelphia newspaper.[109] All of these examples of female correspondence could have been instances of men employing pseudonyms to hide their identities and present entertainment or valuable information much like Benjamin Franklin did with the Silence Dogood letters, but it is highly unlikely.

Women, despite all of the cultural obstructions against them, found a certain measure of independence during the colonial period, according to newspapers. Men sought to suppress that freedom by keeping women within the sphere of the home, but the effort was not successful. Some women functioned very successfully in society in positions of ownership or community involvement. These women, according to the amount of news about them in colonial newspapers, must have comprised a small group, however. While women were making advances in personal autonomy within the eighteenth century, the home remained the realm of influence, and entertainment for and from the home, along with advice on education and marriage made up yet another type of news in colonial newspapers.

The home—entertainment, marriage, and education. The home was the dominion of women, and much of the duty of women included caring for children.[110] Since, as statistics point out, approximately half of the colonial population was under the age of sixteen,[111] the care of children should have occupied a large portion of women's time, and it seems logical, considering these facts, that colonial newspapers would have contained a considerable amount of advice on the proper raising of young people. Colonial newspapers, to the contrary, printed very little information on the proper methods of raising children except on education, discipline, and nurture. In addition, some court records intimate that many women viewed children as a liability.[112] Newspapers printed stories about the abuse of children, which strongly suggests that inhuman treatment of children was deplored, but little else is said about the proper methods of raising children, the education of boys being the exception.

Even though colonial society expected women to provide education for children, newspaper accounts suggested that the method of education employed in homes by women, which taught children to read well enough to be able to understand their Bibles, was not sufficient for young men who needed to enter the world in search of jobs or to assume positions of importance.[113] Without a more formal education, Philanthropos wrote to the *South-Carolina Gazette,* young men would not be able to advance society through their discoveries nor would they be able to cultivate their minds.[114] Newspapers also supported the establishment of colleges to provide even more formal training for young men.[115]

When it came to the training of children in other ways, newspapers spoke of both proper punishment and nurture. Home sites, according to a *Boston Evening-Post* letter, needed a good stand of strong birch saplings in order to provide a plentiful supply of switches of "all Sizes, fit for any Backsides you can imagine, from the fat and plump, down to the most lean and skinny that will hardly bear a whipping" for the proper correction of children.[116] The *Virginia Gazette,* however, suggested that a woman needed to provide love for children in lieu of the mother's own self-interests or any other kind of ill treatment.[117] At other times, newspapers ran nurturing letters from parents to children suggesting the proper modes of conduct as their offspring prepared to leave home and enter the world as gentlemen[118] or as young women.[119]

Newspapers also ran very little about the relationship between husband and wife, except of course for the literature that dealt with the virtuous woman and her responsibility to husband, home, and family. Newspapers did suggest that women had a right to expect a healthy conjugal relationship with their husbands, even though it was not legally required. One woman, the *Boston Evening-Post* reported, had her husband arrested for cruelty because he had not slept with her for fourteen months of marriage.[120] The promotion of equality in marriages was not a source of many newspaper news items either. A *Boston Gazette* poem, however, suggested that since God had formed woman by taking "A Rib out of his Side" that men and women were to approach the marriage relationship side-by-side, not as superior to inferior.[121]

Advice on the home and its proper maintenance was also largely omitted in colonial newspapers. Again, the home was the sphere of women, and no doubt newspapers and society figured that women had been properly trained to manage a household by their own mothers. Newspapers occasionally offered recipes[122] and news that would make home life much more pleasant. In the latter case, the *Pennsylvania Gazette* printed a news item that explained how to rid homes of all types of bugs, which were evidently a source of tremendous problems according to the article. The new treatment, the *Gazette* said, was "not hurtful to Furniture, nor [did it] leave any ill Scent, as in the common way of fuming by Brimstone."[123]

Newspapers may not have provided much in the way of home advice as far as children, marital relations, and home care were concerned, but in the second half of the eighteenth century, newspapers increasingly provided poetry and other pieces of entertainment no doubt aimed directly at women. The Poet's Corner became a regular feature of newspapers. The *North Carolina Gazette,* for example, ran the Poet's Corner as a regular weekly feature with poems on beauty, hope, and other female-aimed topics.[124] Sometimes, the Poet's Corner was filled with poems by women. The *Virginia Gazette* announced before it presented its weekly poem entitled "A WINTER SCENE in the COUNTRY" that the poem had been authored by "a very young LADY." The poem read:

> SOLITARY nature here
> Does in wintry dress appear;
> Wide around, the naked trees,
> Stripp'd of all their leaves, one sees;

Which the winds tempestuous bear,
Whistling thro' the chilly air. . . .
Scarce my pen my hand can hold,
While I write, benumb'd with cold!
Now, my muse, forego thy lyre,
Scenes like these no more inspire;
Sullen winter cease to sing,
Wait to hail the jocund spring.[125]

The inclusion of the Poet's Corner in colonial newspapers aiming poetry, songs, word puzzles, and similar items at a female audience, like almost all facets of colonial newspapers, was a forerunner of nineteenth-century newspapers that regularly printed the Poet's Corner for their female readers.[126] Women in both centuries may have been relegated to the sphere of the home, but newspapers recognized that a part of their audience was female and made sure that some of their information was directed toward them.

CONCLUSION

News directed toward women, their roles in society, and their conduct was fairly constant throughout the colonial period. Newspapers such as the *Boston Evening-Post* and *Pennsylvania Gazette* ran approximately ten items each year dealing with virtuous and vicious women and the importance of education. Other newspapers ran slightly less of this type of news, but all colonial newspapers contained some information aimed directly at female readers. If one considers crime news, sensationalism, and news of Native Americans and slaves that involved women as central to the news, the content of colonial newspapers dealing with women would more than double. In years of increased Indian activity, the amount of news related to females would be even higher.

Women were important—sometimes central—to all of these types of news, but the focus of crime, sensational, Native American, and slave news items that dealt with women differed from the news that sought to manipulate the activity of women. Crime news, however, might well be considered news of the vicious woman because it demonstrated the evil aspect of women. The dichotomy of good women-evil women was very much a part of colonial society and colonial news. Subservience and inferiority were central to the roles of women in colonial newspapers. Woman's duty was to serve selflessly. If this was done, a woman fulfilled her duty to God, husband, society, and self.

Colonial newspapers, however, also present a changing woman in the eighteenth century, a woman who increasingly wanted and demanded some autonomy. This woman, more than the murderer or robber, was portrayed as the vicious woman. She cared more for her own pleasures than her duties to her family and her domain, the home. The male society of colonial America was no doubt concerned by this potential crumbling of the social order, and that is why the letter writer to *Parker's New-York Gazette* in 1760, quoted at the beginning of this chapter, attacked so voraciously independent and free-thinking women and promoted so strongly the virtue of women whose sole purpose it was to make their husbands and children happy.[127]

Society may have felt that women needed to remain subservient, but the news in colonial newspapers was not intended solely for a male audience. If colonial newspapers had been aimed solely at men, it is doubtful that they would have included poetry by both male and female authors on topics that seemed pointed toward females, nor does it seem that newspapers would have ever run correspondence that stated that it was for female readers. The virtuous woman news that newspapers presented also suggests an audience of both sexes. It is doubtful that correspondents would have written to newspapers on this subject if women were not reading newspapers.

Although the amount of correspondence from women never approached the amount received from men, letters from women appeared with enough frequency to lead to the conclusion that eighteenth-century women followed the events of the American colonies in newspapers and felt free to voice their opinions in them. That is why Deborah Sherman wrote to Thomas Fleet of the *Boston Evening-Post* to complain about what she perceived to be "biased news reporting" by the Boston printer.

Why colonial newspapers did not print more information aimed directly at homelife is not known. Newspapers printed very few recipes for preparing and preserving food or information aimed at making life more comfortable. The omission of these types of news may have been because printers were already presenting these pieces of information in their almanacs where it could be collected over the course of the year and published in one volume.[128] By doing this, printers left newspapers open for more "current" information, which is precisely what happened with medical news during the colonial period.[129]

Colonial news directed at a female audience served one major purpose: keeping women within their sphere of influence, the home. That is why so much news adapted to the female world advocated the virtuous woman, the woman who worked selflessly toward bettering the world by serving. That is why any woman who veered from this position as advocated by religion and society was deemed the vicious woman. The portrait of society's understanding of the role of women as presented in colonial newspapers appears to be an accurate reflection of women within colonial society. The home was the place women were expected to be, but women were successfully operating outside of that sphere, much like Sarah Goddard, the Rhode Island printer praised for her hard work in making the *Providence Gazette* a successful newspaper. Women in these roles were accepted probably because there were so few of them. When it did appear that women would make a stronger effort toward gaining personal autonomy, society, speaking through newspaper correspondence, called women back to the home to be nurturers and educators. Women could, as newspapers demonstrated, be independent and successful, but that was not to be their goal in the eighteenth century.

Much of colonial life centered in the home where women cooked, sewed, educated, and nurtured the family. Because of the lack of professionally trained physicians and the abundance of folk remedies, women were no doubt the doctors for most colonial citizens, too. But newspapers say little of women when they speak of disease and cures. A physician of note, however, found out his wife knew more about the practical aspects of medicine than he did when he went to cure a patient with eye troubles. The doctor, after numerous attempts to remove an iron filing from a patient's eye, gave up. Upon turning around, his wife, who was with him, had removed the filing and cured the agonizing patient.[130] Having the ability to find remedies for medical problems, such as the removal of the iron filing, was important during the colonial period. Notices of disease outbreaks and medical advances were, therefore, of vital importance to colonial citizens, and as will be seen in the next chapter, relating information concerning them was one of the more important tasks of the news of colonial newspapers.

7

A Receipt Against the Plague

The Small-pox which has been raging in Boston, after a manner very Extraordinary, is now very much abated. It is thought that far more have been sick of it then were visited with it, when it raged so much twelve years ago. . . . The number of them that have dyed in Boston by this last Visitation is about three hundred' and twenty, which is not perhaps half so many as fell by the former.

—*Publick Occurrences*, 25 September 1690

In the winter of 1760, a smallpox epidemic raged through the South Carolina colony. Each week, the *South-Carolina Gazette* reported new outbreaks of the oft-fatal disease. But in the 23 February 1760 edition, printer Peter Timothy offered his readership more than a table of smallpox deaths for the colony; he presented them with "A Receipt against the PLAGUE," a concoction of "rub, sage, mint, rosemary, wormwood, and lavender," combined in "white-wine vinegar." The resulting elixir was guaranteed by four convicts going to the gallows to protect the user from smallpox.[1]

The *South-Carolina Gazette*'s cure for smallpox is but one example of the many medical remedies presented in colonial newspapers. In an age where bleeding and drawing blisters behind the ears were common prescriptions for maladies, the newspapers offered various cures for their readers to use to heal an assortment of diseases. In addition, the local newspapers kept their readers informed of outbreaks of diseases and described the latest medical breakthroughs made in Europe and America.

This chapter looks at the treatment of medical news in colonial newspapers. Through reports of various medical treatments, news of outbreaks of disease, and news of assorted scientific discoveries, the colonial newspapers entered the battle to eliminate certain maladies and physical shortcomings that tormented the eighteenth-century citizen. Diseases and their cures, therefore, were very much a concern of colonial society, and newspapers served a vital function in the dissemination of timely information to a public waiting to know how to treat certain maladies.

Medical news found a place in American newspapers from their inception. Benjamin Harris in *Publick Occurrences* related that "Epidemical Fevers and Agues grow common."[2] *Publick Occurrences'* report of smallpox "raging in Boston" was only the first of numerous newspaper accounts of the disease in America. Harris, in comparing the 1690 outbreak to the one in 1678 and listing the death toll for the latest outbreak, established the prototype for disease outbreak reports that followed in the eighteenth century.[3]

Medical news was never the most prominent type of information in colonial newspapers, but it was, nonetheless, one of the most vital types of news. Newspaper printers who wanted to be successful during the colonial period generally worked diligently to provide valuable information to readers picked up and ran many items related to curing disease and to the dispersion of notices of disease outbreaks. The *Pennsylvania Gazette* averaged ten news items per year through 1770 on the subjects, and the *Boston Evening-Post,* more than eight in the issues studied. Although these numbers demonstrate that medical news was not the most prominent type of news in colonial newspapers, this news was no doubt of great value to readers because of the potential good such reports could produce.

Timeliness was critical to medical news. Just like news of ship arrivals and hostile Indian activity, it was imperative that newspapers report outbreaks of disease in order to tell readers what cities or regions to avoid because of disease outbreak. In the same way, publication of remedies was also vital to readers, and the continual presentation of methods of inoculation for smallpox, especially, is evidence that colonial citizens looked to newspapers as a source of news of cures, even if, as in the case of some medical remedies printed, those remedies were little more than placebos or worthless concoctions.

Colonial newspapers did present a variety of cures that may seem odd to a modern reader, but many more diseases and afflictions were life-threatening in the eighteeenth century than today. In addition, medical knowledge was limited, and the cause of most ailments was believed to be based in the "humours," that is in bodily fluids like blood and phlegm and in bile. For that reason, a brief overview of the major diseases of the period and the presentation of medical and disease news in colonial print other than in newspapers should help in understanding the reports that ran in colonial newspapers.

THE DISEASES OF COLONIAL AMERICA

Three main diseases preyed upon the inhabitants of colonial America. They were smallpox, typhus, and measles,[4] but these diseases and others like diphtheria, dysentery, and malaria were not new to the English settlers who crossed the Atlantic Ocean to settle in America. The diseases existed in England as well and were brought by the colonists when they emigrated.[5] Smallpox was the most lethal pathogen in Europe, and it continued in that role in America wiping out entire tribes of Native Americans even faster than it claimed the lives of white settlers.[6] The Indians provided the European disease with "virgin soil" in which to grow.[7]

If Native Americans provided "virgin soil" for smallpox and the other European diseases, the first English settlers in America— even though many had been exposed to the diseases in England— became nearly as fertile a field for illnesses. It is estimated that 90 percent of Native Americans succumbed to European diseases, while 80 percent of the English settlers in Virginia died from the same ailments during the colony's first eighteen years.[8] A century later, the death rate among colonists had lowered considerably, but still 6,000 citizens of Boston contracted smallpox in 1721, with 899 dying from it.[9] In addition, smallpox claimed more than 6 percent of Boston's citizens in 1702, 1730, and again in 1752.[10] And the farther south colonists chose to live, the greater the likelihood of contracting a fatal disease because the Southern colonies provided a more ideal environment for the promulgation of viruses.[11]

Fatal diseases were widespread in colonial America. Coupled with the fact that no more than four university-trained physicians practiced in the colonies before 1700, a considerable amount of improvisation or making do in the treatment of diseases naturally occurred.[12] That is where the colonial printers came into play, and in the seventeenth century and into the eighteenth, almanacs that they printed offered a variety of cure-alls. Samuel Atkins's 1686 almanac, *Kalendarium Pennsilvaniense,* advertised cures for assorted "Feavers and Agues, Surfeits, Gripes, Plurisies, &c," the medicines could be obtained from the most unlikely of sources, the almanac's printer, William Bradford.[13]

Other knowledgeable individuals published handbooks of treatments of disease, not unlike the current medical encyclopedias.

These books went through numerous printings. Twelve editions of John Tennent's *Every Man his own Doctor,* for example, were published after the Virginian released it in 1734.[14] Tennent's work was geared toward the Southern colonies and their "Multitude of Marshes, Swamps, and great Waters," all of which "shut the pores all at once, and hinder insensible perspiration. From hence proceed FEVERS, COUGHS, QUINSIES, PLEURISIES, and CONSUMPTION."[15] Tennent's cures were as improvisational as any of the period. He suggested, for instance, taking away "10 Ounces of Blood" for three or four days in a row to cure pleurisy.[16]

Even more popular than Tennent's *Every Man his own Doctor* was the work of the father of Methodism, John Wesley. *Primitive Physick* ran through twenty-two printings. In the twelfth edition published in Philadelphia in 1764, Wesley offered the following terse advice for fighting breast cancer: "Use the Cold Bath. (This has cured many.)"[17]

While household medical guides and annual almanacs provided colonists with assorted cures for maladies, they could not possibly furnish their readers with the latest in discoveries and correctives because they were not published often enough. This niche was quickly filled by the weekly newspaper. The paper could report the emergence of a fatal disease outbreak on a week-by-week basis. The newspaper could relate the occurrence of diseases in other parts of the colonies. It could also present the latest in remedies for diseases and the latest in medical advancements. The weekly newspaper could also warn its readers of which treatments and physicians were dangerous.

DISEASE, MEDICINE, AND COLONIAL NEWSPAPERS

The news of disease and medicine in colonial newspapers falls into three separate but related categories. The first and most urgent of these subjects dealt with reporting disease outbreaks and efforts to halt the spread of infectious diseases. Smallpox was the prime motivator of this news, but diptheria and other disease epidemics prompted newspaper notices of outbreaks. Disease outbreak news usually carried factual information about the numbers of ill or killed and where the illness was raging, but newspapers also reported unsubstantiated news of disease outbreaks that no doubt created a certain amount of panic within certain communities.

The second type of medical news presented assorted remedies that may or may not have helped in the cure of ailments. Many of these remedies were folk cures. Some of these cures were valid; others, as newspapers pointed out, were worthless attempts at curing serious illness or an attempt by someone to make money at the expense of a community seeking relief from epidemics and other types of ailments.

The third type of news concerning disease and medicine reported medical advancements and discoveries. These discoveries were often based upon experimentation that was little more than quackery. Other work that sought cures to diseases, however, employed more scientific methodology producing significant medical advancements that benefitted eighteenth-century society. In contrast to reports of medical breakthroughs, colonial newspapers warned of medical quackery and malpractice, something that was no doubt hard to discern in an age of leaching but demonstrates that colonial society was beginning to disregard some types of folk cures.

Disease. When the lone edition of *Publick Occurrences* hit the streets of Boston on 25 September 1690, the last two paragraphs of the first page honed in upon the diseases prevalent in Massachusetts Bay. In a paragraph loaded with current news, past history, and editorial comment on the future, Benjamin Harris reported:

> The Small-pox which has been raging in Boston, after a manner very Extraordinary, is now very much abated. It is thought that far more have been sick of it then were visited with it, when it raged so much twelve years ago. . . . The number of them that have dyed in Boston by this last Visitation is about three hundred and twenty. . . . It seized upon all sorts of people that came in the way of it, it infected even Children in the bellies of Mothers that had themselves undergone the Disease many years ago for some such were now born full of the Distemper. 'Tis not easy to relate the Trouble and Sorrow that poor Boston has felt by this Epidemical Contagion. But we hope it will be pretty nigh Extinguished, by that time twelve month when it first began to Spread.[18]

For colonial newspaper readers, knowing when and where outbreaks of the fatal diseases occurred was often a life or death matter. In January 1712, for example, "five or six everyday" were carried off by smallpox and other diseases in Rhode Island, the *Boston News-Letter* reported. The *News-Letter* was informing and warning Bostonians to avoid Rhode Island since "it is very Sickly and Mortal there."[19] Disease evidently abated very little in New England during 1712 because a *News-Letter* correspondent wrote to the paper in November that "the malignant Distemper, that proved so Mortal among us, the last Winter; especially in Hartford,

Weatherford, and Glassenbury" had claimed "upwards of Forty, since last August" in Windsor and each of the towns mentioned.[20] A measles epidemic followed in 1714.[21]

While the smallpox epidemic of Boston in 1721 may have been the most deadly of the eighteenth century for the Massachusetts port and the most well documented, the disease extracted a high cost in 1730 as well with at least four hundred deaths.[22] Coverage of the disease in 1730 began cautiously. The selectmen of the city— in an official report—stated that in "the Town of Boston, respecting Small-Pox, We find that it is only in Three Houses in the Town . . . and they are now all well Recovered."[23] The report by the leaders was obviously an optimistic reporting of the facts because smallpox continued to claim lives in Boston and the surrounding countryside for at least nine months. In September, the *New-England Weekly Journal* reported that the selectmen "having made diligent Search thro' this Town, find but Six Persons now Sick of the Small-Pox."[24] Notices of smallpox outbreaks in New England continued throughout the year.[25]

Port cities were a natural point of disease outbreaks because of the large number of ships entering them from other parts of the world, and smallpox was not the only disease to take its toll upon the residents of Boston. In 1735 an unknown disease began spreading through New England putting "universal Terrour into the People." This disease, in reality diphtheria, was described by the *Boston Gazette* so that readers would know the symptoms:

> This disease invades generally such as are very young, they feel at the first somewhat lifeless and heavy for a Day or two, and then begin to complain of a soreness in the Throat, and if you then look into the Mouth you'll discover upon the Uvala and Pares adjacent to the Curicula raised in Spots of different sizes, sometimes to a quarter of an Inch Diameter, and fill'd with a laudable coloured Pus. . . . In a Day or two more they have the same Cough as in the common humourous Quinzey, the next Day a Fever rises, and the Cough is often between whiles very loose; the Patient now begins to Breath hard, and almost loses his Voice, being able only to Whisper, and a Day more makes (with Coughing) only a Whistling kind of Noise, and the next Day pay his Debt to Nature.[26]

In 1739 and 1740, diphtheria again worked its way through New England, beginning with an outbreak in Boston. "Throat distemper," as colonials referred to the disease by this time, claimed casualties in Boston,[27] Newberry,[28] Littleton,[29] and Weston[30] then spread into Connecticut and New York[31] later in the year, according to an on-going report of the disease printed in the *New-England Weekly Journal*. Large epidemics of diseases also occurred in North Carolina in 1735,[32] in South Carolina in 1760,[33] in Maryland in 1765,[34] and in Virginia in 1770.[35] These are but four examples out of many found in colonial newspapers.

Reporting epidemics was important, but stopping them was even more important. Quarantining infected individuals was the first line of defense, and a tragic report in the *Boston Weekly News-Letter* demonstrated what happened if an infected individual was not separated from the populace. When a thirteen-year-old girl developed a fever, her parents summoned a physician who found out, too late, that the girl had contracted smallpox. Not only did the girl die, but the doctor and the girl's father both succumbed to the disease.[36] Inoculation of individuals was the second line of defense, and the one that proved to be the most successful. That is why the issue of inoculation continued to be of major importance in the colonies and did not end with the ebbing of the smallpox crisis of 1721.[37] When smallpox was the disease involved, the inoculation question was often part of the news that surrounded the sickness. Even before the Boston selectmen made their inspection of the houses of Boston for smallpox, the *New-England Weekly Journal* was advocating inoculations to stop the contraction of smallpox.[38] Later in the year, the *Pennsylvania Gazette* explained succinctly the values of inoculation:

> IN a Physical Sense, Inoculation is used for the Transplanting of Distempers from one Subject to another, particularly for the Ingraftment of the Small-Pox, which is a new Practice among us, but of ancient Origin in the Eastern Countries. . . . The Practice seems to be useful, because most proper Age, the favourable Season of the Year, the most regular method of Preparation, and all possible precautions may here be used. . . . Advantages impossible to be had when the Distemper is caught in the natural Way. It has also been constantly observed, that the best Sort of Small-Pox is hereby occasioned, that the Eruptions are few, the Symptoms light, the Danger next to none, the Recovery easy, and that the Patient is equally secured from this Distemper for the future, as he would be by having gone thro' it in the natural Way.[39]

In 1750, a letter appearing in the *Boston Gazette* went so far as to claim that rejecting inoculation was a rejection of God's providential plan for humankind. "To reject the practice of Inoculation," the letter writer declared, "is to reject one of the most providential Discoveries, to save the Lives of Thousands."[40]

The printers of colonial newspapers—following the inoculation controversy in Boston in 1721[41]—apparently believed firmly in inoculation and expended considerable space to convince their readers that having themselves infected with the disease was the only sure way to avoid a bout with death. In 1725, for example, Philadelphia printer Andrew Bradford provided a piece of English news that "Princess Louisa, youngest Daughter to their Royal Highnesses . . . was inoculated for the Small Pox."[42] A month later, the *American Weekly Mercury* stated that the princess faced no danger from the killer disease.[43] If King George saw no danger in inoculating his daughter, the *Weekly Mercury* was intimating, then his subjects in America should see no danger in it either.

In Boston, Samuel Kneeland and Timothy Green began printing notices of smallpox deaths in the *New-England Weekly Journal* by comparing the number that died from inoculation to the number of those who died after contracting the disease in the "natural" way. "To make the utmost of this Computation, to the Prejudice of Inoculation," the *Weekly Journal* stated, "One in four died of the first Sixty in the Way of common Contagion, and four in a hundred have died of those that have been inoculated."[44] If simple arithmetic would not convince citizens to be inoculated, then perhaps publishing the names of all those who had decided to have themselves inoculated might help. On 20 April 1730, the *Weekly Journal* published a list of all of the Boston citizens that had been inoculated. Readers of the paper could search the list for names of important citizens and discover that in March, only two deaths occurred out of seventy-two inoculations.[45]

The concept of injecting one's body with a potentially fatal disease, despite the numerous newspaper accounts demonstrating the value of inoculation, was never universally accepted during the colonial period. Just three months after the *South-Carolina Gazette* offered "A Receipt against the PLAGUE" in 1760 to help curb the smallpox epidemic that was racing through the region, the colony enacted a law that made it illegal to inoculate anyone in Charleston or the surrounding area against the disease. The decree, signed by the governor, said:

WHEREAS the inhabitants of Charles-Town have suffered greatly, not only in their trade and commerce, but from a scarcity of provisions, By the raging of the disease . . . called the Small-Pox, in the said Town: AND WHEREAS the most probable means of preventing the said distemper being continued in the said town . . . it shall not be lawful to or for any person or persons whosoever, within the limits of Charles-Town, or within two miles of the said limits, to inoculate or ingraft, or

to cause, or procure to be inoculated or ingrafted, the disease or distemper commonly called the Small-Pox, in or upon him, her, or themselves, or in or upon any other person or persons whosoever . . . under
pain of forfeiting the sum of One Hundred Pounds proclamation money
for every such offence.[46]

Because inoculation remained a controversial practice, newspapers continued to play the numbers game for their readers as
they attempted to demonstrate the value of smallpox inoculations
over acquiring the disease in "the natural way." The *Pennsylvania
Gazette* reminded its readers that through the inoculation process
given Benjamin Franklin in England that "there has not died more,
than one Person in 700 . . . when in the Common Way of Infection,
one dies out of Five."[47] The *Boston Weekly News-Letter,* in the
same manner as the *Pennsylvania Gazette,* attempted to ease its
readers' fears of inoculation by pointing out that when inoculation
was used in the last outbreak of smallpox in the backcountry region
of New England, those who were inoculated died at a rate of "not
more than one in a thousand," and added, "We ought to be thankful
to GOD for the Discovery of a Medicine so efficacious in antidoting
and subduing the Malignancy of this infectious and formidable Distemper."[48] In 1765, the *Maryland Gazette* was still playing the num-
bersgame for its readers offering for them commonsense odds for
using inoculation versus contracting smallpox in the tradition
manner:

Suppose a Lottery with 116 Chances, and only One Blank in it; and
Another, of 116 Chances with 21 Blanks in it; and the Prizes in Both,
of equal Value; Would any Man, (in his Senses) who could have his
Choice in the Two, chuse to Venture [his LIFE] in the Latter? This
was the exact Case with regard to the Small-Pox in Boston last Year:
From among those who took the Small-Pox by Inoculation, there Died
only in that Proportion, One out of 116; And nearly One out of every
Five who took it in the Natural Way.[49]

While presenting these numbers, the newspaper reported that Annapolis doctors would inoculate for free anyone who so desired,
but newspapers were offering the latest methods of self-inoculation
and self-treatment for diseases. Following in the tradition of the
almanac and home remedy companion, the colonial newspapers
provided home treatments not only for smallpox but for a host
of maladies.

Remedies and cures: fanciful and real. All of the newspaper
accounts listing the odds of surviving smallpox made it seem inevi-

table in colonial America that one would contract it or some other serious disease. True physicians were scarce, and there was little that they could do, in most cases, when someone contracted one of the epidemical diseases.[50] A self-administered inoculation, therefore, provided as good preventative medicine as that performed by doctors. Newspapers printed detailed directions for self-treatment. In 1730, the *New-England Weekly Journal* explained how to perform inoculations using two incisions, pus from a live smallpox sore, and lint. The lint, soaked in pus, was placed in the incisions and wrapped tightly.[51] Similar directions, given to Benjamin Franklin in England, were repeated thirty-five years later in the *South-Carolina Gazette* as the disease swept through that Southern colony. The *Gazette*'s directions were explicit:

> The proper time for taking the matter is just before it would have dried up. In order to take it, any sort of thread must be had ready about the thickness of a common pin. The head of one of the small-pox may be opened with a needle, or pin, and then the thread is to be drawn along this. . . . The thread thus wetted may be put into a common pill-box, into which air can easily get . . . and use it some days after. . . . Half an inch of that part of this thread which had been well soaked in the matter . . . must be cut off at the time of use. The person who is to be inoculated, must have the fine edge of a penknife or lancet, drawn along that part of the arm where issues are usually made; and it must go deep enough to make the blood just begin to appear. . . . In, or rather upon, this, the bit of thread must be put, and a small plaister of what is called the ladies black sticking plaister . . . is all which need be put over it to keep it on.[52]

With these directions, which also explained what must be done for the two weeks following the treatment, any family could inoculate itself.

Newspapers also provided treatments for other fatal contagions. When in 1735 and for several years to follow, diphtheria spread through New England, the *Boston Evening-Post* offered this "effectual Remedy":

> Take Corns of Stone-Horse Feet . . . put them into a Bag and dry them in a Chimney . . . grate off the rough part, powder the remainder, and take five times as much as will lay upon a Shilling heap'd up, put it into a Quart of French White Wine, and let it stand two Days; take a Quarter of a Pint a little warm going to Bed, and two Hours before rising in the Morning.[53]

When the disease flared up again in Boston in late 1739, the *New-England Weekly Journal* offered yet another cure for "Throat Distemper" in January 1740, which the writer of the letter was so positive would work that he said, "I am fully perswaded it will always do so." The *Weekly-Journal*'s method for curing diphtheria combined a mixture of "proven" medical practices of the day and folk herb remedies. The medical practice included raising "six blisters" on the patient, and the herb remedy involved the use of rhubarb and turpentine. In the event that neither the blisters nor the concoction prevented the throat of the patient from swelling, the patient would have to be bled and treated with "Oil of Cedar." This method of fighting diphtheria was employed by Dr. John Clark of Boston to cure the disease.[54]

To stop rabies, which was more certain to be fatal if contracted than diphtheria or smallpox, one colonial newspaper remedy in 1735 called for a mixture of ground liverwort and black pepper in warm cow's milk. After four doses of this, the infected person needed to spend approximately thirty seconds every day for the next nine weeks submerged to his neck in very cold water. The medicine's inventor was convinced the treatment would cure the infected person.[55] Nearly forty years later, newspapers offered similar cures for the bite of a rabid animal with a "RECEIPT to Cure the biting of a MAD DOG":

> TAKE the Leaves of Rus pick'd from the Stalks and bruised, Six Ounces, Garlick picked from the Stalks and bruised; Venice Treacle and Mithridate and the scrapings of Pewter, of each Four Ounces; boil all these over a slow Fire in two Quarts of strong Ale till one Quart be consumed, then keep it in a Bottle close stopped, and give of it Nine Spoonfuls to a Man or Woman warm, seven Mornings Fasting, and Six to a Dog. This the Author believes will not by God's Blessing fail if it be given within Nine Days after the biting of the Dog. This Receipt was taken from the Register of the Church of England.[56]

Several of the treatments found in the colonial newspapers had nothing to do with disease. Instead, they sought to provide relief from everyday afflictions. Toothaches, the *Newport Mercury* stated, could be cured "by the touch of an artificial magnet." All the afflicted had to do was face the North Pole to be "cured by the touch."[57] Frostbite could be remedied by rubbing "the Fat of a Dunghill Fowl" on the exposed areas and then wrapping them in "a Piece of Woolen Cloth, well greased with the said Fat," the *New-York Mercury* informed it readers.[58] Honey rubbed on a child's gums, the *Georgia Gazette* noted, could stop the pain teething caused for infants. As proof, the *Gazette*'s story told of a woman who lost nine children while they were cutting their teeth but had six live after she began rubbing their swollen gums with the honey.[59]

Wells for drinking water were constantly in need of repair, but they were often filled with gases that could render unconscious those who descended them to clean out obstructions. Sharing a tip from coal miners in England, one writer to the *New-York Weekly Journal* explained how to revive a person that had suffocated:

> Cut a hole in the Grassy Ground big enough for a Mans Face, and lay the Man upon his Belly, and his Face in this hole, where he lyes perhaps one Hour, sometimes two, and then (the Earth having drawn from him the Sulphurous matter he had taken in by reason of the Damp) he comes to Life again and is well only small Sickness at his Stomack remains with him two or three Days. Note. The Person so taken has no pulse, Breath, or any other Signs of Life, only that the Body is not Stiff but Limber.[60]

Other serious problems encountered in everyday colonial life involved water, too. Several citizens in Philadelphia, according to newspaper reports, died after drinking extremely cold water during the summer. The newspaper accounts blamed the rapid intake of cold water for the deaths by causing the lungs to stop working. The report explained what happened:

> The Body, from the Season of the Year, as well as from being now so much more heated that usual, is in a very irritable State; so that the cold Water, as soon as it is received into the Stomach, communicates its Effects to the Parts which adjoin the Lungs, whose Irritability is much encreased, and over part of which the Water must pass, in entering into the Stomach.[61]

As a remedy to the lungs' failure, the letter writer offered several treatments and said, "Would not blowing Wind into the Mouth, or into the Anus, by Means of a Pair of Bellows, tend to rouse Circulation, and give the Lungs an Opportunity of playing again?"[62]

Because water provided one of the main forms of transportation in colonial America, colonists were often in boats. As might be expected, numerous drownings occurred. The *Boston Evening-Post* offered a cure for drowning victims that had been performed on a cat in England, the insinuation being that such methods would also work with humans. After being dead for half an hour, the cat was laid before a fire and covered with salt. Next, its body was gently rubbed until it was revived. The cat, after this treatment, began to crawl and make noises.[63] A similar procedure was used successfully to revive a drowned boy in Europe. The account of the successful reviving of the lad was provided by the *Connecticut Courant* so that its readers might use the procedure if so needed. After the three-year-old fell into the water he had no pulse, and his head and hands were swollen. The boy, according to the report, had been this way for forty-five minutes. At that time, a doctor laid the boy upon a bed of ashes filled with salt and other unnamed ingredients and began rubbing him with hot cloths. After thirty minutes of this treatment, the boy was revived and "recovered the use of his senses."[64]

Experimentation for correctives like those performed on the drowned cat and the three-year-old boy were natural in the colonial period since medical practices had so few answers for the maladies of the day. Also, colonists brought with them a number of family and traditional herbal cures for diseases from England.[65] The lack of medical doctors and the penchant for home remedies, therefore, led to a number of "miracle cures" during the colonial period. These "miracle cures" contained the power to heal a great number of diseases or accidental injuries. Some of the strongest claims for curing power went to three potions—tar water, the Negro Cæsar's cure for poison, and Chinese stones.

The Irish philosopher and church bishop George Berkeley penned a treatise on tar water, and the *Virginia Gazette,* for three weeks in May 1745, drew from his "Treatis on Tar-Water," explaining how to make the medication and what maladies it would cure. Tar water was, just as it named implied, water mixed with tar or the resin of pine trees. The *Gazette* opened its series on tar water by explaining how to create the elixir:

> Tar-Water is made, by putting a Quart of cold Water to a Quart of Tar, and stirring them well together in a Vessel, which is left standing 'til the Tar sinks to the Bottom. A Glass of clear Water being pured off for a Draught, is replaced by the same Quantity of fresh Water, the Vessel being shaken and left to stand as before. And this is repeated for every Glass, so long as the Tar continues to impregnate the Water sufficiently.[66]

Once tar water reached its proper consistency, its uses were numerous. It could be taken "as a Preservative or Preparative against the Small-pox," to halt "Distemper," or to heal "Ulceration of the Bowels." Tar water held the cure for "Indigestion" and provided individuals with "a good Appetite." Tar water, according to the

Gazette's publication of Berkeley's treatise, was "an excellent Medicine for Asthma" and produced "quick Circulation to the Juices without heating." For individuals who might need to lose weight, tar water could be used to make "Diet-Drinks."[67]

If curing these maladies were not enough, the following week of the *Virginia Gazette* proclaimed tar water as a cure for the "Bloody Flux," "Gout," and "Gangrene from an internal Cause." In addition, Berkeley's "miracle cure" was "an excellent antihysteric" and worked on "hypochondriacal Disorders." Used as a rub, tar water was "an excellent Preservative of the Teeth and Gums," and it "sweetens the Breath" and "clears and strengthens the Voice."[68]

To prove that tar water worked, the *Gazette*'s printer, William Parks, included an example of the medicine's power against the most deadly of enemies—smallpox. "In one Family there was a remarkable instance of several Children," the paper stated, "who came all very well thro' the Small-pox, except one young Child which could not be brought to drink Tar-Water as the rest had done."[69]

Although not as comprehensive a cure-all as tar water, "The Negro Cæsar's cure for Poison" offered a welcome remedy from snakebites and other types of poisoning. Cæsar's cure was made by boiling "the roots of Plantane and wild Hoare-hound" and was taken by fasting patients. In addition to being taken internally, it was applied to the bite of a rattlesnake with "a leaf of good Tobacco moisten'd with Rum."[70] Just as other wonder cures provided proof of their ability to do as promised, the letter writer to the *South-Carolina Gazette* that provided the information about Cæsar's Cure did the same, saying that the root concoction "never fails" with rattlesnake bites.[71]

While tar water and Cæsar's cure for poison were proclaimed to be potent remedies, another "Chymical Composition, called Chinese Stones" produced all of the cures of the other two and more. Benjamin Franklin must have found Chinese Stones to be a wonderful drug or a source of tremendous amusement because the *Pennsylvania Gazette* of 17 October 1745, dedicated considerable space to the stones.[72] Franklin was not the only one to find the Chinese Stones, introduced by a Mr. Torres, fascinating. The *Pennsylvania Gazette*'s accounts of them came to Philadelphia from Rhode Island, South Carolina, North Carolina, Virginia, and Maryland. The *Maryland Gazette*'s discussion of the stones on 8 November 1745, traveled to Annapolis from Boston. And perhaps not by coincidence, Mr. Torres happened to be in Philadelphia when the *Pennsylvania Gazette* printed this series of articles and offered the stones for sale.

The description of the stones began with a certification that they would "effectually cure the Bites of all venomous or poisonous Creatures; as Rattle (and other) Snakes, Scorpions, mad Dogs, &c." As proof, the article stated, "The Experiment has been made in the Bay of Honduras, on the Bodies of two white Men, and four Negroes, who were bit by Rattle-snakes, the said Stones being applied to the Wound, and the Persons cured immediately."[73]

Not only could snakebites be cured by the Chinese stones, the miracle cure healed a toothache, sore eyes, and a swollen foot overnight in North Carolina. The stones cured rheumatism and sciatic pains in Virginia, and a cancer "was cured with one Bag of this Powder." It appeared to cure appendicitis in Maryland and completely cured hemorrhoids in Philadelphia. For those without an appetite, a bag of Chinese stones "laid on the Pit of the Stomach" immediately created an appetite. Gout, the bloody flux, and all sorts of distempers could be vanquished by Chinese stones, the certified accounts in the *Pennsylvania Gazette* claimed.[74]

Other cure-alls that were presented in colonial newspapers claimed to have just as much power as Chinese stones, Cæsar's poison cure, and tar water. The *Constitutional Gazette* praised the power of "Antiveneral Pills" in 1775. These pills were proclaimed to be able to cure veneral disease, leprosy, and other skin disorders.[75] Even though the antiveneral pills were nothing more than a type of patent medicine, the appearance in a newspaper of this type of news item in the midst of almost exclusive news about the Revolution further enhances the notion that cures for disease were valuable pieces of information to colonial citizens no matter what cause or event was capturing most of the attention of the period.

Medical advancements and discoveries. Even though few actual medical advancements were made during the colonial period and most medical "discoveries" were of the tar water or Chinese stones variety, several real cures occurred during this time period. Two of the most important that appeared in the colonial newspapers dealt with the removal of cataracts and stones.[76] Identical articles in the *New-York Weekly Journal* and *American Weekly Mercury* of Philadelphia in 1735 described how a London doctor had perfected a method for removing cataracts. Dr. Taylor, the articles said, could now remove cataracts without "Waiting for what the vulgar call the Maturity of the Cataract."[77] Cataracts could, evidently, be removed by Dr. Taylor before the patient lost sight because of them. In addition, the article claimed, "this Operation requires little or no Confinement, and cannot be attended or succeeded by any Pain." Dr. Taylor promised that "not one Example can be produced who has been disappointed of this Success."[78] Cataract operations were evidently a regular procedure by American physicians by 1770.[79]

Stones were cut out of patients in America around the same time. The *Essex Gazette* of Salem, Massachusetts, reported such an operation from New Hampshire in 1770. The account of the important medical event appeared as follows:

> Last Monday Morning the Rev. Mr. Samuel Drowne, Pastor of one of the Churches at Portsmouth, New-Hampshire went thro' the dangerous Operation of being cut for the Stone, a Disorder he has for some years past been severely exercised with; and a very large rough one was taken out of his Bladder: He is now in a fair Way of Recovery. Some further Particulars may be made public hereafter.—We hear this ingenious and difficult Operation was performed by Dr. Hall Jackson of that Place.[80]

Because so very little was understood about the causes of diseases during the eighteenth century, some of the best medical advice of the age appears to current observers as foolishness. Since the science of the day attributed most illnesses to the "humours," or the liquids of the body, the removal of blood or causing a patient to vomit continuously were common and acceptable medical practices. In 1770, the *Boston Evening-Post* provided for its readers an essay describing what the loss of too much bodily fluid would do to a person. The essay advised readers to guard against the loss of too much saliva, semen, and urine lest persons find themselves in poor physical health. Too much spitting, the doctor who wrote the essay warned, disturbed digestion. He added, "There is certainly no humor in the body more healthy than the saliva." Semen "discharged too lavishly," the essayist maintained, caused weariness, convulsions, pains in the membranes of the brain, and foolishness, while "too great a discharge by urine occasions dryness, imperviousness and heat of the humors, enextinguishable thirst, crudities, lowness of the spirits, leanness, atrophy, and disorders of the like kind."[81]

Newspapers also reported on cosmetic surgery procedures advanced in the colonial period. The *Massachusetts Gazette* announced that a Boston physician had found a method of surgically repairing a "Hare-Lip." This new surgery was a great help, the news item said, because of the value this cosmetic procedure could have for women in what had been an unsightly birth defect. The paper explained the value of removing the cleft from women's lips:

> The Impression these unhappy Sights are apt to make on married Women, should be an Inducement to have this Defect in Nature rectified early in Life, as there are numerous Instances of the Mother's Affection having impressed her Offspring with the like Deformity.[82]

Newspapers presented the scientific research that went into the efforts to discover cures for maladies. These reports demonstrated the hit-and-miss approach that many "scientists" and doctors employed in attempting to find cures for illnesses and physical defects. They reveal that many times the "enlightened" thinkers of the colonial period had no idea as to what caused a disease or disability. One such example appeared in the *Pennsylvania Gazette* in the summer of 1775. The experiments, conducted in Newport, Rhode Island, ended up finding "cures" for a number maladies, starting with seeking a cure for a man with "foul putrefying matter pent up in his bowels." The experimenting doctor began his cure by mixing different ingredients together until a concoction was devised to purge the patient. Wine, apples, and pears were all tried in the potion until success was achieved. In the same way, the experimenter Thomas Young reported, a cure for asthma was discovered.[83]

Closer to scientific research was the *New-York Gazette*'s account of Dr. Benjamin Rush's work on curing hives. Rush, a Philadelphia doctor and professor at the College of Philadelphia, studied medicine in Edinburgh, London, and Paris.[84] Rush began his investigation of hives by acknowledging that he had no idea of the etymology of the word hives but credited the Irish with applying it to the disorder. Rush's research then defined hives as "a DIFFI-CULTY OF BREATHING, joined with Hoarseness and other symptoms of Oppression and Disorder of the Lungs" and said hives was an affliction apparently unknown in the ancient world. By observing hives, Rush concluded that hives were caused by the nerves producing spasms. Rush's research into hives continued as he examined and attempted to cure a three-year-old patient. Rush noted that the usual remedies applied by physicians, "antinomial emettics, squill mixtures, blisters, warm bath, &c." were of no value in treating hives. The child died anyway.[85] Even though Rush found no cure for hives, no doubt some form of illness similar to asthma, his methodology approached disease in more than a haphazard manner. He concluded that the customary ways of treating the affliction were of no value and that other methods needed to be found in order to cure a patient of hives. Further research, the Pennsylvania doctor noted, was needed.

One of the great discoveries of the colonial period did occur in America and was made by one of Rush's Philadelphia contemporaries. In the mid-1740s, Benjamin Franklin began his experiments with electricity.[86] Although the work with electricity was not done with cures for disease and physical ailments in mind, enterprising researchers in America and Europe sought to apply electricity to the art of healing. A Suffolk, Virginia, gentleman, the *Boston Evening-Post* reported in 1750, had conducted electrical investigations that produced cures for toothaches, headaches, deafness, sprains, and nervous disorders. The experimenter, the news account explained, "applied the Electrical Fire to the human Frame." As a result, "a Negro Boy, about sixteen Years of Age, who had always been so Deaf as scarcely to hear the loudest Sounds, has by the same means been brought to hear, when spoken to in a common Tone of Voice."[87]

In Stockholm, the *Virginia Gazette* noted in 1755, experiments had revealed that electrical shock cured deafness, lameness, toothaches, oozing blood, and dislocations caused by smallpox.[88] John Wesley, the Methodists' founding father and author of the popular remedy text *Primitive Physick,* felt electricity "comes the nearest an universal medicine of any yet known in the world."[89] In addition to electrical experiments to find uses for electricity in curing diseases and physical problems, medical uses for electricity were also discovered by accident. The *Pennsylvania Chronicle,* for example, reported the complete recovery of a man who had lost almost all ability to walk after lightning accidently struck him while he lay in bed. The *Chronicle* explained that "the morning after the shock the lightning gave him, [the man] walked with ease 10 or 12 miles."[90]

The use of electricity to cure the host of diseases described in the pages of colonial newspapers, however, approached quackery, just as the use of tar water and Chinese stones to cure smallpox did. And because the causes of most diseases were completely unknown, the citizens of the eighteenth century turned to quackery out of desperation.[91] Even though newspapers often printed cures that could only work with luck, they also warned their readers of the dangers of quacks and dangerous, useless medicines.

One such warning appeared in the *New-England Weekly Journal* in 1735. The paper reported "that a certain Person . . . has lately turn'd Occulist, and tried his Skill upon several."[92] Becoming a physician was not an uncommon practice in the eighteenth century. Formal training for medical doctors was rare in the colonies, and anyone vaguely familiar with medical literature was often called upon for treatment.[93] The Occulist from "Prince-Town in the Jerseys" probably fell into that category, but his medical treatment produced tragic results. The newspaper stated:

> It seems his Operations have turn'd out contrary to the Desire of his Patients, for instead of restoring their Sight, he intirely takes it away. This Effect his Experiments have had in particular on Mr. Benjamin Randolph, who before this blind Occulist had any thing to do with his Eyes, could See, but now he is quite Blind and in great Pain. *It's to be hop'd People will take Caution by this who they suffer to meddle with their Sight; and not emply those who will put out both their Eyes to make them see clearly.*[94]

The *Boston Evening-Post* issued a similar warning for Bostonians to be on guard against a pair of quack doctors from New York who were currently operating in New England in 1770.[95] Quacks were evidently a large problem in New England. The *Providence Gazette* lamented the fact that "any ignorant plow-boy may live six months or a year with some old Quack, who perhaps started up in the first place from an obscure cow-doctor, and if he can talk pretty glib, and has a good stock of impudence, will gain reputation and practice as soon as the best Physician." As bad as the practice of quackery was, the *Gazette* maintained, even worse was the fact that so many people turned to their "unintelligible nonsense" to seek a cure.[96] The *Massachusetts Spy* warned its readers that a quack was practicing in Boston. The charlatan physician claimed he had discovered a cure for the gout, and the paper described his medical cure as "a white powder of a sweetish taste."[97] And a Boston man, heeding the advice of quackery, attempted to cure a scald on the back of his two-year-old by rubbing the child down in a mixture of milk and soot, which, according to the *Boston Weekly Post-Boy,* led directly to the child's death.[98]

Even some of the great cure-alls were debunked by the very papers that had extolled their virtues. The Chinese stones, for example, were promoted as great remedies in both the *Pennsylvania Gazette* and the *Maryland Gazette,* but both newspapers printed a letter unmasking the wonder cure. Acidus, the letter writer, said that Mr. Torres, who sold a Chinese stone or a bag of ground stone for twenty-five shillings, "ought to be ashamed" for taking advantage of gullible people. The Chinese stones, the letter said, were nothing more than pieces of bone that had been rasped "into what shape you please, and then burn it in hot Embers." All the stones really possessed, the letter writer concluded, were "all the Virtues of—a new Tobacco Pipe."[99]

While cures such as the Chinese stones might be nothing more than placebos and the use of them do no harm to the user, some newspapers warned their readers that the intentional use of another product might well cause harm. That product was tobacco, and the *Massachusetts Gazette* issued perhaps the first warning in America against the use of the "stinking weed" in 1765. The *Gazette*'s report said tobacco produced "nauseous vapors" that were particularly harmful to conjugal relations between husbands and wives. The article said that use of tobacco products should be refrained from completely, but if that was impossible their use should definitely be omitted from the bedroom.[100] A *Boston Evening-Post* medical essay warned that individuals "really injure themselves who smoak too much tobacco."[101] The *Essex Gazette* was even more explicit in attacking the use of tobacco. Often laden with assorted chemicals according to a medical report released in London, the tobacco and chemical combination, "may affect the brain, the stomach, and breast." The *Essex Gazette*'s article then stated:

> persons who are subject to that unwholesome, expensive, and un-cleanly custom of taking snuff . . . ought to be avoided or dismissed by all sensible, cleanly, rational, and delicate persons. All parents, pre-ceptors, &c. should be attentive not to permit youth that dirty, prejudi-cial habit. The present of a snuff-box is the most useless and detrimental gift that can be made to a child, for many young persons have been induced to take snuff from the vanity to show their boxes.[102]

By pointing out the dangers of tobacco and quacks and the foolish-ness of using placebos, colonial newspapers were pointing toward a standardization in medicine and medical practices. Although it would not happen in America during the colonial period, such a movement was already under way in England. Because of the numerous cures such as tar water, Chinese stones, electricity, and Cæsar's cure for poison, a special committee from the college of physicians planned to investigate "the good or bad qualities of each [remedy] previous to their being sent abroad into the world, as often to the ruin of multitudes of the unwary, who from the motive of cheapness . . . are induced to make use of them."[103] American physicians began to adopt a similar approach in the 1790s, but the move toward standardization in medical practices in America did not make many inroads until the nineteenth century.[104]

One medical advancement that did find a place in America was the use of hospitals to treat the ill. Epidemics were the prime concern of the colonial population because of the potential for infecting and killing large numbers during a single outbreak, and outbreaks of contagious epidemics naturally required quarantines. Hospitals, or quarantining facilities for smallpox patients, were in use in the colonies by 1750.[105] But other medical problems that affected individuals had to be dealt with as well, broken bones and rheumatism being two of many possible examples, and a hospital in a city was a logical solution to meeting growing medical needs in high-density population areas.

In the 1750s, Philadelphia sought a way to help individuals with "everyday" medical problems and converted a large house in the city into a hospital. The original intent of Philadelphia's hospital was to see to "the Care and Cure of Lunaticks," but as the *Pennsylvania Gazette* reported, the house acquired for the hospital was really not suitable for that purpose, so the city put it to immediate use in meeting other medical needs. The unit, according to the *Gazette,* treated eighty-nine patients during its first year of operation from April 1754 through April 1755 who were afflicted with everything from aneurysms to "Suppression of Urine," with ulcers being the most common affliction of the patients receiving care in Philadelphia's hospital.[106]

To let the citizens of Philadelphia know what had gone on in the hospital, the *Pennsylvania Gazette* printed a chart listing all the types of medical problems that the hospital staff had encountered for the year. The *Gazette*'s chart[107] allows a glimpse into the types of everyday problems that eighteenth-century citizens faced and how successful the medical practices of the day were in treating those problems. The abstract was thorough in its assessment and presentation of the hospital's operation, and Philadelphia's citizens could take pride in knowing that only nine of the patients who entered the hospital died while forty-seven were cured. While the chart says nothing of the methods of treating ailments, it demonstrates that by the middle of the eighteenth century, American colonies were making a concerted effort to treat maladies in the most effective ways known, that is, through a central medical facility that could pool financial, physical, and intellectual resources to combat the medical probems of their citizens.

CONCLUSION

Diseases and their cures were an important part of colonial life. The inclusion of medical news about illnesses and cures for every-

An *ABSTRACT* of the Cases in the Pennsylvania Hospital, from the 27th of the Fourth Month, 1754, to the 26th of the Fourth Month, 1755.

Diseases.	Admitted.	Cured.	Relieved.	Irregular.	Died.	Incurable.	Remains.
AGUES,	2	2					
Aneurism,	1				1		
Asthma,	1		1		1		
Cancer,	1		1				
Consumption,	1	1			1	1	
Contusion,	1	1					
Cough of long standing,	2	2					
Dropsy,	10	3	1	1	3		2
Empyema,	1	1					
Eyes diseased,	1	1					
Fistula in *Ano*,	1	1					
Fistula in *Perinæo*,	1	1					
Fevers,	2	2					
Flux of long standing,	5	3					
Fracture,	1	1	1		1		1
Hair Lip,	1	1					
Hectic Fever,	2	1	1		1		
Hypocondriack Melancholy,	1		1				
Lunacy,	11	3	1	1		3	5
Palsey,	1	1		1			
Rupture,	1	1	1				
Rheumatism and Sciatica,	5	3	1	1	1		5
Scorbutic and Scrophulous Ulcers,	22	16					6
Suppression of Urine,	1	1	1		1		
Ulcers with Carious Bones,	7	1					
Vertigo,	1	1	1				
Uterine Disorder,	1	1			1		
Weakness habitual,	1	1					
Wounded,	2	1					1
White Swelling,	1	1					
Total,	89	47	7	2	9	4	20

thing from smallpox to "hypochondriacal Disorders" in the colonial newspapers supports this fact. The inclusion of medical news also demonstrates that the colonial newspapers reflected the concerns and needs of society to find a way to halt the spread of these maladies. Unfortunately, cures for diseases were neither discovered nor proper methods for treating them understood by eighteenth-century physicians. That is why Dr. William Douglass remarked in 1760 that "more die of the practitioner than of the natural course of the disease."[108] That is also the reason why so many "miracle cures" appeared in the colonial newspapers. Natural elixirs made of roots, leaves, and horns were believed to be the way to cure diseases, and the assorted articles in the colonial newspapers prove this.

Medical news in the colonial newspapers also demonstrates society's desire for faster and more accurate news on subjects of real importance. Almanacs and medical books existed for the colonial citizen containing assorted cures, but almanacs were published yearly. And books of cures could be printed, but they could not reach the people as quickly or as easily as the same news in a weekly newspaper. In addition, neither almanacs nor medical books could contain notices of where the latest epidemic had erupted or what cures and curers were dangerous. Hundreds of copies of the *Virginia Gazette,* for example, could no doubt be printed, delivered, and shared by large numbers of readers before William Parks or any other colonial printer could produce a similar number of Dr. Berkeley's tar water treatise.

The lack of large numbers of medical items in newspapers should not be construed as a lack of importance for these reports. Papers averaged about nine stories per year on disease and medicine, but outbreaks of infection were periodic. There was no need to provide news of treatments for diseases unless those illnesses were present and necessitated treatment. When large epidemics struck, colonial newspapers responded appropriately. The *Pennsylvania Gazette* covered smallpox epidemics in 1730 with twenty news stories, while the *Weekly Rehearsal* and its successor, the *Boston Evening-Post,* followed the 1735 New England diphtheria outbreak with sixteen items. While South Carolina fought a massive Indian war with the Cherokees in 1760, the *South-Carolina Gazette* regularly reported news of smallpox in the colony providing monthly warnings of outbreaks and "Receipts against the PLAGUE" to help colonists know areas of illness and how the disease might be avoided.

The newspapers of the colonial period sought to provide their

readers with "A Receipt against the PLAGUE," and they attempted to stay abreast of the latest news of disease outbreaks
and epidemics. Even though many local residents already knew of
disease outbreaks, the notices in colonial newspapers served as
official reports—like those of the Boston selectmen—and as ways
to transmit the news of local disease to other colonies. The colonial
newspapers were reasonably effective at transmitting this news
both locally and colony-wide. That is why the *Boston Evening-
Post,* in the midst of news of political unrest and potential revolution in 1775, could also state, "Upon a strict Enquiry no one has
the Distemper in Town."[109] News of disease was important to the
colonial citizen, and the newspapers met the need to know with
varied medical information.

Large numbers of colonial citizens died from smallpox and other
diseases during the colonial period, and many of those deaths were
no doubt attributed to God's providence. Religion played a significant role in the lives of colonial citizens, a role difficult for some
contemporary Americans to understand. As A. L. Morton pointed
out about seventeenth-century England, "religion and the Church
occupied a much larger part of everybody's life than it does even
of Christian believers today."[110] The same may be applied to the
English colonies of America. The question must be asked, however, how much of the religion of the colonial period was reflected
in colonial newspapers? The religiosity of colonial America, as
found in colonial newspapers, was not always obvious, but the
importance of religion in colonial life was still reflected in newspapers in many ways, especially in the life of one preacher, George
Whitefield. More than any other individual, colonial newspapers
followed the activities of this itinerant English preacher. Religion
and colonial newspapers, as will be seen, were intertwined with the
fiery orator for more than thirty years, producing some of colonial
newspapers' most hotly debated topics.

8

The Presence of God Was Much Seen in Their Assemblies

> That mankind have a right to be free in the choice of religion, is a truth that can't be denied, and is a privilege dearer to every sober Christian than any civil privilege whatsoever; and no authority on earth have a right to deprive their subjects of the same.
>
> —*Providence Gazette,* 13 October 1770

EARLY in October 1770, Rhode Island printer John Carter received a letter, its writer requesting it be printed in the *Providence Gazette.* Signed "A PROTESTANT," the writer was outraged that in such an enlightened time, the lands of people were still being confiscated by governments when those people refused to support the government-prescribed form of religion. "To take by force their estates from them, to support a religion or worship that they do not choose, is a piece of oppression that would make even a moral heathen blush," the writer stated about his own colony of Connecticut. "Yet many instances of the same have we had, and still have!"[1] In an era when Americans were in ever greater numbers calling for political freedom, "the free choice of their own religion," as the writer called it, was still being denied to some in colonial America.

For the residents of British colonial America, religion had always been a significant issue. Many of the first English settlers to cross the Atlantic made the hazardous journey for religious reasons, and religion was seen as a vital aspect of life. The Bible was the one book that almost every settler possessed,[2] and religious books and commentaries were basic items on any colonial bookshelf.[3] Parents insisted that children learn to read so that they could understand the Bible,[4] and colleges were begun in colonial American to train ministers.[5] Religion was, as Patricia U. Bonomi has observed, so entwined with life in eighteenth-century America that religion's mark was left indelibly on all aspects of life.[6]

This chapter deals with the religious news that was presented in colonial newspapers and seeks to determine if this all-encompassing power of religion was present in colonial newspapers. A sizable number of religious news items, however, does not mean that all aspects of the news in colonial newspapers were religiously motivated. Nor does it mean that the growing political fervor that captured the attention of many colonial printers from the Stamp Act crisis onward was rooted in the religious beliefs of Americans.[7] Newspapers in the colonial period, regardless of motivation for news, were a reflection of the society that they served, and they were stocked amply with religious news and news on almost any subject imaginable that was indelibly tinted by religion. In fact, colonial newspapers ran more religious news than any other news types studied except news of the sea and crime reporting, both of which contained numerous religious allusions.[8] Religious news was especially heavy in the 1740s when religious revival was rampant in the colonies. Newspapers studied during this decade in Boston, Philadelphia, and Charleston averaged thirty-seven news items per year on religious topics.

Although many eighteenth-century citizens would no doubt have credited much of the religious interest in revival and discussion of religious issues in print to God's providence, one individual acted as the catalyst for this explosion, and his name was George Whitefield. Whitefield revitalized religion in eighteenth-century America and captured the attention of the colonial press like no other individual. An orator of uncommon ability, Whitefield's first preaching tour, which lasted from October 1739 to January 1741, can be traced accurately through colonial newspapers, and every visit Whitefield made to America from that time to his death in Massachusetts in 1770 was noted in newspapers. News of Whitefield, as Charles E. Clark correctly pointed out, helped colonial newspapers focus their news content upon events that either originated in America or had an immediate impact on American readers.[9]

Americans wrote to colonial newspapers concerning Whitefield and the religious issues that surrounded him like no other issue of the day. Every movement that Whitefield made during his first preaching tour, every word he had to say, and how many heard those words ended up in colonial newspapers. And according to that information, no one divided the people like Whitefield. Some swore that "the Presence of God was much seen in the Assemblies" that he conducted.[10] Others were certain he perverted God's message, was out to swindle people of their money, and was intent upon robbing churches of members. They were convinced that the preacher was a persuasive orator "but never [were] of the Opinion that Mr. Whitefield was under God."[11]

Colonial newspapers carried on a relationship with Whitefield for thirty years, but the Grand Itinerant was far from being the sole source of religious information in colonial newspapers. Newspaper articles credited many events to God's providence, and religious liberty remained a source of conversation from about 1730 on.[12] Newspapers printed ordination notices of pastors, hymns, scripture passages, and sermons regularly. The religious nature of colonial governments also found its way continually into newspapers through calls for days of "Fasting, Prayer and Thanksgiving to Almighty God." The religious news of colonial newspapers demonstrates that most colonists were Protestants who brought with them to America an intense hatred of the Roman Catholic Church, a hatred that each generation continued to foster throughout the colonial period. In fact, the page one story in the first *Boston News-Letter* dealt with the threat that Catholicism presented to all British citizens.[13]

If, as Bonomi suggests, religion penetrated all aspects of colonial life, then it is only natural to assume that religion played a vital role in the life and content of colonial newspapers. Before discussing the religious news of colonial newspapers, it will be helpful to understand the nature of religion in the colonial period by gaining a basic understanding of religious liberty, the forms of religion in colonial America, and the nature of the Great Awakening. Understanding these concepts should shed light on the religious news that appeared throughout the colonial period.

RELIGION IN EIGHTEENTH-CENTURY AMERICA

Religion maintained a universal influence upon the colonial American citizen in both the seventeenth and eighteenth centuries, and for that reason, religion was an important motivator for most English emigrants who came to America. Most of these emigrants sought religious toleration, that is, the right to worship in their own manner instead of being forced to worship under a prescribed state religion. Although many would-be Americans left England in search of religious toleration, they did not really believe in the concept.[14] Most believed as did Presbyterian divine Richard Baxter who succinctly stated the common English stance concerning religious toleration when he said, "I abhor unlimited liberty and toleration of all."[15] Once a colony was established in America, the same intolerance for religious beliefs different from those who established the colony again arose.[16] The incongruent but somehow harmonious relationship between religious liberty and religious intolerance was maintained during the seventeenth and eighteenth centuries in both England and America, as J. Sears McGee pointed out, because every Anglican, every Puritan, every Presbyterian, every Quaker, and every Baptist "viewed the other from behind lenses strongly tinted by a particular ideal conception of true Christianity."[17] Each group wanted the right to worship in its own manner but generally denied other groups the same privilege because those other groups did not properly understand the gospel message.

Because of this varying understanding of the Christian message by those immigrating to America, no two American colonies possessed the same religious complexion, and the established state church became the preferred mode of worship for almost every colony.[18] Exceptions to the concept of the established and state supported church were rare in America, and the idea of religious toleration for the residents of a colony was almost unheard of, the colony of Rhode Island being one exception.[19]

Even though a measure of religious toleration was achieved in Rhode Island in the seventeenth century and in the eighteenth century in Pennsylvania as well,[20] efforts at obtaining free worship in America generally failed.[21] Toleration was accepted in the seventeenth century purely as a means of survival for a colony, and if a colony granted religious toleration to its inhabitants, ways were generally found to circumvent the right.[22] The colony of Maryland, established by George Calvert as a refuge for Roman Catholics, is an example. Maryland passed "An Act Concerning Religion" in 1649 calling for religious liberty, but by 1654, Protestant immigrants to Maryland banned free worship. This change was aimed at limiting religious toleration and directed squarely at those who practiced "popery,"[23] and anti-Catholicism was very prominent in colonial newspapers.

The slow acceptance of religious toleration may have been the greatest gift that colonial citizens gave to American religion, and its development may be observed in the religious news of colonial newspapers. But toleration developed within a religious system that differed in each region of colonial America. Puritanism was the religion of New England, and its congregational form of worship became the essential element of society and government.[24] The other form of religion of the colonial period that carried with it political power was that of the Anglican church, the prescribed religion of the Southern colonies that were founded under royal charters. These colonies had less religious structure than the Puritan colonies of New England, and Anglicanism became the competitor of Puritanism through the Society for the Propagation of the Gospel in New England. Slowly in the eighteenth century, all of the colonies in America became royal colonies, and the charters given to groups such as the Quakers and Puritans were terminated.[25] When the eighteenth century began, Quakers, Baptists, Presbyterians, and Catholics, as well as numerous Reformed Protestant groups from Germany and the Netherlands, could be found in America, and colonial newspapers sometimes dealt with events peculiar to each group. More often, however, the religious news of colonial newspapers addressed more general religious topics such as sermons and ordinations, items that tended to portray religion as a part of everyday life.

Theological arguments were not necessarily a part of everyday religious life in America, but they grew to become a part of it as Englightenment thought obtained adherents,[26] and the controversy surrounding religious revival and George Whitefield became important to Americans. The revival that Whitefield sparked created, according to Edwin Scott Gausted, a phenomenon from which "none escaped its influence or avoided its controversy,"[27] and Whitefield's contemporary Jonathan Edwards declared that the English itinerant's preaching was "so extraordinary and wonderful . . . it shall renew the world of mankind."[28] Not only did Whitefield rekindle religious fire and zeal in the colonies, he helped initiate religious schism as well. Ultimately, the Great Awakening produced what Sydney Ahlstrom called "the change in the standing order."[29] As religious groups began to divide, religious discussion became a central focus of colonial newspapers. Not ironically, this oft-heated discussion elevated during Whitefield's first two preaching visits to America, in 1740 and 1745.

The Great Awakening produced a tremendous change in the religious power structure of the period. Before the Awakening, Congregationalism dominated the New England scene, and Anglicanism was the preferred church of the South. Life was ordered for colonists in a neatly wrapped religious and political hierarchy.[30] With Whitefield and the religious splits of the Great Awakening, according to religious historian Harry S. Stout, social categories "were about to explode and splinter in many directions. . . . This generation would be forced to create from the fragments of a once-coherent hierarchical social ethic a more democratic configuration than their predecessors would barely have recognized or endorsed."[31] Divided denominations, new ones, clerics with less authority, and a social structure changing radically from the one known previously in the colonies ultimately would become more important to the future of America than the religious renewal afforded by the Great Awakening.

In the religious environment of the eighteenth century, colonial newspapers were born and grew. What they had to say about religion and ways that religion may have affected their content follows.

RELIGION AND COLONIAL NEWSPAPERS

Did religion permeate colonial news? Based upon the content of colonial newspapers, religion occupied an important place within society and affected some aspects of all types of news. Most leaders in colonial eighteenth-century America, as Patricia Bonomi notes, wanted and expected to build an orderly and reverent society based upon those leaders' preconceived notions of the church, the Puritans offering a prime example. But as settlers ventured out into the rigors of everyday life, fighting disease, Indians, the elements of nature, and foreign adversaries occupied more of the colonial American's time than actual church attendance.[32] Religion was important, vital, but every piece of news that appeared in colonial newspapers was not tainted with religious overtones. If it were, these religious connotations are lost upon readers from later time periods. Instead, there was news about religion, and there was news about important events. At times the two overlapped as in the case of George Whitefield or when the news of colonial newspapers asserted religious implications for an event such as the hand of God in an earthquake in New England.[33] At other times the news about certain occurrences was, as David Paul Nord observed, "simply the news" and completely unencumbered by any religious strings or implications.[34]

When colonial newspapers deal with religious topics, the subject matter of that news falls into five general categories. Within these five areas, one can see how religious thought shaped some opinions, and one can also observe how the politics of the day affected religious perception. Nowhere are these two facets of the religious news of colonial newspapers better seen than in the news concerning Roman Catholics. The way in which colonial newspapers treated Catholics is the first type of religious news found in colonial newspapers to be discussed.

Current religious and political thought also helped shape colonial religiosity. This second body of religious information found in newspapers is comprised of religious documents including scripture quotes, sermons, hymns, ordination announcements, political acts with religious implications, and the combined listings of burials and baptisms within a colonial town.

The third type of religious news deals with God's activity in the everyday affairs of his people. This news, which speaks directly of God's providence, has little to do with political affairs but everything to do with religion shaping the understanding of events. This type of news was much more prevalent during the first third of the eighteenth century than in the remainder, but newspaper articles were still speaking of God's providence in the 1770s. Within this section, the confrontation between Enlightenment thought and God's providential activity, as presented by colonial newspapers, is discussed.

The fourth body of literature on religion found in colonial newspapers revolves around George Whitefield. Whitefield affected news every time he visited America for three decades, but the massive amount of print about the English preacher in the 1740s demonstrates how one topic can absorb the news and crystalize the attention of a populace upon that subject. Political ramifications, religious implications, and hard news reporting may all be found in the Whitefield saga. With the Whitefield story, one observes more than in any other religious news of the eighteenth century just how vital religion was to the lives of colonial Americans. It is hard to imagine that a person could capture as much media attention as Whitefield, especially in a time when news moved by the day, week, and month rather than by the second, unless what the news discussed—namely the religion of a group of people—was of immense importance.

The final subject for the religious news of colonial newspapers is religious liberty. The issue of freedom of conscience in worshipping God was a topic of discussion throughout the colonial period, but the call for religious liberty was also a natural outgrowth of the divisions of religious groups that occurred as a direct result of the Great Awakening. Interestingly, newspapers, despite the move toward religious toleration during the eighteenth century, noted numerous acts of religious intolerance during the period, especially toward newly forming groups like the Methodists. The followers of the ideas of John and Charles Wesley were often held up to ridicule, and just as Roman Catholics, they were considered to be a menace and threat to the established religions of eighteenth-century England and its American colonies.

The Roman Catholic menace. The intense dislike of Catholics by the Protestant Englishmen of colonial British America was evident throughout the colonial period in newspapers. The dislike of Catholicism was no doubt the product of a two-fold bias. First, of course, was the general theological differences between Catholics and Protestants. The second reason for the intense dislike of Catholicism was rooted in the political situation of Europe. England had long been in political confrontation with France and Spain, both Catholic nations. Anti-Catholic news reports in colonial newspapers increased whenever there was a threat from a Catholic nation against England, and the anti-Catholic news did not necessarily have to pertain to any threat against England. Anti-Catholic news in colonial newspapers was presented to demonstrate the errors of Catholicism as viewed through Protestant lenses, and it portrayed both the Roman church and Catholic kingdoms as barbaric and inhuman in their treatment of non-Catholics.

Fear of a Catholic coup in Scotland and subsequently England spurred the first anti-Catholic news story to appear in the *Boston News-Letter* in 1704. Anne Stuart sat upon the English throne, and England had made sure with the Act of Settlement in 1701 that only Protestant successors could assume the crown of Great Britain. Anne was the last Protestant child of James II, who was forced to abdicate the thrown in 1688. But Anne had a half-brother, James III, who was Catholic, and many Englishmen feared that this "Pretender" to the throne would mount an invasion force and enter the British Isles in an attempt to capture the crown for himself.[35] The *News-Letter* apprised Boston citizens of the situation in the Motherland in an article about "the present danger of the Kingdom and of the Protestant Religion." Not only was the Protestant religion in danger in England, but according to the newspaper report, all of Britain was in danger of being invaded by the French with the express goal of a Catholic takeover of the English monarchy and French control of the nation. The story said:

Papists swarm in that Nation [Scotland] . . . many Scores of Priests & Jesuits are come hither from France. . . . That the French Kinch [King] knows there cannot be a more effectual way for himself to arrive at the Universal Monarchy, and to ruine the Protestant Interest, than by setting up the Pretender upon the Throne of England.[36]

Threats to the throne of England by a "popish Pretender"[37] continued throughout the colonial period, and news of these activities inflamed anti-Catholic sentiment in newspapers in America. In 1725, fears that the Pretender might recapture the English throne appeared in newspapers, but this time, the news ran concurrently with news of Catholic atrocities against Protestants in Poland. No doubt readers speculated that a Catholic takeover in England would produce similar attacks on English-speaking Protestants. When Catholic-backed troops entered the Polish town of Thorn, the *American Weekly Mercury* reported, numerous citizens had their hands and heads chopped off in the public square. The executed were then drawn and quartered and left around the town.[38] Two weeks later, the *Mercury* stated that "many Lutherans fall a Sacrifice of their Implacable Enemies the Papists."[39]

The news of the Catholic treatment of the Lutherans in Thorn was followed by other accounts of Catholic action against Protestants, all of which reinforced the potential dangers Protestants believed they saw in Catholics. In Paris, a news report said, children suspected of being Protestant were forced into convents to ensure that they would never be Protestant.[40] Fears of a political takeover of the English government by Catholic-backed insurgents in 1745 led the colony of New York to pass a loyalty test for all citizens. The law strictly forbade all Roman Catholics from preaching unless they could swear allegiance to the Protestant government of England. The decree stated:

> WHereas an Invasion hath lately been attempted against His Majesty's Kingdom and Government, in favour of a Popish Pretender, and we his loyal Subjects of this Colony abhorring such traiterous Conspiracies, and being desirous to prevent the machinations of all Emissaries of that Kind, and to secure this his majesty's Government, as much as in us lies to prevent the Ignorant and Unwary from being led away by Jesuitical and other Pretences of vagrant Teachers: It is therefore Enacted . . . That no vagrant Preacher, Moravian or disguised Papist, shall preach or teach either in publick or private, without first making the Oaths appointed by this Act.[41]

The *Boston Evening-Post*'s printer, Thomas Fleet, added his own anti-Catholic comment after the story on the New York law, asking, "Query, Whether there is not as much or more Reason for passing such an Act in some other Colonies, as in that of New-York?"[42]

The fears of a Roman Catholic takeover of England and her colonies through war efforts by the French or Spanish almost always led to anti-Roman Catholic propaganda in colonial newspapers. When England and Spain went to war in 1739, for example, newspapers in America noted the evil way that Catholic nations treated their Protestant citizens. In Cuba, the *American Weekly Mercury* reported, a Protestant missionary was burned alive using green wood in order to increase the pain inflicted. The news report continued that such torture awaited all Protestants who stood in the way of Spanish Catholic conquest. "No Religion can be propagated by Cruelty and the Sword," the article concluded, but they were "always the Spaniards Method."[43] Newspapers in the colonies were already carrying news about Spanish attacks upon English sailing ships before the war with Spain was ever declared, and the fear of imminent attack in the Southern colonies led to a build-up of fortifications and militia activity, especially in South Carolina.[44] There can be little doubt that news items like the one in the *Weekly Mercury* and essays such as "The Wiles of Popery" that appeared in the *South-Carolina Gazette*[45] helped fuel fear of the Spanish and increase anti-Catholic sentiment.

The news of the evils perpetrated by Catholics began to grow again as French and English hostilities gathered momentum in the mid-1740s, culminating in the French and Indian War (1754–1763). A Catholic priest in Charleston, the *Pennsylvania Gazette* related in 1745, was arrested and charged with conspiracy to burn the town and murder some of its citizens. "He has confessed enough to hang himself," the article stated.[46] The inhuman conditions found in nunneries were described,[47] and articles told that within nunneries captured Protestant women were "whip'd . . . every day with a cat of nine tails, 'till . . . forced into a compliance" with the Roman Catholic religion.[48] Newspaper stories continued to report all sorts of torture and hostility by Catholics against Protestants and even against other Catholics.[49] The reports of Catholic cruelty led to calls for more suppression of Catholics in America and heightened anti-Catholic sentiment when the fighting with the French and Indians escalated in America in 1755. The *Maryland Gazette,* at this time, issued a warning on the dangers of Catholicism in America. In the colony begun as a haven for Roman Catholics, this condemnation of the Roman religion no doubt summed up the feelings of most Protestants in America about the dangers of allowing Roman Catholics into the colonies:

I utterly detest PERSECUTION, on Account of PRIVATE SENTIMENTS in Religion; but there is a wide Difference between THAT and nursing up a Sett of People, who are infatuated till they believe it their DUTY to cut our Throats in Return, and that it is meritorious, and even doing Honour and Service to the All-merciful GOD, for them so to do.

The tender Mercies of the ROMAN CATHOLICS towards HERE-TICS (when in Power) are known to be VERY CRUELTIES. . . . This Nation has found it ABSOLUTELY NECESSARY to restrain RO-MAN CATHOLICS by Law, from sitting in either House of Parliament, from voting for Members of Parliament, from holding any Office or Place of Trust or Profit, from PUBLIC Schools and Mass-houses. . . . But I greatly fear not one of those Laws extends to our Colonies in AMERICA, where they would be MORE NECESSARY.[50]

The French menace was defeated by English and American forces, and by 1763, the French were legally removed from America, even though some French activity continued in the lands west of the Appalachian Mountains. England and the American colonies experienced no more large and united military efforts against them by their Catholic foes during the remainder of the colonial period. Following the French and Indian War, the Ameri-can colonies entered into a period of growing hostilities with an-other enemy, England. Ironically, it was to Catholic nations that the American colonies turned for aid once the Revolution began, demonstrating either that religious tolerance had become more ac-cepted in America by the 1770s or that in the politics of war, the availabiltiy of aid, not religious stripe, produces allies.

Even though Americans of the revolutionary period could sepa-rate religion and military aid, religion and politics were not always separate entities in colonial America. The religious activity of colo-nial governments as found in political decrees is but one of the many examples of the religiosity of colonial America that appeared in colonial newspapers.

Documents of colonial religiosity. Colonial Americans demon-strated their religious beliefs in newspapers in a number of ways. One way was to insert scripture, sermons, and hymns into the newspapers so that they might be shared with all readers. Other ways included weekly tabulations of those baptized and announce-ments of ordinations of preachers.[51] Political decrees based on reli-gious requirements were also prominent during the colonial period. In cities like Boston, dozens of churches existed, and newspapers were an excellent way to share what went on in a particular church with others. These documents of religiosity affirm the fact that colonial Americans were a religious people with no less than 60 percent of them regularly attending church services in the eigh-teenth century.[52]

Scriptural interpretation inserted into newspapers allowed parts of the Bible to fit the colonial situation, as an adaptation of Psalm 23 did. In the colonial version, the shepherd provided food and sustenance that turned the new wilderness of America into a blessed place:

> The Lord my Pasture shall prepare,
> And feed me with a Shepher'd Care:
> His Presence shall my Wants supply,
> And guard me with a watchful Eye;
> My Noon day Walks he shall attend,
> And all my Mid-night Hours defend. . . .
> Tho' in a bear and rugged Way,
> Through devious lonely Wilds I stray,
> Thy Bounty shall my Pains beguile:
> The barren Wilderness shall smile
> With sudden Greens and Herbage crown'd,
> And Streams shall murmur all around.[53]

Hymns were often written and sung in order to fit whatever might be troubling people, and a hymn sung in New York in 1760 demonstrates that fact. This hymn, referring to God's claiming of the Promised Land for the Hebrews, rang with the surety that God would do the very same for his "Chosen People" in America to help them defeat the French and Indian enemy:

> When thou wentest thro' the wilderness the Earth shook.
> Thou dist march through the Land in indignation,
> thou didst thresh the Heathen in thin anger.
> Thou wentest forth for the salvation of thy People,
> ev'n for the salvation of thine anointed.[54]

Hymns also proclaimed times of joy and important events within the life of the church[55] and reinforced biblical beliefs such as the creation,[56] the significance of God's gift of his son,[57] God's mercy,[58] the saving power of Jesus,[59] and the second coming of Christ.[60]

Telling what sermons were preached on a Sunday, the scripture topic, and the preacher was a common feature of colonial newspapers. Sometimes these notices gave a brief exposition of what was said, but usually they contained only a comment about the quality of the sermon such as the "Excellent Sermon on 1 Thes. 4.11" that Reverend Pemberton preached in Boston in 1704[61] or the "very pertinent Discourse at the King's Chapel" reported by the *Pennsylvania Gazette* in 1740.[62]

Sermons, religious documents, and actions taken by church con-

gregations inserted into newspapers were also politically motivated, and as disharmony with England grew in America, ministers
increasingly, according to sermons and hymns in colonial newspapers, turned their efforts toward affirming and supporting revolt
against English rule. Following the Boston Massacre and the growing troubles with England, the *Providence Gazette* noted in a hymn
entitled "The CHRISTIAN SOLDIER," that "the GREAT CAP-
TAIN you have chose Never did a Battle lose."[63] Sermons printed
in newspapers even made it appear that God mandated both
fighting against England and obeying the Continental Congress.
Dunlap's Maryland Gazette ran a sermon in July 1775 calling on
God to "Save us not this Day" if the colonies were in transgression
against the will of God in rebelling against England. Far from being
against the will of God, the sermon reckoned, Americans had
"raised with an express view to perpetuate the name and glory of
that sacred altar" of God on which love of country and liberty were
what God wanted for his people.[64] The *Constitutional Gazette,* in
a bit of political and religious propaganda, printed a sermon that
explained how "the emigrants and adventurers first went to
America" to worship God, "Calvinists, Hugonots, Papists and
Protestants." They all, the sermon stated, "unanimously agreed
that no difference in opinion should disturb the public tranquility."
The "CONCORD" of religious unity, however, was disrupted by
England when shots were fired in Massachusetts.[65] Some churches
even went so far as to excommunicate members who refused to
abide by the laws of America lately drawn up by the Continental
Congress.[66]

Religious sermons were politically inspired in America, and political actions were religiously motivated throughout the eighteenth
century, although religion played a larger part in political activities
in the first third of the century. Legislation, according to colonial
newspapers, addressed moral issues and made everything from
selection of ministers to recreation activities a religiously motivated political issue. When a Springfield, Massachusetts, church
lost its preacher, it selected a new one according to "Province
Law."[67] In 1730, Massachusetts Governor Jonathan Belcher not
only outlawed the playing of any games on Sunday, he also mandated that all citizens attend church and be imprisoned if found
cursing, drinking, or being lewd on Sunday. The governor said:

I do hereby strictly prohibit all His Majesty's Subjects of this Province
of what Degree or Quality soever, from Playing on the LORD's DAY
at any Game whatsoever; and do hereby Command and Require them

decently and reverendly to attend the publick Worship of GOD on every LORD's DAY, on pain of the highest Displeasure of this His Majesty's Government. . . . I do hereby strictly Charge and Command all Judges . . . to be very Vigilant and Strict in the Discovery and effectual prosecution and punishment of all Persons, who shall be guilty of Blasphemy, prophane Cursing and Swearing Prophaning the LORD's DAY, excessive Drinking, Lewdness, or other dissolute and disorderly Practices: And they take care effectually to suppress all Lewd Houses, publick Gaming-Houses and Places, and other Disorderly Houses.[68]

In 1705 the "Profanation of the LORD's DAY" was decried in Massachusetts,[69] and in 1775 activities on Sunday were still considered a violation of religious and civil law, according to a letter written to the *Connecticut Journal:*

THE Sunday before last as I was going to church, I observed a number of men sawing wood near the Governor's gate; and as I returned from church, several persons were skating on a pond in the common. Surely *these things ought not to be.* I hope in the future the civil officers, as well as others, will pay more attention to his Excellency's proclamation *against immorality.*[70]

Although most of the religiously-motivated laws that appeared in colonial newspapers were passed in New England, all colonial governments issued decrees calling for religious acts by their citizens. From *Publick Occurrences* in 1690 onward, governments regularly in the eighteenth century dispensed calls for "a day of solemn FAST, PRAYER, AND HUMILIATION before Almighty God" to the people of the colonies through colonial newspapers.[71] Governments called for days of prayer for numerous reasons: for relief from Native Americans and disease,[72] to gain assistance in war,[73] or to show appreciation to God for successfuly surviving another year.[74] When the colony of Massachusetts issued a call for "a Day of Publick Fasting and Prayer" in March 1720, the *Boston News-Letter* noted the results: "And it is very remarkable that the Earth before that Day extreamly wanted Rain in order to the Grasses Springing, having been a dry Season, on which Day we had a plentiful rain and now Prospect of a good Spring time."[75]

The *News-Letter*'s comment on the results of a day of fasting and prayer pointed toward God's hand in the workings of his people. This providential intervention is what almost all of the calls for fasting, prayer, and thanksgiving sought. The calls for public religious days by colonial governments only confirms the fact that religion was an indelible part of everyday colonial life and that these public days of worship point to yet another feature of religious news in colonial newspapers—the intervention of God in the lives of his people.

God's providence. When Benjamin Harris listed his reasons for beginning a newspaper, the very first one was so "That Memorable Occurrents of Divine Providence may not be neglected or forgotten, as they too often are."[76] Colonial citizens looked upon many of the events that took place within the confines of their world as divine intervention—the supernatural affecting their own physical world.[77] Calls for days of public fasting and prayer were a way that colonial governments attempted to use the collective power of the people to either get God to intercede for them in times of trouble or to thank God for already providing that assistance. In fact, Pennsylvania's governor declared in 1755 that keeping the people apprised of God's providence was the responsibility of government. In a call for a day of fasting and prayer, the governor's decree stated:

WHEREAS it is the Duty of every Government to keep alive among the People a just Sense of their entire Dependence on the Providence of Almighty GOD, and to remind them of the intimate Connection between the Divine Favour and Publick Happiness, between National Calamity and National Vice; in order thereby to propagate that since Love of Religion and Virtue, which, under the Christian Dispensation, is the great Means of recommending a people to the Favour and Protection of Heaven . . . I have . . . thought fit to appoint . . . a Day of publick Humiliation, Fasting, and Prayer.[78]

Colonial newspapers did not neglect acts of God's providence, and the intervention of God into the lives of the people could be both good and bad as an article in *Publick Occurrences* demonstrates. In the spring and summer of 1690, growing conditions had been so ideal that the colony of Massachusetts was looking forward to one of its best agricultural crops in years. *Publick Occurrences* made note of the fact and "looked upon [it] as a Merciful Providence."[79] When storms ravaged the region in 1704, the news report in the *Boston News-Letter* credited the event to "a sad Instance of God's Judgments" upon his people.[80] The idea that God intervened in the lives of people to bless them or to punish them in direct relation to their activities never disappeared from the news of colonial newspapers. One letter writer in 1770 labeled the burdensome taxes placed upon the colonies by Parliament as God's retribution for America's lack of religious zeal. The writer stated:

I apprehend that God is angry with the inhabitants of this land, for the sin of oppression, especially in matters of religion, and in meting out to us such measures as we have been meting out to one another, I mean those oppressive laws that have been made and executed, especially in this colony.[81]

God, according to colonial newspaper reports, could work for or against people in any manner he chose, oppressive taxes imposed on an unreligious people being but one of many examples. Another example of God's intercession took place when a pair of birds dove into the ocean for no apparent reason, according to an account in the *Boston Gazette* in 1735. The actions of the birds were credited to God because a poverty-stricken worker, Silas Remmington, immediately paddled out in his canoe and snatched the stunned birds from the water so that he might supply his family with a meal. He carried them home to his wife who promptly cooked them. The news item concluded with a neighbor asking Remmington's wife if she was not afraid to eat the birds. "No Reply'd the Woman, we are poor People and GOD has sent 'em us."[82]

Even though God was credited with demonstrations of his favor toward people, like the good fortune of the Remmingtons who were delivered from hunger by the meal from God, most newspaper stories that spoke of God's providence referred to God's judgment upon a sinful people. When bad events happened for which people could find no logical solution, an angry God often became the perpetrator. Cotton Mather, according to the *New-England Courant,* issued a call for a synod among the churches of Massachusetts in 1725 because the "Great and Visible decay of Piety in the Country" was causing God to invoke his wrath among the people through the "Growth of many Miscarriages."[83] Earthquakes in 1750 and 1755 were blamed directly on sinful people being punished by an angry God. In 1750, a *Boston Gazette* story concerning an earthquake noted "that it is every man's duty to give attention to all warnings which God in his mercy affords to a sinful people; such warnings we have had by two great shocks of an earthquake."[84] When Boston buildings shook and chimneys crashed to the ground in 1755 from another earthquake, a writer to the *Gazette* said:

Doubtless various natural Causes may be assigned for these extraordinary Convulsions; but surely no one will question the Agency of the supreme Power, who *maketh the Earth to tremble, and whose Voice Shaketh the Wilderness*—If so inconsiderable a Circumstance as the *falling of a Sparrow to the Ground,* is not without the Notice of our heavenly Father . . . it cannot be suppos'd, that such terrible Events, as the laying Waste large & populous Cities, which has been frequently occasion'd by *Earthquakes,* should happen, without his special Influence and Direction.[85]

Natural causes may have been to blame, but God put them into action, the writer explained in the next edition of the *Gazette.* Since the earthquake occurred on a Sunday, the writer speculated, God in his "infinite Wisdom" caused "natural and moral Causes [to] coincide." "I submit it," the letter writer concluded, "Whether it Be not rational to suppose that natural Causes operated to Effect at that Juncture, to awaken us to a more strict Observance of that holy Day."[86]

The entrance of the terms "natural Causes" and "rational" into the discussion of God's providence was important. During the eighteenth century, Enlightenment thought began to question the concept of God's hand in any human activity. Deist thought, which was inspired by writings such as John Locke's *Reasonableness of Christianity,* did not deny the existence of God or that he created the world. Instead, these rational thinkers believed that the law of nature now functioned as the controller of events. Events had to be explained through natural causes, not through God waving his hand and causing earthquakes to shake the foundations of cities or birds to fall from the sky to provide sustenance for hungry people.[87]

Questions dealing with reason and providence appeared in newspapers at various times. In 1730, a writer to the *American Weekly Mercury,* in an essay on the spiritual man versus the natural man, cast aside the case of the natural man without providing any real argument. "NOW the lowest Perswasion of Faith is higher, and of a more noble Nature, than the highest Perswasion of Reason; Because Faith is of an higher Principle, and of a deeper nature and Ground, than Man's Reason is," the essayist stated.[88] A decade later, however, a *Mercury* correspondent said anyone who accepted any action as possible that was not based in reason with provable facts demonstrated "Madness of the Brain."[89]

What often happened, however, in the debate on reason versus God's providence was a melding of the two into a religious stance that allowed for the possibility of God's providence but only if it could be rationally explained through natural occurrences, in much the same manner that the *Boston Gazette*'s writer explained God's use of an earthquake to punish errant people. The *South-Carolina Gazette* provided the portrait of this fusion of natural and providential in an essay entitled "A GOOD MAN." A good man, according to the essay, was first and foremost a Christian who was "neither atheistically profane, nor enthusiastically superstitious." This combination of rational thinker and religious individual was not to set "bounds to religion and circumscribe it to time or place," and he was to constantly enlarge his reason so that he could "knock off the shackles of ignorance and prejudice."[90]

Even though rational thought became the favored stance of many in colonial America, its proponents never completely discredited the providential news items in newspapers, especially when one considers the amount of news about religious revival and George Whitefield that ran in colonial newspapers. Whitefield provided copy for newspapers, and without a doubt Whitefield was seen by many as a man sent by God. As a New York writer, whose poem appeared in the *Virginia Gazette* in 1740 noted about Whitefield, "He comes commission'd from on High." For the next thirty years, God was working directly in America, according to the thought of many such as the writer from New York quoted in Virginia, because of the presence of an itinerant preacher, George Whitefield.

Covering the big story: George Whitefield. Everything about George Whitefield was "big news" in colonial newspapers. As Benjamin Franklin's wife wrote to him in 1770 concerning Whitefield's death, "You will see all a bought him in the Papers."[91] The same was true of Whitefield from the moment he arrived in America and began preaching. The amount of press coverage that Whitefield received may be attributed to several factors. First, as this chapter has pointed out, religion was of prime importance in the lives of colonial Americans. Whitefield offered a powerful religious message. Whitefield also provided ample opportunities for people to hear him. It is estimated that he preached eighteen thousand times during his lifetime, a large number of those sermons being delivered in America and that most Americans had at least one opportunity to hear him speak.[92] But much of the news in papers concerning Whitefield was the product of good public relations. Whitefield traveled with an entourage, and at least during his first preaching tour in 1740, his companion William Seward wrote news accounts of Whitefield's revivals and submitted them to newspapers where Whitefield was currently preaching and to the newspapers in the next major city that he planned to visit.[93] For these reasons, the activities of Whitefield were in the news.

Understanding Whitefield's popularity also requires understanding the nature of the man, his message, and his relationship with America. Whitefield's American experience began when this son of innkeeper parents became associated with John and Charles Wesley at Pembroke College, Oxford. The trio ventured to America in 1738 to evangelize the newly founded Georgia colony. The group soon returned home, and Whitefield vowed to come back and establish an orphanage. Before returning to America, however, Whitefield tried his hand at outdoor preaching to capitalize on his powerful voice. The results were astonishing. Thousands crowded into fields to hear the young Anglican preach.[94]

Whitefield's preaching revolved around the Calvinistic concept of total depravity, or man's inability because of sin to ever know or reach God. Whitefield built this message into his preaching to elicit the response, "What must I do to be saved?" from his audience. Whitefield's answer was receive God's grace through Jesus. As a revival speaker, Whitefield spoke to his hearers as one who had asked the same question of himself. He spoke to their hearts and minds in language they understood.

Whitefield never tied himself to one local church even though he was an Anglican minister. He preferred to spread the gospel as an itinerant, and his success as a traveling evangelist earned him the title the "Grand Itinerant." Because his message was oral, Whitefield chose to speak extemporaneously. He selected his biblical passages and then began to weave his message with a pattern that captivated his listeners. Whitefield would deliver the message and move on, delivering the same concepts in the same basic form to the next set of eager ears. Benjamin Franklin described Whitefield's approach:

> By hearing him often I came to distinguish easily between sermons newly composed and those which he had often preached in the course of his travels. His delivery of the latter was so improved by frequent repetitions that every accent, every emphasis, every modulation of voice was so perfectly well turned and well placed that without being interested in the subject one could not help being pleased with the discourse. . . . This is an advantage itinerant preachers have over those who are stationary.[95]

From 1739 to his death in 1770, Whitefield made seven preaching trips to the colonies. As Harry S. Stout correctly pointed out, with Whitefield "a new form of mass communications appeared in which people were encouraged—even commanded—to speak out concerning the great work of grace in their souls. . . . The audience thrilled not only to the gospel message it heard but also to their own great power visibly manifested in mass assembly."[96] Because

Whitefield produced this kind of response in people, Isaiah Thomas said of him in *The History of Printing in America:*

> This celebrated itinerant preacher, when he visited America, like a comet drew the attention of all classes of people. This blaze of ministration was extended through the continent, and he became the common topic of conversation from Georgia to New Hampshire. All the newspapers were filled with paragraphs of information respecting him, or with pieces of animated disputation pro or con.[97]

With a person of Whitefield's renown, it was only logical that news of him reached America before he did.[98] When Whitefield himself arrived in America in November 1739, newspapers followed his travels by horseback from Philadelphia to Charleston. Along the way, the Grand Itinerant stopped to preach in selected towns such as Williamsburg, Virginia, and Edenton, North Carolina.[99] Once Whitefield arrived in South Carolina in January 1740 and begin his revivals and fund-raising efforts for an orphan house in Georgia, news surrounding his activities increased.

News of George Whitefield changed the priorities of news content in colonial newspapers. With Whitefield, news started to focus more on items of local or intercolonial significance. News of Whitefield's activities in Charleston, Williamsburg, New York, and Boston, for example, became news with which the citizens of Philadelphia were concerned, and the amount of religious news that appeared in the *Pennsylvania Gazette* in 1740 compared to 1735 supports this view. In 1735, the *Gazette* ran sixteen religious news items, accounting for less than 4 percent of the news types that comprise this study. In 1740, the number of religious articles increased to sixty-two, slightly less than 18 percent of the *Gazette*'s weekly output of the same types of news. An identical pattern of increased religious news was repeated in Charleston and Boston. The *South-Carolina Gazette* ran five items of purely religious news in 1735 and forty-eight in 1740, an increase in the religious content from 1.7 percent to 15.7 percent of the news types studied. In Boston, where Whitefield arrived in late September 1740, the controversy concerning him and his brand of religion burned for the next five years.[100] When the Grand Itinerant returned in 1745 for his second preaching tour, he spent much of his time in New England, and the newspapers were filled with discussion of Whitefield and religion. The *Boston Evening-Post*'s religious content jumped from twenty-nine items in 1740 to sixty-eight in 1745, and the *Boston Gazette* ran a similar number of religious news items, sixty-six, in 1745. In both newspapers, the religious news items comprised approximately 20 percent of the news types of this study that were printed in 1745.

Whitefield not only changed the priorities of what was in colonial newspapers, he also changed the nature of the other material printed by colonial printers, no doubt based in part on the interest in Whitefield newspaper articles produced. In 1738, there were a total of 133 imprints made by colonial printers, only 56 of which were on religious topics. By the end of 1741, the total number of imprints had grown to 241, and 146 of those printings dealt with religious subjects. Religious imprints had grown from slightly more than 40 percent of the total publications to slightly more than 60 percent of all publications.[101]

With such intense interest in religious news in general and in Whitefield in particular, it was only natural that all eleven colonial newspapers that were being printed in 1740 carried items on Whitefield's preaching, his message, and the controversy that he spawned. The *Pennsylvania Gazette,* however, carried the most thorough coverage of the Anglican preacher. That may have been because Whitefield and *Gazette* printer Benjamin Franklin were friends,[102] because Philadelphia was more centrally located, served as Whitefield's base of American operations, and received more information on Whitefield, or it may have been because Franklin was a better newsman than his contemporaries, realizing Whitefield was current news of immense interest to readers. All three reasons are probably true.

Whenever possible during 1740—which was usually weekly—the *Pennsylvania Gazette* issued announcements about Whitefield that told where the revivalist was currently preaching, the number of people who heard him, the amount of money that had been raised for the proposed orphanage in Savannah, and his itinerary for the upcoming days. Typical of those news items was one that appeared in April 1740. It said:

> The middle of last Month the Rev. Mr. WHITEFIELD was at Charleston, and preached there five Times, and collected at one Sermon Seventy Pounds Sterling, for the Benefit of the Orphan-House in Georgia; And on Sunday last . . . he landed at New-Castle, where he preached Morning and Evening. On Monday Morning he preach'd to about 3000 at Wilmington, and in the Evening arrived in this City: on Tuesday Evening he preach'd to about 8000 on Society-Hill. . . . Tomorrow Morning he preaches at Whitemarsh, and in the Evening at Germantown.[103]

The numbers of people who heard Whitefield preach at one time may have been the most remarkable of the news about the 1740 preaching tour. The *Pennsylvania Gazette* reported that fifteen thousand heard Whitefield's farewell sermon in New York,[104] while the *New-England Weekly Journal* put the number in attendance at Whitefield's farewell discourse on Boston's common at twenty-three thousand.[105] Franklin, after attending one Whitefield's outdoor revivals, estimated that more than thirty thousand could have heard Whitefield speak at any one time because of his powerful voice.[106] Such extraordinary claims for those who heard Whitefield preach were challenged by his adversaries. An angry writer to the *Pennsylvania Gazette* charged that the number of people reported attending a Whitefield sermon "are always exaggerated, being often doubled and sometimes trebled."[107] A letter from Charleston that ran in the *New-York Weekly Journal* said that many of the reports of Whitefield's preaching that had come from South Carolina were lies because the itinerant was in meetings with members of the Anglican church when he was reported to have been traveling the colony preaching.[108] Not only were the numbers in attendance and the amount of times that Whitefield had preached lies, letter writers said, but so, too, was much that Whitefield had to say. An angry writer to the *South-Carolina Gazette* insisted that Whitefield was nothing more than a liar out for his own gain.[109]

The issue of how many people actually heard Whitefield preach was but a small part of the controversy surrounding the itinerant preacher in 1740 that found its way into colonial newspapers. Whitefield, the *South-Carolina Gazette* reported, angered Anglicans in South Carolina when the visiting preacher, himself a Church of England minister, refused to use the Church's liturgy to conduct services,[110] something Whitefield also did when passing through Virginia.[111] Whitefield further alienated Anglicans by attacking Archbishop John Tillotson, whose preaching and theology were greatly copied by English preachers in the eighteenth century. Whitefield charged that the Archbishop, who died in 1694, knew no more about Christianity than Mahommed.[112] These charges led to Whitefield being banned from the Anglican pulpit in Philadelphia,[113] something no newspaper reported. Whitefield alienated large numbers of Southerners when he issued a letter "to the Inhabitants of Maryland, Virginia, North and South Carolina" calling their practice of owning slaves a sin against God.[114]

In May 1740, the validity of the news surrounding Whitefield was again brought into question. A news item in the *Pennsylvania Gazette* reported:

Since Mr. Whitefield's Preaching here, the Dancing School, Assembly and Concert Room have been shut up, as inconsistent with the Doctrine of the Gospel: An though the Gentleman concern'd caus'd the Door to be broke open again, we are inform'd that no Company came the last Assembly Night.[115]

The next week, a letter appeared accusing William Seward, Whitefield's traveling companion, of sealing the doors and writing the news item to further Whitefield's purposes on return to England. The biting letter charged that Seward

shut up the Door of the Concert Room . . . on the 16th of April. No one can wonder at his low Craft, in getting this Paragraph foisted into the News Papers just before his Departure for England, in order to carry it along with him, and spread his Master's Fame. . . . Nor is this the only Instance of Misrepresentation in Favour of Mr. Whitefield's Success. . . . And considering that these Accounts are said to be put in the Papers by themselves, are they not a further Specimen of their little Regard to Truth? Nay, are they not a Demonstration that these Men have other Designs in View than are agreeable to their Pretenses?[116]

The controversy in Philadelphia continued throughout May with Franklin himself getting into the fray and admitting that he inserted the news item on Whitefield at the insistence of Seward. Franklin even admitted that the story may not have been true:

In my last at the Request of Mr. Seward, I inserted an Article of News, relating to the shutting up of the Concert Room, &c . . . for tho' the Article allow'd to be literally true, yet by the Manner of Expression 'tis thought to insinuate something that is not, viz. That the Gentlemen forbore meeting in the Night mentioned, thinking such Entertainments inconsistent with the Doctrine of the Gospel.[117]

The controversy over the dance hall also appeared in newspapers in Boston[118] and Charleston.[119]

The concert hall controversy produced negative publicity for Whitefield but nothing like the turmoil and trouble that awaited the twenty-five-year-old preacher in Boston. Whitefield arrived in Boston on 18 September and immediately began to preach in the churches and common areas of the Massachusetts city.[120] A week later, an afternoon sermon was planned for the Reverend Mr. Checkley's meetinghouse. Instead of hearing a sermon, the people were greeted with tragedy, and newspapers all over colonial

America picked up the report, described in vivid detail by Thomas Fleet in the *Boston Evening-Post:*

> Last Monday about Four O'Clock after Noon, a most melancholy and surprising Accident happen'd here, viz. The Rev. Mr. Whitefield being to preach in the Rev. Mr. Checkley's Meeting-House, the People crowded so thick into it, that before the Time of Mr. Whitefield's coming, the Galleries were so thronged, that many People apprehended some Danger of their falling; and being thus pre-posses'd with Fear, and a Board on which several People stood, breaking, the Word was soon given by some ignorant and disorderly persons, that the Galleries gave Way; upon which the whole Congregation was immediately thrown into the utmost Confusion and Disorder, and each one being desirous to save themselves, some jump'd from the Galleries into the Pews and Allies below, others threw themselves out at the Windows, and those below pressing hard to get out at the Porch Doors, many (especially women) were thrown down and trod upon by those that were crowding out, no Regard had to the terrible Screeches and Outcries of those in Danger of their Lives, or other; so that a great Number were sore wounded and bruised, and many had their Bones broke: Two married Women, viz. Mrs. Story and Mrs. Ingersole, and Servant Lad were so crush'd that they died a few Minutes after.[121]

Fleet followed the news item with an acerbic editorial comment, "And this morning the Rev. Mr. Whitefield set out on his Progress to the Eastward, so that the Town is in a hopeful Way of being restor'd to its former State of Order, Peace and Industry."[122] Fleet's comment about Whitefield's unsettling ways brought an attack printed in the next edition of the *Boston Weekly News-Letter*,[123] to which Fleet responded in his next edition by saying he meant no disrespect to Whitefield.[124] Regardless of Fleet's intention, the war between pro- and anti-Whitefield forces was now in full force in Boston, and no doubt the anti-Whitefield forces were fueled by the preacher's seeming lack of concern for those killed in the Checkley incident that was made known when Whitefield's *Journal* was printed and made available to the public.[125]

The controversy in Boston escalated again in 1745 when Whitefield returned, and the anti-Whitefield elements continued to find an open line of communication through the *Boston Evening-Post*.[126] The *Evening-Post* reported that a concerted effort was being made in Boston to keep Whitefield out of the pulpits of local churches. "Last Friday Evening," the paper informed its readers, "Mr. Whitefield preach'd the Lecture at the Old-South Meeting-House for Mr. Prince, notwithstanding his Promise not to invite Mr. Whitefield into his Pulpit. . . . We hear that a Man at Topsfield has lately been presented for breaking into the Meeting House . . . and letting in Mr. Whitefield."[127] Other newspapers, like the *Boston Gazette,* defended Whitefield against the negative news that they had "seen in the Evening-Post."[128]

One of the great controversies surrounding Whitefield in 1745 centered on the dividing of religious groups, something that was blamed on him in colonial newspapers by letter writers and was the reason why so many churches closed their doors to the itinerant preacher. In 1735, newspaper articles were calling for all religious groups of all persuasions to put aside their differences and join together in "an Union between the Churches."[129] By 1745, numerous religious bodies had divided, and Whitefield and his itinerant way of preaching was seen as the cause. A letter in the *South-Carolina Gazette* explained:

> It is not easy to conceive how this poor Country is pester'd with Itinerants and strolling Preachers: They pour in upon us like Egyptian Caterpillars. They sow Discord and Dissentions wherever they come, by exclaiming against the settled Ministers whatever Denomination they are of. They ask us what sort of Preachers can be expected from our Nurseries of Learning, which they say are covered with Darkness, yea Darkness that may be felt, tho' they themselves are Men of no Education. . . . They are always crying out stink, shewing putrified Sores, raw Bones, Infants wallowing in their Blood, flowing Corruptions, and boggy Sepulchers, all in a Quag-Mire. These Things they frequently discharge at our Tables as well as in the Pulpit.[130]

A writer to the *Boston Evening-Post* said "that Mr. Whitefield has been the great Instrument of causing the Divisions and Separations which have disturbed and rent in Pieces so many of the Churches of this Land." Another writer, whose letter appeared in the same edition, said that neither Whitefield or any "New-Light" that followed him was "a true Christian." And a final letter writer in the *Evening-Post* noted that Whitefield's use of meeting houses helped divide the people and proved that Whitefield would lie to achieve his purposes.[131]

By August 1745, the *Boston Evening-Post* noted that the religious controversy in New England had subsided a great deal.[132] The reason for the easing of tensions rested on the fact that Whitefield had left for Philadelphia.[133] With the end of 1745 and Whitefield's impending return to England, the great religious controversies surrounding him subsided in America. Whitefield returned to the colonies again in 1747, 1751, 1755, 1765, and 1770, but no great controversy surrounding the minister occurred during those preaching tours that took place during the years of this study, although newspapers reported on Whitefield's presence and his preaching during each of those revival tours.[134]

Whitefield did make one more tremendous splash across the pages of colonial newspapers, but it took his death to accomplish that feat. The orator, who had come to America as a bold twenty-five-year-old spark plug, was now sixty-five. Asthma continually bothered him, and after a prayer session in Newburyport, Massachusetts, he retired to his room, opened the window to get a bit of air, sat down, and died. The same newspaper that had been Whitefield's great nemesis in 1745, the *Boston Evening-Post,* proclaimed:

> It is questionable whether any one since the days of the Apostles, or even they, had more hearers, he having delivered above seventeen thousand Discourses, to five, ten, fifteen, & twenty thousand persons at a time, both in Europe & America.—He kep up his zeal and popularity to the last discourse, which he delivered the day before before his death to an audience of at least six thousand in open air. . . . He seem'd to have a clear view of the entertainments of another life; and would commonly converse so familiarly of death, as tho' he was a kind friend he was waiting for, and even long'd to receive the summons; and was unwilling to tarry here any longer than he could be serviceable to mankind.—Such was the character of the Person whose departure we lament.[135]

At least fifteen thousand people, the *Connecticut Journal* reported, attended Whitefield's funeral,[136] and his obituary ran in papers throughout colonial America.[137]

By the end of Whitefield's thirty-year preaching affair with America, everyone in the colonies knew of the man and his ministry, and as Deborah Franklin wrote to husband Benjamin concerning Whitefield's death, the papers were full of news of the English preacher. The face of religion had changed in America during the period of Whitefield's relation with the colonies. Whitefield believed strongly in a free conscience in worshipping God, and his preaching no doubt helped to strengthen the concept of religious liberty in America.

Religious liberty. The colonial record of religious liberty as found in newspapers makes it obvious that religious liberty and toleration of various sects were relative concepts thoughout much of eighteenth-century America. As the writer to the *Providence Gazette* pointed out in 1770, some colonies claimed that the free choice of religion was available to all of its citizens, but in reality, the people of the colony were forced to support a state church or risk the loss of their personal property.[138] The treatment of Roman Catholics is also a prime example that talk of religious liberty and its application were understood in terms of Protestants only. Few people in colonial America believed in religious liberty in the manner of Roger Williams who advocated complete religious freedom for Roman Catholics, Protestants, Jews, Moslems, and even atheists.[139] Most Americans, instead, believed as Williams's contemporary John Milton did. "This is more Christian," Milton wrote in *Areopagetica,* "that many be tolerated, rather than all compelled. I mean not tolerated popery and open superstition, which, as it extirpates all religions and civil supremacies, so itself should be extirpate."[140] Milton placed limits upon religious toleration, and so did most colonial Americans. There was a continual suppression of new religious groups and ideas throughout the colonial period, according to newspapers.

Despite the fact that intolerance existed, the acceptance of liberty of conscience in colonial America did make inroads, and the move toward the freedom of religion later found in the Constitution's First Amendment is chronicled in the acts of colonies and religious groups in colonial newspapers. The fact that news articles about the suppression and intolerance of groups such as Catholics and Methodists ran concurrently with articles calling for religious liberty and with reports of acts of freedom of conscience supported by colonial governments only confirms the fact that the concept of complete separation of church and state was an evolving process, one that did not reach full maturity in the colonial period.

Intolerance was a by-product of fear and misunderstanding and as has been seen in the case of Roman Catholics produced an almost universal call for the suppression of free worship in colonial America so long as "papists" were involved. But colonial newspapers ran articles that demonstrated that Protestants in America were often intolerant of other Protestants as well. This intolerance occurred, as has already been pointed out, because all religious groups viewed one another through a strict "conception of true Christianity" that generally disavowed the validity of any other understanding of true Christianity.[141] Considering this fact, it is remarkable that any religious toleration ever was granted during the colonial period.

The strong theological lens through which various religious groups viewed life led to numerous confrontations, which were aimed at suppression. Anglicans attacked Presbyterians in 1707, the *Boston News-Letter* reported.[142] In Providence, Presbyterians were the target of an attack upon their meetinghouse in 1725. Just who the perpetraitors were was not known by the correspondent who reported the event, but whoever sought to stop the Presbyterians did so by putting "a stinking Sturgeon of about 8 Foot in Length" in the pulpit during the middle of the week. The rotting fish successfully ended the Presbyterian worship for the week because "it was so much corrupted and putrified, that it swarm'd with Vermine, and caused such a nausious Stench, that the People could not assemble in the Meeting House."[143] Quakers disrupted an Anglican service in Boston, and a Quaker minister—one Anne Flower—refused to let the Anglican minister speak, insinuating that he and his religion did not possess the true spirit.[144] And Congregationalists in New England suppressed the religion of Baptists[145] and Quakers.[146]

Other than the extremely strong aversion for Catholics, Methodists appeared to be the most detested religious group during the colonial period, according to colonial newspapers. The dislike for Methodism may have grown from the fact that John and Charles Wesley's method called for a change within the Anglican church, and religious beliefs that challenge or alter current practices generally evoke hostility. It may have stemmed from the ties between the Wesleys and George Whitefield, whose own evangelical system was highly disliked by many churchmen. Whatever the reason, Methodism added yet another lens for theological understanding in the eighteenth century, and as a new form of Protestantism it raised the ire of many other groups.

Methodism's formative period, 1738–1744, coincided with the Great Awakening in America,[147] and attacks upon the Wesleyan movement began during this period. Riots took place in London, a 1740 newspaper report stated, after one Methodist called the Anglican church "the Scarlet Whore, prophesied of in the Revelations."[148] Usually, however, the news reports on Methodists categorized them as foolish in matters of religion or as disrupters of the commonweal. The *New-York Weekly Journal* reported that the Methodist message had ruined the woolen industry in London.[149] A Methodist minister in Charleston was jailed for laying "dangerous Plots against this Province," the *South-Carolina Gazette* noted.[150]

Methodists were made to appear foolish in newspapers. One Methodist preacher, a news item said, led his followers to destruction instead of salvation. Saying he knew impending doom was in store for London, the minister, called Dr. Whimwam in the news account, led his people to the safety of a high hill. Instead of finding a safe haven, the followers of the Methodist preacher fell victim to an electrical storm, which killed and maimed many. The people then "set the false prophet on an ass, and led him, in derision; thro' the whole Town."[151] Readers also laughed at the foolishness of Methodists who gave their money to a robber when they thought the bandit was taking the collection.[152] When a respected individual announced his conversion to Methodism, an *Essex Gazette* news story intimated that the man had fallen prey to a demonic evil.[153] Newspaper reports described the intolerance of Methodists in a number of other ways. John Wesley was pelted with stones in Ireland,[154] and other Methodists were daubed with dung as they entered their meetinghouse.[155]

Even though little tolerance appeared to be shown for Methodists and some other religious groups, newspapers indicated that religious freedom was indeed making inroads in America. A strong statement on the concept of freedom of conscience appeared in the *Pennsylvania Gazette* in 1730. The essay stated:

> Every Man has a Right, a divine Right to interpret for himself. . . . If you consider what terrible Work the different Sentiments about the Meaning of certain texts have occasioned; how piously Christians, as they have affected to call themselves, have cut one anothers Throats by Turns, about hard words, and Sounds without Sense; if you consider, for how many Ages the most absurd Tenets have been forced upon mankind, and all who could not believe, or were not wicked enough to say they believed were burnt here, and doomed to eternal Flames hereafter. . . . A Spirit of liberty is growing amonst us.[156]

The concept of religious toleration was the basis for a call for unification of religious denominations in 1735. Although there were theological differences in those who believed in infant baptism and those who accepted believer baptism as the proper mode of baptism, a letter writer in Boston noted, "the very Essence of Religion" was the same for all. For that reason the people should be able to support each group and accept its adherents.[157] Freedom of conscience led to an extended battle in New York in 1755 over control of a proposed college for the colony. The colony's government sought to establish the college with control of it falling to the Church of England. The *New-York Mercury,* however, took exception to this plan, and printer Hugh Gaine fought against the proposal and for religious liberty through "THE WATCH-TOWER," a regular editorial essay feature of the newspaper. Gaine stated in one of his essays, "IT is evident that Religion of whatever kind, can have no other Connection with the affairs of civil Society, than as it has a natural Tendency to refine, and improve the Morals of its Members." Gaine was attempting to point out that a college supported by public funds should not, under any circumstances, be controlled by any one religious group, but instead be open to all religious persuasions.[158]

Toleration made gains in the colonies, and newspapers reported these small victories along the path to religious liberty. Jews were granted religious toleration in Pennsylvania in 1740.[159] Quakers, who had been hanged in Massachusetts a century earlier, applied to the Boston selectmen for the use of Faneuil Hall for a meeting. The request was granted according to a newspaper account, and both the positive response to the request and the sermon preached met "the Satisfaction of People of all Denominations."[160]

The final push for religious liberty prior to the Revolution came from Baptists, who never gained full liberty of conscience during the colonial period, at least in New England. Baptists, under the guidance of Issac Backus, mounted a political campaign against paying support for churches in Massachusetts. Backus, recalling the writings of his Baptist forefather Roger Williams, sought a complete separation of church and state.[161] In 1770, an announcement that appeared in the *Providence Gazette,* presented the Baptists' plan for ending the Massachusetts Bay system of taxes to support churches. The announcement called for all Baptists, instead of paying taxes "you have paid to build meeting-houses, to settle ministers and support them" to take that money and turn it in to the local Baptist association. If the money was continuously withheld by all Baptists, the plan proposed, then governmental support for religion could be broken.[162] Baptists received support from other colonies in their efforts to obtain religious freedom in Massachusetts. One writer to the *Pennsylvania Chronicle* praised Baptist efforts at attempting to solve the problem by first going through the proper political channels and did not blame them for their current plan of action. "I am sorry that ever any denomination of christians," the writer said, "when vested with civil power, has acted so far according to the best of their judgment, and the light of their consciences; or that any peaceable subjects . . . have ever been deprived of this privilege . . . on account of their religious opinions."[163]

By carrying essays on religious toleration and reports on the efforts of some religious groups to establish complete religious liberty in America, colonial newspapers demonstrated that sensitivity to the religious beliefs of others was slowly becoming a part of colonial life. In printing part of the proceedings of the Continental Congress in 1775, the *Essex Journal* related a debate in that body over religious beliefs and how the new government could be sensitive to those beliefs and still begin a war. The congressional debate declared:

> As there are some people, who from religious principles cannot bear arms in any case, this Congress intend no violence to their consciences, but earnestly recommend it to them to contribute liberally in this time of universal calamity to the relief of their distressed brethren in the several colonies, and to do all other services to their oppressed country, which they can consistent with their religious principles.[164]

Intolerance and tolerance stood juxtaposed in colonial newspapers and in the mindset of colonial citizens. Even though religious tolerance was not yet the law of the land, newspapers present a portrait of a people torn between upholding their own beliefs, which they were certain were correct, and allowing others to espouse a religious position to which they could not agree.

CONCLUSION

Religion was an important subject to Americans of the colonial period, as the religious news in colonial newspapers demonstrates. Religious implications were applied to news of war and natural disasters. Sermons, ordination notices, and hymns appeared regularly on the pages of newspapers. News concerning George Whitefield and the religious controversy surrounding him captured the attention of colonial newspapers like news of no other individual in the colonial period, and the religious news of colonial newspapers increased in the Middle and Southern colonies in 1740 and in New England in 1745 in direct relation to Whitefield's visits to those colonies. Neither the Stamp Act crisis nor any other political controversy for that matter ever completelly eradicated religious news from newspapers, and newspapers from 1730 on provided a forum for arguments for and against religious liberty.

But does news of religious controversy and individuals such as George Whitefield support the concept that religion was so pervasive in colonial America that it was the foundation of everything, including all the news? The answer is no, but the negative response must be qualified. Issues of religious liberty, God's providence, and countless insertions of hymns, religious poems, sermons, and scripture were not the only ways in which religion entered the news of colonial newspapers. Every type of news contained some religious elements. Ship captains gave God credit for rescuing them from a tumultuous ocean,[165] and providence ensured death at sea as well.[166] Colonial Americans saw Native Americans as both a punishment for unrighteous colonists[167] and as a fertile field of evangelism.[168]

The shock value of sensational news was based, at least in part, on the concept of divine intervention.[169] Crime in early colonial America equaled sin,[170] and newspapers reported that it was important for criminals convicted of capital offenses to die forgiven of all "past Sins."[171] The idea of a life for a life, which was the foundation for the execution of murderers, was biblically based[172] and rigorously enforced in colonial America according to newspapers. The basis for the proslavery argument of the eighteenth century was biblically based,[173] as was antislavery rhetoric.[174] The concept of women as either virtuous or vicious as displayed in colonial newspapers was directly proportional to their relation with God.[175] And it was God's providence that provided an inoculation for smallpox and other diseases.[176]

Considering eighteenth-century religion's role in all of these types of news, it is safe to say that God permeated the thoughts and discussions of almost all subjects of news in colonial newspapers, but religious implications were not present in all news stories. This omission of religion explains the qualified no for religion's role in all news. It would also probably be safe to say that religion affected a reader's understanding of almost every piece of news, even if there were no overt religious references in it.

Religion, according to the news of colonial newspapers, was as vital a part of colonial life as finding cures for diseases and protecting oneself from enemies like Native Americans. Most colonial Americans viewed a relationship with God as important to their well-being—and perhaps even more so—as finding cures to diseases or protection from Indians. If one was in proper relation to God, God's providence would be there to protect a person, newspaper stories intimated. The phenomenon of George Whitefield also lends support to the value and importance of religion. The news about Whitefield was like the news of no other person or event prior to 1740. Whitefield attained "star status," something he never relinquished in America for thirty years, and the religious news of Whitefield demonstrates how one individual or event could capture the media's attention.

Whitefield also helped shape the way colonial newspapers reported their news, and through him there was always a theological tint to news, even if news of Whitefield did not state anything other than where he preached. That is because during 1740, every newspaper—and consequently every citizen—became acquainted with this itinerant and his message. The effects of his preaching were visible for years to come, and in fact, as newspapers reported the divisions of religious groups, which took place at least in part because of Whitefield and the revival he sparked, they were reporting a change in America that would affect the future nation and its religious stance on toleration and separation of church and state forever.

One could say, as Deborah Franklin did, that news about Whitefield was found in all the papers, but that would also be true of religion in general. Religion was vital to the lives of most colonial citizens, and newspapers provided reports of religious controversy and presented news tinted by religious belief throughout the colonial period.

If God played a role in all types of news and religious controversy was a staple of colonial newspapers, it is safe to assume that religion affected even the smallest of subjects in colonial newspapers. This statement is true. Religion played a role in the news of weather, agriculture, natural occurrences, and in obituaries of colonial newspapers. These topics, the assorted news items of colonial newspapers, form the basis for the final section of news that appeared in colonial newspapers. As much as any large topic such as religion, they reflect the varied nature of the character and content of colonial newspapers.

9

The Chief Amusement of This City

A newspaper is like a feast,
Some dish there is for every guest;
Some large, some small, some strong, some tender,
For every stomach, stout or slender.
            —*Virginia Gazette,* 18 January 1770

In 1770, American printers published twenty-seven newspapers in fourteen different cities and towns.[1] Newspapers were expanding their information content in attempts to provide more timely material to readers. A triweekly, the *Massachusetts Spy,* joined the host of weeklies and the few biweeklies, as newspapers reached citizens in every colony.[2] By 1770, newspapers were providing colonial citizens with information on almost every subject imaginable. Perhaps realizing the growing power of the press, a poem entitled "The NEWS-PAPER" appeared in 1770. Many American printers, recognizing a good promotional tool when they saw it, picked up the rhyme, and applied it to their own editions. The poem proclaimed the newspaper as the only real source citizens needed to meet a multitude of purposes. Even though the poem may have been a promotional tool, much of what it claimed for eighteenth-century newspapers was true. The poem declared:

News'papers are the spring of knowledge,
The gen'ral source throughout the nation,
Of ev'ry modern conversation.
What would this mighty people do,
If there, alas! were nothing new?
    A New-paper is like a feast,
Some dish there is for ev'ry guest;
Some large, some small, some strong, some tender,
For ev'ry stomach, stout or slender;
Those who roast beef and ale delight in,

231

Are pleas'd with trumpets, drums and fighting;
For those who are more puny made,
Are arts and sciences, and trade;
For fanciful and am'rous blood,
We have a soft poetic food;
For witty and satyric folks,
High-season'd, acid, BITTER JOKES;
And when we strive to please the mob,
A jest, a quarrel, or a job.
  If any gentleman wants a wife,
(A partner, as 'tis term'd, for life)
An advertisement does the thing,
And quickly brings the pretty thing.
  If you want health, consult our pages,
You shall be well, and live for ages. . . .
  Our services you can't express,
The good we do you hardly guess;
There's not a want of human kind,
But we a remedy can find.[3]

As the poem "The NEWS-PAPER" intimates and the preceding chapters have shown, the information presented in colonial newspapers covered a wide variety of topics. The massive amounts of ship, crime, and religious news—along with large amount of political news—captured most of the space in newspapers, but news of sporting events, obituaries, poetry, agricultural news, and accident reports also appeared. No subject seemingly was ignored. In fact, the less frequently discussed topics in colonial newspapers often became "the chief Amusement of this City," which is the way one *American Weekly Mercury* story described the information it provided about a young man who was stopped from robbing his uncle's estate by the ghost of his recently departed relative.[4]

More than most of the major categories of news in colonial newspapers, the assorted types of news that appeared regularly in newspapers often served as both amusement and as valuable information to readers. This chapter covers the basic types of news that do not fit into any of the major groupings in colonial newspapers discussed earlier. These topics include: accidents, agriculture, animals, literature, poetry, oddities, gaming and sporting events, natural occurrences and disasters, social news, science and discoveries, and weather. In many instances the information presented in these categories overlaps, weather and accidents being one example where severe weather might cause a fire. In other cases and especially in the literary endeavors of newspapers, the subject matter may be drawn from other topics of the day, poems on George Whitefield, as discussed in chapter 8, being a prime example.

Many of the subjects discussed in the assorted news types of colonial newspapers contained entertaining elements. These news stories often presented information in a manner that made the information less important as news and more important as a diversion from everyday affairs. An excellent example is a weather report that appeared in the *American Weekly Mercury* in 1740. The news account related the severity of the Dutch winter and described it with several examples of just how cold it had been. As a piece of news, the report allowed newspaper readers to compare what they had experienced locally with a news account from another region. The report could have made Philadelphia readers thankful that their winter had not been as harsh, but the account from Europe worked much better as entertainment. The item related how water froze while being poured from a glass and how spittle froze before it landed on the ground.[5]

Other types of news discussed in this chapter, like much of the sensational news discussed in chapter 3, are concerned less with timeliness and newsworthiness than with providing information that could amuse or entertain readers. In this chapter, news of this type includes literature, poetry, oddities of nature, foolish actions by people, gaming, and sporting events. These news subjects are referred to as "entertainment" because diversion and amusement are their prime objectives, but it must be remembered that most of the assorted news of colonial American newspapers offered informational aspects as well.

While the amount of weather news and most of the other assorted news that ran in newspapers never approached the amount of news in the major categories of this study such as ships and crime, the body of assorted news in colonial newspapers was actually quite large. The *Pennsylvania Gazette,* for example, averaged about 130 of these stories per year from 1730–1770. And in some newspapers, accident reports, social news including obituaries, and pure entertainment pieces rivaled the larger subdivisions of news. The *Boston Evening-Post* never ran fewer than thirty accident reports per year in the years studied from 1735–1770. Weather news in the *Evening-Post* numbered between fourteen and twenty-five items per year for the same period. The *Evening-Post*'s Boston rival, the *Boston Gazette,* might have been considered Massachusett's social register in 1735 with nearly two hundred pieces of social news.

Social news in colonial newspapers, which included obituaries, birthdays, social functions, and marriages, was very popular in all major newspapers, averaging approximately forty news items per year through 1770.[6] The social news that appeared in newspapers served as the official notice of a marriage or death,[7] in much the same way that other types of information that appeared in colonial newspapers served as the official notice of an occurrence, too. It is, in fact, reasonable to assume that the appearance of most news that may or may not have been known by the residents in a colonial city became "official" once it appeared in a colonial newspaper.[8]

The varied types of news discussed in this chapter truly demonstrate that colonial newspapers were the prototype of American newspapers of the nineteenth and twentieth centuries because of the diversity of news topics and the value that such diversity possessed. A large assortment of news meant that a paper would appeal to a wider readership, and diversity of news led one newspaper, the *Essex Journal,* to imply that perhaps it carried too much news, more in fact than readers could absorb in a week's time. The *Essex Journal* declared:

> We have enlarged our Paper to such a Size, that not one of our Customers can find fault unless it be that it is too lengthy; which we shall endeavour to apologize for by making a collection of the most material pieces contained in the Portsmouth, Salem, Boston, Connecticut, Rhode-Island, New-York, Philadelphia, Maryland, South Carolina, and Quebec news-papers, which we are now regularly supplied with, together with those Original pieces our good Town and Country correspondents are pleased favour us with; and whose favours we still earnestly intreat.[9]

Although it may seem presumptuous for a weekly newspaper to claim that it contained too much news, the *Essex Journal,* as well as many other colonial newspapers of the 1770s, contained much more news than their earlier counterparts. New and smaller type,[10] more columns per page—the *Essex Journal* printed four per page in comparison to the usual three or two—and extended weekly runs through supplements measuring two to six pages increased the amount of news that colonial newspapers contained. Some newspapers, such as the *South-Carolina and American General Gazette* regularly ran eight-page weekly editions. Reading an edition of these expanded newspapers, therefore, could not be accomplished in one short sitting.[11]

The assorted news in colonial newspapers that focused more upon entertainment than upon timely pieces of information was presented in many different ways. Sometimes these items were short; at other times they were lengthy, sometimes extending over weeks and months. Colonial newspaper printers, despite the method of presentation, were fairly certain that they were presenting information that would capture the attention of readers. The character of the assorted news of colonial newspapers follows.

THE ASSORTED NEWS OF COLONIAL NEWSPAPERS

Newspapers, as information sources dependent on public acceptance, must provide valuable information and be able to capture the public's interest at the same time. The nature of the news is often sufficient to accomplish this feat, but colonial printers quickly realized that one story about the political affairs of Europe after another was not enough to pique the interests of readers. Certainly the *Boston News-Letter* as the only available newspaper in the colonies for the first two decades of the eighteenth century was able to get by without much variation in news types, but competition changed that. When the *Boston Gazette* offered competion to the *News-Letter* in 1720, Boston's older paper attempted to hold on to its readership by offering Bostonians a biweekly. Even though the attempt was not successful and the *News-Letter* returned to the weekly format, the attempt proves that capturing and holding an audience was important from the beginning for newspapers, and papers tried many different methods to obtain readers.

Samuel Keimer, who began Philadelphia's second newspaper the *Universal Instructor in all Arts and Sciences; And Pennsylvania Gazette* in December 1728, attempted to pull readers away from the *American Weekly Mercury* by printing pure entertainment. Week after week Keimer ran articles from *Chambers' Cyclopædia; Or an Universal Dictionary of the Arts and Sciences.* Keimer's last edition contained the encyclopedia entry on "Air,"[12] but readers rejected a newspaper devoid of any news that addressed local issues and full only of entertainment. Newspapers, in order to hold readers, had to diversify their content, and that meant providing news that was both informative, entertaining, and timely. John Mein's *Boston Chronicle,* for example, tended to overlook all news that had local relevance in the tenuous year of 1770, and Mein's biweekly, which began printing in 1767, failed to finish out the year.[13] Colonial newspapers had to learn how to balance timely information with entertaining news.

The information in colonial newspapers did not always have to be timely in order to be newsworthy or acceptable to readers, even though much of the assorted news of colonial papers was entertaining, newsworthy, and timely. But as Keimer's failed effort proved, printing nothing but pure entertainment was not a valid method for running a newspaper, a product that by its very name places the emphasis on news. Newspapers did, however, sometimes offer pure entertainment in the form of literature and poetry in lieu of current news, but this replacement took place more in the newspapers of the first forty years of the eighteenth century than after. Elizabeth Christine Cook was mistaken, however, when she argued that pure entertainment in newspapers was a welcome respite from the "stale news" of Europe contained in many newspapers.[14] Three-month-old European news was not always stale news in America. The key again for American newspapers was balance, balance between what was timely and valuable news that affected the lives of readers and what was entertainment. The most successful colonial newspapers achieved this balance; those that were less successful like the *Boston Chronicle* and the *Universal Instructor* died. The assorted news of colonial newspapers established a balance between timely news and entertainment as well. A description of colonial newspaper stories that primarily served as entertainment follows.

Entertainment. Entertainment news appeared in various forms in colonial newspapers. One of those forms was literature, and newspapers, Cook believes, were more important than any books in colonial America up to 1750.[15] Another form of entertainment that colonial printers ran was rooted in the humorous and odd events of everyday life. This type of entertainment was a favorite of colonial newspapers. These pieces were much baser in their appeal than was the literature and poetry that appeared in colonial newspapers. The *New-York Weekly Journal,* for example, was not attempting to stimulate the intellect of readers when it presented the details of a fight in Norwich where one man bit off the nose of another during an argument.[16]

Literary pieces in colonial newspapers were more the product of the first half of the eighteenth century than the latter. The reasons for this fact are several. First, there was less news arriving in colonial ports in the early part of the century, which meant there was more room for entertainment, especially longer literary pieces. As the century developed, the political situation of the colonies grew more complex, and newspapers began to focus more upon these events—the French and Indian War and the Stamp Act crisis being two examples—forcing pure entertainment to assume a secondary role in the content of newspapers. There were also more ships arriving in America in the middle of the century than there had been in the first three decades.[17] The desire for timely news and its growing inclusion in newspapers did not diminish the need for entertaining reading, however. Colonial Americans continued to read literature, but in books available from booksellers and from libraries that began to be opened throughout America. Savannah, for example, only thirty years after the first Georgia colonization efforts, had at least five major libraries.[18] The increasing availability of literature outside the newspaper, the growing complexity of the colonial situation that necessitated closer and more timely newspaper scrutiny of events affecting the colonies, and greater access for printers to news helped decrease the amount of entertainment in newspapers. Yet it is still important to note, even after all of this discussion, that stories that amused and provided diversions from everyday life decreased but did not disappear from newspapers during the colonial period.

The weekly essay was the most-often-used literary device in colonial newspapers. Copying the styles used by the essayists of England's *Tatler, Spectator,* and *Guardian,*[19] colonial printers ran pieces on many topics such as the good fortune of people[20] and happiness.[21] The *American Weekly Mercury* ran the "Busy-Body" series written by Benjamin Franklin for printer Andrew Bradford, while other newspapers applied other names to their essays such as "The Monitor" in the *Virginia Gazette* and "The Watchtower" in the *New-York Mercury.*[22] All of these literary essays did not deal with purely entertaining topics, however, and many of them were tinged with political and religious overtones.[23]

Running serials or weekly installments of pieces of literature was also a practice of colonial newspapers. From 9 October 1725, through the end of the year, the *New-England Courant* provided readers in Boston with weekly portions of *The Life of Jonathan Wild.* Wild, who had swung from the gallows as a common thief, lived an extraordinary life, and the weekly installments in the *Courant* allowed readers to follow the criminal's exploits around the world. The *Providence Gazette* used installments to tell the history of Providence Plantation over a three-month period in 1765.[24]

Because the newspaper offered an open forum to anyone who wished to contribute or pay for the insertion of information, literary works in colonial newspapers ranged from the works of the well-known to those of the obscure. The *American Weekly Mer-*

cury, for example, ran excerpts from Bacon's treatise on natural philosophy,[25] while in contrast, the *South-Carolina Gazette* presented notice that it would begin to present a series of literary works produced by a group of locals who called themselves "the Meddlers' Club."[26]

Prose was not the only form of literature that appeared in newspapers. Poets, also of wide-ranging ability, used colonial newspapers as avenues to make their works accessible to readers. The works of such notables as Shakespeare, Swift, and Defoe appeared in colonial newspapers,[27] and newspapers, in addition to printing the works of these writers, used their well-known lines for parody. Isaiah Thomas played upon the words of Hamlet in the *Massachusetts Spy* when the Boston printer pondered whether he should print an essay that might be considered libelous. Thomas declared:

> TO print or not to print—-that is the question.
> Whether 'tis better in a trunk to bury
> The quirks and crotchets of outrageous fancy,
> Or send a well-wrote Essay to the press.[28]

Poetry, unlike the extended serial, remained a fairly stable form of diversion and amusement in colonial newspapers throughout the period,[29] the "Poet's Corner" becoming a regular feature of many newspapers in the 1770s. The "Poet's Corner" usually occupied the top left corner of the fourth page of those newspapers that ran it.[30]

Colonial newspapers' poetry, just like its prose, explored many varied topics. Prolific poets such as Charles Wesley praised God and the work of men like George Whitefield in their poetry.[31] Yet for every work by a great writer, there were dozens of poems that thrust doggerel upon newspaper readers. As one poem dealing with having one's cake and eating it too crudely stated:

> All the few Cakes we have are puffed up with Yeast;
> and the nicest Gingerbread is spotted with Flyshits![32]

In another poem, a novice poet paid homage to his bed, the one place of solace that the writer had found throughout his life:

> THOU Bed, in which I first began
> To be that various creature, Man;
> And, when again the Fates decree,
> The place where I must cease to be;
> When sickness comes, to whom I fly,

To sooth my pain and close my eye;
When cares surround me, where I weep,
Or lose them all in balmy sleep;
When sore with labour, whom I court,
And to thy downy breast resort;
Where too extatic joys I find,
When designs my Delia to be kind,
And, full of love, in all her charms,
Thou giv'st the fair one to my arms;
The Centre thou, where joy and pain,
Disease and rest, alternate reign!
Oh! if within thy little space
So many different scenes have place,
Lessons as useful shalt thou teach
As Sages dictate, Churchmen preach;
And Men, convinc'd by thee alone,
This great important truth shall own,
That thin partitions do divide
The bounds where good and ill reside;
That nought is perfect here below,
But bliss still borders upon Wo.[33]

The poetry provided by aspiring writers to colonial newspapers also contained acrostics and riddles. A reader of the *New-York Weekly Journal,* for example, proposed in 1740 to provide the paper with monthly word puzzles for the entertainment of those who read John Peter Zenger's newspaper, the first of which proclaimed:

OF Seven Parts they me Compose,
I've many Eyes, yet ne'er a Nose.
I'm neither flat nor tall not thin,
Yet Women's Choice have always been.
I shun the cold and love the Fire,
Yet never to the South retire.
I often gaze on Man's Delight,
And have been with it Day and Night.
I never seek to find the fair.
To look for me is all their Care.
Yet such my fate in Summer's heat,
Slighted by all I then retreat.

In Winters Frost return again,
And with the Fair till Summer reign.[34]

The answer to the riddle, "The January Riddle I swear by jove, Is as blind with many Eyes as a Stove," was provided several weeks later,[35] but the rhyming puzzles were evidently not a favorite of the *Weekly Journal*'s patrons—or the author died or left New York—because they did not last six months.

Almost any event in the lives of people was a suitable occasion for poetry in colonial newspapers, but death sparked the largest number of poems about everyday life. Epitaphs and eulogies to famous individuals were common. The *Pennsylvania Gazette,* for example, carried a eulogy to the deceased son of New York's governor in 1750,[36] and many newspapers printed poems honoring George Whitefield after his death.[37] But eulogies praising the lives of less-known individuals were, naturally, more common since "ordinary" people outnumberd the "famous." The *Boston Gazette* printed an epitaph "To a young Lady lately Dead,"[38] but most epitaphs in colonial newspapers named the individual that was being eulogized. The poetry that followed an obituary was not usually of high quality, but it nonetheless provided diversity while honoring a member of the community no longer living. William Rind's *Virginia Gazette* offered a typical colonial newspaper epitaph following the death of Elizabeth Prentis:

> If love for worth of ev'ry kind,
> Which all can with; which few can find,
> E'er claim'd the tribute of a tear:
> (Here lies a maid whom virtue warm'd,
> With ev'ry pleasing grace adorn'd)
> Stop traveller and drop it here.[39]

Cultural entries, whether they were of quality or not, were joined in the colonial newspapers by another form of diversion, which appealed to baser instincts, made fun of human misfortune or mistakes, took delight in foolishness, and loved oddities nature produced in humans. These pieces also demonstrated a fascination for relics from the past, especially from the time period of the Roman Empire. Because this news generally played upon the mistakes and misfortunes of life, it held little intellectual value, but these stories no doubt appealed to a wider group of people than many of the more intellectual essays in colonial newspapers. These entertainment pieces also never lost their appeal throughout the colonial period.

When a Connecticut minister misquoted scripture in a sermon, for example, most readers probably received a hearty chuckle at the pastor's expense. "Verily, verily I say unto you," the preacher declared, "it is easier for a rich man to go through the eye of a

needle, than for a camel to enter the kingdom of heaven."[40] Making
fun of a preacher's slip of the tongue, however, was mild for this
type of story in colonial newspapers. The *Boston Evening-Post*
humorously reported the death of a woman who either fell or
jumped from a church belfry as an attempt to fly,[41] while a *Maryland Gazette* news item took great delight in retelling the story
of a gentleman whose physical features were somewhat less than
masculine. The feature called the man a "maccaroni of distinction"
and described his public humiliation at a concert.[42]

Personal and mental misfortunes by people were only part of
the news in colonial newspapers that focused upon amusement and
diversion. Newspapers were especially fond of demonstrating the
foolishness of individuals. Most of these stories were rooted in the
occurrences of daily life. The stupidity of over-indulging in alcohol
was often made apparent by colonial newspapers, and in one news
item, the "bravado of drunken heroism" was replaced by reality
when a shoemaker held his finger over a candle until the appendage
"was burnt to the bone." The reality of the situation, as discovered
the following day, was that the cobbler would probably lose his
arm because of his alcohol-induced foolishness.[43] When a sailor
made port in Boston in 1735, the *Weekly Rehearsal* reported, his
desire to find female companionship led the pair to a nasty rendez-
vous in a near-by "necessary House." To the lovers' surprise, the
floor gave way leaving the "Woman slumped up to her Neck in
Ordure" and the man seeking help to extract his lover from the
mire.[44]

The ignorance of people sometimes cost them money, newspapers reported. A New England "Country Fellow" lost his crop
of apples that was being brought to town for sale when a sailor
slipped the reigns from a horse to himself and gave the horse and
the apples to his friends. When the horse's owner turned around,
he saw a man wearing the bridle and was told by his "horse" that
a witch had changed him into a horse seven years previous. The
time of the spell was now up, and the man—who had been a horse
moments before—was returned to his original state.[45] Another
time, a group of fishermen mistook a sea turtle "for some hideous
Monster come to devour them," they attacked the creature with
axes and pitchforks, thoroughly mangling the nearly seven-foot
long creature. The story then declared, "Had it been bro't to Town
alive, the Proprietors might easily have made an hundred or two
Pounds of it: Whereas by their Ignorance and Folly in mangleing
it to Death, it was entirely lost."[46]

Oddities like the large sea turtle were not the only types of amusing features that newspapers presented. Newspaper readers evidently liked stories that told of human oddity and deformity or of longevity, and these news stories sometimes bordered upon the sensational. These pieces were no doubt popular for the same reason that sensationalism was so popular in colonial newspapers. What was presented in these news items removed the readers from everyday existence and placed them within a sphere that was surreal. What was reported was often shocking, but it almost always provided a brief escape from the realities of life. Newspapers told of a seven-foot woman in England,[47] a twenty-eight-inch-tall man in Maryland,[48] a woman who grew a horn in the middle of her forehead,[49] Siamese twins born in Barbados,[50] a three-year-old who was already four-feet tall,[51] and a European husband and wife aged 172 and 194 respectively.[52]

The fascination with oddities by newspaper readers was further pandered to with stories of the discoveries of relics from the past. A report coming out of London in 1765 declared that "the Existence of Giants is proved" after a grave of inhuman proportions was opened in France and the bones found therein had been studied by "Anatomists." "When the Tomb was opened," the story proclaimed, "they found a human Skeleton entire, 25 Feet and a Half long, 10 Feet wide across the Shoulders, and 5 Feet deep from the Breast Bone to the Back."[53] Also during 1765, readers were treated to another archaeological discovery in England, that of a cache of Roman coins from a campaign into the British Isles during the reign of Emperor Titus, 79–81 A. D.

One of the most amazing stories concerning the unearthing of Roman relics that appeared in colonial newspapers had nothing to do with the fact that the coins unearthed in the English countryside were approximately sixteen hundred years old but that the identical feature appeared in colonial newspapers thirty-five years apart. In 1735, the following story ran in newspapers in Boston, New York, and Philadelphia:

A few Days ago, a poor Man as he was working in a lead Mine near Wirksworth, found above 100 Pieces of Roman Silver Coin, being the Roman Danii [denarii]: The newest of the Pieces must be above 1600 Years old. The Busts of the five first Emperors of Rome appear exceeding full and clear upon several of them, and the inscription very legible.[54]

The identical story reappeared in the *Virginia Gazette* in 1770, only the location of the find had changed. The *Gazette*'s report claimed:

We hear from Cornwall that some time ago a poor man, as he was working in a mine there, found above a hundred pieces of silver coin, being the Roman denarii, the newest of these pieces must be above 1600 years old. The busts of the five first Emperours of Rome appear exceeding full and clear upon several of them, and the inscription very legible.[55]

Interesting stories where timeliness did not play a role in reporting were obviously worth repeating. And more than likely, few people would remember that such a news item had run decades before. The story could have also been circulating again through the countryside and made its way to London a second time. It is worth noting that the original story claimed "A few Days ago," while the 1770 version only said that "some time ago" the coins were discovered, leaving just how long ago open to speculation.

The denarii story was probably printed by Purdie and Dixon without any knowledge of the account that ran thirty-five years earlier, but the Williamsburg printers could have had a copy of an old newspaper from Philadelphia, Boston, or New York on hand, pulled it and provided the nebulous "some time ago" to the dateline. The insertion of identical news items so far apart chronologically, however, does raise the question of validity of news, especially of wild claims like that made for the discovery of giants that obviously were not true. Even though newspapers had improved the focus of their content by 1770 so that most of their hard news dealt almost exclusively with news vital to the colonies, readers throughout the colonial period had to trust that printers were presenting truthful pieces in their newspapers when the news originated from any region outside that of the reader.

Truth was no doubt less important in the amusing features of colonial newspapers than in hard news items, but even in much of the news that has been classified as entertainment that appeared in newspapers, the basics of providing facts applied. The who, what, when, where, why, and how was especially applicable in another type of news that offered a diversion from everyday life. That news dealt with gaming and sports.

Gaming and sports. The leisure activities reported in colonial newspapers generally pitted feats of strength, human or animal, against similar opponents, and betting usually was waged on the competition. The bets could be made by one of the participants, or they could be placed on those taking part. Races by men and horses and wrestling and boxing matches were the most common sporting activities described in colonial newspapers, but they were not the sole forms of sporting activities reported. Team competition was also mentioned in newspapers. The *American Weekly Mercury,* for example, reported that boys were playing football in the streets in 1725.[56] Cricket matches were also covered, and in 1735, the *Boston Weekly Post-Boy* provided Boston readers with what was probably one of the first true sports stories to appear in American newspapers when it described a London cricket match:

> Yesterday a great Match at Cricket was play'd on Bromley-Common in Kent for One Thousand Pounds, between His Royal Highness the Prince of Wales and the Earl of Middlesex, the Londoners playing for the former, and the Kentish Men for the Latter. . . . The Stumps were pitch'd, and the London Gamesters went in first, when the Betts were equal, and they got by their first Innings 73; then the Countrymen went in, and having but indifferent Success at first, the Odds turn'd to the Londoners six to four, however the Countrymen made 97, leading the others 24, which turn'd the Scale again: The London Gamesters at their second Innings made but 32, leading their Adversaries only eight, which they got, and beat them without one Hand being out the second Time.[57]

Newspapers also described individual sports competition. In 1750, the *Boston Evening-Post* related that two of Europe's best boxers would square off in a decisive third meeting between the two to decide the champion. The match was "to be determin'd by the most bleeding Wounds in nine Bouts."[58] In another fight described in a newspaper, the knockout came "14 minutes and 11 seconds" into the fight."[59]

Competitions on either the team or individual level must have been large social events during the colonial period, according to the way in which they were reported in colonial newspapers. The nobility in large numbers attended a boxing match in London in 1750, according to colonial newspapers.[60] Sometimes the sporting event pitted nation against nation, as boxing matches often did. In 1725, Boston newspapers reported an Italian and Englishmen squared off in Figg's Ampitheatre where the Englishman "beat his Adversary all to nothing."[61]

Almost all reports about sports in colonial newspapers spoke of the betting that took place on the events, and indeed, the gambling aspect was usually the most important part of the news accounts. One horse race in 1765, for example, brought bets in excess of £100,000, according to the *Boston Evening-Post.*[62] These competitions for money evidently took place quite often. The *Newport Mercury* informed its readers that "the Bull Horse, belonging to

Mr. Giles Sanford" had just won its eleventh straight race pulling in bets totalling "about 300 Dollars."[63] Cockfights, like horse races, were popular forms of entertainment that pitted town against town and animal against animal, and bets were placed on cockfights. The *Virginia Gazette* related one of these events to its readers in 1755. "The great Cock Match between Gloucester and New-Kent" was the way the *Gazette* referred to the competition that saw numerous bets placed on both sides with New-Kent winning the overall competition ten to seven.[64]

Betting, according to newspaper reports, was evidently a popular activity, and it increased greatly after 1750 because of the introduction of lotteries in America. Even though lotteries had been held in England throughout the eighteenth century, their general acceptance in America came later, partly because lotteries were illegal in some colonies in the first half of the eighteenth century.[65] Lotteries raised questions in American in relation to whether they were wholesale gambling by people or a means to raise needed funds for projects that were being undertaken to open schools and universities or to expand churches. The fact that so many lotteries took place in the last twenty-five years of colonial America's existence attests to Americans' penchant for placing wagers and to the fact that most colonials saw no great danger in purchasing lottery tickets. But Thomas Fleet of the *Boston Evening-Post* objected to lotteries, and he made them a moral issue in 1750 with an essay that attacked the evils of gambling:

> In short, a Gaming-Table is the School of Iniquity, where all the Vices of the Age are taught and practic'd; the Temple of Lucifer, in which Immorality and Prophaness, Drunkeness and Debauchery, Cheating and Lying, Rapine and Murder, have their Place of Residence; nor can any Man enter, without great Danger of infection: But what is still worse, the Distemper is of such malignant Nature, that whoever has the Misfortune to catch it, remains uncurable; for there is not one in a Thousand that ever recovers.[66]

In order to drive home his point, Fleet quoted from Massachusetts' anti-lottery law of 1719:

> Quere, Whether a LOTTERY is not the most extensively mischievous Sort of a Game? It is certain the General Assembly of this Province were of this Opinion, when they passed an Act for suppressing of Lotteries, in the Year 1719, the Preamble of which is as follows: Whereas there have been lately set up within this Province certain mischievous and unlawful Games called Lotteries, whereby the Children and Ser-

vants of several Gentlemen, Merchants and Traders, and other unwary People have been drawn into a vain and foolish Expence of Money; Which tends to the utter Ruin and Impoverishment of many Families, and is to the Reproach of this Government, and against the common Good, Trade, Welfare and Peace of the Province. And the first Clause in that Act declares, 'That all such Lotteries, and all other Lotteries are common and publick Nusances.'[67]

The arguments by Fleet and others against lotteries were overshadowed by those desiring to have them. At least one lottery took place in Boston in 1745[68] and another again in 1750.[69] Lotteries were proposed as a way to support America's war effort against the French and Indians in 1755,[70] used to build up the fledgling colony of Nova Scotia,[71] and employed as a way to remove political debt from a colony.[72] But most lotteries held in America raised money for benevolent purposes. New Jersey held a lottery in 1750 for the New Jersey College.[73] Philadelphia did the same thing as a means of support for its college the same year.[74] Baptists in Rhode Island held a lottery in order to gather sufficient funds to build a new meeting house.[75]

Newspapers were used to promote lotteries,[76] sell lottery tickets[77] and to announce the winners.[78] When all of a lottery's tickets were sold, newspapers ran the list of numbers and the amount of money the winning numbers would receive. A typical numbers sheet, pictured in Figure 2, ran in the *Pennsyvlania Gazette* to announce the winners of the city's Academy Lottery, used to support a new school in Philadelphia.[79] Those who bought lottery tickets could look at the chart to determine if their number was a winner. According to the Philadelphia Academy lottery, thousands of tickets were sold, and most winning numbers received a relatively small prize. Still, a sizable amount of money was awarded by lotteries, and the large number of lotteries that were held in America from 1750–1775 evidently means lotteries were profitable for those sponsoring them. Lotteries, like entertainment pieces and sporting news with gambling reports, were part of the social aspect of the colonies, but the social news of colonial newspapers encompassed more. Colonial newspaper social news served as an official ledger of events for the upper levels of the social hierarchy through announcements of social functions and especially deaths and marriages.

Social news. Social news, at least as far as numbers of items are concerned, represents a sizable facet of the news of colonial newspapers. The *Boston Gazette*'s nearly two hundred social list-

Prizes in the *ACADEMY* Lottery.

No.	Pz.	No.	Pz.	No.	Pz.	No.	Pz.	No.	Pz.	No.	Pz.	No.	Pz.
2276	5	2590	5	2919	5	3240	5	3513	5	3782	5	4117	5
80	5	95	5	20	5	41	5	14	5	87	5	26	5
82	5	2602	5	22	5	45	5	19	5	92	5	32	5
94	5	11	5	26	5	50	5	20	125	93	5	35	5
2301	5	12	5	31	5	51	5	22	5	94	5	43	5
6	5	13	5	38	5	55	5	26	5	96	5	45	5
10	5	23	5	52	5	58	5	28	5	97	5	48	5
18	5	26	5	63	5	59	5	37	5	3812	5	55	5
32	5	32	5	65	5	61	5	39	259	15	5	64	5
34	5	35	5	67	5	65	62¼	41	5	25	5	66	5
35	5	37	5	68	5	71	5	47	5	28	62¼	67	5
37	5	41	5	73	5	78	5	49	5	31	5	69	5
40	5	46	5	74	5	80	5	50	5	34	5	73	5
45	62¼	48	5	79	5	84	5	54	5	42	5	76	5
50	5	55	62¼	93	5	85	5	64	5	44	5	80	5
54	5	56	5	94	5	89	5	67	5	45	5	82	5
56	62¼	63	5	3002	5	3301	5	69	5	47	5	84	5
61	c	67	5	15	5	5	5	70	5	53	5	92	5

ings for 1735 were abnormal but not too abnormal for Boston. The *Boston Evening-Post* easily presented more than one hundred social notices per year from 1765 on, according to the newspapers of 1765, 1770, and 1775.

Social news combined entertainment and news of community, and as such it often became an extension of pure entertainment news, not in the way an essay or poem provided pure entertainment but as a report that this type of entertainment would take place or had occurred at a particular location. Social news about concerts or banquets, then, was both news reporting and entertainment combined. When the *South-Carolina Gazette,* for example, reported to its Charleston readership that "a Consort of Vocal and Instrument Musick" would be held in two weeks, it was providing news of an upcoming event and of a social function. It was also revealing a piece of knowledge about the entertainment in the South Carolina port.[80] A similar report in the *Pennsylvania Gazette* about a social gala in London provided entertainment as it described those at the party and the fact that "Mr. Handel performed on the Harpsicord,"[81] and the news item also provided notice of an event that had taken place in which people might be interested.

When colonial newspapers reported on social functions, they were no doubt providing a social register for the community that the newspaper served. They were also providing a bit of news and entertainment that would allow those who did not move in the upper levels of colonial society a glimpse of the upper crust of colonial society, and as such this news served much the same function of the news of the "rich and famous" currently in vogue. A glimpse into colonial "aristocracy" is exactly what the *American Weekly Mercury* furnished its readers when it told of "a very handsome Entertainment" conducted by "the Honourable John Penn, Esq; one of the Proprietaries of this Province."[82] The *Virginia Gazette* allowed its readers a view into social functions when it described "a most elegant ball at the Capitol" hosted by the governor's council.[83] And on some occasions, social news could provide news, entertain, and also make readers proud, which is what happened in 1755 in Charleston. The *South-Carolina Gazette* reported that

CHARLES PINCKNEY, Esq; one of his Majesty's Council of SOUTH CAROLINA, has lately had the Honour to wait on her Royal Highness the Princess of Wales at Leicester House, with a Piece of Silk Damask of the Growth and Product of his own Plantation . . . which her Royal Highness was pleased to receive very favourably.[84]

News of visiting dignitaries in a colony was another type of social news that appeared in colonial newspapers. When North Carolina Governor Josiah Martin arrived in Williamsburg with his wife and children, the *Virginia Gazette* related that information to its readers.[85] Social news of the arrival of individuals did not always have to deal with politically prominent people. In much the way that news of balls and banquets provided news of the activities of the social elite within a community, social news also informed newspaper readers that important members of the community were traveling abroad or returning home. The *Maryland Gazette* informed its readers that Archibald Buchanan, an influential merchant from Baltimore County, had just returned to Maryland from London.[86] In this way colonial newspapers dispensed news about the people considered the most important within the community and offered a small amout of diversion from everyday life at the same time.

Even though news of concerts, parties, and the travels of "important" people contributed to the understanding of the social fabric of colonies and at the same time entertained readers, these stories were not nearly as vital to the social news of colonial newspapers as marriage notices and obituaries were. Obituaries and marriage reports within colonial newspapers could be as long or as short as the social position of the person required, and in the case of obituaries for women, the size of the obituary was often proportional to the social standing of the widower within the community. And, as has been said, the newspaper report of marriages and obituaries generally became the official notice of an event in colonial life. A news item from the *South-Carolina Gazette* of February 1735 was a typical newspaper announcement of the wedding of individuals from the upper levels of colonial society. The news of the wedding declared:

On Thursday last Mr. JOHN GARRET, an eminent Merchant of this Town, was married to Mrs. ELISABETH HILL, a young, beautiful and genteel Lady, with a considerable Fortune, eldest Daughter of Ch. Hill Esq; deceased. A splendid Entertainment in the Evening was prepared for a large Company, who diverted themselves all Night, and in the morning the hearty Wishes of Happiness and Welfare to the new married Couple were followed by the firing off the Guns of several Vessels in this Harbour.[87]

As the colonial period progressed, wedding notices tended to become less descriptive of the revelry that often accompanied a marriage of two socially prominent people, but the importance of those involved in the wedding was not omitted. The difference may be observed in the announcement of John Hancock's wedding in 1775 in the *Essex Journal:*

> On Monday evening last week, was married at the seat of Thaddeus Burr, Esq; in Fairfield in Connecticut, by the Rev. Mr. Eliot, the Hon. JOHN HANCOCK, Esq; President of the Continental Congress, to Miss DOROTHY QUINCY, daughter of EDMUND QUINCY, Esq; of Boston.[88]

Even though most wedding reports from later in the colonial period tended to omit the social frills, they did not fail to emphasize the importance of those involved in the wedding. Wedding news in colonial newspapers, even though it was part of the official register of events, never completely lost its ability to offer entertaining features, as the wedding announcement of David Coupland and Nancy Harrison from Virginia did. Following the wedding notice, a poem about the newlyweds offered hope for a blessed married life.[89]

Newspaper printers also began to realize their obligation as the official announcer of the events of a community such as weddings and deaths extended beyond the limits of the socially and politically powerful. By 1770, many newspapers regularly ran listings of deaths and marriages. These lists only stated who was married and where, or they stated who had died and where that person had resided if the location was different from the place of the paper's publication.[90]

Colonial newspaper obituaries followed closely the style of marriage reports by reporting the deaths of the most important individuals within a colony—the physicians,[91] ministers,[92] and other prominent citizens.[93] The inclusion of an individual's obituary in a newspaper was based on the social, political, and economic hierarchy of the region, and individuals often received flowing death notices that praised their virtue. Those citizens with more middling or common origins were overlooked until much later in the period when death listings became a regular part of the public record appearing in colonial newspapers. The colonial obituary of prominent citizens often reflected upon the individual's accomplishments and praised the individual for a well-lived life, as did an obituary in the *South-Carolina Gazette:*

> On Saturday last died here Capt. Anthony Mathews, an eminent Merchant & Settler of this Province, who by his Industry, Frugality & Improvement in Mercantile Affairs, acquired one of the greatest Estates in this Country. He first arrived in this Province about the Year

1980 [1680]. Now near 55 Years since, and died lamented in the 73d Year of his age, and was decently burried on Monday last.[94]

The obituaries of women were not excluded from colonial newspapers, and the inclusion of a death notice about a female in colonial newspapers was based upon her social and economic standing or that of her husband. Death notices for Dorcas Bradford and Anne Catharine Green, wives of printers Andrew Bradford and Jonas Green respectively, were recorded in colonial newspapers based upon their relationship to their husbands.[95] When Margaret Child died in Boston in 1720, the obituary explained that she was the wife of Captain Thomas Child and the daughter of the late Reverend Samuel Willard. Nothing else was mentioned about her.[96] But, for example, when Rebeccah Fisk died in 1750, the *Boston Evening-Post* elaborated upon her Christian character, praising her as a virtuous woman, one to imitated:

This Day was decently interred here, Mrs. Rebeccah Fisk, Consort of Capt. Thomas Fisk, late of Wenham, and Daughter of the Rev. Mr. Perkins of Topsfield; a Woman of good Education, uncommon Courtesy and Civility, a sincere hearty Friend, given to hospitality, a lover of good Men, the Ministers of Christ particularly, and of a blameless Christian Life and Conversation. Having acted her Part upon the Stage agreeable to such noble and divine Principles, she is gone off with Approbation from her Acquaintance, and to the Grief of her particular Friends, who while they lament her Death, should carefully imitate the Vertues of her Life.[97]

Obituaries of this kind could have been pure praise, or they could have been a way to focus women's attention upon the concept of the virtuous woman who served others. It is impossible to know exactly, but the amount of news in colonial newspapers that promoted the virtuous woman leads to speculation that obituaries served the same purpose.[98]

Marriages and obituaries sometimes served a purely entertaining function in colonial newspapers. Newspaper readers evidently enjoyed odd and peculiar occurrences, so it became a common practice in the colonial period to report marriages or obituaries that contained unusual individuals or situations in colonial newspapers. When a deaf and mute man married, for example, a clever news report followed:

Last week a young man, a shoemaker, who is both deaf and dumb, was married to a sprightly young girl; at the wedding there were present three of the bridgroom's sisters, with two young men, who were all born deaf and dumb, so that there were six dumb persons convened on this occasion.—The minister asked the bride how he would marry them, she told him to do the best he could to buckle them together.[99]

Age played a large role in this entertaining aspect of marriage and obituary news. Weddings of elderly individuals and obituaries of those living long lives appeared on a fairly regular basis in newspapers.[100] The fear of death, or more specifcally the fear of being buried alive, led to several interesting obituary features. The *New-England Weekly Journal* and the *Pennsylvania Gazette* reported in 1730 that as the coffin of a woman was being carried out the door, a disturbance was heard from within the box. The coffin was immediately opened and the woman, "having been in lethargy only," sat up.[101] The fear of being buried alive was apparently so great for one woman, according to a newspaper report, that she ordered a large pane of glass be built into the lid of her coffin, and it observed for eight days after she was placed into it.[102]

Animals and agriculture. Because of the agrarian nature of colonial America, news of animals and agriculture should have played a more prominent role in the news of colonial newspapers than they did. The *Pennsylvania Gazette,* for example, averaged about fourteen of these stories per year from 1735–1755. During the same period, the *South-Carolina Gazette* printed on average only eight per year. The explanation for what appears to be an obvious omission by newspapers may lie in the fact that agricultural methods did not change rapidly and could be provided on a yearly basis in printers' almanacs[103] and in the fact that newspapers were more concerned with mercantile efforts as witnessed in the hundreds of shipping items in newspapers each year. Newspapers were also largely directed toward a city audience, and most residents of cities with newspapers such as Boston, Philadelphia, New York, and other New England municipalities worked as tradesmen or mariners.[104] In Southern cities such as Charleston and Williamsburg, agriculture played a more active role in the economic well-being of individuals, but it must be remembered that a large number of those reading colonial newspapers were involved in the growing and selling of agricultural goods, but not necessarily in subsistence farming.[105]

Even though agricultural news was not the most prominent news in colonial newspapers, news of crop conditions was not completely absent from newspapers, and the success or failure of crops was obviously important to colonial society. Newspaper stories reported on the possiblity of favorable harvests throughout the colonial period,[106] and they related failed crops,[107] drought conditions,[108] and crops damaged by adverse weather to readers.[109] Agricultural news also warned of disease and pestilence. Squirrels posed a threat to the New England corn crop in 1725, according to a letter appearing in the *American Weekly Mercury.*[110] Caterpillars[111] and locusts[112] destroyed crops in 1750. Connecticut crops, the *Connecticut Courant* stated, were destroyed by brown worms in 1770.[113] When corn blasts affected crops in 1760, the *New-London Summary* provided readers with a method to control the deterioration of the ears of corn.[114] Newspapers also tried to keep readers abreast of new agricultural machinery and techniques. The *Pennsylvania Gazette,* for example, touted a new plow that could significantly cut down the work time of farmers. "Dane's mathematical or universal plow, which plows three complete furrows at the same time," the news report said, "can sow, harrow or roll all as it goes on, which in about 5 minutes may be made to heel week or level ground, and . . . can be done with it without any more horses than what is usual to a common plow."[115] Other agricultural reports explained the best land for growing flax,[116] the use of salt as a winter preservative of crops,[117] and a method of making molasses from pumpkins.[118]

News of animals in colonial newspapers may have dealt with farm animals, or it may have provided odd news and entertainment. The *Boston Evening-Post,* for example, explained a new method for feeding calves in 1750,[119] and the *Virginia Gazette* reported on a disease that was spreading among horned animals in 1770.[120] Extremely large animals and odd occurrences that dealt with both livestock and wild animals made much of the news associated with animals very entertaining. When the *Maryland Gazette* told that a butcher had lately slaughtered a hog weighing 973 pounds, it was only relating a type of news common to nearly every colonial newspaper.[121] Stories of whales and sharks were evidently equally entertaining to newspaper readers.[122] News accounts about these animals points to interest in the odd and unusual, something that seemed to be appealing to newspaper readers no matter what the subject.

Accidents. Perhaps more than any of the other assorted categories of news of this study, accident news provided the most entertainment and news in one package. Accident reports could be sensational in nature or they could be humorous. They could be timely in recording the events of a local occurrence, or they could come from another section of the colonies or even Europe. The appeal of accident reports was evident in the increase in them seen in the content of the *American Weekly Mercury*. In 1720, Andrew Bradford's newspaper ran four accident news items, but that number grew to fifty-eight by 1735. When items of controversy such as Indian wars or the first preaching tour of George Whitefield captured the attention of the people, accident news tended to decrease, which affirms the fact that printers used accident news as a means to gaining readers, and readers, in turn, enjoyed news items that sparked emotion.[123]

Accident reports often played upon human emotion and fallacy, and they used human tragedy to build an interesting news item. Accident reports also reveal much about colonial life. The cities in which newspapers were printed were located on bodies of water, something required during the colonial period for transportation, livelihood, and as an avenue of correspondence. As a result, news of accidental drownings regularly appeared in newspapers. Another necessity for life in the colonial period was fire. Required yearlong, fires were sources of continual danger for individuals and cities. Colonial newspapers reported numerous fires. A third type of accident report that became a regular feature of colonial newspapers related tragedy in relation to children. Both fire and water were involved in these tragedies with children. Another type of accident news dealt with accidental shootings. Many hunting accidents and other types of accidental shootings, pointed to the need for and use of firearms during the period.

Benjamin Franklin offered Philadelphia readers a slice of entertainment with news of accidents that the printer gleaned from London newspapers. His collected news stated:

> The following Accidents have happen'd the Week past: A big Boy tumbled out of a flying Chair at Bartholomew Fair, and was kill'd. A Boy and a Girl fell off a Woman's Lap in a Hackney-Coach going to the Fair, and the Hind-Wheel run over his Thigh: The Girl was not Hurt. Mr. Higgin's Daughter in Swallow-street, choak'd herself with a Bit of Half-penny Loaf and Butter. A Gentleman fell in Fleet-ditch Head foremost.[124]

Forty years later, the *Gazette*'s chief Philadelphia competitor, the *Pennsylvania Journal,* supplied the city's readers with an emotion-charged accident account that took place at a funeral. The paper explained that a number of people had gathered for the funeral of a Mr. Hideen, who was to be buried that evening, and "just as the Rev. Mr. Parsons began prayer, the floor fell in, which much surprised them, and bruised many persons."[125] And the *Weekly Re-*

hearsal, with one sentence, illustrated the dangers that everyday life presented when it reported that "a Woman, who had been washing, going to empty a Tub of Water out of a Chamber Window, fell down her self, by which she was so much bruised, that 'tis thought she cannot live."[126]

Accident reports revolving around water could be slightly humorous, such as the news account that told of a man bathing in the river who drowned,[127] or they could involve great tragedy, in much the way of one Boston couple who returned from church only to find their sons missing. After a frantic search, the boys' bodies were found in a near-by pond, the pair having drowned in their parents' absence.[128] The dangers of water in everyday travel claimed a pair of sisters in New Haven when the ferry on which they were riding to Saybrook filled with water, and the girls went down with the ferry.[129]

Fire was a major problem for colonial towns, according to colonial newspapers, and large blazes leveled portions of Annapolis,[130] Boston,[131] Charleston,[132] and Philadelphia.[133] The spread of fire was a problem of immense proportions. Within a two-week period, according to *Publick Occurrences,* fire consumed twenty-six houses in Boston, killed one man, and destroyed "the best furnished PRINTING-PRESS of those few we know of in America."[134] Fires were evidently such a problem in Charleston that the city formed a landowners' group to provide fire insurance. Printer Louis Timothy wrote, "I can with Pleasure inform my Readers, that there was one Day last Week a Meeting of several of the Freeholders of this Town, who then entered into an Agreement . . . for a mutual insuring their Houses against Fire."[135] Insurance, however, could not protect Charleston from fire, and in 1740, a massive fire broke out in the South Carolina port. The *South-Carolina Gazette* reported, "The Wind blowing pretty fresh at North-west, carried the Flake of Fire so far, and by that Means set Houses on Fire at such a distance, that it was not possible to prevent the Spreading of it."[136] After the description of how the fire spread through the city, the *Gazette* listed the damage done by the blaze:

> The Number of Houses burnt, are computed to be above 300, besides Store-houses, Stables, &c. and several Wharfs, and had it not been high Water, all or most of the Shipping would have been burnt. The Damage only in Merchandize, is computed to be above the Value of 100,000*l.* Sterling.[137]

In order to fight fires, Charleston acquired fire engines from London, but the crude pumpers were no match for a fire and a strong wind, as the city discovered in 1760 when fire again ripped the city's houses. "Although the fire masters, with the masters of the engines, &c. and all degrees of people were extremely active to stop the progress of the flames," the *Gazette* reported, "*The want of public wells and pumps in the streets of that part of the town was felt on this occasion, as it was difficult, for some time, to find water to supply the engines.*"[138] The fire engines did, however according to the newspaper, save a few of Charleston's houses that were in danger of being consumed by the fire.

The massive fires within cities destroyed numerous homes, but individual house fires were also a regular part of the accident news of colonial newspapers. Newspapers made a point of informing readers if the occupants of the burned house had escaped with their lives and with their possessions, especially their furniture. Furniture was no doubt a valuable commodity in colonial America, and the loss of household possessions was evidently a great tragedy.[139] No one was immune from the destruction caused by fire in colonial America, and accident reports often told readers of fires at the homes of important people and what they lost in the fire. The fact that these individuals—Cotton Mather,[140] Andrew Hamilton,[141] and Thomas Jefferson[142] to name three—were well-known throughout the colonies only increased the interest in these news accounts of fires. But fire accounts worked best to capture reader interest when they were able to pull upon the emotions of the readers and capitalize upon an event's sensational nature. In one Connecticut fire, for example, the bravery of a mother saved her family but cost her her life:

> About five Weeks ago, the House of one Johnson . . . took Fire in the Night, while the Family were asleep, and had got to a great Head before it was discovered. There were at home only a Woman and four Children, the Man happening to be abroad at that Time; and altho' the Room wherein the Children lay was all on Fire, yet the tender Mother ventured in and threw them all safe out at the Window, but in getting out her self, a horn of Gun-Powder which happened to hang over the Window, took Fire, and (Oh! hard Fate!) blew her back into the room, where she was consumed in the Flames, no Part of her being to be seen the next Day, but two or three of her Bones. There was Fifty Bushels of Wheat burnt in the said House, belonging to a Gentleman from whom we had this Relation.[143]

Similar emotions and sensationalism were employed to describe the tragic burning of children, which seemed to happen fairly often according to colonial newspapers. A young child left by an open fire by its mother who went next door to help a neighbor, the *American Weekly Mercury* reported, was discovered moments later "burnt almost to Death." The child died within minutes.[144] And a child pinned to a chair by its mother so that she could help a sick neighbor burned to death, driving its mother "raving Mad."[145]

In addition to the dangers of fire and water, gun accidents made for interesting accident reading in newspapers. Hunting accidents were the most common type of gun accident stories,[146] but accidents with guns appeared to be almost as varied and numerous as there were firearms. A Charleston man, for example, after cleaning his rifle brought it into the house to show his wife. The clean gun accidentally fired and "shot her in the right Breast through he Body, whereby she instantly died."[147] In another instance, a man brought his newly acquired pistols to the "Publick House." One of the pistols accidentally fired, hitting a butcher in the head "in such a Manner that some of his Brains came out."[148] And the *Connecticut Gazette* reported how one foolish soldier, in an effort to create a louder "Report," stuck his gun into his mouth in order to wet down the load. The gun "accidentally went off, in his mouth, and tore his head asunder."[149]

If accidents with guns, fires, and drownings were not enough to make life in colonial America sufficiently dangerous, newspapers also reported "traffic accidents." These accidents involved people being run over by wagons,[150] wagons and carts overturning,[151] and accidents with horses.[152] Other accidents[153] occurred within everyday life, too, but many of these accidents were caused by the weather, another type of news found in newspapers.

Weather. Even though colonial newspapers recorded some of the everyday aspects of weather such as high tides,[154] unusual and extreme weather comprised the majority of news items that dealt with climatic conditions. News of abnormal weather allowed readers to know the weather in other portions of the colonies and in Europe once that news was picked up by local newspapers, and severe weather accounts provided readers with interesting reading based in the reality of everyday life. When extreme weather from another region appeared in newspapers, it permitted residents of one city to compare the reported weather with that of their own locale, which is exactly what the Boston newspapers did when they related a series of violent gales and torrential rains in New London that caused a meeting-house to collapse.[155] Evidently, there was no similar weather in Boston—approximately two hundred miles from the Connecticut port—since Boston papers did not mention it. The *Pennsylvania Journal,* in similar fashion, picked up news of a violent wind storm in Charleston that damaged many ships and the wharfs.[156]

The Charleston storm that the *Pennsylvania Journal* described was reported in the *South-Carolina Gazette*. As with other types of news, the local account served as official notice for what had occurred, such as hail storms,[157] blizzards,[158] damaging rains,[159] drought,[160] and the coldest month in memory.[161] By running these news reports, colonial newspapers allowed local readers to read about events of local interest and concern, and they provided a means of sharing the news with other regions as newspapers were carried by ship from port-to-port or by post carrier on the colonial mail routes. Often, these weather reports from other areas were highly entertaining reading, and an especially severe winter in Europe in 1740 provided colonial readers with one such report. The cold in Holland during the winter was so severe that nothing could hold back the cold, several newspapers reported. Whether intended as a joke or actually what happened as a result of the low temperatures, the results were, as the news reports stated, quite remarkable:

> Our chief Study and Care is how to thaw our Eatables & Drinkables, as Water, Milk, Beer, &c. My Wine is tolerably strong, yet the whole Bottle freezes into a solid Mass; Bread cannot be cut without being first set by the Fire near an Hour; in the same Manner we serve our Butter, and also our oranges, which are otherwise as hard as Stones: Boiling strong Punch put into a Bowl, presents us with Ice in eight Minutes: My Barber coming Yesterday to shave me, put a little hot Water into his Bason below Stairs, and in the Time he was coming up to my Chamber, it began to freeze: Warm Urine from a Man's Body freezes in six Minutes; Spittle directly as it falls to the Ground. But what is yet more remarkable, a Gentleman of my Acquaintance, having a Bottle of Water from a Pump that was not frozen, going directly to pour some into a Glass, it was immediately Ice; but what is more surprising, part of the Stream from the Bottle to the Glass froze, and stood up like an Icicle, the like certainly never known in these Climates.[162]

Even though unusual weather often provided interesting reading, news of violent and extreme weather made for the most entertaining reading. Weather news of this type usually involved lightning, and the resulting reports were entertaining. An excellent example ran in the *Essex Gazette* in 1770. Lightning, the paper stated,

> struck a Woman who was kneeling at the side of the Chimney, who did not survive afterwards longer than to repeat three Times, My God,

I am dying: Help! On examining her Body, the Bones of her Arms were found to be broken, without any outward Marks; in the Back Part of her Shift was a Hole the Size and Form of a Canon-Ball, and on her Back a Mark of the same Size and Figure without any Scratch.[163]

In a similar accident involving lightning, a New Bern man was struck in the head as he walked down the street of North Carolina's capital city. The lightning killed him instantaneously and "melted the buckles in his knees and shoes."[164] In 1765, the *Boston Evening-Post* presented a series of six articles all relating to severe weather accidents involving lightning. In those articles, lightning struck people, sheep, and vessels, killing humans and animals and destroying several ships.[165]

Natural occurrences and disasters. News of earthquakes, volcanos, and phenomena that appeared in the sky was often closely related to weather news that dealt with extreme weather and accidents because all three involved tragedy. News of natural occurrences such as comets provided readers with timely and interesting news about events that were often mysterious. Earthquakes were evidently cause for great concern during the colonial period, and newspapers recounted that earthquakes occurred in many locations around the world including Boston,[166] Constantinople,[167] Providence,[168] Peru,[169] Oxford,[170] Italy,[171] Haiti,[172] New Haven,[173] Rhode Island,[174] Philadelphia,[175] Cadiz,[176] New York,[177] Hispaniola,[178] Paris,[179]Rome,[180] Calais,[181] Kingston,[182] London,[183] Annapolis,[184] Albany,[185] Syria,[186] Fyal,[187] and Antigua.[188]

Although it is impossible to ascertain from the earthquake information given in newspapers whether a quake actually occurred every time a newspaper reported one, newspapers do reveal that sizable seismic activity took place in America and in Western Europe in 1750 and 1755. During this period, newspapers stated that earthquakes caused considerable damage from Maryland through New England in America and in England and France in Europe. Major quakes rocked the Caribbean in 1770. Earthquakes evoked many images among colonial citizens, and God's judgment was often credited with causing an earthquake as a way to punish sinful people.[189] The *Boston Evening-Post*'s description of the 1755 tremors and destruction in Boston confirms that an earthquake did strike the Middle and New England colonies. The *Evening-Post*'s news report is also typical of those on earthquakes. The paper stated:

About half an Hour past Four o'Clock last Tuesday Morning, we were surpised with the most violent Shock of an Earthquake that ever was felt in these Parts of the World. . . . There was a first a rumbling Noise like low Thunder, which was immediately followed with such violent shaking of the Earth and Buildings, as threw every one into the greatest Amasement, expecting every moment to be buried in the Ruins of their Houses. This violent Tremor continued for about the Space of one Minute (some say two) in which Time the Tops of a great Number of Chimnies, and many of them quite down to the Roofs of the Houses were thrown down, and many of the Roofs on which they fell, beat in. . . . The Ends and Sides of several Brick Buildings were thrown down, and, in a Word, the Instances of Damage done to our Houses and Chimnies are so many, that it would be endless to recount them.— Much Damage has also been sustained by the Destruction of Glass, China, Earthen Ware, &c. . . . About three Quarters of an Hour after the amazing Shock, there was a fainter one, and some Persons imagine they have felt several since. Last Saturday Evening, between seven and eight o'Clock, we were surprised with another hard Shock, attended with a rumbling Noise.[190]

Neither newspapers nor those writing to them offered much speculation upon the cause of earthquakes other than God's providence, and few reasons were given in newspapers for the many unexplained sightings in the skies over America either. Comets caused some excitement among citizens in 1760[191] and 1770,[192] but they were expected phenomena. Many unexplained events also crossed the heavens. In 1735, for example, newspapers reported that "Brimstone," or "yellow Sulphur fell with the Rain."[193] A ball of fire was seen racing across the northern sky in 1750,[194] and in 1765, the *Newport Mercury* related how the night sky lit up like daylight when "a globe of fire, apparently of about 18 inches in diameter, with a tail several yards long" passed near West Chester, New York. Those who saw it deduced that it must have been a meteor.[195] Other sightings in the heavens obviously carried more political connotation than physical possibility. In Poland, where warring factions needed a sign to ensure victory, for example, the *Boston Gazette* reported that "a surprizing Phænomenon appeared in the Air," which included "a red Cross with two Moons on each side, upon each of which were a hand a a Foot, with two Swords and two knives."[196] The sightings in the heavens that appeared in colonial newspapers provided ample entertainment and opportunities for speculation at their origins by those who read the news accounts.

Science and discoveries. From electricity to new islands, colonial newspapers informed readers of the latest that science and exploration had to offer. Many discoveries that appeared in colonial newspapers dealt with medicine and the treatment of diseases. Important discoveries such as electricity were immediately applied to the medical sphere.[197] The discovery of electricity by Benjamin Franklin was probably the most important scientific breakthrough to appear in colonial papers. In direct relationship to the discovery of electricity, Franklin developed lightning rods or "Franklin rods" as they were called in the 1750s,[198] whose use was explained "in a *South-Carolina Gazette* article in 1755. A house with "an electrical Rod fixed to one of the Chimnies" received a direct hit from lightning. Usually a lightning strike to a house produced fire, explosions, and large amounts of structural damage, but this house, equipped with "Points for securing Houses against the Effects of Lightning," "received no Damage from the Explosion." The news article concluded by saying the lightning strike confirmed the belief that lightning rods could protect buildings from lightning damage.[199]

Many scientific findings were applied directly to travel, especially sea voyages. A man in England developed a treatment to keep ship timbers from rotting in the water.[200] An invention in 1730, the *Pennsylvania Gazette* stated, could keep track of ships' voyages at sea. The invention was "called the Marine Log."[201] Dr. Halley, in 1735, the *Boston News-Letter* reported, "found out Longitude," giving sea travellers another way to pinpoint their location on the ocean.[202] The new inventions that were applied to sea travel helped exploration. One British captain reported finding thirty-four new islands in the "Northern Ocean," and many of them, he declared in a news report, were inhabited by "Savages" not known to the civilized world.[203] Many other news items about exploration ended up in colonial newspapers including accounts of the English captain James Cook, who explored Australia and Antarctica.[204]

Many other inventions and discoveries discussed in colonial newspapers were part of technological efforts to improve living conditions. News stories, for example, on a new grate for fireplaces to keep them from filling houses with smoke[205] and on the development of the anemometer, a device proported to be able to measure "all alterations of the weather,"[206] promised readers a better life. The new technology on which newspapers reported allowed scientists and tinkerers to invent new war weapons that fired thousands of rounds in minutes[207] and household security systems.[208]

CONCLUSION

The assorted news of colonial newspapers did make them a "Feast" that provided a dish for every guest, to paraphrase "The

NEWS-PAPER," the 1770 poem used by many American newspaper printers to describe their wares. This multi-topical news in colonial papers emphasized entertainment, but entertainment was not its sole purpose. News of weddings, deaths, and to a certain extent accidents all served as official notice of an event's occurrence, and for that reason the information was newsworthy. If these events could be made entertaining in the process, then good journalistic practices, according to eighteenth-century standards, were met. Timeliness played a role in the assorted news of colonial newspapers, too, but it held less importance in most of the assorted news than in news of Native American attacks, disease outbreaks, and ship arrivals, for example. Getting information to readers quickly was more important for assorted news when it dealt with weather, natural disasters, and some accidents than it was with pure entertainment, sporting events, and oddities.

The diversity in subject matter in colonial newspapers appears to have reached its zenith by 1750, but appearances in this case are deceiving. Newspapers of the first half of the eighteenth century generally used large type and fewer columns and therefore ran fewer stories per edition than the newspapers of the last twenty-five years of the colonial period. Because of this fact, the assorted news of the earlier newspapers seems to be more prevalent. In reality, the expanded format of newspapers in the latter part of the colonial period provided more room for all sorts of news. Expanded pages per edition, increased numbers of columns, and smaller type naturally allowed for more political news, but it also provided increased space for all types of news. All news types did not increase in this expanded format, sensationalism being a prime example of a type of news that flourished more prior to 1750 than after.

Assorted news in this expanded format appeared to decrease, but the amount in newspapers remained fairly constant, and perhaps it even increased, especially when the ever-growing quantity of social news that newspapers ran from 1750–1775 is considered. The *Boston Evening-Post,* for example, ran just as much assorted news during and after the French and Indian War as it did from 1735–1750, and the paper's social news more than quadrupled from 1735 to 1770. Even in 1775, when the *Evening-Post* ceased printing immediately after shots were fired at Lexington and Concord, more social news ran in those four months of printing than in all of the *Evening-Post*'s 1740 editions.

The greatest difference in the assorted news of the latter quarter of the colonial period and that of the years from 1720–1750 lay in the exclusion of most pure entertainment, such as essays and literary prose in the form of long reprintings of books and the like. This type of entertaining news decreased as colonial newspapers focused their news upon topics of colonial interest such as George Whitefield, the French and Indian War, and the Stamp Act crisis because of the amount of space these extended entertainment pieces required. This pure entertainment also decreased in colonial newspapers because of the increasing numbers of books available in the colonies through importation, colonial printing, and the growing number of libraries in the colonies. Literary entertainment did not cease completely, however. Shorter literary prose could still occasionally be found in newspapers,[209] and newspaper poetry, often printed in a weekly feature called "the Poet's Corner," remained strong with poetry increasing in inclusion in newspapers in the 1770s.

The decline of literary entertainment was not matched by a decline in entertainment pieces that appealed to baser instincts. News that exploited human misfortune or foolishness, relayed oddities of nature, and reported accidents that were both tragic and entertaining remained fairly constant during the colonial period. People needed a respite from the news of politics and war; therefore, colonial newspapers continued to present news that provided a diversion. Americans had, after all, been fighting the British for six months when John Dixon and Alexander Purdie offered Williamsburg readers the frivolous "ADDRESS of the Author to his Bed" in "the Poet's Corner" following three pages of news that addressed almost exclusively issues of war.[210]

The assorted news of colonial newspapers broached nearly every topic conceivable. In the process it entertained readers, provided an oft-welcome diversion, contributed the official record of occurrences within colonies, provided timely news of tragic events, related new discoveries, and reported major events such as weather that affected everyone. The assorted news of colonial newspapers filled the gaps and rounded out news of eighteenth-century America. News of political controversy and physical harm through war with the Indians, the Spanish, the French, and eventually the British may have been the big topics of discussion for newspapers, but those topics were tempered with the varied assorted news making newspapers "the gen'ral source throughout the nation, of ev'ry modern conversation."[211]

Conclusion

This Taste, we Englishmen, have for News, is a very odd one;
yet it must be fed; and tho' it seems to be a Jest to Foreigners,
yet it is an Amusement we can't be without.
—*New-York Gazette,* 22 January 1750

AMERICANS' love for news grew in the eighteenth century. From a single newspaper in 1704 and only three in 1720, America's newspaper output expanded to forty newspapers regularly printed in 1775 with more than twenty-five others having lived and died during the years between *Public Occurrences* and the Revolution. The growth in the number of newspapers in colonial America opened, as Richard Brown has said, the dispersal of information to anyone with access to a newspaper,[1] and in fact, the large number of newspapers meant that almost everyone in colonial America had access to news by the end of the colonial period and perhaps even by midcentury. Literate people everywhere, Warren Johnson says, could obtain a copy of a newspaper, and illiterate people were given the opportunity to hear the news when newspapers were read aloud in taverns.[2]

America's desire for "the freshest Advices Foreign and Domestic" developed into a thirst for news, something that the *New-York Gazette* said that the people "can't be without."[3] Benjamin Franklin was correct in 1728 when he remarked that "a good paper would scarcely fail" because the desire for information in colonial America was so great that only the worst of colonial sheets expired, and their death almost always signaled the birth of new newspapers to take their places. By colonial standards, a good newspaper addressed items of local concern, items of intercolonial interest, and transatlantic matters that affected colonial life or the world situation. Good newspapers provided a diversity in news types and subject matter. They offered diversions from the rigors and problems of everyday life without ignoring those problems. And good newspapers developed into the official records of local and intercolonial events.

These ideals for a good colonial newspaper did not develop immediately. Newspapers were still essentially a new development in the 1700s, despite the fact that newspapers had been produced in England and other European countries for almost a century. Creating newspapers that could meet the information needs of a diverse and ever-growing American population required the passage of several decades and the efforts of several astute individuals. Men such as Andrew Bradford, Thomas Fleet, Samuel Kneeland, Timothy Green, and William Parks produced successful newspapers in America prior to 1730, but it took the insight of Benjamin Franklin to achieve the rich diversity of news types and hone the concept that local news items were a valid and essential part of colonial newspapers. Franklin obtained his own newspaper in Philadelphia late in 1729 when he purchased Samuel Keimer's failing *Universal Instructor in All Arts and Sciences; and the Pennsylvania Gazette.* How Franklin helped change the face of news in colonial newspapers may be explained by the opening comment used in the first edition of the *Universal Instructor,* when the London-born Keimer stated, "We have little News of Consequence at present, the English Prints being generally Stufft with Robberies, Cheats, Fires, Murders, Bankrupcies, Promotions of some, and Hangings of Others."[4] Keimer had missed the importance and value of newspapers. English newspapers were full of news on various subjects, and it took Franklin and those printers who copied him in the 1730s and 1740s to grasp the fact that this news on a host of topics was "News of Consequence" and of interest to readers. Franklin and those who followed his lead realized newspapers needed to make this news available to readers on a weekly basis. That is why Franklin perceptively requested that people keep him—and consequently everyone through the *Pennsylvania Gazette*—apprised of "every remarkable Accident, Occurrence, &c. fit for public Notice."[5]

With the growth of the American colonies in population, trade, and economic importance to England and much of Western Europe, astute printers realized that an ample amount of news of robberies, murders, accidents, and court news existed within the American colonies. In addition, the peculiarities of colonial life provided news that could not be ignored. News of Native American activities, diseases, and slaves—items that to a large degree were not a part of life in England—gave colonial printers sources of news that needed to be shared with local populations and with colonials up and down the Atlantic seaboard. And these news types became very popular with printers in the 1730s and 1740s, again following Franklin's lead. Before 1730 only Andrew Bradford with Philadelphia's *American Weekly Mercury* came close to grasping the idea that news of crimes and executions was information that would attract readers. Accident reports, however, were insignificant in newspapers. Franklin's *Pennsylvania Gazette* erased the concept that these types of news were of little interest or value to readers. Franklin nearly doubled the number of crime and court reports from the total that Bradford ran in 1730 with 129, and he printed more than three times the amount of crime news as appeared in Boston newspapers. The number of accidents described in the *Gazette* in 1730, seventy-nine, was four times greater than the number of accidents listed in any Boston newspaper. By 1735, most colonial newspapers were following the *Pennsylvania Gazette*'s lead and printing large amounts of crime and accident reports, many tinged with sensational accounts of executions and gruesome "Melancholy Accidents."

From 1730 to the period of the Stamp Act crisis, colonial printers honed the "good newspaper" into a weekly sheet of assorted news, and a rich diversity developed in the content of papers. European news and high matters of state remained important topics of discussion, but other news subjects contributed significantly to the content of colonial newspapers making them multifaceted, something newspapers replete with only politics could not accomplish. As this study has demonstrated, news of the seas was vital and prominent in colonial newspapers. Shipping news affected economics and politics. That is why hundreds of items about ships, customs houses, and the price current in ports ran in almost every colonial newspaper yearly. The content of colonial newspapers was limited only by the topics of interest and concern during the period. News of Native Americans, crime, sensationalism, slaves, women, the home and family, medicine, disease, religion, accidents, animals, agriculture, literature, stories of diversion dealing with human misfortune and foolishness, oddities of nature, gaming, sports, natural occurrences, weather, discoveries, science, and social news helped make the news content of colonial newspapers rich, varied, and anything but purely political, the perception many media historians hold about the news of colonial sheets.

The variety of news printed in colonial newspapers served as the prototype for all American newspapers to follow in the nineteenth and twentieth centuries. In fact, with the possible exception of regular editorial cartoons and comic strips, products of the 1830s and 1880s respectively,[6] and photographs, all the types of news, topics to be discussed, and presentation devices appeared first in colonial newspapers. And even the editorial cartoon received its start during the colonial period with the *Pennsylvania Gazette*'s 9 May 1754, woodcut "Join, or Die," which depicted the colonies as a snake. The severed snake, the cartoon intimated, would never survive in small pieces, but joined, the snake could thwart a French and Indian invasion. By the revolutionary period, the "Join, or Die" snake had been applied to American resistance of English tyranny and was used by some printers regularly, as did Isaiah Thomas in the nameplate of the *Massachusetts Spy*.

The practice of running varied contents by colonial printers provided printers and editors of the nineteenth century with a perfect example of the blending of important political and world news with other subjects that readers desired. Whether nineteenth-century printers and editors ever looked to the colonial newspapers for examples is not known, but when the Penny Press newspapers of the 1830s began to include police and crime reports, local news, and human interest news on a daily basis,[7] they were not producing a "new" content for newspapers.[8] Newspaper readers in Philadelphia, and to a lesser extent readers in Boston and New York, had been introduced to the same content a century earlier. When James Gordon Bennett "shocked" readers with his account of the prostitute Ellen Jewett's murder,[9] Bennett and his Penny Press compatriots who followed his lead were not introducing a new type of news—sensationalism—to American readers. Colonial printers had dashed brains, blood, bowels, and body parts across the pages of their papers for decades. The fascination with such gruesome news, as Mitchell Stephens has demonstrated, is as old as humankind's desire to know what is going on around them,[10] so the perception by many media historians that sensationalism developed with the Penny Press and was elevated to new heights by "yellow journalism" later in the nineteenth century is incorrect.

Although the content of colonial newspapers was quite varied and served as a prototype for American newspapers to follow, ascertaining the actual content of newspapers is more difficult. Johnson believes that one-half the content of colonial newspapers to 1763 was international in flavor,[11] but Johnson's speculation is made by using fifteen colonial newspapers. The content of colonial newspapers changed as printers incorporated more news topics into their weekly editions. In the early colonial period of newspapers, that is from the beginning of colonial newspapers to around 1725, European affairs and legislative and executive decrees that appeared in newspapers probably consumed about 75 percent of the actual content of a weekly newspaper.[12]

The anomoly in this generalization, however, is America's first newspaper, *Publick Occurrences*. This newspaper, which appeared as one lone edition before governmental authorities suppressed it, contained only local news. Had *Publick Occurrences* been allowed to continue, its news content would no doubt have greatly affected future attempts at newspapers and their contents. *Publick Occurrences* may have offered a different approach to news because its printer, Benjamin Harris, had already worked as a newspaper printer in England, beginning his work in 1679.[13] Other newspaper owners and printers of the early eighteenth century were new to the profession. It was much easier to clip or copy news from Europe and pass it along the way John Campbell had done with his handwritten newsletter, which he sent to the governors of the colonies,[14] a practice his printed *Boston News-Letter* continued.

By 1730, competition among newspapers for readers and the insightful understanding of men like Benjamin Franklin, who realized that varied news content meant a more appealing product that could meet the needs of a diversified readership, ensured a larger amount of space for varied news content in colonial newspapers. From 1730 up to the period of the Stamp Act crisis, newspapers probably ran between 40–50 percent news per week that dealt with subjects other than European affairs or high matters of state for the colonies and England. Some newspapers during this period printed news that almost totally ignored the European political connection. Several factors contributed to this change in news content. The newspapers of the 1730s and 1740s especially were still produced as two-column editions, even though the *Pennsylvania Gazette,* for example, increased to three columns by 1745, and type, especially on page one, continued to be rather large. These factors limited the amount of news that could appear in a weekly edition.

With a rise in issues of intercolonial importance, such as George Whitefield's first preaching tour, the French and Indian War, and the other Indian wars of the period, the political flavor of the news that marked the copied European news and legislative and executive decrees that dominated news in the first three decades of the eighteenth century lost its position of importance. Events that were peculiar to the colonies were of more concern to readers than political news of Europe because the American colonies were coming of age politically and economically during the middle third of the eighteenth century. When colonial newspapers of this period focused their attention upon international political affairs such as military and political confrontations between England and Spain and England and France, newspapers were beginning to report on matters that were now also of domestic concern. The American colonies were playing an increasingly important role the economic situation of Europe, and when fighting between England and her European rivals interrupted American shipping, Americans became very interested in those confrontations. The Anglo-Spanish War that was being waged in 1740 greatly affected American trade as ships heading to the Caribbean were seized, sunk, and plundered. Spain, as colonial newspapers reported, even invaded colonial America.[15] As the focus of news from 1730–1765 turned toward topics that affected the American colonies, a wide number of issues of importance to America naturally increased as well. The inclusion of news of local concern to readers of newspapers had by the middle of the eighteenth century been applied to almost all news in colonial papers.

With the Stamp Act crisis, American colonies began to reach a maturation stage. Trade with Europe and the desire for American goods made America very important to England, but many Americans began to believe that America did not need England in order to exist and advocated separation from the mother country. Once again, the focus of news in colonial newspapers took a decidedly political turn. By 1765, the confrontations with Native Americans had been almost completely eliminated east of the Appalachian Mountains, and even though news of Indian activity in the Ohio and Mississippi valleys, crime news, accident reports, and most other types of news continued to appear in newspapers in approximately the same amounts as they had in previous years, improvements in newspaper printing technology made it possible to insert more news than ever before into colonial papers. Smaller print, more columns and more pages per week all added up to more news in most newspapers. That news was devoted to political issues and European events of concern to colonists. Yet in reality, political events such as the Stamp Act and nonimportation agreements were still entwined with the economic aspects of the colonies and as a result affected ship news. The political implications, however, outweighed shipping influences for this study, and stories on nonimportation and the Stamp Act were excluded from counts of ship news. From 1765–1775, even though assorted news topics continued to be important to readers, they slowly lost their hold on the space they occupied in colonial newspapers. By 1775 and the outbreak of armed rebellion in America against England, the political news of colonial newspapers exceeded 75 percent, and as expected war news almost consumed the news content of newspapers.

The fact that news of European events and high matters of state dominated the content of colonial newspapers during the early part of the eighteenth century and again at the end of the period is significant because it is from both of these periods that most of the assumptions concerning colonial newspapers have been drawn by scholars. Even though Elizabeth Christine Cook studied the literary content of colonial newspapers to 1750, she concluded that colonial newspapers contained "no news." Cook based her conclusion solely on the very earliest newspapers of eighteenth-century America.[16] Similarly, Sidney Kobre, whose insight into colonial newspapers was probably greater than any other scholar, chose to describe the *Boston News-Letter*'s initial editions as typical of colonial newspapers rather than using a newspaper from later in the eighteenth century after American newspapers had better developed. That choice made it appear that all colonial newspapers were filled predominently with news taken from English newspapers or from the workings of colonial governments with only terse comments on other news topics and local information.[17]

In other major studies of colonial newspapers, the political crises from the Stamp Act period through the Revolution have made it appear again that colonial newspapers were almost exclusively political organs,[18] the same perception created by the large amount of research into free press issues in the colonial period[19] and the John Peter Zenger trial.[20] While these studies are accurate in their attempts to describe the political role newspapers played in the period from 1765–1775 and in efforts to promote freedom of the press, they inaccurately portray the content of colonial newspapers because colonial newspapers in the middle of the eighteenth century were, as this study has shown, anything but pure political machines. In addition, the significance of the Zenger trial for freedom of the press has assumed greater importance in the twentieth century as scholars have attempted to explain freedom of the press as a part of the fabric of America's history than it did in the eighteenth century. Although beyond the limits of this study, it is significant to note that newspapers outside of New York ignored news stories on the Zenger trial until several years after the 1735 trial.[21] Most news surrounding the Zenger trial dealt solely with the fact that Zenger's lawyers, James Alexander and William Smith, had been disbarred, and they never mentioned Zenger in these articles.[22] Although newspaper content at the beginning and end of the colonial period was predominantly political in nature and the Zenger trial of 1735 formed the foundation for free press arguments, newspapers never ignored completely in their formative years nor abandoned totally during the closing years of the period the inclusion of diversified news content.

Another misperception concerning the content of colonial newspapers is that colonial newspapers neglected local news since the publisher felt everyone was aware of local events and thus believed it unnecessary to print those occurrences.[23] Colonial newspapers addressed local concerns. If one, for example, looks at the dozens of news items dealing with marriages, obituaries, and the like that appeared in colonial newspapers yearly, it becomes apparent that local news was not completely overlooked by colonial printers. No doubt all of a city knew when a prominent person died, but the official record appeared in the newspaper, and by the last third of the colonial period, newspapers regularly ran lists of death notices obviously in an effort to make known all of the deaths that had occurred within a city or region. The same conclusion about the inclusion of local news may be reached about other local news items. When Boston citizens, for example, stampeded out of Reverend Checkley's meeting house in September 1740, killing several and severely wounding others after the church had become filled beyond capacity with those desiring to hear George Whitefield preach, the Boston newspapers reported the incident.[24] There can be little doubt, however, that almost every citizen of Boston had already heard of the tragedy before the news report appeared in print. Some local news items were left out, but many others were included no doubt because people enjoyed reading about occurrences about which they already had some knowledge in much the same way community newspapers of later periods provided news about events that were already public knowledge.

Newspapers may have begun their existence in eighteenth-century colonial America as Richard Brown says, as "non-essential, minor commercial ventures,"[25] but they did not remain "non-essential." They were a mirror of their times, according to Anna DeArmond,[26] and as such they reflect the growing interest of newspaper readers in a wide variety of subjects, entertaining news, and items of local significance.

The content of colonial newspapers tells us that American journalism was in a state of evolution during the colonial period. Most printers prior to 1730 had little experience in producing newspapers. They did have English newspapers to copy, but life in America was not the same as that in London. A newspaper suitable for America, therefore, necessitated a more varied approach to news coverage even though the first efforts at newspaper production in eighteenth-century America did not achieve this goal. While

English prints might concern themselves with shipping troubles with Spain and France and rebellion in Scotland, American newspapers, in addition to sharing many of these same concerns, needed to keep readers abreast with the colonies' own sea troubles and other problems such as Native American activity. The fact that the first printers did not accomplish this feat demonstrates newspaper evolution because as has been seen, the newspapers of the period from 1730–1765 were able to cover most aspects of colonial life. The change in the content of colonial newspapers from almost exclusively European political news and essays to subjects more diverse in nature and more in tune with local interests was the result of the maturation process of life in America. The innovation in news coverage initiated by Benjamin Franklin was a response to this maturation in society, and it naturally led to competition, and this competition among newspapers for readers and advertising business led to improved newspapers.

One of the greatest steps in the evolutionary process of colonial newspapers occurred around 1740. That is when news items of great significance to colonial life began to capture the focus of colonial news. The phenomenon was not initiated by an individual printer like Franklin. Instead, it seems to have been a step in the logical progression in the quality of colonial newspapers, one that printers grasped, no doubt, because of the enormity of the news that spawned it and also because Franklin had shown them that news did not have to be purely political to be important. The concept of the "hot topic" in news in the eighteenth century grew from the news surrounding the itinerant preacher George Whitefield who captured the interest of not only newspapers in 1740 but of almost everyone in America. The controversy that Whitefield created within the religious environment of America, especially in Boston, carried over to 1745 when the *Boston Evening-Post* and the *Boston Gazette* weekly fueled religious debate in Massachusetts through a religious war of words in the newspapers.[27] Both newspapers published in excess of sixty religious news items during the year, almost every single one of them on the religious controversy surrounding Whitefield, and fueled controversy weekly by keeping the issue in front of the people.

Another example of "hot news" in colonial newspapers was the meteoric rise in Native American news from 1755–1760. Indians had been a source of concern in colonial America since the beginning of colonization and were a continuing topic for colonial newspapers. *Publick Occurrences* carried extensive news of Native Americans, and John Campbell's *Boston News-Letter* kept closer tabs on Indian activity during the first two decades of the eighteenth century than on any other news topic with the exception of reprinting news of European affairs. But the threat that Indians represented to the British inhabitants of America during the eighteenth century reached its zenith with the French and Indian War and the Cherokee war. In 1750, colonial newspapers studied averaged twenty-four news items per year on Native Americans. By 1755, that average rose to more than eighty-seven per year, an increase of more than 300 percent.

The introduction of "hot topics" naturally led to more local news because the topics of chief concern were almost always issues that directly affected communities and gave rise to comment on those items from the local citizenry. Because of the importance of this news to a city, colony, or colonies, newspapers evolved into the official registers for colonial America. Items became "official" once they appeared in a newspaper. Often this news confirmed what was already common knowledge,[28] but as the colonial period continued, these official notices no doubt provided more information than was known by citizens of a city or a colony.

The growth of local news in newspapers served yet another purpose in the development of newspapers in the colonial period. Local news presented in newspapers helped to develop a "colonial news service." Whether initiated intentially by printers or as a step in the evolutionary process, local news placed in a local newspaper helped disseminate information to other colonies. News concerning the Cherokee war in 1760, for example, was taken by printers in Philadelphia, New York, Boston, and other cities from the accounts that ran weekly in the *South-Carolina Gazette*. Often times newspapers credited the *Gazette* as the source of the news, but even if printers did not acknowledge the South Carolina paper as the source of their news, they felt they could count on its accuracy. That is also how the *Boston Evening-Post*'s printers treated news of slave rebellions in Jamaica in 1760. The Fleet brothers considered the reports "authoritative" when they could confidently assure their readers that the news of the rebellions came from the newspapers of Jamaica and not from a visitor to the island or a casual observer.[29]

The best example of the dispersal of information by the "colonial news service," however, may be observed in the slave news of the eighteenth century. Virtually every piece of news about slave revolts recorded in a newspaper in one colony was extracted and reprinted in the newspapers of other colonies. In fact, except for the precarious situation of South Carolina where slaves greatly outnumbered the white population and the fear of slave rebellions tended to suppress news of slave rebellions, it was rare for a city with a newspaper not to share news of slave revolts or slave crimes with readers once that news was received. When, for example, a Kittery slave threw his master's child down a well in apparent retribution for what the slave believed to be ill treatment, the news quickly spread from Boston to Annapolis, and the "paper" trail of the news story is easily traceable from an 11 August 1755, report that ran in the *Boston Evening-Post* and *Boston Gazette.* The identical story appeared in New Haven on 16 August,[30] New York on 18 August,[31] Philadelphia 21 August,[32] and Annapolis 28 August.[33]

By the time America reached the period of conflict with Great Britain, colonial newspapers had developed into sheets that provided a wide variety of information on many different topics. More importantly, newspapers had learned that information that affected local conditions was much more valuable to readers than any other type of news. It did not always matter whether this news was generated locally; what was important was that the information was of value to local readers. Much of this news during the middle of the eighteenth century had no direct politial ties, and a method of transmitting this news developed. Printers inserted local news into newspapers, and that news was in turn shipped throughout the American colonies and used by other printers to keep all Americans apprised of the events of colonial America. The evolution of newspapers into this type of news service helped to create a cohesiveness in America, a feeling that the citizens of South Carolina and New York, for example, had something in common. This unification began with news of George Whitefield, and it ended with the news of revolution.

Although beyond the parameters of this study, the content of colonial newspapers also reveals important insights into the nature of colonial newspapers and the relationship between news content and advertising practices. As newspapers developed, some printers realized that advertising made newspapers profitable, and advertisers realized that people would not see their ads if papers did not carry news that was of value locally. For that reason printers had to make sure they ran an ample amount of news on the "hot topics" of the day. When the *Boston Chronicle,* for example, only referred to the Boston Massacre as "an unfortunate affair"[34] and ignored other news about the shooting on Boston's streets, opting instead for bits of news and essays from Europe, its advertising copy exhibited a noticeable drop. By 25 June 1770, the newspaper was dead.[35]

The common assumption about advertising in colonial newspapers concludes that printers ran ads on the last page of the news-paper, and sometimes those ads ran on page three. While this practice was essentially true early in the colonial period, the more ads that ran in a paper, the more money printers made; the equa-tion was simple. By 1735, Benjamin Franklin began running ads on page one and four.[36] This allowed newspapers to present ads in large blocks to readers. But by midcentury, printers hit upon a better plan for displaying advertising. Printers at that time started to spread advertisements throughout their papers, placing ads at the bottom of columns of news on most pages. Now instead of being able to ignore all of the ads if one chose to do so by turning to the inside pages of a newspaper, readers discovered ads and news together. Even though clever advertising displays were lim-ited to woodcuts, the interspersing of news and ads demonstrates that as colonial printers developed new methods of information dispersal they also developed ways to better transmit the advertis-ing that paid for newspapers.

Placing advertisements among the news on the inside pages also allowed printers to receive ads later than if the ads were to appear on pages one and four. This fact was related to the printing prac-tices for colonial newspapers. The logistics of printing in the colo-nial period and the newspapers themselves support this conclusion. Printing houses could produce 250 printed sheets per hour. Each one of these sheets had to be hung up to dry in the shop. Once dry, the sheets were taken down and the other side printed.[37] When circulation figures for colonial newspapers are con-sidered, then it becomes apparent that before the end of the period when printers were selling more than three thousand five hundred editions weekly,[38] printers had to produce at least part of their newspapers before the day of publication in order to get their news-papers out on time. The same was probably true by midcentury when six hundred was an average circulation figure for newspapers except in print shops with two or three presses.[39] Ads that ran several weeks in a row could be set and left in the stick and printing frame. If a printer received a new ad, he could insert it on page two or three, the side of the newspaper printed last. The fact that this was where new ads were generally placed for ease of operation and to attract attention to them is demonstrated by the *South-Carolina Gazette; and Country Journal,* which often labeled its advertisements on the inside "New Advertisements."[40]

The fact that the latest advertisements were placed on the inside of the newspaper is supported by the fact that colonial newspapers ran most of their local news and latest correspondence on pages two and three of their four-page weekly editions. Again, news and advertising were used in tandem by colonial printers as the process of developing "a good newspaper" continued. News and ads were on the inside of newspapers, pages two and three, not because news was known by everyone already or because that was the most convenient place to put the ads but because the inside pages were where colonial citizens expected the latest news to be. It is a mistake of current journalistic practices to assume that the most important news should appear on page one in eighteenth-century America.[41] The "freshest Advices," according to colonial standards, appeared on the last pages set by a colonial printer each week—pages two and three.[42]

The nature of the content of colonial newspapers also raises several questions that need to be addressed but are beyond the scope of this research. Who, after all, read colonial newspapers? This study has alluded to the fact that the varied types of news contained in colonial newspapers made them attractive reading to all citizens of colonial America. Determining exactly who read the newspapers, however, cannot be ascertained from this research. Similarly, knowing the sources of colonial news is important. Within this study, the importance of local news has been stressed, as well as the development of local interest of all news in newspapers, but this study has not attempted to categorize news sources to compare quantitatively locally generated news versus clipped news. Such a study would no doubt greatly support the conclusions reached here and demonstrate, as did Donald Shaw with newspapers from 1820–1860, that the content of the newspapers of the period began to focus more on items of local interest and used less clipped news as they developed and matured.[43]

This study has also maintained that newspapers evolved during the colonial period, and their evolution was directly related to developing into "good newspapers," sheets that met the needs of communities with a wide variety of news items on numerous topics. Working to provide a community with news of local concern was prime, and the fact that newspapers did become the official record keepers for the communities they served affirms the notion that the developing newspapers of the colonial period grew into products that served their communities. But continual evolution does not necessarily mean something better is produced; it only means that an item continues to change and adapt. It is not the purpose of this study to judge the quality of newspapers, although some judging has been done. This study has attempted to present the character and content of the news of colonial newspapers outside the areas of European political news, free-press issues, and news of high matters of state. From 1730–1765, "the freshest Advices Foreign and Domestic" were the most varied of any time during the colonial period. Newspapers of the period of political turmoil from 1765–1775 were more one dimensional, turning into political agents. They were, however, evolving into documents that continued to meet the needs of the people, and history tells us that most Americans of the last decade of the colonial period were very much interested in relations with England.[44] Viewed from a two-century-plus perspective, these newspapers that closed the period were not nearly as interesting reading as those produced in the middle of the eighteenth century, in much the same way the newspapers from 1800–1830 were much more singular in purpose and less entertaining than the newspapers produced by the Penny Press, which contained all types of news.

"The freshest Advices Foreign and Domestic" included news that was as varied as could be imagined or as diverse as life itself. The diversified news of colonial newspapers told of America's religion, crimes, deaths, weather, and agricultural situation. The news apprised colonial citizens of the activities of Native American and slaves, and it warned of disease outbreaks and provided methods for curing those maladies. News shocked readers with graphic accounts of murder and cruelty and related the most spectacular accidents as well as the most mundane follies of people. News emphasized the role of women within society and in the process provided a glimpse at what was expected of women in a male-dominated world. And news emphasized the importance of the sea to colonial America. Americans may have begun moving westward during the later stages of the colonial period, but the colonies looked to the Atlantic and the eastern destinations of ships according to the newspapers. The sea was the lifeblood of colonial America, according to the news, and upon it moved almost all correspondence, trade, and economic prosperity.

To assume that colonial newspapers were poorly printed, clipped sheets of stale news is to short change "The freshest Advices Foreign and Domestic" of colonial newspapers. To conclude that their study holds no value for understanding eighteenth-century America or no lessons for media today is also a grievous error. America's first newspapers have served as prototype for all newspapers that have followed. As colonial newspapers evolved and began to include a wider variety of nonpolitical news, they were responding to the information needs of those who read the papers. The great success of colonial newspapers should offer a lesson for print media of the twenty-first century as editors, publishers, and reporters seek ways to make their product better meet the needs of those for whom newspapers are intended to serve. The study of colonial newspapers as a guide for the troubled print media today, however, is the stuff of future research.

This study has uncovered the vast array of news and its presentation during the colonial period. In the process it has provided a small glimpse into the nature of colonial society, but it has granted anyone willing to look a magnifying-glass view of the true character and content of the news of America's first efforts at mass communication with the printed page. Combined with the numerous studies of the political content of newspapers of the colonial period, a true portrait of colonial news is available. Americans by the middle of the eighteenth century had, as the *New-York Gazette* proclaimed in 1750, developed an unsatiable appetite for news. And as a host of newspapers boldly stated in 1770:

> News'papers are the spring of knowledge,
> The gen'ral source throughout the nation,
> Of ev'ry modern conversation.
> What would this mighty people do,
> If there, alas! were nothing new?
> A News-paper is like a feast,
> Some dish there is for ev'ry guest;
> Some large, some small, some strong, some tender,
> For ev'ry stomach stout, or slender.[45]

"The freshest Advices Foreign and Domestic" as newspapers developed in the eighteenth century came to represent the commitment of printers to present varied news on a diverse range of topics, offered in a sincere effort to help meet the information needs of Americans who were living in an ever-changing and evolving society. Newspapers changed and evolved as well, and in the course of the eighteenth century, America's news sheets no doubt affected society's changes as much as society affected them.

Appendix 1
Methodology

THE newspapers used in this study were the English-language newspapers of British America, that is, the thirteen colonies that became the United States. The study does not look at the newspapers of Canada or of the Caribbean nor does it attempt to examine any of the foreign-language papers of eighteenth-century America.[1] For the purpose of this study, content includes news items, essays, letters, and editorials. Advertisements, although a valuable tool in understanding colonial newspapers, are excluded from the study.

Ascertaining exactly how many newspapers existed in the colonial period necessitated consulting a number of sources. By combining the count of newspapers in Sidney Kobre's *The Development of the Colonial Newspaper* with the names of newspapers in Isaiah Thomas's *The History of Printing* and the newspaper listings in Clarence S. Brigham's *A History and Bibliography of American Newspapers, 1690–1820,* an inventory of newspapers was obtained. Copies of these newspapers were located by using *Newspapers of Microfilm.*[2] The names of newspapers and their total number remained consistent throughout much of the period. By 1730, the colonies had seven newspapers. By 1735, twelve different newspapers were published, and from 1735–1755, the number of newspapers in the colonies fluctuated between twelve and fourteen, reaching seventeen in 1760.

With the Stamp Act and the political crisis leading to its implementation in 1765, the political climate of the colonies precipitated the founding of numerous newspapers, and by 1775 and the outbreak of armed resistance by the colonists the number of newspapers increased greatly. Exactly how many newspapers were printed in 1775, however, is a point of contention. Thomas concluded that a total of thirty-five English language papers were printed at that time.[3] Brigham listed forty newspapers that were printed in 1775. Kobre put the number at forty-eight, but when he listed them by name as either Tory or patriot newspapers, his count included only thirty-nine newspapers that were printed in 1775.[4] In this study, forty newspapers were found in 1775, and a full list of all newspapers used in this research may be found in the bibliography.

The best estimate for the total number of newspapers that were printed during the colonial era is approximately eighty. Seventy-two of those newspapers were read for this study and out of a total of more than thirty-six thousand issues, approximately seven thousand four hundred were read.[5]

The goal of this study was to read enough newspapers between 1690–1776 to give an accurate representation of colonial newspapers and their content while keeping the number manageable. These criteria were met by setting up a sampling method that accurately reflected the content of colonial newspapers over the entire period as reflected in the total number of newspaper issues available. In using this method, either every extant newspaper or a sampling of extant newspapers was read at five-year intervals beginning in 1720 and continuing to 1775. No sampling methods were used in reading the news content of the papers, however. In every edition of the approximately seven thousand four hundred used for the study, each news item other than those that dealt specifically with European affairs or free-press issues was read, regardless of the whether two, four, six, or eight pages of news were included in an edition. Such a study is very inclusive. Newspapers of the colonial period that began and ceased publication in years excluded from this study are few in number, and none of them published longer than two years.[6] In addition, the number of newspapers printed during the years to be sampled that were not available on microfilm[7] or no longer extant[8] is very small.

In any year that a sampling of the total number of newspapers was taken, the margin of error was less than 4 percent, meaning that there was a 4 percent chance in 100 of missing a significant item for the year sampled. For most of the years studied, the chance of error was zero because the total number of issues of newspapers that appeared in that year was small enough that every edition of each newspaper was read. Whenever sampling became necessary for a specific year, between five hundred and six hundred issues representing every available paper printed during that year were read. Social science research has demonstrated that a survey sample of this size produces a margin of error of 4 percent or less, thereby providing an accurate portrait of the total population.[9]

Because the number of newspapers that existed during the colonial period fluctuated, a three-step procedure was employed to select those newspapers to read. The purpose of each step was to provide as accurate as possible representation of the colonial newspapers and their contents. The procedure, which divided the period into three groups based on the number of individual newspapers printed and total number of newspapers issued, is as follows:

1) *All newspapers before 1720.* With the exception of the one edition of *Publick Occurrences* in 1690 and two editions each of the *Boston Gazette* and the *American Weekly Mercury* of Philadelphia in December 1719, the only newspaper in colonial America prior to the 1720s was the *Boston News-Letter.* In order to have an accurate representation of the contents of colonial newspapers prior to 1720, each edition of the *News-Letter,* along with *Publick Occurrences,* was read. The resulting number of newspapers was approximately one thousand. The margin of error within this period is zero.

2) *All newspapers every five years from 1720–1755.* Because the total number of newspapers printed during this period varies but never reaches an unmanageable number for any single year, each extant issue during the selected years, a possible total of thirty-eight hundred editions, was read. This provides a margin of error of zero for each of the selected years.

3) *Selected issues of every newspaper printed from 1760–1775.* By 1760, seventeen different newspapers were being printed in the British American colonies bringing the total yearly editions to almost nine hundred. By 1775, the yearly output, which now included several multi-weekly papers, approached two thousand. By reading at least five or six hundred individual issues from the years being sampled, or approximately twenty-six hundred issues, an accurate representation of the news content should be revealed.

The overall results of sampling every five years of colonial newspapers from 1720–1775 and reading all newspapers before 1720—approximately seventy-four hundred issues—produced a standard error of 1 percent. This means that there is only a 1 percent chance of missing any significant story or change in the colonial papers printed from 1690–1776. The same standard error would be produced if twenty-five thousand of the thirty-six thousand colonial newspapers were read.[10]

The selection of individual editions of newspapers within each sample was systematic with the same weeks of each newspaper read and charted for comparisons among newspapers. The weeks selected in each year of sampling may be found below. Properly sampling the newspapers from 1775, for example, necessitated reading an issue of each newspaper every three weeks. That provided a sample of approximately six hundred newspapers. In order to achieve the proper sample size for 1760, two issues of each newspaper were read and the third issue skipped, providing a similar sampling size. The same type of sampling strategy was employed in 1765 and 1770 to keep the sample error below 4 percent.

This process provides an accurate overview of colonial newspapers and reveals their content. While no factual statements can be made about any specific years in which newspapers were not read, changes in the nature and character of news over the entire period should be discernible using this method since changes in news—that dealing with Native Americans, slaves, and women for instance—should occur at a more gradual rate than news pertaining to the volatile political issues that developed with the Stamp Act and continued to end of the colonial period, issues that have been studied in depth by other scholars.[11]

The above methodology solves the problem of reading a sufficient number of newspapers to form accurate conclusions on the news of the colonial period. But because the colonial newspapers varied greatly in size of type used, page size, and number of columns per page, making an accurate comparison of amounts of certain types of news is difficult. A newspaper's front page, for example, might contain one story in large type, while the inside pages might contain thirty to fifty news items each in varied type sizes. Comparing inches of type of stories in such a case would not be accurate because the larger type faces consume more space. In addition, measuring inches on microfilm and microcard copies is not possible.

Similarly, counting the stories and drawing conclusions about the news content will not always be accurate. In the example posed above, twenty of the inside news items may have been political in nature and therefore outside the parameters of this study. Another group of ten may have given ship news with another twenty on other topics. Only one news item from the newspaper dealt with crime, but it was the front page story of a trial dealing with a particularly heinous murder. If only news items are counted, political news in this case greatly outnumbered the other types of news, but crime news occupied a full page. Numbers of articles, however, can be helpful in identifying trends over time and those people or events that capture the attention of the news at certain points in time, and for that reason the news content discovered by this study for selected newspapers may be compared by consulting appendix 2.

Because of the problems encountered with both methods of comparing the amounts of news in the colonial papers, no accurate figures based on concise measurement are likely. While such a comparison is important, the fact that so many varied types and topics of news appeared in the colonial press reveals more about the newspapers than any statistical measurement and leads to a discussion of current scholarly perceptions of colonial newspapers.

Dates Used for Sampling: 1760–1775

1760

January 1–6
January 7–13
January 21–27
January 28–February 3
February 11–17
February 18–24
March 4–10
March 11–17
March 25–31
April 1–6
April 15–21
April 22–28
May 6–12
May 13–19
May 27–June 2
June 3–9
June 17–23
June 24–30
July 8–14
July 15–21
July 29–August 4
August 5–11
August 19–25
August 26–September 1
September 9–15
September 19–25
September 30–October 6
October 7–13
October 21–27
October 28–November 3
November 11–17
November 18–24
December 2–8
December 9–15
December 23–29

1765

January 1–5
January 13–19

January 27–February 2
February 10–16
February 24–March 2
March 10–16
March 24–30
April 7–13
April 21–27
May 5–11
May 19–25
June 2–8
June 16–22
June 30–July 6
July 14–20
July 28–August 3
August 11–17
August 25–31
September 8–14
September 22–28
October 6–12
October 20–26
November 3–9
November 17–23
December 1–7
December 15–21
December 29–31

1770

January 1–6
January 14–20
February 4–10
February 18–24
March 4–10
March 18–24
April 1–7
April 15–21
May 6–12
May 20–26
June 3–9
June 17–23
July 1–7

July 15–21
August 5–11
August 19–25
September 2–8
September 16–22
October 7–13
October 21–27
November 4–10
November 18–24
December 2–8
December 16–22

1775
January 2–7
January 22–28

February 5–11
February 27–March 4
March 19–25
April 9–15
April 30–May 6
May 21–27
June 11–17
July 2–8
July 23–29
August 13–19
September 3–9
September 24–30
October 15–21
November 5–11
November 26–December 2
December 17–23

Appendix 2
Content Breakdown, Selected Colonial Newspapers

THE content of colonial newspapers uncovered in this study falls into fifteen categories. The news in some of the categories, such as the sea and crime, remained fairly consistent in newspaper presentation throughout the period. Other topics, such as news of Native Americans and religion, increased or decreased whenever events warranted. This appendix contains charts to help readers see the breakdown of the news content of this study from 1720–1775 in representative newspapers. By placing the charts together in an appendix, one can compare year by year, the coverage of certain types of news in the colonies.

In observing these charts one must remember that counting numbers of articles is not perfect in determining the amount or importance of news in colonial newspapers. As noted in Appendix 1, the inconsistency of type sizes, columns per newspaper, variation in the size of news sheets, and length of stories make standardization in measurement of colonial newspapers impossible. Comparing the total number of news items in selected newspapers, however, does allow one to determine which topics were mentioned most during the selected years of this study. The comparison also provides an easy method to determine whether the same topics were mentioned with the same frequency in newspapers in all regions of the colonies.

The comparisons allow one to observe which subjects were "hot topics," and in which newspapers the topics were of prime concern and during what period. For instance, the breakdown reveals that Native Americans became a topic of prime concern for newspapers in all regions in 1755 and 1760, the years of the French and Indian War and the Cherokee War in the South. The number of news articles on Native Americans in New York and Pennsylvania in 1755 is much greater than the total count in Southern newspapers and slightly higher than New England sheets, which leads to rightful speculation that the fighting between the French and Indians and British colonists was much more intense in the Middle colonies in 1755 than in the Southern colonies especially. The fighting in New England, according to the numbers of articles, was only slightly less than in New York and Pennsylvania.

Even though the comparisons work well for studying Native American news content of colonial newspapers, the charts are not always so revealing, and those using them should be apprised of at least one caveat. Within the news of colonial newspapers, there is a certain amount of overlapping. This means that some Native American news, slave news, and news of the seas—as demonstrated in the chapters of this study—contain information that is very sensational in nature. This news, even though it is sensationalistic and meets the criteria for sensationalism, has been counted as news of Native Americans, slaves, or news of the sea because that is the prime nature of the news item. The same is true for other topics and other areas where subject matter overlaps. For that reason, a topic such as sensationalism appears to be of less consequence than in reality it is in the newspapers.

The newspapers included in the charts that follow represent each region of the colonies, and for the most part they are the newspapers with the longest continual runs. The *New-York Gazette,* however, is represented by two different newspapers. The first is the *Gazette* begun by William Bradford in November 1725, and the second is James Parker's *New-York Gazette,* which began in 1743 as the *New-York Weekly Post-Boy.* The *Maryland Gazette* entries include those printed by William Parks and Jonas Green or members of his family. The other newspapers included in this Appendix breakdown are as follows: Boston-*Boston News-Letter* (name changes to *Massachusetts Gazette* in 1770 and 1775 tables), *Boston Evening-Post* (includes items from the *Weekly Rehearsal,* the name of the *Post* in the first half of 1735), *Boston Gazette;* Philadelphia-*American Weekly Mercury* 1720–1740, *Pennsylvania Journal* 1745–1775, *Pennsylvania Gazette;* and Charleston-*South-Carolina Gazette* for a total of eight newspaper entries. Not all newspapers for each year of the study were extant. Those years are so marked.

Subject matter included in each topic is as follows: Sea-ship news, customhouse news, price current, and tide reports; Native American-all news pertaining to Indians; Sensationalism-news stories that shocked the senses but did not fall into any other subject category; Crime/Courts-all crimes and court reports; Slaves-all items dealing with African slaves including some slave crimes; Women-all subject matter dealing with women, the home, family relations, children, education, and crime when being female was the prime motivation for the news item; Disease-any news item that deals with medicine and disease reports and obituaries that emphasize a particular disease such as smallpox as the cause of death; Religion-all religious topics; accidents-all accidents such as drownings; Animals/Agriculture-all news items dealing with animals either domestic or wild and crop news; Natural Events-all natural disasters and occurrences such as earthquakes and sightings of comets and other natural phenomena; Entertainment-all literary and amusement pieces, gaming and sports, and oddities such as abnormal humans; Social news-weddings, obituaries, and social events; Weather-all weather-related stories including severe weather such as lightning; Discoveries-science, inventions, and natural discoveries such as electricity.

Each chart is broken down by year, subject matter, and newspaper. If a newspaper column is empty for a particular year, such as 1735 for the *Maryland Gazette,* it means that the newspaper did not print during that year. The numbers in each column represent the percent of news items found in a particular newspaper on a specific topic for the year of the chart. If, for example, one looks at the *American Weekly Mercury* for 1720, one discovers that approximately 4.5 percent of its 375 news items dealt with crime and court reports. The percentage represents seventeen news items. The charts do not include European political news nor those items that dealt purely with government decrees in America.

Table 1

News Content of Colonial Newspapers by Percentage

1720

Topic	Weekly Mercury	Boston Gazette	News Letter
Sea	82.4	66.0	35.6
N. Americans	0.2	2.8	1.0
Sensationalism	0.2	0.8	0.6
Crime/courts	4.5	4.4	4.4
Slaves	0	0	0.3
Women	0	0.5	0
Disease	0.8	0.5	2.2
Religion	2.7	2.5	14.9
Accidents	1.0	3.0	6.3
Animals/agri.	0.2	0.5	1.3
Entertainment	0	1.6	1.0
Natural events	0	0.2	1.6
Social news	5.6	15.3	23.8
Weather	1.9	1.4	6.3
Discoveries	0.2	0	0.3
Total items	375	360	314

Table 2

News Content of Colonial Newspapers by Percentage

1725

Topic	Weekly Mercury	Boston Gazette	News Letter
Sea	58.3	60.5	36.7
N. Americans	3.2	4.0	2.8
Sensationalism	0	1.3	0.8
Crime/courts	13.6	4.0	3.6
Slaves	0.2	0.5	0.2
Women	1.4	0.8	0.8
Disease	1.0	1.7	1.3
Religion	6.8	4.9	11.0
Accidents	2.6	0.8	6.7
Animals/agri.	2.2	0.8	1.9
Entertainment	2.2	0.8	3.3
Natural events	0.5	0	0.8
Social news	6.6	17.5	26.1
Weather	1.0	0.5	2.2
Discoveries	0.5	0	0.2
Total items	499	223	359

Table 3

Content of Colonial Newspapers by Percentage

1730

Topics	Weekly Mercury	Boston Gazette	News Letter	N.Y. Gazette	Pa. Gazette	Md.[a] Gazette
Sea	55.0	47.6	25.8	44.8	20.1	33.9
N. Americans	1.3	1.0	0.9	2.1	1.2	3.5
Sensational	0.5	0.5	1.8	0	2.2	0
Crime/courts	13.0	7.3	6.7	19.8	16.3	7.1
Slaves	1.0	1.0	1.2	2.5	1.7	0
Women	1.6	1.7	1.8	2.5	2.9	3.5
Disease	1.5	3.0	6.7	2.5	2.5	3.5
Religion	3.2	3.5	8.6	5.6	13.1	1.7
Accidents	4.7	2.8	6.7	4.7	10.0	1.7
Animals/agri.	0.8	0.5	5.2	0.8	2.8	3.5
Entertainment	6.2	3.5	4.0	3.0	7.4	17.8
Natural events	2.7	0.2	2.4	0.8	0.8	0
Social news	5.7	25.5	21.8	8.6	11.9	21.4
Weather	0.6	1.3	4.9	1.3	4.3	1.7
Discoveries	0.3	0.2	0.9	0.4	1.5	0
Total items	592	395	325	232	790	56

[a]Only ten editions of the *Maryland Gazette* are extant for 1730.

Table 4

Content of Colonial Newspapers by Percentage

1735

Topics	Weekly Merc.	Ev'ning Post	Boston Gazette	News Letter	N.Y. Gazette	Pa. Gazette	S.C. Gazette	Md.[a] Gazette
Sea	52.0	27.2	39.3	25.0	49.1	31.3	56.0	
N. Americans	1.3	2.3	0.8	1.7	1.7	1.3	1.4	
Sensational	1.2	1.3	0.8	3.5	0.8	4.1	2.1	
Crime/court	11.2	15.1	9.1	9.1	7.5	15.6	11.7	
Slaves	2.2	1.9	2.4	1.7	1.7	2.9	4.2	
Women	2.2	3.7	1.3	3.8	3.1	2.7	1.0	
Disease	0.8	3.1	3.4	2.7	2.0	2.0	0.3	
Religion	2.2	5.3	5.2	6.8	1.1	3.6	1.7	
Accidents	9.8	12.7	8.1	14.2	4.6	3.6	1.7	
Animals/agri.	0.5	3.5	1.4	2.0	2.9	3.4	0.3	
Entertainment	2.5	5.8	2.2	1.7	5.2	7.9	6.3	
Natural events	4.2	1.3	0.3	1.5	1.4	0.9	0.3	
Social news	8.6	9.8	22.1	16.7	12.5	15.4	8.1	
Weather	0.8	6.2	2.5	8.1	4.6	3.8	2.8	
Discoveries	0	0.1	0.4	0.7	1.1	0.9	1.4	
Total items	588	510	821	394	344	440	282	

[a] The *Maryland Gazette* under William Parks ceased publication in 1734. Jonas Green resumed publication of the newspaper in 1745.

Table 5

Content of Colonial Newspapers by Percentage

1740

Topics	Weekly Merc.	Ev'ning Post	Boston Gazette	News Letter	N.Y. Gazette	Pa. Gazette	S.C. Gazette	Md.[a] Gazette
Sea	65.8	55.5	62.0	57.0	55.7	51.7	71.8	
N. Americans	0	1.3	0.4	2.4	0	2.1	0	
Sensational	0	1.6	0.4	1.3	0	0.5	0.3	
Crime/court	2.3	5.3	3.7	2.8	7.3	4.2	1.0	
Slaves	0.7	2.2	0.4	1.0	0	1.4	0.6	
Women	0.3	1.8	2.4	1.7	0	1.4	0	
Disease	0	1.6	0.4	2.2	2.1	1.1	0.3	
Religion	14.5	5.3	2.9	9.6	16.8	17.7	15.7	
Accidents	4.3	6.7	12.0	5.2	2.1	0.5	2.6	
Animals/agri.	1.0	2.2	1.2	2.2	1.0	2.2	0.6	
Entertainment	4.3	3.1	2.0	2.4	3.1	1.4	1.6	
Natural events	1.9	0.5	0	0	0	0	0	
Social news	1.9	7.8	10.3	9.2	5.2	6.2	4.9	
Weather	2.3	4.5	1.6	4.8	5.2	3.1	0.3	
Discoveries	0	0.1	0	0	1.0	0.2	0	
Total items	255	546	242	455	95	350	305	

[a] The *Maryland Gazette* under William Parks ceased publication in 1734. Jonas Green resumed publication of the newspaper in 1745.

Table 6

Content of Colonial Newspapers by Percentage

1745

Topics	Pa.[a] Journal	Ev'ning Post	Boston Gazette	News Letter	N.Y. Gazette	Pa. Gazette	S.C. Gazette	Md. Gazette
Sea	71.5	44.0	56.8	55.8	80.0	75.8	69.8	34.1
N. Americans	7.7	6.5	4.3	6.4	4.1	4.4	2.3	2.1
Sensational	1.0	2.3	0.8	1.6	0.6	0.3	0	1.0
Crime/court	3.1	2.6	1.4	2.9	2.3	3.1	3.6	2.8
Slaves	0.5	1.1	0.3	1.3	0.5	0.5	0.6	0.7
Women	0.5	2.0	0.5	0.5	1.0	0.3	0.3	1.4
Disease	3.6	1.7	0.5	1.3	1.0	3.3	1.0	1.7
Religion	2.6	20.1	19.1	5.5	2.6	3.1	5.6	0.7
Accidents	1.5	5.3	3.4	6.9	1.8	2.2	0	2.8
Animals/agri.	0	1.4	0	1.3	0.1	0.3	4.3	1.0
Entertainment	3.1	3.2	1.4	3.2	1.5	1.0	5.6	4.5
Natural events	0	0	0	0	0	0	0	0
Social news	2.6	3.5	8.1	8.2	3.8	3.4	5.0	6.0
Weather	2.0	5.3	2.9	4.5	1.0	1.6	1.9	5.6
Discoveries	0	0.2	0	0.2	0	0.5	0	0
Total items	193	337	345	376	670	547	302	284

[a]These numbers represent five months of the *Pennsylvania Journal, or the Weekly Advertiser.*

Table 7

Content of Colonial Newspapers

1750

Topics	Pa. Journal	Ev'ning Post	Boston Gazette	News Letter	N.Y. Gazette	Pa. Gazette	S.C. Gazette	Md. Gazette
Sea	52.8%	23.4	26.4	56.8	50.7	40.8	43.3	23.7
N. Americans	8.6	5.2	4.2	14.7	5.8	6.4	4.0	2.0
Sensational	1.7	1.4	1.0	1.4	0.4	0.9	0.8	1.8
Crime/court	8.8	12.5	6.6	10.4	10.7	15.3	4.4	19.7
Slaves	1.7	1.9	2.0	3.8	1.5	1.5	1.2	4.0
Women	1.2	2.8	1.8	6.1	1.3	1.9	2.4	3.8
Disease	1.4	2.1	0.6	4.2	0.7	0.5	2.8	1.6
Religion	5.4	7.3	17.0	16.1	2.5	2.3	2.4	3.6
Accidents	5.9	11.5	13.0	15.6	6.6	6.0	1.6	8.3
Animals/agri.	1.7	5.6	1.0	6.6	1.0	4.6	7.6	3.8
Entertainment	1.2	6.8	2.8	12.3	6.2	4.4	8.8	6.7
Natural events	2.4	3.5	3.2	3.3	1.7	2.5	2.8	3.8
Social news	4.1	8.9	15.2	28.9	5.8	7.5	13.6	10.7
Weather	2.2	5.2	4.8	4.7	3.7	5.4	2.0	5.3
Discoveries	0.5	1.4	0.2	1.9	0.5	0.9	2.0	0.8
Total items	407	423	499	211	510	514	249	501

Table 8

Content of Colonial Newspapers by Percentage

1755

Topics	Pa. Journal	Ev'ning Post	Boston Gazette	News Letter	N.Y. Gazette	Pa. Gazette	S.C. Gazette	Md. Gazette
Sea	64.2	27.5	44.7	42.8	50.4	53.8	62.9	26.1
N. Americans	15.0	13.4	15.3	14.7	22.3	16.8	12.8	13.6
Sensational	0.8	1.7	0.6	1.5	1.4	0.4	0	1.4
Crime/court	2.4	8.8	1.9	4.1	5.4	4.9	1.0	9.8
Slaves	0.7	1.5	0.1	1.5	0.6	0.3	0.4	2.5
Women	0.4	2.5	1.4	2.3	2.0	1.6	0.6	2.5
Disease	0.4	0.7	0.5	1.8	1.0	1.6	1.0	1.0
Religion	2.0	6.0	13.7	4.9	2.0	2.5	2.7	5.6
Accidents	1.9	8.5	4.2	6.7	3.1	3.0	0	5.4
Animals/agri.	0.4	2.0	0.1	1.0	0.7	1.6	1.2	1.8
Entertainment	3.0	5.8	3.4	3.3	3.8	5.7	2.1	2.7
Natural events	1.4	4.0	2.9	1.0	1.1	1.6	1.9	3.3
Social news	3.7	12.1	6.7	10.0	3.4	3.8	10.7	14.0
Weather	3.0	4.8	2.1	2.5	2.0	2.0	1.5	9.2
Discoveries	0	0.2	0.2	1.3	1.3	0.1	0.1	0.6
Total items	685	396	612	387	676	685	467	478

Table 9

Content of Colonial Newspapers by Percentage

1760

Topics	Pa. Journal	Ev'ning Post	Boston Gazette	News Letter	N.Y. Gazette	Pa. Gazette	S.C. Gazette	Md. Gazette
Sea	70.9	37.2	50.2	50.1	50.8	62.7	33.8	26.8
N. Americans	12.0	13.4	9.3	11.0	15.5	18.3	30.6	13.2
Sensational	0	1.5	0.2	1.5	0.6	0.1	2.2	1.2
Crime/court	1.7	4.6	2.0	4.4	3.8	1.9	1.0	6.8
Slaves	1.8	2.3	1.6	2.5	1.0	2.1	0.6	4.8
Women	0.4	2.3	0.5	0.9	0.7	1.1	0.6	1.2
Disease	1.0	1.7	1.4	1.5	1.7	1.9	3.3	4.8
Religion	1.7	5.4	12.4	3.9	2.4	1.3	0.6	1.9
Accidents	1.4	7.9	5.9	8.3	6.0	3.9	0.6	8.7
Animals/agri.	0	0.2	0.9	0.4	1.0	0.4	0	0.9
Entertainment	0.7	3.8	5.4	2.4	6.1	0.4	3.1	7.5
Natural events	1.0	2.1	0.5	0.9	1.2	0.8	1.6	3.6
Social news	4.2	12.6	9.4	9.5	6.0	3.4	4.7	10.7
Weather	2.3	3.6	1.3	1.9	2.6	0.4	15.9	7.0
Discoveries	0.4	0.9	0.5	0.1	0	0.6	1.0	0.2
Total items	643	516	537	835	649	612	502	410

Figures for 1760 represent a computed number. Two-thirds of all editions of colonial newspapers for this year were read. The numbers in the chart are based on the total number of items counted in those newspapers plus one-third of that number.

Table 10

Content of Colonial Newspapers by Percentage

1765

Topics	Pa. Journal	Ev'ning Post	Boston Gazette	News Letter	N.Y. Gazette	Pa. Gazette	S.C. Gazette	Md. Gazette
Sea	58.0	24.3	40.2	35.7	49.2	54.5	40.5	17.1
N. Americans	3.9	4.6	3.2	4.7	2.7	6.9	8.4	4.6
Sensational	0.4	2.3	0.3	1.0	1.5	0.2	0.0	1.9
Crime/court	3.4	11.6	6.1	8.2	7.8	6.6	2.8	11.1
Slaves	0	1.0	0.7	1.5	1.5	0.5	0.7	0
Women	1.9	1.5	1.7	1.3	1.9	2.4	1.4	4.6
Disease	0.9	1.8	2.1	3.2	2.7	1.8	2.8	12.5
Religion	5.3	7.8	14.3	6.5	3.1	4.8	2.8	3.2
Accidents	3.9	7.8	5.4	5.2	11.0	2.9	0.7	4.6
Animals/agri.	3.9	2.8	2.5	2.7	0.7	2.9	2.8	4.6
Entertainment	1.9	6.5	3.2	4.5	6.2	1.8	13.2	8.5
Natural events	0	0.2	0.7	1.0	0.4	0	0	3.2
Social news	8.3	22.0	14.0	17.5	4.7	7.2	21.0	5.9
Weather	7.8	4.4	3.6	5.9	5.5	6.4	1.4	5.9
Discoveries	0	1.0	0.7	0.8	0.4	0.5	1.4	2.6
Total items	410	772	556	1188	508	748	286	304

Figures for 1765 represent a computed number. One-half of all editions of colonial newspapers for this year were read. The numbers in the chart are based on the total number of items counted in those newspapers doubled.

Table 11

Content of Colonial Newspapers by Percentage

1770

Topics	Pa. Journal	Ev'ning Post	Boston Gazette	Mass. Gazette	N.Y. Gazette	Pa. Gazette	S.C. Gazette	Md. Gazette
Sea	64.8	19.4	25.7	26.0	41.9	62.0	36.3	23.3
N. Americans	1.4	1.2	1.8	1.3	1.0	0.3	2.2	.0
Sensational	0	0.8	0	1.5	0.5	0.3	.0	0
Crime/court	9.8	15.4	10.0	13.0	13.9	8.9	3.9	9.5
Slaves	0.3	0.4	0.6	0.8	0.5	0	1.7	0
Women	1.8	2.0	0.6	2.0	1.6	1.8	3.9	8.2
Disease	2.9	3.9	2.5	3.9	2.1	1.8	0.5	1.3
Religion	7.2	11.1	11.9	7.9	1.0	3.5	2.8	6.8
Accidents	1.0	3.5	6.2	9.4	3.2	2.5	1.1	2.7
Animals/agri.	1.0	1.5	1.2	2.0	0.5	1.4	2.8	0
Entertainment	1.4	3.1	3.7	1.1	20.9	2.5	2.8	17.8
Natural events	0.3	1.2	0.6	1.7	1.0	1.8	1.1	5.4
Social news	6.1	34.1	30.8	25.5	8.0	7.1	36.9	24.6
Weather	3.6	1.2	2.5	3.9	2.6	2.8	2.2	0
Discoveries	0.3	0.8	1.2	3.9	0.5	2.8	1.1	0
Total items	551	504	318	907	372	558	352	146

Figures for 1770 represent a computed number. One-half of all editions of colonial newspapers for this year were read. The numbers in the chart are based on the total number of items counted in those newspapers doubled.

Table 12

Content of Colonial Newspapers by Percentage

1775

Topics	Pa. Journal	Ev'ning Post[a]	Boston Gazette	Mass. Gazette	N.Y.[b] Gazette	Pa. Gazette	S.C. Gazette	Md. Gazette
Sea	52.9	13.8	26.6	32.8		55.0	46.1	54.8
N. Americans	11.1	5.0	4.7	2.9		4.7	7.6	4.1
Sensational	1.3	1.2	0	0		0	0	0
Crime/court	1.3	1.8	1.9	1.4		1.7	10.2	0
Slaves	1.3	0	1.9	0		1.1	0	0
Women	1.9	0	1.9	1.4		1.7	0	4.1
Disease	1.3	1.2	1.9	0		1.7	0	0
Religion	5.2	9.4	7.6	2.1		4.1	5.1	2.7
Accidents	1.3	3.1	1.9	0		1.1	0	4.1
Animals/agri.	1.9	1.8	2.8	3.6		3.5	10.2	0
Entertainment	3.2	5.0	9.5	2.1		1.7	5.1	9.5
Natural events	0	0	0	0		0	0	0
Social news	8.5	56.6	33.3	53.2		15.9	10.2	10.9
Weather	5.2	0	2.8	0		4.1	5.1	6.8
Discoveries	3.2	1.2	2.8	0		2.9	0	2.7
Total items	153	159	105	137		169	39	73

Figures for 1775 represent a computed number. One-half of all editions of colonial newspapers for this year were read. The numbers in the chart are based on the total number of items counted in those newspapers plus two-thirds of that number.

[a]The *Boston Evening-Post* ceased publication after shots were fired at Lexington and Concord in the third week of April 1775.

[b]The *New-York Gazette or the Weekly Post-Boy* ceased publication in 1772.

Appendix 3
The Names of Colonial Newspapers

THE names of colonial newspapers are often confusing. Printers sometimes changed the names of their papers, or newspapers were bought by another printer. In either case, the same paper under a slightly different name continued to serve a city. In other instances, all newspapers that were printed in a city employed essentially the same name. The Virginia House of Burgesses, for example, decreed that all official printing in that colony would be done by the *Virginia Gazette.* For that reason, every newspaper in colonial Virginia was named the *Virginia Gazette,* and there were three *Gazettes* in Williamsburg in 1775 and another in near-by Norfolk. The only way to tell the Williamsburg newspapers apart was to consult the name of the printer.

The best sources for determining the lineage of colonial newspapers are the newspapers themselves and Isaiah Thomas's *The History of Printing in America.* Thomas, both an apprentice and printer during the colonial era, became involved in printing in 1756 at the age of seven when he was apprenticed to a Boston printer. The following discussion, based on the name changes found in the newspapers and in Thomas, should help readers in better following the geneology of certain newspapers.

Boston Gazette: The *Gazette*'s name was expanded to the *Boston Gazette, or Weekly Journal* in 1741 when the paper was acquired by the owners of the *New-England Weekly Journal.* By 1750, the name was again altered to the *Boston Gazette, or Weekly Advertiser.* In April 1755, the name changed again to the *Boston Gazette, or Country Journal,* and altered to the *Boston Gazette, and Country Journal* 12 April 1756. The newspaper continued under that name for the remainder of the colonial period, but it moved its base of operations from Boston to Watertown following the beginning of the Revolution, suspending publication during the move for two months.

Boston News-Letter: The *News-Letter* operated under that title from 1704 until 1726 when *Weekly* was added to the name. The *Boston Weekly News-Letter* underwent another name change in 1762 to the *Boston News-Letter, and New-England Chronicle,* a name not used in this study. In 1764, the paper's name changed significantly to the *Massachusetts Gazette (And Boston News-Letter).* After 1 November 1765, the date the Stamp Act was to go into effect, the newspaper dropped *Boston News-Letter* from its name.

Boston Weekly Post-Boy: The *Boston Weekly Post-Boy* operated under the name *Post-Boy* from 1734 throughout the rest of the colonial period. Additions and changes to the name occurred three times, however. By 1760, the paper's name changed to *Green & Russell's Boston Post-Boy & Advertiser,* Green and Russell being the new publishers of the newspaper. By 1765, the two printers dropped their names from the paper's title calling it the *Boston Post-Boy and Advertiser.* In 1768, the newspaper, in conjunction with the *Massachusetts Gazette,* became an official printing arm for the colony of Massachusetts. At that time the name of the newspaper changed to the *Massachusetts Gazette, and the Boston Post-Boy and Advertiser.*

Connecticut Courant: Begun in Hartford in 1764, the *Courant's* name changed in 1773 to the *Connecticut Courant, and Hartford Weekly Intelligencer.*

Essex Gazette: The first newspaper of Salem, Massachusetts, the *Gazette* continued under the same name until May 1775. At that time the name of the newspaper changed to the *New-England Chronicle: or, the Essex Gazette* with a move to Cambridge.

Essex Journal: Begun by Isaiah Thomas and Henry Walter-Tinges in 1773 in Newbury-Port, Massachusetts, the *Essex Journal and Merrimack Packet: Or, the Massachusetts and New-Hampshire General Advertiser* altered its name in July 1775, to the *Essex Journal or, the New-Hampshire Packet.*

Massachusetts Spy: The *Spy,* begun in 1770 as a tri-weekly, changed its name to *The Massachusetts Spy or Thomas's Boston Journal* by 1775. The name change recognized the paper's printer, Isaiah Thomas. When the Revolution forced Thomas to move out of Boston to Worcester, he renamed his newspaper *Massachusett's Spy; or, American Oracle of Liberty.*

New Hampshire Gazette: This paper, printed in Portsmouth, continued under the same name until 1775 when *And Historical Chronicle* was appended to the title.

New-London Summary: The *New-London Summary, or The Weekly Advertiser* printed under that name from 1758–1763 when the paper's name changed to the *New-London Gazette.* In 1775, printer Timothy Green changed the name of his newspaper to the *Connecticut Gazette; and the Universal Intelligencer.* This newspaper should not be confused with the *Connecticut Gazette* printed in New Haven from 1755–1767.

New-York Gazette: Several printers operated numerous newspapers under this title. William Bradford started the first *New-York Gazette* in November 1725. That newspaper continued until 1744, at least in principle, by William DeForeest who had been Bradford's printing partner since 1742, in DeForeest's *New-York Evening-Post.* Other *New-York Gazettes* followed. The first began as the *New-York Weekly Post-Boy,* printed by James Parker. Parker changed the name of the newspaper in January 1747 to the *New-York Gazette Revived in the Weekly Post-Boy.* By 1755, the paper dropped *Revived* from its title and went by the name *New-York Gazette: or the Weekly Post-Boy.* In February 1759, the *Gazette*'s name changed again, this time to *Parker's New-York Gazette; or the Weekly Post-Boy,* the Parker being added to show that Samuel Parker, nephew to James Parker, now printed the newspaper. In 1765, John Holt printed the *Gazette* and returned the name of the newspaper to the *New-York Gazette: or the Weekly Post-Boy,* the name under which the newspaper operated until in ceased publishing in 1773. Another *New-York Gazette* was printed during this time as well that was connected with Parker's newspaper. William Weyman, a partner with James Parker, started the *New-York Gazette* in February 1759. Commonly referred to as *Weyman's New-York Gazette,* the newspaper ceased publication at the end of 1767.

New-York Mercury: The *Mercury* began printing in 1752. In 1763, the newspaper's name changed to the *New-York Gazette; and the Weekly Mercury.*

South-Carolina Gazette; and Country Journal: Begun in opposition to the Stamp Act in 1765, the *Country Journal* printed its first two editions as the *South-Carolina Gazetteer. Gazetteer* was then changed to *Gazette.*

Pennsylvania Mercury: This newspaper, called the *Pennsylvania Mercury; and the Universal Advertiser* added the names of its printers, Story and Humphreys to the title after one edition.

Virginia Gazette: The official newspaper of Williamsburg was begun in 1736 by William Parks. Parks printed the newspaper until his death in 1750. A single *Virginia Gazette* continued to be printed by various printers until 1766. In 1770, two *Gazettes* were printed in Williamsburg, one by William Rind and another by Alexander

Purdie and John Dixon. By 1775, three *Gazettes* were printed by printers Purdie, Dixon and William Hunter, and John Pinkney.

Weekly Rehearsal: Begun in 1731 in Boston by John Draper, the *Weekly Rehearsal* was purchased in 1733 by Thomas Fleet, who had been printing the newspaper since 1732. In August 1735, Fleet announced that he would begin printing the newspaper in the evenings. The paper's name was then changed to the *Boston Evening-Post*.

Notes

INTRODUCTION

1. Webb turned out to be a poor confidant because he informed another Philadelphia printer, Samuel Keimer, of Franklin's plans to begin a newspaper. Keimer quickly put into operation his own scheme to start a newspaper. Keimer's newspaper, the *Universal Instructor in all Arts and Sciences; And Pennsylvania Gazette,* was hardly "a good paper," and Franklin, through a series of pieces entitled the "Busy Body," in Philadelphia's first newspaper, the *American Weekly Mercury,* denounced Keimer's newspaper as an affront to women because of a piece Keimer ran on abortion. The attack on Keimer continued, and Franklin bought the paper from the eccentric Keimer in less than a year. See Benjamin Franklin, *Autobiography of Benjamin Franklin: A Genetic Text,* J. A. Leo Lemay and P. M Zall, eds. (Knoxville: University of Tennessee Press, 1981), 63–64. and Anna Janney DeArmond, *Andrew Bradford: Colonial Journalist* (New York: Greenwood Press, 1969), 16 n. 42, 194 n. 65.

2. *Universal Daily Register* (London), 1 January 1785, quoted in Mitchell Stephens, *A History of News: From the Drum to the Satellite* (New York: Penguin Books, 1988), 165.

3. Joseph Frank, *The Beginnings of the English Newspaper 1620–1660* (Cambridge: Harvard University Press, 1961), 3.

4. *Boston Gazette,* 21 December 1719, 1.

5. *Pennsylvania Chronicle, and Universal Advertiser* (Philadelphia), 26 January 1767, nameplate.

6. *Pennsylvania Gazette* (Philadelphia) 16 October 1729.

7. Frank Luther Mott, *American Journalism A History: 1690–1960,* 3rd ed. (New York: The MacMillan Company, 1962), 51, 52.

8. These works include: Edmund S. Morgan and Helen M. Morgan, *The Stamp Act Crisis: Prologue to Revolution* (Chapel Hill: University of North Carolina, 1953); Gary B. Nash, *The Urban Crucible. Social Change, Political Consciousness, and the Origins of the American Revolution* (Cambridge: Harvard University Press, 1979); Arthur M. Schlesinger, *Prelude to Independence: The Newspaper War on Britain 1764–1776* (New York: Random House, 1958); Livingston Rowe Schuyler, *The Liberty of the Press in the American Colonies before the Revolution* (New York: Thomas Whittaker, 1905); Clyde A. Duniway, *The Development of Freedom of the Press in Massachusetts* (Cambridge: Harvard University Press, 1906); Lawrence H. Leder, *Liberty and Authority. Early American Political Ideology, 1689–1763* (Chicago: Quadrangle Books, 1968); Stephen Botein, "'Meer Mechanics' and an Open Press: The Business and Political Strategies of Colonial American Printers," in *Perspectives in American History* IX, eds. Donald Fleming and Bernard Bailyn (Cambridge: Harvard University Press, 1975), 127–225; Leonard Levy, *Legacy of Suppression* (Cambridge: Harvard Uni-

versity Press, 1960); Leonard Levy, *The Emergence of a Free Press* (New York and Oxford: Oxford University Press, 1985); Jeffery A. Smith, *Printers and Press Freedom: The Ideology of Early American Journalism* (New York and Oxford: Oxford University Press, 1988); James Alexander, *A Brief Narrative of the Case and Trial of John Peter Zenger of the New York Weekly Journal;* Livingston Rutherfurd, *John Peter Zenger. His Press. His Trial and Bibliography;* Vincent Buranelli, "Peter Zenger, Editor," *American Quarterly* 7 (1955): 174–81; Vincent Buranelli, ed., *The Trial of Peter Zenger* (New York: New York University Press, 1957); Cathy Covert, "Passion Is Ye Prevailing Motive: The Feud Behind the Zenger Case," *Journalism Quarterly* 32 (1973): 3–10; Warren C. Price, "Reflections on the Trial of John Peter Zenger," *Journalism Quarterly* 32 (1955): 47–53.

9. Three examples of media histories that approach an understanding of news in relation to history are Michael Shudson, *Discovering the News: A Social History of American Newspapers* (New York: Basic Books, Inc., 1978); Dan Schiller, *Objectivity and the News: The Public and the Rise of Commercial Journalism* (Philadelphia: University of Pennsylvania Press, 1981); and Stephens, *A History of News.* The work of Shudson was a quick response to call of James Carey, but both Shudson and Schiller begin their discussions with the Penny Press in the 1830s. Stephens attempts to cover all human communication from the very first efforts of humankind into the 1980s. Stephens acknowledges that more than half of his work is devoted to communication before the printing press. In addition, the colonial era is almost completely absent from Stephens' study.

10. James W. Carey, "The Problem of Journalism History," *Journalism History* 1 (Spring 1974): 3–5, 27. Carey, former dean of the College of Communications at the University of Illinois, has written in the field of journalism history and is one of the most influential voices in the field.

11. Ibid., 4–5.

12. In two of the more popular media history texts, Michael Emery and Edwin Emery, *The Press and America: An Interpretive History of the Mass Media,* 6th ed. (Englewood Cliffs, N.J.: Prentice Hall, 1988), 22–31; and Jean Folkerts and Dwight L. Teeter, *Voices of a Nation: A History of the Media in the United States* (New York: MacMillan Publishing Company, 1989), 17–43, topics in the colonial press section include the following headings: "*Publick Occurrences,* 1690," "John Campbell's *News-Letter,* 1704," "James Franklin Begins a Crusade," "The *New England Courant,*" "Benjamin Franklin," and "The Zenger Trial." While each heading is not the same in each text, the content is similar and follows the pattern used by media histories described by Carey. Those histories include: Frederic Hudson, *Journalism in the United States, From 1690–1872* (New York: Harper & Brothers, 1873); George Henry Payne, *History of Journalism in the United States* (New York and London: D. Appleton, 1920); James Melvin Lee, *History of American Journalism* (Garden City, N.Y.: Garden City Publishing, 1923); and William Grosevenor Bleyer, *Main Currents in the History of American Journalism* (Boston: Houghton Mifflin, 1927). Two textbooks, Mott, *American Journalism,* 3rd ed. (1962) and Sidney Kobre, *Development of American Journalism* (Dubuque: Wm. C. Brown, 1969), attempt to expand the discussion of colonial newspapers, but neither directly addresses the varied types of news that are contained in colonial newspapers over the entire colonial period. Wm. David Sloan, James G. Stovall and James D. Startt, eds. *The Media in America: A History,* 2d ed. (Scottsdale, Ariz.: Publishing Horizons, 1993), 25, accurately points out that informing readers of events was the purpose of the news in colonial newspapers,

but religion is the only topic—other than politics—that is mentioned as being a regular part of the news of colonial newspapers.

13. *Publick Occurrences* (Boston) 25 September 1690. According to Charles E. Clark, "The Newspapers of Provincial America," *Proceedings of the American Antiquarian Society* 100 (1990): 375, only one copy of *Publick Occurrences* remains in existence and is in the Public Records Office in London. Copies exist on microfilm, and the entire contents of the paper may be found in James Melvin Lee, *History of American Journalism* (Garden City and New York: Garden City Publishing, 1923), 19–20.

14. The reasoning behind the suppression of *Publick Occurrences,* according to most media historians, has been blamed the Puritan leaders of Massachusetts Bay. *See,* Mott, *American Journalism,* 9, 18; Emery and Emery, *The Press and America,* 22–23; Kobre, *The Development of the Colonial Newspaper,* 16; George Henry Payne, *History of Journalism in the United States* (New York: D. Appleton, 1920; reprint, Westport, Conn.: Greenwood Press, 1970), 16–17. Wm. David Sloan, "Chaos, Polemics, and America's First Newspaper," *Journalism Quarterly* 70 (Autumn 1993): 667, sees the suppression of *Publick Occurrences* as an action taken by the Anglican government of Massachusetts Bay. Sloan believes that the Puritan clergy of Massachusetts Bay supported Harris in his efforts to publish a newspaper.

15. Kobre, *The Development of the Colonial Newspaper,* 96.

16. Henry L. Snyder, "Newsletters in England, 1689–1715 with Special Reference to John Dyer—A Byway in the History of England," in *Newsletters to Newspapers: Eighteenth-Century Journalism,* Donovan H. Bond and W. Reynolds McLeod, eds. (Morganton: West Virginia University, 1977), 3–19.

17. Frank, *The Beginnings of the English Newspaper 1620–1660,* 3.

18. According to Stephens, *A History of News,* 157, n. 48, the term coranto refers to newssheets and newspapers of many countries. Stephens speculates that like the English word current, coranto is of Italian origin, probably meaning a runner or messenger.

19. Frank, *The Beginnings of the English Newspaper,* 6.

20. Jim Allee Hart, *The Developing Views on the News Editorial Syndrome 1500–1800* (Carbondale: Southern Illinois University Press, 1970), 95.

21. Ian K. Steele, *The English Atlantic 1675–1740. An Exploration of Communication and Community* (New York and Oxford: Oxford University Press, 1986), 31–33.

22. Ibid., 40.

23. *Pennsylvania Gazette* (Philadelphia), 16 October 1729.

24. Shortly after taking ownership of the *Universal Instructor* from Samuel Keimer, Benjamin Franklin ran a short notice about "the present dearth of news." *Pennsylvania Gazette* (Philadelphia), 24 November 1729.

25. Steele, *The English Atlantic,* 32.

26. Hart, *The Developing Views on the News Editorial Syndrome 1500–1800,* 120–21.

27. Ibid., 122–39; and Kobre, *The Development of the Colonial Newspaper.*

28. The *Boston News-Letter* printed on a half sheet producing a two-page weekly paper until 1719 according to Mott, *American Journalism,* 13. Many colonial newspapers, including the *Boston News-Letter,* continued to print two-page newspapers throughout the period, although four—and sometimes more—pages per week was the more likely.

29. *South-Carolina Gazette* (Charleston), 18 May 1734; *Pennsylvania Gazette* (Philadelphia), 31 July 1735, are but two examples.

30. Kobre, *Development of American Journalism,* 49.

31. William S. Reese, "The First Hundred Years of Printing in America: Printers and Collectors," *Proceedings of the American Antiquarian Society* 99 (1989): 340.

32. Stephen Botein, "'Meer Mechanics' and an Open Press: The Business and Political Strategies of Colonial American Printers," in *Perspectives in American History* IX, eds. Donald Fleming and Bernard Bailyn (Cambridge: Harvard University Press, 1975), 146–50. See also Reese, "The First Hundred Years of Printing in British North America: Printers and Collectors," 337–73.

33. Although printing was a strenuous profession, some master printers were quite successful financially. Franklin, the biography of Andrew Bradford tells us, admired the fortune Philadelphia's first newspaper printer amassed. DeArmond, *Andrew Bradford, Colonial Journalist,* 35. The estate of Thomas Fleet, the printer of the *Boston Evening-Post* who died in 1758 and left the printing business to his sons John and Thomas Jr., was probated at $110,000. Mary Ann Yodelis, "Who Paid the Piper? Publishing Economics in Boston, 1763–1775," *Journalism Monographs* 38 (February 1975): 41.

34. Lawrence Wroth, *The Colonial Printer* (Portland, Maine: The Southworth-Anthoenson Press, 1938), 161.

35. *Virginia Gazette* (Williamsburg), 26 July 1744. The request is quoted in Wroth, *The Colonial Printer,* 147, who in turn copied it from another source. The paper, Wroth says, is no longer extant.

36. Mott, *American Journalism,* 59.

37. William A. Dill, *Growth of Newspapers in the United States* (Lawrence: University of Kansas Press, 1928), 11.

38. Warren B. Johnson, "The Content of American Colonial Newspapers Relative to International Affairs" (Ph.D. diss.: University of Washington, 1962), iii.

39. Richard D. Brown, *Knowledge Is Power: The Diffusion of Information in Early America, 1700–1865* (New York and Oxford: Oxford University Press, 1989), 4.

40. Stephens, *A History of News,* 2.

41. *South-Carolina Gazette* (Charleston), 8 January 1732, 3–4.

42. *Connecticut Gazette* (New Haven), 21 June 1755, 2.

43. High matters of state is a term used by Donald Avery in "The Colonial Press," in *The Media and America.* Although Avery does not elaborate upon what high matters of state might include, the term is appropriate in describing the political events and actions of colonial governments that newspapers printed. For this study, high matters of state includes assembly proceedings, general announcements by colonial governors, and political decrees from England that might announce the appointment of a person to a colonial office.

44. Robert A. Gross, "Printing, Politics, and the People," *Proceedings of the American Antiquarian Society* 99 (1989): 377.

45. Thomas C. Parramore, *Carolina Quest* (Englewood Cliffs, N.J.: Prentice-Hall, 1978), 185.

46. *Boston Evening-Post,* 27 March 1741.

47. *Virginia Gazette* (Williamsburg), 10 August 1739.

CHAPTER 1. *THERE IS A VESSEL LATELY ARRIVED FROM ENGLAND, OR INFESTED BY THOSE HELL-HOUNDS THE PIRATES*

1. *Pennsylvania Gazette* (Philadelphia), 22 January 1744–5, 1.

2. These figures are based on a precise counting of news items that dealt

with the sea. The complete tabulations for ship news, in addition to totals for each of the topics in the selected years of this study, may be found in appendix 2. The newspapers used to obtain these figures represent newspapers from all regions of the American colonies. An effort was made to use the American newspapers with the longest continual runs during the period in order to give the figures continuity. The newspapers were also selected in an effort to accurately represent the total numbers of newspapers printed in the geographical regions of America.

3. *Boston News-Letter,* 26 December 1720, 2.

4. *Boston News-Letter,* 14 January 1705–6, 2.

5. It should be noted that colonial newspapers printed prior to 1770 were located in towns on major waterways. All had connections to the Atlantic Ocean. Hartford, Connecticut, which was approximately forty miles up the Connecticut River, was the farthest inland of any colonial town to have a newspaper until the beginning of a newspaper in Albany, New York, in 1772. Albany, located north of New York on the Hudson River, was still easily accessible by ship. Waterways were essential to the success of colonial towns both economically and in providing a means to receive news. In turn, the ability to receive news as quickly as possible ensured the success of towns.

6. John J. McCusker and Russell R. Menard, *The Economy of British America, 1607–1789* (Chapel Hill and London: University of North Carolina Press, 1985), 71.

7. Sidney Kobre, *The Development of the Colonial Newspaper* (1944; reprint, Gloucester: Peter Smith, 1960), 20, pointed out the fact that the *Boston News-Letter* routinely ran ship news of this type. Kobre's study of colonial newspapers, however, is the only media history to deal with the news of the sea and colonial newspapers. Kobre's conclusions on news of the sea do not explore the vast amount of sea news that appeared in colonial newspapers nor do they examine the various facets of that news.

8. William A. Dill, *The Growth of Newspapers in the United States* (Lawrence: University of Kansas Press, 1928), 11.

9. David Hackett Fischer, *Albion's Seed: Four British Folkways in America* (New York and Oxford: Oxford University Press, 1989), 642.

10. Gary M. Walton and James F. Shepherd, *The Economic Rise of Early America* (Cambridge: Cambridge University Press, 1979), 38.

11. Albert Anthony Giesecke, *American Commercial Legislation Before 1789* (1910; reprint, New York: Burt Franklin, 1970), 4.

12. Victor L. Johnson, "Fair Traders and Smugglers in Philadelphia 1754–1763," *The Pennsylvania Magazine of History and Biography* 83 (1959): 126–27.

13. Oscar Theodore Barck and Hugh Talmage Lefler, *Colonial America* (New York: The Macmillan Company, 1958), 364.

14. Allan Kulikoff, *Tobacco and Slaves: The Development of Southern Cultures in the Chesapeake, 1680–1800* (Chapel Hill and London: University of North Carolina Press, 1986), 5.

15. McCusker and Menard, *The Economy of British America 1607–1789,* 79.

16. David A. Smith, "Dependent Urbanization in Colonial America: The Case of Charleston, South Carolina," *Social Forces* 66 (September 1987): 10–11.

17. See Jacob M. Price, "The Transatlantic Economy," in *Colonial British America: Essays in the New History of the Early Modern Era,* Jack P. Greene and J. R. Pole, eds. (Baltimore and London: The Johns Hopkins University Press, 1984), 18–42.

18. Ian K. Steele, *The English Atlantic 1675–1740: An Exploration of Communication and Community* (New York and Oxford: Oxford University Press, 1986), 159.

19. Ibid., 40, 275.

20. Ibid., 275.

21. James F. Shepherd and Gary M. Walton, *Shipping, Maritime Trade, and the Economic Development of Colonial North America* (Cambridge: Cambridge University Press, 1972), 49.

22. Frank Luther Mott, "The Newspaper Coverage of Lexington and Concord," in *Highlights in the History of the American Press,* Edwin H. Ford and Edwin Emery, eds. (Minneapolis: University of Minnesota Press, 1954). Mott computes the amount of time it took for the news of the opening shots of the American Revolution to reach each of the major ports with newspapers in America.

23. Ibid.

24. *Boston News-Letter,* 14 January 1705–6, 2, provided notice of Belcher's wedding.

25. Examples of different types of ship news used are representative of news items that appeared in all of the colonial newspapers.

26. *American Weekly Mercury* (Philadelphia), 5 March 1729–30, 1.

27. *New-England Weekly Journal* (Boston), 16 November 1730, 2.

28. Ibid., 24 March 1735, 2; 5 May 1735, 2.

29. *Connecticut Journal, and New-Haven Post-Boy,* 23 November 1770, 3.

30. *Boston Gazette,* 4 January 1719–20, 2.

31. See, for example, *Boston Gazette,* 14 March 1719–20; 25 April 1720 and 9 May 1720. When giving the price current for Rhode Island ports, the *Gazette* listed the colony as a collective, not by the name of a particular town.

32. *South-Carolina Gazette* (Charleston), 4 January 1734–5, 2.

33. Ibid., 19 April 1770, 4, is but one example.

34. See, for example, *New-York Journal; or the General Advertiser* (Holt's), 19 July 1770.

35. *Boston News-Letter,* 17 October 1720, 2.

36. *Pennsylvania Gazette* (Philadelphia), 6 September 1775, 2.

37. *Connecticut Gazette* (New-Haven), 19 April 1755, 4.

38. *Publick Occurrences Both Forreign and Domestick* (Boston), 25 September 1690.

39. *Maryland Gazette* (Annapolis), 19 June 1760, 3.

40. This type of ship news appeared with great frequency and in numerous editions of colonial newspapers. The *New-York Mercury,* 11 March 1765, 2, advised New Yorkers that the anticipated fleet from London had been detained, therefore it should not be expected as soon as had been anticipated. The *North-Carolina Gazette* (Wilmington), 20 November 1765, 6, provided news on ships sailing from Philadelphia and Antigua. During the French and Indian War, ships provided weekly information on the shipping situation from Nova Scotia to the West Indies.

41. *New-York Evening-Post,* 4 February 1744–5, 2–3.

42. *New-London Summary; or the Weekly Advertiser,* 31 October 1760, 3, advised its readers that a ship safely landed in Philadelphia after fighting through a storm at Hatteras. Ship reports from New York and Jamaica, however, noted that the vessels were lost and overset respectively.

43. *Connecticut Journal, and New-Haven Post-Boy,* 19 January 1770, 3.

44. *Boston News-Letter,* 12 June 1704, 1.

45. *Boston Gazette,* 1 August 1720, 3.

46. A description of the types of ships used during the colonial period may be found in Charles Gray, *Pirates of the Eastern Seas (1618–1723),* George Mac-Munn ed. (Port Washington, N.Y. and London: Kennikat Press, 1933), ix.

47. *Maryland Gazette* (Annapolis), 24 April 1755, 2.

48. *South-Carolina Gazette* (Charleston), 4 April 1740, 2.

49. *Boston Evening-Post,* 2 June 1755, 4.

50. *Virginia Gazette,* (Williamsburg, Dixon and Purdie), 22 February 1770, 2.

51. *Boston Evening-Post,* 13 October 1755, 2.

52. *New-England Weekly Journal* (Boston), 19 August 1735, 2.

53. Daniel Vickers, "Nantucket Whalemen in the Deep-Sea Fishery: The Changing Anatomy of an Early American Labor Force," *Journal of American History* 72 (September 1985): 281.

54. *Boston News-Letter,* 30 May 1720, 2.

55. Lesley Dow, *Whales* (New York: Facts on File, 1990), 49.

56. Ibid.

57. *American Weekly Mercury* (Philadelphia), 27 March 1735, 3.

58. *Pennsylvania Gazette* (Philadelphia), 10 January 1760, 2.

59. *Boston Evening-Post,* 21 January 1740, 1.

60. *Boston Gazette, and Country Journal,* 10 March 1760, 1.

61. *New-York Weekly Journal,* 21 April 1740, 1; and *Boston Weekly Post-Boy,* 12 May 1740, 2.

62. *Boston Evening-Post,* 4 June 1750, 2.

63. *Boston Weekly News-Letter,* 30 October 1755, 1.

64. *Boston News-Letter,* 26 December 1720, 2.

65. Frank Sherry, *Raiders and Rebels: The Golden Age of Piracy* (New York: Hearst Marine Books, 1986), 20.

66. Ibid.; John Esquemeling, *The Buccaneers of America* (1684; reprint, London: George Allen & Unwin, 1951), xv. The introduction of this work, for which no author is given, is the source of the information used here, not Esquemeling who died in 1707.

67. Steele, *The English Atlantic,* 225.

68. John Esquemeling, *The Buccaneers of America* first appeared in English in 1684. First printed in Dutch in 1678, the book appeared in numerous other editions with information added to that provided by Esquemeling. Esquemeling is described as "one of the Buccaneers who was present at these tragedies." The second edition of *The General History of the Pyrates* was offered for sale in 1725 in Philadelphia by Andrew Bradford in the *American Weekly Mercury,* 12 January 1724–25, 4.

69. Esquemeling, *The Buccaneers of America,* 229.

70. *Boston News-Letter,* 29 July 1725, 2.

71. *American Weekly Mercury* (Philadelphia), 17 March 1719–20, 3.

72. Sherry, *Raiders and Rebels,* 58–59.

73. Numerous examples of news of privateers exist throughout the newspapers of the colonial period. Privateering activity peaked during the French and Indian War years.

74. *Boston Weekly News-Letter,* 18 July 1745, 4.

75. *Pennsylvania Gazette* (Philadelphia), 9 May 1745, 3.

76. *Newport Mercury, or the Weekly Advertiser,* 25 March 1765, 2.

77. *New-York Journal; or the General Advertiser,* 19 July 1770, 2.

78. *New-England Weekly Journal* (Boston), 8 June 1730, 2.

79. *Boston News-Letter,* 17 March 1720, 2.

80. Ibid., 28 October 1717, 2.

81. *Pennsylvania Gazette* (Philadelphia), 9 May 1745, 3.

82. *Massachusetts Gazette,* 8 March 1770, 2.

83. Thumbscrews were devices used to rip fingers from their sockets. Sherry, *Raiders and Rebels,* 48.

84. *Pennsylvania Gazette* (Philadelphia), 20 January 1729–30, 3.

85. *Boston Evening-Post,* 23 January 1775, 2; *South-Carolina and American General Gazette* (Charleston), 3 March 1775, 2.

86. The *American Weekly Mercury* (Philadelphia), 16 February 1719–20, 2, told of a Portuguese ship that missed its port and wandered the ocean for forty days. Only two of the crew survived, six others were used for food.

87. *Boston News-Letter,* 22 August 1715, 2.

88. *Virginia Gazette* (Williamsburg), 21 March 1744–45, 4.

89. *Pennsylvania Journal, or Weekly Advertiser* (Philadelphia), 13 March 1760, 2; and *Boston Evening-Post,* 17 March 1760, 4.

90. *Boston Evening-Post,* 23 June 1760, 2.

91. *Maryland Gazette* (Annapolis), 21 November 1750, 3.

92. *New-York Evening-Post,* 5 November 1750, 3.

93. *Maryland Gazette* (Annapolis), 7 March 1750, 2.

94. *Essex Journal and Merrimack Packet: Or, the Massachusetts and New-Hampshire General Advertiser* (Newbury-Port), 4 January 1775, 2.

95. Newspapers were carried from one port to another in colonial America. Because they were, the news that was generated in Boston or received from a ship arriving at the Massachusetts port that appeared in a Boston newspaper eventually found its way to New York, Philadelphia, Annapolis, Williamsburg, Charleston, Savannah, and every other port between where ships from Boston docked. Numerous news items confirm this, especially the news of slaves. Slave news from Boston, for example, can be traced moving down the coast (See chapter 5, pages 139–40, 147). News that appeared in colonial newspapers became the "official" notice of events, and the sharing of newspapers was the manner in which these official reports were shared with other regions of the colonies.

96. The figures in this section are based on the newspapers in appendix 2.

CHAPTER 2. *THE SCULKING INDIAN ENEMY*

1. *Pennsylvania Gazette* (Philadelphia), 24 February 1729–30, 3.

2. John Smith, *The General Historie of Virginia, New England and the Summer Isles,* in *English Scholar's Library of Old and Modern Works,* Edward Arber ed. (New York: AMS, 1967), 10–11.

3. See, for example, *Boston News-Letter,* 29 July 1706, 2. Referring to Native American's method of fighting as "sculking" was a common descriptive term during the colonial period, especially in the seventeenth century. See Patrick M. Malone, *The Skulking Way of War: Technology and Tactics among the New England Indians* (Baltimore and London: Johns Hopkins University Press, 1993).

4. Smallpox was the most lethal disease introduced by Europeans to America, but measles, influenza, typhus, and diphtheria—to name some of the other diseases inflicted upon Indians—were killers as well. Epidemics of diseases broke out throughout the colonial period often destroying Native Americans far

beyond their contact with white settlers. For a complete discussion the effect of disease upon Native Americans, see Henry F. Dobyns, *Their Numbers Become Thinned: Native American Population Dynamics in Eastern North America* (Knoxville: University of Tennessee Press, 1983), 7–26.

5. During the eighteenth century, Native American population counts were never very high. Members of the Five Nations of the Iroquois Confederacy, one of the most influential Native American groups upon all white settlers, never numbered more than ten thousand. Daniel K. Richter and James H. Merrell, eds., *Beyond the Covenant Chain: The Iroquois and Their Neighbors in Indian North America, 1600–1800* (Syracuse, N.Y.: Syracuse University Press, 1987), 5.

6. For a discussion of media treatment of Native Americans in the nineteenth and twentieth centuries, see Sharon Murphy, "American Indians and the Media Stereotype," *Journalism History* 6, 2 (Summer 1979): 39–43.

7. Thomas More, *Utopia* (1517; reprint, London, 1955), 17, quoted in Alfred A. Cave, "Canaanites in a Promised Land: The American Indian and the Providential Theory of Empire," *American Indian Quarterly* 112 (Fall 1988): 278.

8. John Rastell, *Interlude of the Four Elements* (London, 1519), quoted in Cave, "Canaanites in a Promised Land," 278.

9. Cave, "Canaanites in a Promised Land," 279.

10. James Axtell believes part of the hostility that Native Americans exhibited for the English colonists from the very beginning stemmed from at least fifty to one hundred years of prior contact with white Europeans. James Axtell, *Beyond 1492: Encounters in Colonial North America* (New York and Oxford: Oxford University Press, 1992), 29.

11. *Mercurius Civicus* (London), 22 May 1645, in Joseph Frank, *The Beginnings of the English Newspaper, 1620–1690* (Cambridge: Harvard University Press, 1961), 86–87.

12. A description of the treatment of Native Americans in American literature, especially fictional literature, may be found in Wynette L. Hamilton, "The Correlation between Societal Attitudes and Those of American Authors in the Depiction of American Indians, 1607–1860," *American Indian Quarterly* 1 (Spring 1974): 1–26.

13. Mary Rowlandson, *A True HISTORY of the Captivity and Restoration of Mrs. MARY ROWLANDSON, a Minister's Wife in New-England. Wherein is set forth, The Cruel and Inhumane Usage she underwent amongst the Heathens, for Eleven Weeks time: And her Deliverance from Them* (New-England, 1682), 3.

14. Ibid., 1, 8.

15. Cotton Mather, *Humiliations follow'd with Deliverances, A Brief Discourse on the MATTER and METHOD, of that HUMILIATION which would be an Hopeful Symptom of our Deliverance from Calamity. Accompanied and Accommodated with A NARRATIVE, of a notable Deliverance lately Received by some English Captives, From the Hands of Cruel Indians* (Boston, 1697), 43.

16. Quoted in Arrell Morgan Gibson, *The American Indian: Prehistory to the Present* (Lexington, Mass.: D. C. Heath and Company, 1980), 189.

17. The Rev. Gilbert Tennent, one of the ministers who joined George Whitefield in promoting religion and revival during the Great Awakening, offered a recommendation for a captivity narrative written by a deacon in his church. See Robert Eastburn, *A Faithful NARRATIVE of The Many Dangers and Sufferings, as well as wonderful Deliverance of ROBERT EASTBURN, during his late Captivity among the INDIANS: Together with some Remarks upon the Country*

of Canada, and the Religion, and Policy of its Inhabitants; tho whole intermixed with devout Reflections (Philadelphia, 1758).

18. Peter Williamson, *French and Indian Cruelty; Exemplified in the LIFE And various Wicistitudes of Fortune, of PETER WILLIAMSON, A Disbanded Soldier* (York, 1757).

19. Yasuhide Kawashima, "Forest Diplomats: The Role of Interpreters in the Indian-White Relations on the Early American Frontier," *American Indian Quarterly* 13 (Winter 1989): 4.

20. Axtell, *Beyond 1492*, 119.

21. Gregory Evans Dowd, *A Spirited Resistance: The North American Indian Struggle for Unity, 1745–1815* (Baltimore and London: The Johns Hopkins University Press, 1992), 35, 40.

22. *Boston News-Letter,* 19 August 1706, 2.

23. *South-Carolina Gazette* (Charleston), 21 June 1735, 1.

24. *Boston Evening-Post,* 26 August 1745, 2.

25. Ibid., 20 January 1755, 1.

26. *South-Carolina Gazette* (Charleston), 5 April 1735, 2.

27. *Boston News-Letter,* 1 May 1704, 3.

28. The Tuscaroras were the largest tribe of Native Americans in the coastal region of North and South Carolina in the early 1700s. Their population numbered about four thousand at this time. The Indians began the war by attacking settlements around New Bern, the largest town in North Carolina on 22 September 1711. With assistance from South Carolina, the Tuscaroras were defeated after two years of fighting, and those remaining eventually migrated to New York and became a part of the confederacy of tribes there. Thomas C. Parramore, *Carolina Quest* (Englewood Cliffs, N.J.: Prentice-Hall, 1978), 65.

29. *Boston News-Letter,* 26 November 1711, 2.

30. Ibid., 11 May 1713, 2.

31. Ibid., 20 July 1713, 2.

32. Ibid., 13 June 1715, 2.

33. *New-England Courant* (Boston), 14 August 1725, 2.

34. *American Weekly Mercury* (Philadelphia), 28 August 1735, 3.

35. *Pennsylvania Gazette* (Philadelphia), 28 August 1735, 3.

36. *Boston Evening-Post,* 8 September 1735, 2.

37. Ibid., 29 July 1745, 2.

38. *Maryland Gazette* (Annapolis), 6 November 1755, 3.

39. Ibid., 20 November 1755, 2.

40. Ibid., 18 December 1755, 3.

41. *Virginia Gazette* (Williamsburg), 19 September 1755–17 October 1755.

42. *Boston Evening-Post,* 14 January 1765, 3.

43. *Virginia Gazette* (Williamsburg), 19 September 1755, 2.

44. *South-Carolina Gazette* (Charleston), 23 February 1760, 2. The Cherokee War probably was initiated by Indian bounty hunters in the mountains of Virginia early in 1760. A group of forty Cherokees returning from military service in the British army were ambushed and scalped for the reward that the colonial government of Virginia paid for the scalps of enemy Indians. Gibson, *The American Indian*, 228.

45. James H. Merrell, *The Indians' New World: Catawbas and Their Neighbors from European Contact through the Era of Removal* (Chapel Hill and London: University of North Carolina Press, 1989), 117.

46. *Boston Evening-Post,* 17 March 1760, 4.

47. Ibid., 28 April 1760, 3.

48. *South-Carolina Gazette* (Charleston), 15 March 1760, 2.

49. Ibid., 12 April 1760, 1.

50. Ibid., 7 June 1760, 2.

51. Ibid., 23 August 1760, 2.

52. Ibid., 4 October 1760, 2.

53. Ibid., 28 November 1761.

54. Ibid., 19 December 1761, 1.

55. The French and Indian War and its repercussions upon relationships between Native Americans and British American colonists is discussed fully below.

56. The colonial newspapers were consistent in the spelling of Pondiac. In every news items uncovered concerning the chief, his name was spelled Pondiac, rather than Pontiac.

57. Dowd, *A Spirited Resistance,* 35–36.

58. *Boston Gazette, and Country Journal,* 14 January 1765, 3.

59. *Newport Mercury, or the Weekly Advertiser,* 8 April 1765, 3.

60. *Georgia Gazette* (Savannah), 9 May 1765, 1.

61. Ibid., 11 April 1765, 2.

62. *Newport Mercury, or the Weekly Advertiser,* 31 June 1765, 3.

63. Ibid., 15 July 1765, 2; and *Massachusetts Gazette (And Boston News-Letter),* 18 July 1765, 2.

64. *Newport Gazette, or the Weekly Advertiser,* 26 August 1765, 2.

65. *Green & Russell's Boston Post-Boy & Advertiser,* 26 August 1765, 3.

66. *New-York Gazette* (Weyman's), 2 December 1765, 2.

67. Dowd, *A Spirited Resistance,* 43–44.

68. *Boston Evening-Post,* 20 August 1770, 2.

69. *South-Carolina and American General Gazette* (Charleston), 8 June 1770, 3.

70. *South-Carolina Gazette; and Country Journal* (Charleston), 18 September 1770, 1.

71. *Green & Russell's Boston Post-Boy & Advertiser,* 2 January 1775, 4.

72. *Maryland Gazette* (Annapolis), 20 June 1765, 2.

73. Gibson, *The American Indian,* 122–23.

74. *Publick Occurrences* (Boston), 25 September 1690, 3.

75. Cotton Mather, *Decennium Luctuosum. An HISTORY of Remarkable Occurrences, in the Long WAR, which NEW-ENGLAND hath had with the Indian Salvages, From the Year, 1688. To the Year, 1698* (Boston, 1699), 13. This was King William's War, the first of four wars in North America between the English and the French and their Native American allies.

76. The term French Indians is employed consistently in colonial newspapers to refer to any Indians that entered into alliance with the French. These Indians were often from Canada, but even Southern Indians sometimes were referred to as French Indians. *Publick Occurrences* used the term when it reported that a rescue party had traveled down the Oyster River in search of English captives. The group met with "the French, and the French Indians."

77. *Boston News-Letter,* 3 July 1704, 1.

78. Ibid., 1 August 1704, 1.

79. Ibid., 9 October 1704, 2.

80. Ibid., 25 June 1711, 2.

81. *American Weekly Mercury* (Philadelphia), 30 September 1725, 2.

82. *New-England Weekly Journal* (Boston), 19 February 1740, 1.

83. *Virginia Gazette* (Williamsburg), 5 December 1745, 4.

84. *Boston Gazette, or Weekly Journal,* 26 November 1745, 2.

85. Ibid., 17 December 1745, 2.

86. *Maryland Gazette* (Annapolis), 4 July 1750, 3.

87. *Pennsylvania Gazette* (Philadelphia), 27 September 1750, 2.

88. *Boston Evening-Post,* 3 March 1755, 2.

89. Ibid., 24 March 1755, 1.

90. *Virginia Gazette* (Williamsburg), 28 February 1755, 3.

91. Ibid., 5 September 1755, 1.

92. *Boston Evening-Post,* 13 October 1755, 2; *Maryland Gazette* (Annapolis), 30 October 1755, 2; and *Pennsylvania Journal, or Weekly Advertiser* (Philadelphia), 16 October 1755, 2.

93. October 13–17, 1755.

94. 13 October 1755.

95. 13 October 1755.

96. 16 October 1755.

97. 16 October 1755.

98. 17 October 1755.

99. 16 October 1755.

100. *Maryland Gazette* (Annapolis), 26 June 1760, 3.

101. *Georgia Gazette* (Savannah), 14 March 1765, 3.

102. Ibid., 18 July 1765, 2.

103. *Pennsylvania Journal, or the Weekly Advertiser* (Philadelphia), 5 July 1770, 3.

104. Gibson, 195.

105. *Boston News-Letter,* 26 June 1704, 2.

106. Ibid., 29 December 1712, 2.

107. Ibid., 9 March 1713, 2.

108. *Pennsylvania Gazette* (Philadelphia), 29 May 1740, 3.

109. *Virginia Gazette* (Williamsburg) 26 September 1755, 2; 17 October 1755, 2.

110. *Maryland Gazette* (Annapolis), 16 October 1755, 2.

111. *South-Carolina Gazette* (Charleston), 11 October 1760, 3.

112. It should be remembered that all of the Native American activities during the eighteenth century did not revolve around the white colonists, even though a look at Native Americans through the colonial press makes it appear that way. Native Americans continued for many years to follow their own diplomatic and military agendas among themselves, in addition to their relationships with the English colonists (Richter, *Beyond the Covenant Chain,* 6).

113. *Boston News-Letter,* 5 November 1716, 1.

114. *Pennsylvania Gazette* (Philadelphia), 5 March 1730, 4; *Virginia Gazette* (Williamsburg), 10 October 1745, 3.

115. *Boston Evening-Post,* 23 September 1745, 2.

116. Ibid., 15 July 1765, 2.

117. Ibid., 1 July 1765, 2 emphasis included. The identical news item appeared in the *Massachusetts Gazette (And Boston News-Letter)* 4 July 1765, 2 and in *Green & Russell's Boston Post-Boy & Advertiser,* 15 July 1765, 3. The story also appeared in the *Newport Mercury, or the Weekly Advertiser,* 31 June 1765 (1 July), 3. The *Mercury*'s story, however, noted that "four of them were unhappily drowned" instead of "happily drowned." The report of unhappily drowning is more than likely a mistake by whomever set the type, since the *Mercury* contained an abundance of news of "the Sculking Indian Enemy" during this period. It is

doubtful, therefore, that the change was an intentional editorial decision, although it could have been the sentiments of a sympathetic apprentice or printer's assistant or the unrealized workings of his conscience.

118. *Pennsylvania Gazette* (Philadelphia), 16 January 1750, 1.

119. In December 1763, twenty "friendly Indians" were massacred in Lancaster County, Pennsylvania. Benjamin Franklin penned an essay on the matter, but, according to Pete Steffens, "at no time during December or January did either of the two papers in Philadelphia . . . print news of the two massacres" except for what was in a proclamation denouncing the killings. Pete Steffens, "Franklin's Early Attack on Racism: An Essay Against a Massacre of Indians," *Journalism History* 5 (Spring 1978): 10.

120. *Pennsylvania Gazette* (Philadelphia), 6 March 1760, 1.

121. *Essex Gazette* (Salem, Massachusetts), 7 August 1770, 1.

122. *Connecticut Journal,* and *New-Haven Post-Boy,* 20 April 1770, 3.

123. *Georgia Gazette* (Savannah), 28 March 1765, 1.

124. *South-Carolina Gazette;* and *Country Journal* (Charleston), 3 April 1770, 2.

125. *Publick Occurrences* (Boston), 25 September 1690, 2.

126. *Boston News-Letter,* 11 August 1712, 2.

127. *American Weekly Mercury* (Philadelphia), 14 January 1735, 2.

128. Ibid., 4 February 1735, 3.

129. *New-England Weekly Journal* (Boston), 26 August 1735, 2.

130. Ibid., 2 September 1735, 2.

131. *Boston Gazette,* 23 November 1730,2; and *New-York Gazette,* 15 December 1730, 2; 28 January 1734(5), 3.

132. *Boston Gazette,* 15 September 1740, 3; *Boston Gazette, or Weekly Journal,* 5 March 1745, 2; and *New-York Evening-Post,* 4 November 1745, 3.

133. *Boston Gazette, or Weekly Advertiser,* 28 January 1755, 3.

134. *Georgia Gazette* (Savannah), 3 January 1765, 2.

135. Ibid., 17 January 1765, 1.

136. *Connecticut Courant* (Hartford), 20 May 1765, 3.

137. Ibid., 2.

138. *Providence Gazette;* and *Country Journal,* 16 March 1765, 2.

139. Even though the relationship between Native American tribes and colonies in 1775 is deemed political here, it is not considered political news in the context of the political content that has been studied by scholars and is, therefore, excluded from this study. Arthur Schlesinger, *Prelude to Independence: The Newspaper War on Britain 1764–1776* (New York: Random House, 1957) does not treat the Native American-American alliances. This news does not really differ from other treaties and agreements made between Native Americans and American colonists during the colonial period. The only difference is the fact that now colonists were enlisting Indian assistance against Great Britain in a war that was very much politically motivated.

140. *Massachusetts Gazette (*And the *Boston News-Letter),* 25 May 1775, 2.

141. *Providence Gazette;* and *Country Journal,* 8 July 1775, 3.

142. *Constitutional Gazette* (New York), 19 August 1775, 1; *South-Carolina Gazette* (Charleston), 17 October 1775, 2.

143. *Pennsylvania Ledger; Or the Virginia, Maryland, Pennsylvania, & New-Jersey Weekly Advertiser* (Philadelphia), 9 September 1775, 3.

144. *Pennsylvania Evening Post* (Philadelphia), 5 September 1775, 4.

145. Ibid.

146. Ibid., 30 November 1775, 1.

147. *New-York Gazette and Weekly Mercury,* 14 August 1775, 2.

148. *Virginia Gazette or Norfolk Intelligencer,* 6 September 1775, 1.

149. *New Hampshire Gazette, and Historical Chronicle* (Portsmouth), 5 May 1775, 2.

150. The number counts are based upon the newspapers in appendix 2.

151. It is significant to note that all of the secondary sources used in preparation of this chapter failed to consult the colonial newspapers for information concerning Native Americans, even though many of them dealt with the relationships between white settlers and the Indians. The colonial records were the primary source of informatiton for these scholars. The information on Indians in the newspapers, in many instances, can shed additional light on a subject, provide verification for statements or bring to light new information.

152. *Pennsylvania Gazette* (Philadelphia), 2 January 1750, 2.

CHAPTER 3. *MELANCHOLY ACCIDENTS AND DEPLORABLE NEWS*

1. *Boston Weekly Post-Boy,* 13 October 1735, 3.

2. Warren Francke, "An Argument in Defense of Sensationalism: Probing the Popular and Historiographical Concept," *Journalism History* 5 (1978): 72.

3. *Boston Evening-Post,* 23 January 1775, 2; *South-Carolina and American General Gazette* (Charleston), 3 March 1775, 2. See chapter 2, 36–37.

4. *Pennsylvania Gazette* (Philadelphia), 24 February 1729–30, 3. See chapter 2, 42.

5. The *New York Herald* began its coverage of Jewett's murder on 11 April 1836. A prostitute, Jewett was found murdered in her bed, which had afterwards been set on fire. A wealthy citizen of New York, Richard Robinson, was accused of the murder after his cloak was found in the murder victim's room. Through the trial of Robinson, which began on 2 June 1836, Bennett ran little else in the *Herald.* See Sidney Kobre, *Development of American Journalism* (Dubuque, Iowa: Wm. C. Brown Company Publishers, 1969), 234–35; and Frank Luther Mott, *American Journalism. A History: 1690–1960,* 3d ed. (New York: The Macmillan Company, 1962), 232–33.

6. See John D. Stevens, *Sensationalism and the New York Press* (New York: Columbia University Press, 1991), 55–100; Jean Folkerts and Dwight L. Teeter Jr., *Voices of a Nation* (New York: Macmillan Publishing Company, 1989), 265–74; Michael Emery and Edwin Emery, *The Press and America. An Interpretive History of the Mass Media,* 6th ed. (Englewood Cliffs: Prentice Hall, 1988), 231–34; and Mott, *American Journalism,* 519–609.

7. See Stevens, *Sensationalism and the New York Press;* and Mitchell Stephens, *A History of News. From the Drum to the Satellite* (New York: Viking Penquin, Inc., 1988).

8. Mott, *American Journalism,* 442.

9. Mitchell Stephens, "Sensationalism and Moralizing in 16th- and 17th-Century Newsbooks and News Ballads," *Journalism History* 12 (1985): 93 (emphasis included).

10. David Paul Nord, "Teleology and News: The Religious Roots of American Journalism, 1630–1730," *Journal of American History* 77 (June 1990), 9.

11. At least one study has been done on sensationalism in the colonial period.

Kenneth D. Nordin, "The Entertaining Press: Sensationalism in Eighteenth-Century Boston Newspapers," *Communication Research* 6 (1979): 295–320, uses a content-analysis approach to determine the amount of sensational news found in Boston newspapers from 1710–1784. In defining sensationalism for the purpose of news items to include in the analysis, Nordin employed two broad categories—stories of violence and nonviolent human interest stories. He based these categories on D. G. Clark and W. B. Blankenburg, "Trends in Violent Content in Selected Mass Media," in *Television and Social Behavior,* vol. I, G. A. Comstock and E. A. Rubinstein, eds. (Washington, D.C.: National Institute for Mental Health, 1972). As a result, any mention of war became a sensational story. Nordin's approach was refuted in Francke, "An Argument in Defense of Sensationalism," 71. Franke said of "The Entertaining Press," "The amount of space is the crudest measurement of treatment. Only by neglecting treatment, as the Boston study does, and discarding dictionary definitions can all war news be categorized as sensational." Sensational news in Philadelphia is discussed in Ronald A. Bosco, "'*Scandal,* like other Virtues, is in part its own Reward': Franklin Working the Crime Beat," in *Reappraising Benjamin Franklin: A Bicentennial Perspective,* ed. J. A. Leo Lemay, (Newark: University of Delaware Press, 1993), 79–97.

12. Nord, "Teleology and the News," 9.

13. Stephens, "Sensationalism and Moralizing in 16th- and 17th-Century Newsbooks and News Ballads," 93.

14. *Pennsylvania Gazette* (Philadelphia), 16 October 1729.

15. Mott, *American Journalism,* 442.

16. Perry H. Tannenbaum and Mervin D. Lynch, "Sensationalism: The Concept and Its Measurement," *Journalism Quarterly* 37 (1960): 382.

17. Donald L. Shaw and John W. Slater, "In the Eye of the Beholder? Sensationalism in the American Press News, 1820–1860," *Journalism History* 12 (1985): 87.

18. Emery and Emery, *The Press and America,* 115.

19. Stevens, *Sensationalism and the New York Press,* 5.

20. George Juergens, *Joseph Pulitzer and the New York World* (Princeton: Princeton University Press, 1966), viii–ix, in Stevens, *Sensationalism and the New York Press,* 5.

21. Stephens, *A History of News,* 108.

22. *New York Herald,* 11 April 1836, quoted in Stephens, *A History of News,* 244.

23. *Boston News-Letter,* 15 January 1730, 2.

24. Puddings refers to intestines. Bowels may mean the same but also includes most of the internal organs as described in colonial papers.

25. *Publick Occurrences* (Boston), 25 September 1690, 3.

26. *American Weekly Mercury* (Philadelphia), 23 October 1735, 1.

27. *New-York Mercury,* 23 June 1755, 2.

28. *Boston News-Letter,* 16 October 1740, 1.

29. *American Weekly Mercury* (Philadelphia), 6 January 1729–30, 4.

30. *Pennsylvania Gazette* (Philadelphia), 20 March 1739–40, 2.

31. *Connecticut Gazette* (New-Haven), 12 April 1755, 2.

32. *American Weekly Mercury* (Philadelphia), 8 May 1725, 2.

33. *Boston Weekly News-Letter,* 7 August 1760, 2.

34. *Green & Russell's Boston Post-Boy & Advertiser,* 12 August 1765, 2.

35. *Weekly Rehearsal* (Boston), 21 July 1735, 2; and *American Weekly Mercury* (Philadelphia), 14 August 1735, 2.

36. Peter C. Hoffer and N. E. H. Hull, *Murdering Mothers: Infanticide in England and New England 1558–1803* (New York and London: New York University Press, 1984), xiv–xix.

37. *New-England Courant* (Boston), 26 April 1725, 2.

38. *New-York Evening-Post,* 3 September 1750, 3.

39. *Pennsylvania Gazette* (Philadelphia), 18 September 1735, 1.

40. *South-Carolina Gazette* (Charleston), 22 February 1734–35, 3.

41. Nord in "Teleology and the News," 36, says that news stories that created an "Oh, my God" response lost all religious implications around 1729 and became simply news that produced a similar response void of religious overtones.

42. *Boston News-Letter,* 15 October 1730, 1.

43. *New-London Summary; or The Weekly Advertiser,* 10 October 1760, 2.

44. *New-York Mercury,* 3 February 1755, 3.

45. *Georgia Gazette* (Savannah), 28 February 1765, 1. These stories of stillborn infants with double features no doubt were examples of Siamese twins who died in the womb. A similar story may be found in the *New-York Mercury,* 3 June 1765, 2.

46. Nord, "Teleology and the News," 36.

47. Patricia U. Bonomi, *Under the Cope of Heaven: Religion, Society, and Politics in the Colonial Era* (New York and Oxford: Oxford University Press, 1986), 3, says that religion gave meaning to all aspects of eighteenth-century life. She believes that this fact gave a certain tone to everything about life during the century. Although newspapers do not reflect this fact overtly and none of the content of colonial papers discussed so far has revealed this religiosity, understanding the supernatural events of colonial newspapers can best be understood by applying a spiritual or religious lens.

48. *Pennsylvania Gazette* (Philadelphia), 6 January 1729–30, 3.

49. *Boston Weekly News-Letter,* 19 December 1745, 2. Interestingly, the *Boston Evening-Post* ran the same story on 23 December 1745, 4. In an editorial comment by either Thomas Fleet or the person providing the news, the supernatural aspects of this account were doubted. Still, the *Evening-Post*'s account referred to "a filthy nasty Spirit" and "Damons."

50. *Boston News-Letter,* 6 May 1735, 2.

51. Mark A. Noll and others, eds., *Christianity in America* (Grand Rapids, Mich.: William B. Eerdmans, 1983), 68–69.

52. Ibid., 71.

53. Henry F. May, *The Enlightenment in America* (New York and London: Oxford University Press, 1976), 55.

54. *Boston News-Letter,* 21 November 1720, 1.

55. *Pennsylvania Gazette* (Philadelphia), 22 October 1730, 3–4 (emphasis included).

56. Ibid., 19 March 1730, 3.

57. *New-England Weekly Journal* (Boston), 12 August 1735, 1.

58. *Maryland Gazette* (Annapolis), 7 November 1750, 1.

59. *South-Carolina Gazette* (Charleston), 9 August 1735, 3.

60. *Pennsylvania Gazette* (Philadelphia), 15 December 1730, 1.

61. *Maryland Gazette* (Annapolis), 29 August 1765, 2.

62. *Boston Evening-Post,* 11 March 1765, 1.

63. Ibid.

64. *Boston Weekly News-Letter,* 8 August 1745, 1; *New-York Evening-Post,* 26 August 1745, 2.

65. *Boston Evening-Post,* 17 March 1760, 4.

66. *Boston News-Letter,* 20 November 1735, 1.

67. *Boston Weekly News-Letter,* 13 June 1745, 1.

68. *Maryland Gazette* (Annapolis), 15 May 1760, 1.

69. *Pennsylvania Gazette* (Philadelphia), 19 November 1730, 4.

70. Ibid., 31 October 1745, 2; and *Virginia Gazette* (Williamsburg), 12 December 1745, 3.

71. *Maryland Gazette* (Annapolis), 19 June 1755, 3.

72. *American Weekly Mercury* (Philadelphia), 20 November 1735, 1.

73. *Essex Gazette* (Salem, Mass.), 2 September 1770, 4

74. *Virginia Gazette* (Williamsburg, Purdie), 3 March 1775, 1.

75. *Boston Gazette,* 31 March 1735, 3.

76. *Pennsylvania Gazette* (Philadelphia), 21 August 1735, 3.

77. For example, the *South-Carolina Gazette,* 15 March 1760, 2, 3 described how colonists in the back country at two different places chopped up the bodies of Indians in view of Native Americans. One time the scalp was run up the flag pole to infuriate the Indians. At another place, the settlers fed the pieces of the Indians to the dogs. In the *Gazette* of 4 October 1760, 2, a news account described the way Indians tortured Captain Demeré by first scalping him and then making him dance. The Indians then cut off his arms and legs.

78. Warren Francke, "Sensationalism and the Development of 19th-Century Reporting: The Broom Sweeps Sensory Details," *Journalism History* 12 (1985): 81.

79. *Boston Evening-Post,* 26 August 1765, 3.

Chapter 4. *Whipt Through the Streets and Burnt with a Hot Iron*

1. *Virginia Gazette* (Williamsburg, Dixon and Purdie), 8 November 1770, 2.

2. *Virginia Gazette* (Williamsburg), 10 October 1745, 1.

3. This is the same conclusion reached by A. G. Roeber, "Authority, Law, and Custom: The Rituals of Court Day in Tidewater Virginia, 1720 to 1750," *William and Mary Quarterly* 37 (1980): 29–52. Roeber maintains that county court day in Tidewater Virginia served as a means of enforcing the importance of obeying the law for all those attending the court session. The immediate and public punishment of criminals was necessary to keep the law in the colony.

4. *New-York Gazette: or, the Weekly Post-Boy,* 25 August 1755, 3. The paper's story, taken from the *London Magazine* of May 1755, was based on British subjects in the colonies. It used "Militia Rolls, Poll-Taxes, Bills of Mortality, Returns from Governors, and other authentick Authorities" to reach this figure. The number does not include slaves nor immigrants from other countries.

5. Lester J. Cappon, Barbara Bartz Petchenik and John Hamilton Long, eds. *Atlas of Early American History* (Princeton: Princeton University Press, 1976), 97.

6. *American Weekly Mercury* (Philadelphia), 28 January 1735, 2.

7. Numerous laws were applied in colonial America. Land laws, laws concerning succession at death, poor laws, laws concerning indentured servants and slaves, commercial law, legislative law, and economic laws were all a part of the

legal landscape. Lawrence M. Friedman, *A History of American Law*, 2nd ed. (New York: Simon & Schuster, 1985), 58–90.

8. It should be noted that John Peter Zenger's trial in 1735 in New York was not discussed in colonial newspapers outside of New York. Several newspapers, including the *American Weekly Mercury* (Philadelphia), 27 November 1735, 2 and 4 December 1735, 2, mentioned the censuring of Zenger's lawyers, James Alexander and William Smith, but neither Zenger's name nor the nature of his trial were ever discussed. The *South-Carolina Gazette* (Charleston), 18 January 1734–35, 3, reported that New York Governor William Cosby had offered a reward for information concerning the person or persons responsible for the libel against him published in Zenger's newspaper.

9. The press's role in the Stamp Act crisis and the legal and political issues that ensued and led to the Revolution are discussed in Edmund S. Morgan and Helen M. Morgan, *The Stamp Act Crisis: Prologue to Revolution* (Chapel Hill: University of North Carolina Press, 1953); and Arthur M. Schlesinger, *Prelude to Independence: The Newspaper War on Britain 1764–1776* (New York: Vintage Books, 1965).

10. For a listing of media history works dealing with newspapers and the legal issues surrounding the trial of John Peter Zenger as well as free press and legal-political issues, see Introduction, note 8.

11. Herbert William Keith Fitzroy, "The Punishment of Crime in Provincial Pennsylvania," *Pennsylvania Magazine of History and Biography* 60 (1936): 242.

12. Thomas Hobbes, *Leviathan, or the Matter, Forme and Power of a Commonwealth, Ecclesiastical and Civill* (1651, reprint; Cambridge: Cambridge University Press, 1904), quoted in ibid., note 2.

13. Douglas Greenberg, "Crime, Law Enforcement, and Social Control in Colonial America," *The American Journal of Legal History* 26 (1982): 296.

14. Friedman, *A History of American Law*, 33–34.

15. Kathryn Preyer, "Penal Measures in the American Colonies: An Overview," *The American Journal of Legal History* 26 (1982): 326.

16. George L. Haskins, *Law and Authority in Early Massachusetts* (New York: Macmillan, 1960), 6.

17. Friedman, *A History of American Law*, 37.

18. Greenberg, "Crime, Law Enforcement, and Social Control in Colonial America," 300.

19. David H. Flaherty, "Law and the Enforcement of Morals in Early America," *Perspectives in American History* 5 (1971): 209.

20. Samuel Walker, *Popular Justice: A History of American Criminal Justice* (New York and Oxford: Oxford University Press, 1980), 11–13.

21. Preyer, "Penal Measures in the American Colonies: An Overview," 328–29.

22. *The Book of the General Lawes and Libertyes Concerning the Inhabitants of the Massachusetts (1641)*, quoted in Friedman, *A History of American Law*, 70.

23. Preyer, "Penal Measures in the American Colonies: An Overview," 344–45.

24. Greenberg, "Crime, Law Enforcement, and Social Control in Colonial America," 298.

25. Preyer, "Penal Measures in the American Colonies: An Overview," 333.

26. Fitzroy, "Punishment of Crime in Provincial Pennsylvania," 249.

27. Ibid., 254, note 48.

28. Preyer, "Penal Measures in the American Colonies: An Overview," 342.

29. Richard B. Morris, *Studies in the History of American Law,* 2d ed. (1959), 62.

30. William E. Nelson, "Emerging Notions of Modern Criminal Law in the Revolutionary Era: An Historical Perspective," *New York University Law Review* 42 (1967): 451.

31. William Blackstone, *Commentaries,* IV, 41–42, quoted in Flaherty, "Law and the Enforcement of Morals in Early America," 249–50.

32. Flaherty, "Law and Morals in Early America," 248.

33. Walker, *Popular Justice: A History of American Criminal Justice,* 18.

34. James Richardson, *The New York Police: From Colonial Times to 1901* (New York: Oxford University Press, 1970), 16.

35. David Hackett Fischer, *Albion's Seed: Four British Folkways in America* (New York and Oxford: Oxford University Press, 1989), 765–66.

36. Ibid., 765.

37. Ibid., 766–69.

38. Daniel J. Boorstin, *The Americans: The Colonial Experience* (New York: Vintage Books, 1958), 197; and Friedman, *A History of American Law,* 97–98. A full discussion of lawyers in the colonial period may be found in Boorstin, 195–202 and Friedman, 94–102.

39. Boorstin, *The Americans,* 196.

40. Susan C. Towne, "The Historical Origins of Bench Trial for Serious Crime," *The American Journal of Legal History* 26 (1982): 123, 159.

41. Ibid., 129.

42. Walker, *Popular Justice,* 26.

43. Jules Zanger, "Crime and Punishment in Early Massachusetts," *William and Mary Quarterly* 22 (1965): 473.

44. Psalm 51:1 states: "Have mercy upon me, O God, according to thy loving kindness; according to the multitude of thy tender mercies blot out my transgressions."

45. Friedman, *A History of American Law,* 71.

46. Preyer, "Penal Measures in the American Colonies," 331–32 note 9.

47. Friedman, *A History of American Law,* 71.

48. Melvin I. Urofsky, *A March to Liberty: A Constitutional History of the United States,* 2 vols. (New York: Alfred A. Knopf, 1988), I:30.

49. See, chapter 1, pages 30–36, 39–40.

50. *Pennsylvania Journal, and Weekly Advertiser* (Philadelphia), 18 October 1750, 2, reported that a Halifax, Nova Scotia, man was arrested for breach of the Sabbath. This crime included the selling of "spiritous Liquors" on Sunday. His punishment was a fine of £4 and one hour in the stocks.

51. *American Weekly Mercury* (Philadelphia), 8 October 1730, 1.

52. *South-Carolina Gazette* (Charleston), 29 March 1740, 3.

53. *American Weekly Mercury* (Philadelphia), 17 September 1730, 3.

54. *Pennsylvania Gazette* (Philadelphia), 10 September 1730, 3.

55. Ibid., 15 December 1730, 1.

56. *American Weekly Mercury* (Philadelphia), 8 October 1730, 1.

57. *New-England Courant* (Boston), 14 August 1725, 1.

58. Many colonial governments, especially those in New England, required the testimony of two or three witnesses before anyone could be put to death for a crime. Preyer, "Penal Measures in the American Colonies: An Overview," 333.

59. *Boston Evening-Post,* 16 June 1755, 3.

60. *Pennsylvania Gazette* (Philadelphia), 4 October 1750, 2.

61. *New-England Weekly Journal* (Boston), 4 August 1735, 1.

62. Prostitution appeared to be more of an accepted practice in eighteenth-century America than in the seventeenth. Cotton Mather noted of Boston that there were "several Houses in this Towne, where there are young Women of a very debauched character . . . unto whom there is a very great Resort of young Men." Cotton Mather, *Diary of Cotton Mather,* ed. Worthington C. Ford (Boston: Massachusetts Historical Society, 1912), II, 160, quoted in Flaherty, "Law and the Enforcement of Morals in Early America.

63. Diary of Lt. John Peebles, Dec. 31, 1776, quoted in Flaherty, "Law and the Enforcement of Morals in Early America," 236.

64. *Boston Evening-Post,* 22 April 1765, 3.

65. Ibid., 2 July 1770, 3.

66. *Maryland Gazette* (Annapolis), 28 March 1765, 1.

67. *Pennsylvania Gazette* (Philadelphia), 16 July 1730, 4.

68. *Boston Weekly News-Letter,* 12 April 1750, 2.

69. Ibid., 26 April 1750, 2.

70. *Publick Occurrences* (Boston), 25 September 1690, 1.

71. *Boston Evening-Post,* 29 September 1735, 2.

72. *Parker's New-York Gazette; or the Weekly Post-Boy,* 21 January 1760, 2.

73. Ibid., 23 February 1719–20, 2.

74. *New-York Mercury,* 4 November 1765, 1.

75. *Essex Gazette* (Salem), 8 May 1770, 2.

76. *Essex Journal and Merrimack Packet: Or, the Massachusetts and New-Hampshire General Advertiser* (Newbury-Port), 8 February 1775, 2.

77. See, for example, *Maryland Gazette* (Annapolis), 20 March 1755, 3.

78. Ibid., 15 August 1750, 3.

79. *New-York Gazette: or the Weekly Post-Boy,* 13 January 1755, 2.

80. Ibid., 10 October 1750, 2.

81. *Newport Mercury, or the Weekly Advertiser,* 29 July 1765, 3.

82. *Maryland Gazette* (Annapolis), 8 May 1760, 3.

83. *Essex Gazette* (Salem), 16 January 1770, 3.

84. *Boston Evening-Post,* 12 November 1750, 1.

85. *New-York Gazette,* 4 August 1735, 3.

86. *American Weekly Mercury* (Philadelphia), 5 November 1730, 4.

87. *New-York Weekly Post-Boy,* 23 September 1745, 3.

88. *Maryland Gazette* (Annapolis), 9 June 1730, 1–3 (emphasis included).

89. See, for example, the *South-Carolina Gazette* for 1760. During that year, 154 news stories of Indian wars, most including murders, appeared in the fifty-two weekly editions of the Charleston paper. Also, nearly every edition of the *Boston News-Letter* in 1704, its first year of publication, contained news of murders either by Native Americans or by colonists against the Indians.

90. *New-London Gazette,* 21 September 1770, 1.

91. *Boston Evening-Post,* 18 August 1735, 2.

92. *Boston Gazette, or Weekly Journal,* 19 November 1745, 3.

93. *New-York Mercury,* 6 May 1765, 2.

94. *Pennsylvania Gazette* (Philadelphia), 20 March 1749–50, 2.

95. Ibid., 22 December 1730, 2.

96. *American Weekly Mercury* (Philadelphia), 22 July 1725, 3.

97. *New-England Courant* (Boston), 31 July 1725, 2.

98. *Georgia Gazette* (Savannah), 4 July 1765, 2.

99. *Maryland Gazette* (Annapolis), 13 February 1755, 2.

100. *Boston Weekly Post-Boy,* 17 November 1735, 3.
101. *Virginia Gazette* (Williamsburg, Dixon and Purdie), 8 November 1770, 2.
102. See, for example, *New-York Evening-Post,* 11 June 1750, 1.
103. *Maryland Gazette* (Annapolis), 17 May 1745, 4.
104. *Parker's New-York Gazette; or the Weekly Post-Boy,* 20 November 1760, 3.
105. Rhys Isaac, *The Transformation of Virginia 1740–1790* (Chapel Hill: University of North Carolina Press, 1982), 72–73.
106. *New-York Journal; or the General Advertiser,* 18 January 1770, 3.
107. *Boston Evening-Post,* 28 January 1760, 3.
108. *Connecticut Journal, and New-Haven Post-Boy,* 2 February 1770, 3.
109. *Boston News-Letter,* 31 July 1704, 1.
110. Ibid., 23 July 1730, 2.
111. *Boston Gazette,* 17 August 1730, 2.
112. *Pennsylvania Gazette* (Philadelphia), 15 November 1750, 2.
113. *South-Carolina Gazette* (Charleston), 26 July 1735, 2.
114. Fitzroy, "Punishment of Crime in Provincial Pennsylvania," 254.
115. See, for example, *Boston News-Letter,* 2 June 1712, 1.
116. *Pennsylvania Chronicle, and Universal Advertiser* (Philadelphia), 5 November 1770, 2.
117. *Massachusetts Gazette,* 8 November 1770, 1.
118. *Maryland Gazette* (Annapolis), 4 December 1755, 2 (emphasis included).
119. *American Weekly Mercury* (Philadelphia), 16 October 1735, 2–3.
120. Ibid., 3.
121. *American Weekly Mercury* (Philadelphia), 15 July 1725, 2.
122. Fitzroy, "The Punishment of Crime in Provincial Pennsylvania," 254, note 48.
123. *Pennsylvania Packet, or the General Advertiser* (Philadelphia), 2 January 1775, 3.
124. See, for example, *New-York Weekly Post-Boy,* 1 April 1745, 3.
125. *Green & Russell's Boston Post-Boy & Advertiser,* 22 April 1765, 2.
126. Peter C. Hoffer and N. E. H. Hull, *Murdering Mothers: Infanticide in England and New England 1558–1803* (New York and London: New York University Press, 1984), 12–14.
127. Flaherty, "Law and the Enforcement of Morals in Early America," 226.
128. Ibid.
129. From Hoffer and Hull, *Murdering Mothers: Infanticide in England and New England 1558–1803.*"
130. *American Weekly Mercury* (Philadelphia), 28 August 1735, 3.
131. *Boston Evening-Post,* 14 April 1755, 2; *Connecticut Gazette* (New Haven), 19 April 1755, 1; and *Maryland Gazette* (Annapolis), 8 May 1755, 2.
132. See, for example, *Boston Evening-Post,* 22 October 1770, 3.
133. *Boston News-Letter,* 3 January 1740, 2.
134. See, for example, *Boston Evening-Post,* 1 September 1760, 3.
135. *Weekly Rehearsal* (Boston), 23 June 1735, 2.
136. *New-England Courant* (Boston), 8 February 1725, 2.
137. Ibid., 11 September 1765, 2.
138. *Virginia Gazette* (Williamsburg, Pinkney), 12 June 1775, 2–3.
139. *Parker's New-York Gazette; or the Weekly Post-Boy,* 11 February 1760, 3 (emphasis included).
140. *Boston News-Letter,* 19 June 1740, 2.
141. *Boston Weekly Post-Boy,* 4 August 1740, 2.

142. *New-York Gazette Revived in the Weekly Post-Boy,* 5 March 1749–50, 1.

143. *New-England Weekly Journal* (Boston), 24 February 1735, 2. Numerous accounts of slaves and the courts of colonial America appeared in colonial newspapers in addition to this one. Courts and slaves will be discussed in the next chapter.

144. See Greenberg, "Crime, Law Enforcement, and Social Control in Colonial America," 333; and Greenberg, *Crime and Law Enforcement in the Colony of New York, 1691–1776,* 130.

145. Greenberg, *Crime and Law Enforcement in the Colony of New York, 1691–1776,* 130. The exact amount of criminals whose death sentence was commuted is listed at 51.7 percent by Greenberg.

146. *Virginia Gazette* (Williamsburg, Dixon and Purdie), 8 November 1770, 2.

147. *Pennsylvania Gazette* (Philadelphia), 20 January 1729–30, 3 (emphasis included).

148. Ibid.

149. For an account of convicts arriving by ship in America, see, for example, *Boston Gazette, or Country Journal,* 21 April 1755, 3. Convicts sent to America served as laborers until their sentences were completed. Peter Charles Hoffer, *Law and People in Colonial America* (Baltimore and London: Johns Hopkins University Press, 1992), 90.

150. *Boston Gazette,* 9 February 1730, 2.

151. *New-York Weekly Post-Boy,* 28 January 1744–45, 4.

152. *New York Mercury,* 14 July 1760, 3; *South-Carolina Gazette* (Charleston), 9 August 1760, 2.

153. *Pennsylvania Gazette* (Philadelphia), 29 December 1730, 1.

154. *Maryland Gazette* (Annapolis), 31 January 1765, 1.

155. *Virginia Gazette* (Williamsburg, Purdie), 10 February 1775, 1.

156. See, *Virginia Gazette* (Williamsburg, Pinckney), 12 June 1775, 2.

157. *New-York Mercury,* 4 November 1765, 1.

CHAPTER 5. *THE PROCEEDINGS OF THE REBELLIOUS NEGROES*

1. *Boston Evening-Post,* 10 March 1755, 1.

2. See, for example, *American Weekly Mercury* (Philadelphia), 14 January 1734–35, 3; *South-Carolina Gazette* (Charleston), 18 January 1735, 4; *New-York Weekly Journal,* 20 January 1735, 2; *Weekly Rehearsal* (Boston), 3 February 1735, 2; *Boston News-Letter,* 22 February 1735, 2; *New-England Weekly Journal* (Boston), 30 June 1735, 2; *Boston Evening-Post,* 25 August 1735, 2; *Virginia Gazette* (Williamsburg), 18 January 1739–40, 3; *Boston Gazette, or Country Journal,* 28 January 1755, 2; *Pennsylvania Gazette* (Philadelphia), 5 June 1760, 2; *Pennsylvania Journal, or Weekly Advertiser* (Philadelphia), 5 June 1760, 3; and *Massachusetts Gazette (And Boston News-Letter),* 18 July 1765, 2.

3. *South-Carolina Gazette* (Charleston), 26 January 1740, 2.

4. It should be noted that an antislavery address in Virginia was published in the *Virginia Gazette* (Williamsburg), 19 March 1767. This address was an exception in Southern colonial newspapers.

5. *Pennsylvania Gazette* (Philadelphia), 17 April 1740, 1, reprinted George Whitefield's letter to the colonies of Maryland, Virginia, North Carolina, and

South Carolina denouncing slavery as an act abhorrent to God. See discussion below.

6. See, Darold D. Wax, "The Image of the Negro in the *Maryland Gazette, 1745–75," Journalism Quarterly* 46 (1969): 73–80, 86; and Samuel Allinson, Billy G. Smith, and Richard Wojtowicz, "The Precarious Freedom of Blacks in the Mid-Atlantic Region: Excerpts from the *Pennsylvania Gazette, 1728–1776," The Pennsylvania Magazine of History and Biography* 113 (1989): 237–264. This second article reprints numerous advertisements concerning slaves who had run away or were for sale. In addition, the *Boston News-Letter* contained an advertisement or advertisements concerning slaves in nearly every edition prior to 1720.

7. Wax, "The Image of the Negro in the *Maryland Gazette, 1745–75,"* 86.

8. This point of view is affirmed in Jeffery J. Crow, "Slave Rebelliousness and Social Conflict in North Carolina, 1775 to 1802," *William and Mary Quarterly* 37 (1980): 79–102.

9. *Boston News-Letter,* 22 October 1730, 4.

10. Ibid., 13 June 1720, 4.

11. George Brown Tindall, *America* (New York and London: W. W. Norton, 1984), 129.

12. Stanley M. Elkins, *Slavery: A Problem in American Institutional and Intellectual Life,* 3d ed. (Chicago and London: University of Chicago Press, 1976), 94 note 17.

13. David Brion Davis, "The Comparative Approach to American History: Slavery," in *Slavery in the New World: A Reader in Comparative History,* eds. Laura Foner and Eugene D. Genovese (Englewood Cliffs, N.J.: Prentice-Hall, 1969), 61.

14. Thomas C. Parramore, *Carolina Quest* (Englewood Cliffs, N.J.: Prentice-Hall, 1978), 185.

15. Wilbert Moore, "Slave Law and the Social Structure," *Journal of Negro History* 26 (1941): 184–88.

16. Edmund S. Morgan, *American Slavery, American Freedom: The Ordeal of Colonial Virginia* (New York: W. W. Norton, 1975), 129. The growing proficiency in growing tobacco and its effects upon slaves are discussed in Allan Kulikoff, *Tobacco and Slaves: The Development of Southern Cultures in the Chesapeake, 1680–1800* (Chapel Hill and London: University of North Carolina Press, 1986), 5. Winthrop D. Jordan, "Enslavement of Negroes in America to 1700," *Colonial America: Essays in Politics and Social Development,* 3d ed., eds. Stanley N. Katz and John M. Murrin (New York: Alfred A. Knopf, 1983), 251–52, agrees that the first decade of Africans' existence in America began the debasement of blacks that led to perpetual bondage.

17. Gary B. Nash, *The Urban Crucible: Social Change, Political Consciousness, and the Origins of the American Revolution* (Cambridge and London: Harvard University Press, 1979), 13.

18. *Historical Statistics of the United States: Colonial Times to 1970* (Washington, 1975), 1168.

19. Elkins, *Slavery,* 48–49.

20. James Truslow Adams, *Provincial Society 1690–1763* (New York: The Macmillan Company, 1927), 229–30. Various shipping triangles are also discussed in Ian K. Steele, *The English Atlantic 1675–1740: An Exploration of Communication and Community* (New York and Oxford: Oxford University Press, 1986). It should be noted that Gary M. Walton and James F. Shepherd, *The Economic Rise of Early America* (Cambridge: Cambridge University Press, 1979), 91, say that

describing the trading patterns of colonial America as triangles is inaccurate. Walton and Shepherd base their conclusions on data from the years 1768–1772 only. Triangular trade is a simplified explanation for the trading patterns that were used in the eighteenth century. American ships sailed several triangles. Besides the African triangle, ships ran from America to England to the Caribbean. Often there were many more stops along the way, but the basic configuration of the trade routes was triangular. Eric Foner and John A. Garraty, eds., *The Reader's Companion to American History* (Boston: Houghton Mifflin, 1991), s.v. "Triangular Trade."

21. Oscar Theodore Barck, Jr. and Hugh Talmage Lefler, *Colonial America* (New York: The Macmillan Company, 1958), 305.

22. Curtis P. Nettels, *The Roots of American Civilization*, 2d ed. (New York: Appelton-Century-Crofts, 1963), 419.

23. Steven Deyle, "'By farr the most profitable trade': Slave Trading in British Colonial North America," *Slavery & Abolition* 10 (1989): 112.

24. James F. Shepherd and Gary M. Walton, *Shipping, Maritime Trade, and the Economic Development of Colonial North America* (Cambridge: Cambridge University Press, 1972), 42 note 2.

25. Philip D. Curtin, *The Atlantic Slave Trade: A Census* (Madison: University of Wisconsin Press, 1969), 216.

26. *Historical Statistics of the United States,* 1168.

27. David Hackett Fischer, *Albion's Seed: Four British Folkways in America* (New York and Oxford: Oxford University Press, 1989), 810.

28. Davis, "The Comparative Approach to American History: Slavery," 62.

29. A. Leon Higginbotham, *In the Matter of Color: Race and the American Legal Process, The Colonial Period* (New York: Oxford University Press, 1978), 81.

30. *Historical Statistics of the United States,* 1168.

31. Marvin Harris, "The Origin of the Descent Rule," in *Slavery in the New World: A Reader in Comparative History,* eds. Laura Foner and Eugene D. Genovese (Englewood Cliffs, N.J.: Prentice-Hall, 1969), 52.

32. Deyle, "'By farr the most profitable trade,'" 111.

33. Gary B. Nash, *Forging Freedom: The Formation of Philadelphia's Black Community 1720–1840* (Cambridge and London: Harvard University Press, 1988), 11.

34. Elkins, *Slavery,* 49 note 33.

35. John Codman Hurd, *The Law of Freedom and Bondage in the United States* (Boston: Little, Brown, 1858), 303.

36. Ibid., 232.

37. Nash, *The Urban Crucible,* 14. See also, Winthrop Jordan, *White Over Black: American Attitudes Toward the Negro, 1550–1812* (Chapel Hill: University of North Carolina Press, 1968).

38. Barck and Lefler, *Colonial America,* 305.

39. Louis Filler, *The Crusade against Slavery 1830–1860* (New York: Harper & Row, 1960), 13.

40. Ibid.; Nash, *Forging Freedom,* 9; and Deyle, "'By farr the most profitable trade,'" 119 note 64.

41. Nash, *Forging Freedom,* 9.

42. Kulikoff, *Tobacco and Slaves,* 6.

43. Deyle, "'By farr the most profitable trade,'" 115–16.

44. *Boston News-Letter,* 21 April 1712, 2.

45. *New-York Journal; or the General Advertiser,* 23 June 1770, 1 supplement. The revolt, even though slaves murdered several whites, was not successful. Similar reports of slave revolts on board ships may be found throughout the colonial period. See, for example, *New-York Weekly Journal,* 5 October 1735, 3; *Pennsylvania Gazette* (Philadelphia), 13 January 1730, 4; 9 August 1750, 2.

46. *Boston Evening-Post,* 13 August 1750, 2.

47. *Boston Weekly Post-Boy,* 7 July 1740, 2.

48. The Stono Rebellion took place in September 1739. Slaves, estimated at sixty to one hundred, fought whites after breaking into a store and stealing guns and ammunition. The Stono Rebellion will be discussed more fully later in the chapter. For a full discussion of the Stono Rebellion, see Peter H. Wood, *Black Majority* (New York: W. W. Norton, 1974), 314–23.

49. *Boston News-Letter,* 22 October 1730, 2.

50. The idea of a slave insurrection was always a concern for white colonists, but when accounts of rebellions mentioned the fact that blacks planned only to murder white males and keep white females for mating and marriage purposes, white hysteria was often raised even more. See, for example, *Essex Gazette* (Salem), 8 May 1770, 2.

51. The Cherokee War of 1760 and the reports concerning it that appeared in colonial newspapers may be found in Chapter Two.

52. H. Orlando Patterson, "The General Causes of Jamaican Slave Revolts," in *Slavery in the New World,* eds. Laura Foner and Eugene D. Genovese (Englewood Cliffs, N.J.: Prentice-Hall, 1969), 211–12.

53. *New-York Weekly Post-Boy,* 8 April 1745, 2; and *New-York Evening-Post,* 8 April 1745, 3.

54. *Pennsylvania Gazette* (Philadelphia), 12 April 1745, 2.

55. *Virginia Gazette* (Williamsburg), 23 May 1745, 2.

56. *New-York Gazette Revived in the Weekly Post-Boy,* 6 August 1750, 3.

57. *Boston Evening-Post,* 13 August 1750, 2 and *Boston Weekly Post-Boy,* 13 August 1750, 2.

58. *Pennsylvania Gazette* (Philadelphia), 9 August 1750, 2 and *Pennsylvania Journal, or Weekly Advertiser* 9, August 1750, 2.

59. *Maryland Gazette* (Annapolis), 5 September 1750, 2.

60. The noticeable omission by the *South-Carolina Gazette* of numerous slave revolt news items that appeared in many colonial newspapers will be discussed later in this chapter.

61. The story may have appeared in the *Virginia Gazette* like the Jamaican rebellion story of 1745, but the 1750 editions of the paper are no longer extant.

62. *New-York Evening-Post,* 6 August 1750, 3.

63. *Virginia Gazette* (Williamsburg), 18 January 1740, 3; *South-Carolina Gazette (Charleston), 26 January 1740, 2; American Weekly Mercury* (Philadelphia), 4 March 1740, 2; *New-York Weekly Journal,* 10 March 1740, 1; and *Boston News-Letter,* 28 March 1740, 1.

64. *Pennsylvania Gazette* (Philadelphia), 5 June 1760, 2; *Pennsylvania Journal, or Weekly Advertiser* (Philadelphia), 5 June 1760, 3; *Boston Weekly News-Letter,* 19 June 1760, 1.

65. Part of the letter reported, "There were such Dissentions among them that several were killed in their own Quarrels." Since no trials for the rebelling slaves had yet been held, this type of news was grounded in rumor.

66. *Boston News-Letter,* 6 March 1760, 1.

67. *Boston Evening-Post,* 14 July 1760, 3; *Boston Weekly News-Letter,* 17 July

1760, 2; *Weyman's New-York Gazette,* 21 July 1760, 2; *New-York Mercury,* 21 July 1760, 2.

68. *Maryland Gazette* (Annapolis), 10 July 1760, 3.
69. *Boston Evening-Post,* 24 November 1760, 2.
70. *Maryland Gazette* (Annapolis), 26 June 1760, 3.
71. *Historical Statistics of the United States,* 1168.
72. *New-York Gazette,* 9 November 1730, 2. The *Gazette*'s information about the insurrection was obtained from a later and different source than that printed in other colonial newspapers. The other papers referred only to "an Account of a bloody Tragedy which was to have been executed here." *Boston News-Letter,* 22 October 1730, 2; *New-England Weekly Journal* (Boston), 12 October 1730, 2; and *Pennsylvania Gazette* (Philadelphia), 22 October 1730, 4.
73. *Boston Evening-Post,* 7 July 1740, 3; *Boston Weekly Post-Boy,* 7 July 1740, 2; *Pennsylvania Gazette* (Philadelphia), 26 June 1740, 3. Another suspected slave rebellion was uncovered in 1745, according to the *Pennsylvania Journal, or Weekly Advertiser* (Philadelphia), 22 August 1745, 2. The news of this suspected slave revolt was not reported in Charleston either.
74. The information on the Stono Rebellion is taken from Wood, *Black Majority,* 314–23 and Higginbotham, *In the Matter of Color,* 192–95.
75. *Statutes at Large of South Carolina,* vol 7, 397, 399, 386, quoted in Higginbotham, *In the Matter of Color,* 193–94, 195.
76. *South-Carolina Gazette* (Charleston), 15 April 1745, 1.
77. *Boston Evening-Post,* 14 July 1740, 4.
78. *New-York Journal; or the General Advertiser,* 22 February 1770, 2.
79. Higginbotham, *In the Matter of Color,* 77.
80. *Boston Gazette,* 7 December 1730, 2.
81. *Boston Evening-Post,* 20 January 1755, 1.
82. *New-York Gazette: or, the Weekly Post-Boy,* 10 February 1755, 3.
83. *South-Carolina Gazette* (Charleston), 22 March 1744–45, 1.
84. *American Weekly Mercury* (Philadelphia), 11 March 1734–35, 2.
85. *Boston News-Letter,* 10 June 1706, 4.
86. *American Weekly Mercury* (Philadelphia), 31 July 1735, 2.
87. *North-Carolina Magazine; Or Universal Intelligence* (New Bern), 4 January 1765, 3.
88. *Boston Gazette, and Country Journal,* 1 July 1765, 3.
89. *Massachusetts Gazette (And Boston News-Letter),* 19 July 1770, 2.
90. *Boston Weekly Post-Boy,* 21 July 1735, 3; and *American Weekly Mercury* (Philadelphia), 7 August 1735, 3.
91. *Dunlap's Maryland Gazette; or the Baltimore General Advertiser,* 28 November 1775, 2; and *Virginia Gazette* (Williamsburg, Dixon and Hunter), 2 December 1775, 3.
92. *American Weekly Mercury* (Philadelphia), 24 July 1735, 4; *New-England Weekly Journal* (Boston), 4 August 1735, 1; and *New-York Gazette* 4 August 1735, 3.
93. *Pennsylvania Gazette* (Philadelphia), 4 June 1730, 4.
94. *Boston Evening-Post,* 12 November 1750, 1.
95. *Maryland Gazette* (Annapolis), 29 August 1750, 3 and 19 December 1750, 3; and *South-Carolina Gazette* (Charleston), 8 April 1745, 2.
96. See, for example, Ibid., 10 October 1750, 2 and 20 March 1755, 3.
97. Although the dates of the newspapers consulted are outside the time pa-

rameters of this study, see Higginbotham, *In the Matter of Color*, 76, for more on slaves and arson.

98. Joshua Coffin, *Slave Insurrections* (New York: American Anti Slavery Society, 1860), 11–13.

99. *American Weekly Mercury* (Philadelphia), 27 August 1730, 3.

100. *Boston Evening-Post*, 28 January 1760, 3.

101. *Boston News-Letter*, 9 February 1707–08, 2

102. *Weekly Rehearsal* (Boston), 4 August 1735, 2; *Boston Weekly Post-Boy*, 4 August 1735, 4; *American Weekly Mercury* (Philadelphia), 14 August 1735, 3; *New-England Weekly Journal* (Boston), 2 September 1735, 2; and *South-Carolina Gazette* (Charleston), 20 September 1735, 2.

103. *Boston Evening-Post*, 7 July 1755, 4.

104. Ibid., 25 August 1755, 3.

105. Ibid., 21 July 1755, 1.

106. See, for example, *Maryland Gazette* (Annapolis), 18 July 1750, 2.

107. *Boston Evening-Post*, 16 September 1745, 4.

108. *American Weekly Mercury* (Philadelphia), 4 June 1730, 4.

109. *Boston Evening-Post*, 11 August 1755, 4; *Boston Gazette, or Country Journal*, 11 August 1755, 3; *Connecticut Gazette* (New Haven), 16 August 1755, 3; *New-York Gazette: or, the Weekly Post-Boy*, 18 August 1755, 1; *New-York Mercury*, 18 August 1755, 3; *Pennsylvania Gazette* (Philadelphia), 21 August 1755, 3; *Pennsylvania Journal, or Weekly Advertiser* (Philadelphia), 21 August 1755, 2; and *Maryland Gazette* (Annapolis), 28 August 1755, 2.

110. For a description of the way in which white colonists were treated when convicted of murder, see Chapter Four.

111. *Pennsylvania Journal, or Weekly Advertiser* (Philadelphia), 26 July 1750, 1; and *Pennsylvania Gazette* (Philadelphia), 2 August 1750, 2.

112. *New-York Mercury*, 14 July 1755, 2.

113. *Pennsylvania Gazette* (Philadelphia), 5 July 1750, 2; *Pennsylvania Journal, or Weekly Advertiser* (Philadelphia), 5 July 1750, 2; and *Boston Evening-Post*, 9 July 1750, 4.

114. A. G. Roeber, "Authority, Law, and Custom: The Rituals of Court Day in Tidewater Virginia, 1720 to 1750," *William and Mary Quarterly* 37 (1980): 49–50. According to Roeber, slaves and the lower ranks of society could feel a part of communal affairs, at least in Tidewater, Virginia, through participation in court day.

115. *New-England Weekly Journal* (Boston), 24 February 1735, 2.

116. Elkins, *Slavery*, 49 note 33; Hurd, *The Law of Freedom and Bondage in the United States*, 303; Peter Charles Hoffer, *Law and People in Colonial America* (Baltimore and London: Johns Hopkins University Press, 1992), 91.

117. This conclusion is affirmed by Hoffer, *Law and People in Colonial America*, 91. Hoffer, in looking at colonial court records discovered that slave owners were tried for murder in Virginia after beating slaves to death.

118. *Pennsylvania Journal, or Weekly Advertiser* (Philadelphia), 21 January 1755, 2; and *Maryland Gazette* (Annapolis), 13 February 1755, 2.

119. Hoffer, *Law and People in Colonial America*, 92.

120. *Boston Evening-Post*, 10 March 1755, 1.

121. Bradley, "Connecticut Newspapers and the Dialogue on Slavery: 1770–1776," 4, says that the Boston newspapers did not take part in the dialogue on slavery because the issue was one that was part of the patriot-tory controversy. Patriot newspapers could not, Bradley intimates, oppose slavery when so many

of America's patriots were themselves slave owners. While this argument is valid, another reason may also play a role in the omission the antislavery dialogue by Boston's newspapers, that is, the political situation of Massachusetts' chief city. By 1770, the port of Boston was already embroiled for all practical purposes in revolution with England. The Tea Party of 1773 and the Stamp Act controversy of 1765 had inflamed Bostonians, and the 5 March 1770 Boston Massacre only increased hard feelings among colonial citizens and British troops. Troop deployment to the port city continually grew and embargoes of the port beginning with the Boston Port Act of 1772 made Boston, for all intents and purposes, a city under seige from that date forward. The *Boston Gazette* did run pieces on slavery prior to the Revolution, but these pieces were used as revolutionary propaganda to unite opposition to American "slavery" under British rule. See Patricia Bradley, "The Boston Gazette and Slavery as Revolutionary Propaganda," *Journalism & Mass Communications Quarterly* 72 (1995): 581–96.

122. *Pennsylvania Gazette* (Philadelphia), 17 April 1740, 1.

123. Barck and Lefler, *Colonial America*, 305; Filler, *The Crusade against Slavery*, 13; Nash, *Forging Freedom*, 9.

124. Benjamin Franklin, *The Autobiography of Benjamin Franklin: A Genetic Text*, J. A. Leo Lemay and P. M. Zall, eds. (Knoxville: University of Tennessee Press, 1981), 105–6. Franklin, after meeting Whitfield in 1739, considered him a friend for life, and Whitefield had an open invitation to stay with Franklin whenever the preacher was in Philadelphia.

125. Carl Van Doren, *Benjamin Franklin* (New York: Viking Press, 1938), 129, 216, 479. Franklin, according to Van Doren, began ridding himself of his slaves and advocating the abolition of the practice as early as 1731 (129 note 5).

126. *Boston Evening-Post,* 15 December 1740, 1.

127. *South-Carolina Gazette* (Charleston), 18 July 1740, 3.

128. *New-York Evening-Post,* 28 May 1750, 3.

129. See, Edmund S. Morgan and Helen Morgan, *The Stamp Act Crisis: Prologue to Independence* (Chapel Hill: University of North Carolina Press, 1953); Arthur M. Schlesinger, *Prelude to Independence: The Newspaper War on Britain 1764–1776* (New York: Random House, 1958); and Jeffery A. Smith, *Printers and Press Freedom: The Ideology of Early American Journalism* (New York and Oxford: Oxford University Press, 1988).

130. *Pennsylvania Ledger: Or the Virginia, Maryland, Pennsylvania, & New-Jersey Weekly Advertiser* (Philadelphia), 28 January 1775, 4; and *Providence Gazette; and Country Journal,* 28 January 1775, 4.

131. Bradley, "Connecticut Newspapers and the Dialogue on Slavery: 1770–1776," 12.

132. *Essex Gazette* (Salem), 19 June 1770, 2.

133. *New-London Gazette,* 10 August 1770, 1.

134. *Connecticut Journal, and New-Haven Post-Boy,* 6 July 1770, 3.

135. *Connecticut Gazette; and the Universal Intelligencer* (New London), 6 January 1775, 1.

136. Ibid.

137. This is the same conclusion reached by Bradley, "Connecticut Newspapers and the Dialogue on Slavery, 1770–1776," 4.

138. *Providence Gazette; and Country Journal,* 29 July 1775. A similar report on the incident appeared in the *Connecticut Gazette;* and the *Universal Intelligencer* (New London), 28 July 1775, 2.

139. *Boston-Gazette, and Country Journal,* 27 February 1775, 2 supplement.

140. *Providence Gazette; and Country Journal,* 9 September 1775, 1.

141. Quoted in Lorenzo J. Greene, *The Negro in Colonial America, 1620–1776* (New York, 1942), 60.

142. *Essex Gazette* (Salem), 19 June 1770, 2.

143. The content of the *American Weekly Mercury* of Philadelphia in 1730 offers a typical breakdown of these types of news as they appeared in colonial newspapers. This breakdown does not include war and political news of Europe. The count of news items for the year on these topics were: ship news-326, court and crime news-77, social news 34, accident reports-28, entertainment pieces-35, slave news- 7. See appendix 2 for a more thorough comparison of slave news with other types of nonpolitical news in other newspapers and in other years.

144. *Boston Evening-Post,* 11 August 1755, 4; *Boston Gazette, or Country Journal,* 11 August 1755, 3; *Connecticut Gazette* (New Haven), 16 August 1755, 3; *New-York Gazette: or, the Weekly Post-Boy,* 18 August 1755, 1; *New-York Mercury,* 18 August 1755, 3; *Pennsylvania Gazette* (Philadelphia), 21 August 1755, 3; *Pennsylvania Journal, or Weekly Advertiser* (Philadelphia), 21 August 1755, 2; and *Maryland Gazette* (Annapolis), 28 August 1755, 2.

145. See note 73 for a listing of the newspapers.

146. David A. Copeland, "Covering the Big Story: George Whitefield's First Preaching Tour, News Manipulation, and the Colonial Press," paper presented at the American Journalism Historians Association annual conference, Lawrence, Kansas, 1992, 22. The announcement of the arrest was made in the *Gazette,* 15 January 1741. The belief that Elizabeth Timothy was imprisoned instead of her son, Peter, is not universally accepted. See Wm. David Sloan and Julie Hedgepeth Williams, *The Early American Press, 1690–1783* (Westport, Conn.: Greenwood Press, 1994), 97.

147. Richard D. Brown, *Knowledge Is Power: The Diffusion of Information in Early America, 1700–1865* (New York and Oxford: Oxford University Press, 1989), 17–19.

148. *Boston Evening-Post,* 24 November 1760, 2.

149. *Historical Statistics of the United States,* 1168.

150. Bradley, "Connecticut Newspapers and the Dialogue on Slavery: 1770–1776," 21, notes that up to sixteen separate insertions were made in some colonial newspapers that dealt with antislavery dialogue. In "Slavery in Colonial Newspapers: The Somerset Case," 6, Bradley found that at least one-fourth of those antislavery reports dealt with 1772 Somerset case. According to Charles Evans, *American Bibliography* (Chicago, 1904), at least eight books or pamphlets with antislavery viewpoints stated in the titles were printed in 1774. This was determined by examining the list of colonial publications for the year. Many more of the works may have contained antislavery rhetoric, but it is impossible to ascertain their exact content from the titles.

151. Filler, *The Crusade against Slavery,* 10–11.

152. When Noah Webster began publishing his daily newspaper, the *Minerva,* in 1793, it ran antislavery pieces, works that sounded very similar to the antislavery correspondence of the colonial newspapers. See, Frederic Hudson, *Journalism in the United States, from 1690 to 1872* (New York: Harper & Brothers, 1873), 191–92.

153. George Henry Payne, *History of Journalism in the United States* (New York and London: D. Appleton, 1920), 223–24.

CHAPTER 6. *ADAPTED TO THE FEMALE WORLD*

1. *Parker's New-York Gazette; or the Weekly Post-Boy,* 4 December 1760, 1.

2. On women and sensationalism, see chapter 3. Women and crime may be

found in chapter 4. Women and Native Americans are dealt with in chapter 2. Slave news and women are discussed in chapter 5. Women and their role in religion may be found in chapter 8. Women in relation to literature, poetry, and social news is contained in chapter 9.

3. *Pennsylvania Gazette* (Philadelphia), 26 November 1730, 1; and *New-York Gazette,* 8 September 1735, 1.

4. *New-York Weekly Journal,* 19 May 1735, 1.

5. Cotton Mather, *Ornaments for the Daughters of Zion. Or, The Character and Happiness of a Virtuous Woman* (1692; reprint, Delmar, N.Y.: Scholar's Facsimiles & Reprints), 1–2.

6. Quoted in Sara M. Evans, *Born for Liberty: A History of Women in America* (New York: The Free Press, 1989), 22.

7. Mary Beth Norton, "The Evolution of the White Women's Experience in Early America," *American Historical Review* 89 (1984): 610.

8. The witchcraft trials of the colonial period are an example of the evil of women. See, Evans, *Born for Liberty,* 33; Norton, "The Evolution of White Women's Experience in Early America," 610; John Putnam Demos, *Entertaining Satan: Witchcraft and the Culture of Early New England* (New York: Oxford University Press, 1983), 198; N. E. H. Hull, *Female Felons: Women and Serious Crime in Colonial Massachusetts* (Urbana and Chicago: University of Chicago Press, 1987), 13–14.

9. Women in the role of savior may be found throughout the colonial period, but the concept of the "republican mother," the woman who would instill all of the necessary ingredients into her sons to help in the success of America, was very prevalent during and after the Revolution. See, Evans, *Born for Freedom,* 57.

10. Laurel Thatcher Ulrich, *Good Wives: Image and Reality in the Lives of Women in Northern New England 1650–1750* (New York: Alfred A. Knopf, 1982), 13.

11. Ibid., 596, and Hull, *Female Felons,* 4. David Hackett Fischer, *Albion's Seed: Four British Folkways in America* (New York and Oxford: Oxford University Press, 1989), 490, believes that the dominance of males over females in colonial society may have been absent within many Quaker families. Norton, "The Evolution of White Women's Experience in Early America," 603, includes Quakers with other groups who saw a dominant male controlling the nuclear families of America.

12. Norton, "The Evolution of White Women's Experience in Early America," 603.

13. Laurel Thatcher Ulrich, "Vertuous Women Found: New England Ministerial Literature, 1668–1735," *Amerian Quarterly* 31 (1974): 55–78.

14. Norton, "The Evolution of White Women's Experience in Early America," 617.

15. Thomas C. Parramore, *Carolina Quest* (Englewood Cliffs, N.J.: Prentice-Hall, 1978), 118.

16. Robert V. Wells, *Revolution in American's Lives: A Demographic Perspective on the History of Americans, Their Families, and Their Society* (Westport, Conn.: Greenwood Press, 1982), 30.

17. Lorena S. Walsh and Russell R. Menard, "Death in the Cheseapeake," *Maryland Historical Magazine* 69 (1974): 222.

18. For a discussion of various methods of raising children in America, see Philip Greven, *The Protestant Temperament: Patterns of Child-Rearing, Religious Experience, and the Self in Early America* (New York: Alfred A. Knopf, 1977).

19. Nancy F. Cott, "Eighteenth-Century Family and Social Life Revealed in Massachusetts Divorce Records," *Journal of Social History* 10 (1976): 29–30.

20. N. Ray Hiner, "Cotton Mather and His Female Children: Notes on the Relationship between Private Experience and Public Thought," *The Journal of Psychohistory* 13 (1985): 33.

21. Lawrence A. Cremin, *American Education: The Colonial Experience 1607–1783* (New York: Harper & Row, 1970), 135.

22. Maris A. Vinoskis, "Family and Schooling in Colonial and Nineteenth-Century America," *Journal of Family History* 12 (1987): 23.

23. Norton, "Evolution of White Women's Experience in Early America," 608–9. For a complete discussion of women in the role of religious providers for their children, see Perry Miller, *The New England Mind: From Colony to Province* (Cambridge: Harvard University Press, 1953).

24. Richard Shiels, "The Feminization of American Congregationalism, 1730–1835," *American Quarterly* 33 (1981): 46–62.

25. Kenneth A. Lockridge, *Literacy in Colonial New England: An Enquiry into the Social Context of Literacy in the Early Modern West* (New York: Norton, 1974), quoted in Vinoskis, "Family and Schooling in Colonial and Nineteenth-Century America," 23.

26. Joan R. Gunderson and Gwen Victor Gampel, "Married Women's Legal Status in Eighteenth-Century New York and Virginia," *William and Mary Quarterly* 39 (1982): 114.

27. Evans, *Born of Liberty,* 35; and Norton, "The Evolution of White Women's Experience in Early America," 605. Continuing in the trade of a deceased husband is exactly what many women whose husbands had been printers did in colonial America. See Ira L. Baker, "Elizabeth Timothy: America's First Woman Printer," *Journalism Quarterly* 54 (1977): 280–85; Susan Henry, "Exception to the Female Model: Colonial Printer Mary Crouch," *Journalism Quarterly* 62 (1985): 725–33; Susan Henry, "Sarah Goddard, Gentlewoman Printer," *Journalism Quarterly* 57)1980): 23–30; and Susan Henry, "Ann Franklin: Rhode Island's Woman Printer," in *Newsletters to Newspapers: Eighteenth-Century Journalism,* Donovan H. Bond and W. Reynolds McLeod, eds. (Morganton: West Virginia University, 1977), 129–44.

28. Bonnie Thornton Dill, "Our Mothers' Grief: Racial Ethnic Women and the Maintenance of Families," *Journal of Family History* 13 (1988): 416.

29. Hugh T. Lefler and Patricia Stanford, *North Carolina,* 2d ed. (New York: Harcourt Brace Jovanovich, 1972), 151–52. For more on women's roles in public affairs, see Mary Beth Norton, "Eighteenth-Century American Women in Peace and War: The Case of the Loyalists," *William and Mary Quarterly* 33 (1976): 386–409.

30. For an extended discussion of women's roles in the fight for independence, see Linda Kerber, *Women of the Republic: Intellect and Ideology in Revolutionary America* (Chapel Hill: University of North Carolina Press, 1980) and Mary Beth Norton, *Liberty's Daughters: The Revolutionary Experience of American Women, 1750–1800* (Boston: Little, Brown, 1980).

31. Evans, *Born for Liberty,* 49.

32. From the travels of Duc de la Rochefoucauld, in Mary Sumner Benson, *Women in Eighteenth Century America* (New York: Columbia University Press, 1935), reprinted in Barbara Welter, *The Woman Question in American History* (Hinsdale, Ill.: The Dryden Press, 1973), 23.

33. 17 October 1775, 1.

34. A discussion of the Dogood letters may be found in Mark Lipper, "Benjamin Franklin's 'Silence Dogood' as an Eighteenth-Century 'Censor Morum,'" in *Newsletters to Newspapers: Eighteenth-Century Journalism,* 73–83.

35. Peter Charles Hoffer, in his introduction to *Early American History: Colonial Women and Domesticity* (New York and London: Garland Publishing, 1988), vii, concludes that newspapers, like all official records of the colonial period, were written only by men. Although most of the news in colonial newspapers, probably in excess of 95 percent, was written by men, women could and did submit correspondence that was printed by newspapers.

36. *Boston Evening-Post,* 21 January 1745, 1; 15 April 1745, 1.

37. *New-England Courant* (Boston), 22 February 1725, 1.

38. See, for example, *New-York Journal; or General Advertiser,* 8 March 1770, 4.

39. If, as Mary Beth Norton maintains in "The Evolution of White Women's Experience in Early America," 609, most men were completely unchurched by the eighteenth century, it seems logical to assume that women, who were to train children in their religious ways, would be more interested in religious news and doctrinal issues than men, provided the religious items were not saturated with political overtones. And although it is not safe to assume studies from the twentieth century on news readership would hold true in the eighteenth, George Gallop discovered in 1930 that women were more likely to read news of births, deaths, and news concerning health than men. Considering the fact that birth, death, disease, and medical news were so much a part of the domestic sphere in the eighteenth century, it seems probable that women in the eighteenth century would have had a special interest in these news items, too. George Gallop, "A Scientific Method for Determining Readership-Interest," *Journalism Quarterly* 7 (1930): 11. In another study, David H. Weaver and John B. Mauro, "Newspaper Readership Patterns," *Journalism Quarterly* 55 (1978): 84–91, 134, showed that women preferred accident, crime, and military news more than men. All three types of news appeared regularly in colonial newspapers.

40. *Boston Chronicle,* 18 June 1770, 1 (emphasis included).

41. *Green & Russell's Massachusetts Gazette & Boston Post-Boy and Advertiser,* 20 August 1770, 4 (emphasis included).

42. *American Weekly Mercury* (Philadelphia), 3 January 1739–40, 2.

43. *Pennsylvania Gazette* (Philadelphia) 8 October 1730, 1.

44. *Providence Gazette; and Country Journal,* 6 January 1770, 1 (emphasis included).

45. Ibid.

46. *Boston Evening-Post,* 8 October 1750, 1–2.

47. *Maryland Gazette* (Annapolis), 24 December 1745, 2.

48. *New-York Journal; or the General Advertiser,* 9 August 1770, 4.

49. *Providence Gazette; and Country Journal,* 19 January 1765, 3.

50. *Rivington's New-York Gazetteer,* 27 July 1775, 3.

51. *Boston Evening-Post,* 24 March 1740, 1.

52. See, for example, *American Weekly Mercury* (Philadelphia), 17 November 1735, 2; *Boston Evening-Post,* 17 December 1750, 2; and *Pennsylvania Gazette* (Philadelphia), 18 September 1735, 2.

53. *New-England Courant* (Boston), 11 December 1725, 2.

54. *New-York Journal,* 19 May 1735, 1.

55. *South-Carolina and American General Gazette* (Charleston), 20 April 1770, 3.

56. *New-London Gazette,* 8 June 1770, 2.

57. *Virginia Gazette* (Williamsburg, Rind), 11 October 1770, 3.

58. *Boston Evening-Post,* 1 October 1750, 2.

59. *Providence Gazette; and Country Journal,* 16 February 1765, 2.

60. See, for example, *Pennsylvania Gazette* (Philadelphia), 8 October 1730.

61. Hull, *Female Felons,* 62. Using court records of Massachusetts, Hull estimated that women committed almost 18 percent of the crime in that colony from 1673–1774. In chapter 4 of this work, the way in which colonial newspapers presented crime by females is examined. Crimes by women, if Hull's percentage for crimes committed by females may be applied to all of the colonies, suggests that newspapers ran stories on women's crimes in a greater percentage than the actual number of female-perpetrated crimes actually were. Part of the reason for that, no doubt, lies in the virtuous versus vicious dichotomy of women understood by colonial society.

62. Mather, *Ornaments for the Daughters of Zion,* 3.

63. *Boston Evening-Post,* 31 March 1755, 4; and *New-York Mercury,* 7 April 1755, 3 (emphasis included).

64. Genesis 3:14.

65. In the *Pennsylvannia Gazette* of 1730, for example, there were nearly three times as many news items concerning vicious women and women's crimes as there were news items on the virtuous woman out of a total of thirty-three items dealing directly with women.

66. *Pennsylvania Gazette* (Philadelphia), 26 November 1730, 1 (emphasis included); and *New-York Gazette,* 8 September 1735, 1. This piece originally ran in the *Spectator* in London in 1730.

67. *Pennsylvannia Gazette* (Philadelphia), 4 March 1734–35, 2.

68. *American Weekly Mercury* (Philadelphia), 13 August 1730, 1–3.

69. *Boston Weekly Post-Boy,* 12 November 1750, 1.

70. *Boston News-Letter,* 2 January 1735, 1.

71. *Boston Gazette,* 8 December 1735, 1.

72. *Weyman's New-York Gazette,* 8 April 1765, 1.

73. *Connecticut Gazette; and the Universal Intelligencer* (New London), 24 March 1775, 3.

74. *New-London Gazette,* 21 December 1770, 2.

75. Ibid.

76. *American Weekly Mercury* (Philadlephia), 15 May 1735, 3.

77. See, for example, *Boston Evening-Post,* 6 January 1755, 2; and *Virginia Gazette* (Williamsburg, Dixon and Purdie), 19 April 1770, 1.

78. *Virginia Gazette* (Williamsburg, Rind), 8 March 1770, 2.

79. *New-York Evening-Post,* 12 March 1750, 2.

80. Norton, "Evolution of White Women's Experience in Early America," 613.

81. These subjects will be treated below.

82. See *Boston Evening-Post,* 23 June 1740, 2; and *Pennsylvania Gazette* (Philadelphia), 28 August 1740, 2.

83. *South-Carolina Gazette* (Charleston), 8 October 1750, 1.

84. *Pennsylvania Gazette* (Philadelphia), 13 September 1750, 1.

85. Ibid.

86. *Boston Weekly News-Letter,* 6 December 1750, 1.

87. *South-Carolina Gazette* (Charleston), 22 February 1734–35, 3.

88. *American Weekly Mercury* (Philadelphia), 30 September 1725, 2.

89. *Pennsylvania Gazette* (Philadelphia), 17 April 1735, 4.

90. *Boston Gazette,* 24 March 1740, 1.

91. Lawrence Wroth, *The Colonial Printer* (Portland, Me.: The Southworth-Anthoensen Press, 1938), 154–56.

92. See note 27, p. 334 for numerous scholarly works on women printers of the colonial period.

93. *American Weekly Mercury* (Philadelphia), 17 September 1730, 1.

94. *Massachusetts Spy* (Boston), 8 November 1770, 1.

95. *Virginia Gazette* (Williamsburg, Dixon and Purdie), 22 February 1770, 1.

96. Cott, "Divorce and the Changing Status of Women in Eighteenth-Century Massachusetts," 592. The trend toward divorce continued in eighteenth-century America and is worth noting even though the information goes beyond the time parameters of this study. By 1784, divorces increased by 87 percent in Massachusetts over the 1774 divorce rate with women petitioning for more than two-thirds of them.

97. *Georgia Gazette* (Savannah), 7 March 1770, 2.

98. The "Poet's Corner" was a weekly feature that began to appear in many colonial newspapers in the second half of the eighteenth century. Within the corner, which usually ran on the fourth page of the newspaper, poems appeared on topics that seemed to have a very feminine appeal such as beauty, a snowfall, and happiness. Sometimes, the authors were women. This feature further supports the fact that women in at least some parts of colonial society were gaining more control of their own lives. The "Poet's Corner" will be discussed later in the chapter.

99. *New-York Journal; or the General Advertiser,* 25 October 1770, 4; and *New-London Gazette,* 9 November 1770, 4.

100. *Parker's New-York Gazette; or the Weekly Post-Boy,* 4 December 1760, 1.

101. Henry, "Sarah Goddard, Gentlewoman Printer," 23.

102. *Providence Gazette; and Country Journal* , 10 February 1770, 3.

103. See, for example, *South-Carolina Gazette* (Charleston) 20 September 1770, 2.

104. See, for example, *Massachusetts Spy* (Boston), 25 August 1770, 2.

105. *Connecticut Courant* (Hartford), 20 August 1770, 1.

106. *Virginia Gazette* (Williamsburg, Purdie), 16 June 1775, 4 supplement.

107. *Boston Evening-Post,* 21 January 1745, 1. Sherman chastised Fleet by saying, "you have promis'd to be fair, and print both sides."

108. *New-England Courant* (Boston), 22 February 1725, 1.

109. *Story & Humphrey's Pennsylvania Mercury; and the Universal Advertiser* (Philadelphia), 14 April 1775, 1.

110. See, Greven, *The Protestant Temperament.*

111. Hiner, "Cotton Mather and his Female Children," 33.

112. Cott, "Eighteenth-Century Family and Social Life Revealed in Massachusetts Divorce Records," 30–31.

113. *American Weekly Mercury* (Philadelphia), 7 January 1735, 1.

114. *South-Carolina Gazette* (Charleston), 6 August 1750, 1.

115. See, for example, *New-York Mercury,* 25 August 1755, 1.

116. *Boston Evening-Post,* 26 August 1745, 2.

117. *Virginia Gazette* (Williamsburg, Purdie and Dixon), 18 January 1770, 1.

118. *Dunlap's Maryland Gazette; or the Baltimore Advertiser,* 17 October 1775, 4.

119. *Essex Journal and Merrimack Packet: Or, the Massachusetts and New-Hampshire General Advertiser* (Newburyport), 4 January 1775, 4.

120. *Boston Evening-Post*, 26 May 1755, 2.

121. *Boston Gazette, or Weekly Journal*, 30 January 1750, 2.

122. *New-York Gazette: or the Weekly Post-Boy*, 23 June 1755, 1.

123. *Pennsylvania Gazette* (Philadelphia), 28 August 1740, 2.

124. *North Carolina Gazette* (New Bern), 5 May 1755, 4. Numerous examples of the Poet's Corner exist throughout many colonial newspapers.

125. *Virginia Gazette* (Williamsburg, Pinkney), 9 February 1775, 3.

126. The *Raleigh Register*, for example, was the only newspaper to print continuously in North Carolina during the nineteenth century, and it included the Poet's Corner as a regular weekly feature.

127. *Parker's New-York Gazette; or the Weekly Post-Boy*, 4 December 1760, 1.

128. For a discussion of the contents of almanacs, see Marion Barber Stowell, *Early American Almanacs: The Colonial Weekday Bible* (New York: Burt Franklin, 1977); and Robb Sagendorph, *America and her Almanacs: Wit, Wisdom & Weather 1639–1970* (Boston: Little, Brown, 1970).

129. Almanacs contained cure-alls, but they could not present the latest in medical breakthroughs because of their yearly printing schedule. Colonial newspapers picked up the newly reported cures and ran them instead of waiting to publish them in a yearlong compendium because of their immediate value to readers. News of medicine in the colonial period will be discussed fully in chapter 7.

130. *Pennsylvania Chronicle, and Universal Advertiser* (Philadelphia), 5 February 1770, 2.

Chapter 7. *A Receipt Against the Plague*

1. *South-Carolina Gazette* (Charleston), 23 February 1760, 2. The table of smallpox deaths appeared in the *Gazette* on 16 February 1760, 1.

2. *Publick Occurrences* (Boston), 25 September 1690, 1.

3. Ibid., 1–2.

4. P. M. Ashburn, *The Ranks of Death: A Medical History of the Conquest of America* (New York: Coward-McCann, 1947), 80–82.

5. Mary J. Dobson, "Mortality Gradients and Disease Exchanges: Comparisons from Old England and Colonial America," *Social History of Medicine* 2 (1989): 259–97.

6. Henry F. Dobyns, *Their Numbers Become Thinned: Native American Population Dynamics in Eastern North America* (Knoxville: University of Tennessee Press, 1983), 11.

7. Alfred W. Crosby, Jr., "Virgin Soil Epidemics as a Factor in the Aboriginal Depopulation in America," *William and Mary Quarterly* 33 (1976): 289–99.

8. James H. Cassedy, *Medicine in America: A Short History* (Baltimore and London: The Johns Hopkins University Press, 1991), 4–5.

9. Duffy, *Epidemics in Colonial America*, 51.

10. Dobson, "Mortality Gradients and Disease Exchanges," 284.

11. Ibid., 269–73.

12. Richard Harrison Shryock, *Medicine and Society in America, 1660–1860* (New York: New York University Press, 1960), 7; Cassedy, *Medicine in America*, 10–11.

13. *Kalendarium Pennsilvaniense,* printed in Marion Barber Stowell, *Early American ALMANACS: The Colonial WEEKDAY BIBLE* (New York: Burt Franklin, 1977), 187.

14. Cassedy, *Medicine in America,* 15.

15. John Tennent, *Every Man his own Doctor: or, The Poor Planter's Physician* (Williamsburg, 1734), 4 (emphasis included).

16. Ibid., 9.

17. John Wesley, *Primitive Physick: or, an Easy and Natural METHOD of curing Most Diseases,* 12th ed. (Philadelphia, 1764), 26.

18. *Publick Occurrences* (Boston), 25 September 1690, 1–2.

19. *Boston News-Letter,* 21 January 1711(2), 2.

20. Ibid., 24 November 1712, 2.

21. Ibid., 25 January 1713–14, 2; 15 March 1713–14, 2; and 5 April 1714, 2.

22. John B. Blake, *Public Health in the Town of Boston, 1630–1822* (Cambridge: Harvard University Press, 1959), 47–51, in Gary B. Nash, *The Urban Crucible: Social Change, Political Consciousness, and the Origins of the American Revolution* (Cambridge and London: Harvard University Press, 1979), 104.

23. *New-England Weekly Journal* (Boston), 12 January 1730, 2.,

24. Ibid., 21 September 1730, 2.

25. Ibid., 21 December 1730, 2.

26. *Boston Gazette,* 6 October 1735, 3.

27. *New-England Weekly Journal* (Boston), 1 January 1740, 3; and 8 July 1740, 2.

28. Ibid., 20 May 1740, 2.

29. Ibid., 26 August 1740, 2.

30. Ibid., 8 July 1740, 2.

31. Ibid., 7 October 1740, 2.

32. Ibid., (Boston), 24 March 1735, 2.

33. *South-Carolina Gazette* (Charleston), 16 February 1760, 1.

34. *Maryland Gazette* (Annapolis), 25 April 1765, 3.

35. *Virginia Gazette* (Williamsburg, Dixon and Purdie), 22 February 1770, 3.

36. *Boston Weekly News-Letter,* 31 January 1760, 1.

37. Wilson, "The Boston Inoculation Controversy: A Revisionist Interpretation," *Journalism History* 7 (1980): 19, says that the issue of inoculation "fizzled out" by the summer of 1721 and implies that it was no real issue in 1730. Inoculation was still a controversial issue in 1730 and later, as newspapers demonstrate.

38. *New-England Weekly Journal* (Boston), 5 January 1730, 1.

39. *Pennsylvania Gazette* (Philadelphia), 28 May 1730, 1.

40. *Boston Gazette, or Weekly Journal,* 20 November 1750, 1.

41. The inoculation controversy of 1721 pitted the anti–inoculation forces of Boston, led by Dr. William Douglass and printer James Franklin, against the pro-inoculation group headed by Dr. Zabdiel Boylston and the Puritan divine Cotton Mather. Although Douglass was the only physician in Boston with a medical degree, he absolutely refused to inoculate. Mather, on the other hand, studied the practice and had Boylston inoculate his children. Because of the strong stances taken by both sides and because printer James Franklin sided with the anti–inoculation forces, the Boston inoculation controversy became a war of words in the Boston newspapers during 1721. For a more complete discussion of the 1721 controversy, see Wilson, "The Boston Inoculation Controversy"; and Duffy, *Epidemics in Colonial America,* 23–33.

42. *American Weekly Mercury* (Philadelphia), 22 July 1735, 2.

43. Ibid., 19 August 1725, 2.
44. *New-England Weekly Journal* (Boston), 6 April 1730, 2.
45. Ibid., 20 April 1730, 1.
46. *South-Carolina Gazette* (Charleston), 31 May 1760, 1.
47. *Pennsylvania Gazette* (Philadelphia), 26 June 1760, 1.
48. *Boston Weekly News-Letter*, 25 December 1760, 4.
49. *Maryland Gazette* (Annapolis), 14 March 1765, 2. On page one, the *Gazette* offered another mathematical computation on smallpox. "Upon deliberate Examination it appears by our public Accounts, that of 3434 Persons Inoculated in the Inoculating Hospital, only Ten have died; whereas of the Number of 6000 and odd having the Small Pox in the natural Way, dying in the same Hospital, upon the lowest Computation it is Twenty-five in an Hundred. The Question is, if in common Life this is not Ten or Twenty per Cent short of the ordinary Mortality by the Disease?"
50. Shryock, *Medicine and Society in America*, 5.
51. *New-England Weekly Journal* (Boston), 2 March 1730, 1.
52. *South-Carolina Gazette* (Charleston), 19 April 1760, 1.
53. *Boston Evening-Post*, 4 February 1740, 1.
54. *New-England Weekly Journal* (Boston), 1 January 1740, 3.
55. Ibid., 18 November 1735, 1.
56. *Massachusetts Gazette & Boston Post-Boy & Advertiser*, 2 April 1770, 1.
57. *Newport Mercury*, 25 February 1765, 1.
58. *New-York Mercury*, 14 January 1765, 2.
59. *Georgia Gazette* (Savannah), 18 July 1765, 2.
60. *New-York Weekly Journal*, 14 April 1740, 1.
61. *Pennsylvania Gazette* (Philadelphia), 9 August 1770, 1; and *Pennsylvania Journal; and the Weekly Advertiser* (Philadelphia), 9 August 1770, 2.
62. *Pennsylvania Gazette* (Philadelphia), 9 August 1770, 1.
63. *Boston Evening-Post*, 6 May 1765, 3.
64. *Connecticut Courant* (Hartford), 26 August 1765, 1.
65. Cassedy, *Medicine in America*, 10. For a discussion of numerous back-country cures practiced in America, see David Hackett Fischer, *Albion's Seed: Four British Folkways in America* (New York and Oxford: Oxford University Press, 1989), 711–14.
66. *Virginia Gazette* (Williamsburg), 9 May 1745, 1.
67. Ibid.
68. Ibid., 16 May 1745, 1.
69. Ibid., 9 May 1745, 1.
70. *South-Carolina Gazette* (Charleston), 14 May 1750, 1.
71. Ibid.
72. It should be noted that the *Pennsylvania Gazette* was not the only Philadelphia newspaper to run an account of the Chinese stones. The *Pennsylvania Journal, or Weekly Advertiser* also carried a notice of the Chinese stones and their miracle curing power. When the information about the Chinese stones appeared in the *Journal* on 5 September 1745, the word "advertisement" was printed above it. The advertisement filled the fifth page of the paper. The *Gazette*'s account of the Chinese stones was included within the body of the paper and had news items both before and after the Chinese stones information. Franklin may well have been paid to insert the news of the Chinese stones in the *Gazette*, but there is no evidence that payment was made nor that the *Gazette* considered the Chinese

stones information anything other than news. It was up to the readers to discern whether the stones were valid medicine or quackery.

73. *Pennsylvania Gazette* (Philadelphia), 17 October 1745, 3.

74. Ibid.

75. *Constitutional Gazette* (New York), 18 October 1775, 4.

76. It should be noted that during the eighteenth century most surgery was performed for emergencies, that is, for superficial growths, amputations, and the like. Surgery for cataracts—even though they technically would be a superficial growth—could be considered fairly advanced since most disorders were considered to reside in the humors—blood, bile, and phlegm. Shryock, *Medicine and Society in America, 1660–1860,* 59.

77. *New-York Weekly Journal,* 8 December 1735, 2; *American Weekly Mercury* (Philadelphia), 18 December 1735, 2.

78. Ibid.

79. *Massachusetts Gazette, and the Boston Post-Boy & Advertiser,* 19 November 1770, 1; and *Essex Gazette* (Salem, Mass.), 20 November 1770, 4.

80. *Essex Gazette* (Salem, Mass.), 16 January 1770, 3.

81. *Boston Evening-Post,* 15 January 1770, 1.

82. *Massachusetts Gazette (And Boston-News Letter),* 6 September 1770, 3.

83. *Pennsylvania Gazette* (Philadelphia), 16 August 1775, 4.

84. Michael Martin and Leonard Gelber, *Dictionary of American History* (Savage, Md.: Littlefield Adams, 1978), s.v. "Benjamin Rush."

85. *New-York Gazette: or the Weekly Post-Boy,* 15 January 1770, 1.

86. Carl Van Doren, *Benjamin Franklin* (New York: The Viking Press, 1938), 156.

87. *Boston Evening-Post,* 1 January 1750, 1.

88. *Virginia Gazette* (Williamsburg), 14 March 1755, 2.

89. John Wesley, *Diary of John Wesley,* quoted in Maurice Bear Gordon, *Æsculapius Comes to the Colonies* (Ventnor, N.J.: Ventnor Publishers, Inc., 1949), 498.

90. *Pennsylvania Chronicle, and Universal Advertiser* (Philadelphia), 17 September 1770, 1.

91. Shryock, *Medicine and Society in America, 1660–1860,* 5.

92. *New-England Weekly Journal* (Boston), 21 October 1735, 2

93. Cassedy, *Medicine in America,* 10–11. True doctors in the eighteenth century were university trained like Benjamin Rush.

94. *New-England Weekly Journal* (Boston), 21 October 1735, 2 (emphasis included).

95. *Boston Evening-Post,* 7 May 1770, 3.

96. *Providence Gazette; and Country Journal,* 8 September 1770, 1.

97. *Massachusetts Spy* (Boston), 20 September 1770, 1.

98. *Boston Weekly Post-Boy,* 17 September 1750, 2.

99. *Pennsylvania Gazette* (Philadelphia), 31 October 1745, 2; and *Maryland Gazette* (Annapolis), 8 November 1745, 4.

100. *Massachusetts Gazette (And Boston News-Letter),* 14 February 1765, 4.

101. *Boston Evening-Post,* 15 January 1770, 1.

102. *Essex Gazette* (Salem, Massachusetts), 2 January 1770, 4.

103. *Newport Mercury,* 17 June 1765, 2.

104. Shryock, *Medicine and Society in America, 1660–1860,* 117–166.

105. *Boston Gazette, or Weekly Journal,* 20 November 1750, 1.

106. *Pennsylvania Gazette* (Philadelphia), 10 July 1755, 1.

107. Ibid.

108. William Douglass, *A Summary, historical and political, of the first planting, progressive improvements, and present state of the British Settlements in North America* (London, 1760); quoted in Duffy, *Epidemics in Colonial America*, 4.

109. *Boston Evening-Post,* 23 January 1775, 3.

110. A. L. Morton, *The World of the Ranters: Religious Radicalism in the English Revolution* (London: Lawrence & Wishart, 1970), 9.

CHAPTER 8. *THE PRESENCE OF GOD WAS MUCH SEEN IN THEIR ASSEMBLIES*

1. *Providence Gazette; and Country Journal,* 13 October 1770, 2.

2. Oscar Theodore Barck, Jr. and Hugh Talmage Lefler, *Colonial America* (New York: The Macmillan Company, 1958), 379.

3. Richard Beale Davis, *A Colonial Southern Bookshelf: Readings in the Eighteenth Century* (Athens: University of Georgia Press, 1979), 75–90.

4. The importance of being able to read the Bible and the subsequent necessity of an education for colonial children is discussed in chapter 6.

5. David D. Hall, "Religion and Society: Problems and Reconsiderations," in *Colonial British America: Essays in the New History of the Early Modern Period,* eds. Jack P. Greene and J. R. Pole (Baltimore and London: Johns Hopkins University, 1984), 322.

6. Patricia U. Bonomi, *Under the Cope of Heaven: Religion, Society, and Politics in Colonial America* (New York and Oxford: Oxford University Press, 1986), 3.

7. Ibid., 6–10. Cedric B. Cowing, *The Great Awakening and the American Revolution: Colonial Thought in the 18th Century* (Chicago: Rand McNally, 1971), 178–225. Bonomi and Cowing believe that from the Great Awakening on, religion played a larger and larger role in American political thought and shaped America's effort at revolution. Works that have looked at newspapers' role in the revolutionary process, however, do not point to an overt religiosity in news articles. See Arthur M. Schlesinger, *Prelude to Independence: The Newspaper War on Britain 1764–1776* (New York: Random House, 1957); and Edmund S. Morgan and Helen M. Morgan, *The Stamp Act Crisis: Prologue to Revolution* (Chapel Hill: University of North Carolina Press, 1953).

8. See chapter 1 for news of the sea and chapter 4 for crime news. In both types of news, God's providence was very important. It was God who saved ships and sailors at sea from sure destruction during storms, and it was imperative for criminals condemned to die to seek repentence so that they could die at peace with God.

9. Charles E. Clark, "The Newspapers of Colonial America," *Proceedings of the American Antiquarian Society* 100 (1990): 382. Clark draws this conclusion but offers no tangible examples to support the claim.

10. *New-England Weekly Journal* (Boston), 3 June 1740, 2.

11. *Boston Evening-Post,* 4 February 1745, 1.

12. Exactly why the issue of religious liberty was not discussed to any great extent prior to 1730 may be explained by the fact that few newspapers existed prior to that time. Of the newspapers being printed prior to 1730, all except the *American Weekly Mercury, Pennsylvania Gazette,* and *New-York Gazette* were

printed in Boston, probably the most religiously controlled city of the colonies. Calls for religious liberty in Boston would obviously have been seen as libelous publications. Religious liberty, on the other hand, was a basic part of the chartering of Pennsylvania, and the pluralistic nature of New York, which was a cultural mixture of continental European and English settlers by the eighteenth century, was never as concerned about religious issues as were New Englanders.

13. *Boston News-Letter,* 24 April 1704, 1.

14. Louis B. Wright, *The Cultural Life of the American Colonies 1607–1763* (New York: Harper & Row, 1962), 72–73.

15. Richard Baxter, *Plain Scripture Proof* (London, 1651), 251.

16. Wright, *The Cultural Life of the American Colonies,* 73.

17. J. Sears McGee, *The Godly Man in Stuart England: Anglicans, Puritans, and the Two Tables, 1620–1670* (New Haven and London: Yale University Press, 1976), 2.

18. John E. Semonche, *Religion & Constitutional Government in the United States: A Historical Overview with Sources* (Carrboro, N. C.: Signal Books, 1986), 6–7.

19. H. Leon McBeth, *The Baptist Heritage: Four Centuries of Baptist Witness* (Nashville, Tenn.: Broadman Press, 1987), 124–32. Rhode Island was established by Roger Williams, who began life as an Anglican, came to America as a Puritan, converted to the Baptist faith, and eventually became a "seeker" of the true path to God. Rhode Island adopted Williams's idea of a separation of church and state that he began preaching in the 1630s and transcribed to print in a 1644 work entitled *The Bloudy Tenent of Persecution for Cause of Conscience Discussed in a Conference between Peace and Truth.* Rhode Island's official charter of 1663 declared that

> no person within said colony, at any time hereafter shall be in any wise molested, punished, disquieted, or called in question for any differences in opinion in matters of religion . . . and at all times hereafter freely and fully have and enjoy his and their own judgments and consciences in matters of religious concernment.

Quoted in Joseph Martin Dawson, *Baptists and the American Republic* (Nashville, Tenn.: Broadman Press, 1956), 34.

20. Bonomi, *Under the Cope of Heaven,* 33.

21. See Sydney E. Ahlstrom, *A Religious History of the American People* (New Haven and London: Yale University Press, 1972), 166–83.

22. George Dargo, *Roots of the Republic: A New Perspective on Early American Constitutionalism* (New York and Washington: Praeger Publishers, 1974), 81, 84.

23. Charles M. Andrews, *The Colonial Period of American History: The Settlements* (New Haven: Yale University Press, 1936), II, 318; Semonche, *Religion & Constitutional Government in the United States,* 7; and Wright, *The Cultural Life of the American Colonies,* 76.

24. David Chidester, *Patterns of Power: Religion and Politics in American Culture* (Englewood Cliffs, N.J.: Prentice Hall, 1988), 20–21; Mark A. Noll and others, eds., *Christianity in America* (Grand Rapids, Mich.: William B. Eerdmans, 1983), 33–35; and Wright, *The Cultural Life of the American Colonies,* 79–80. As central to all aspects of life, religion in Puritan New England was maintained through the Puritan's covenantal theology. Under the Covenant of Grace, persons were saved and converted into God's chosen people. This conversion was then applied to the political realm through the Civil Covenant, which held that no one could participate in the affairs of government, that is, vote or hold office unless

one was a member of the covenantal community. Religion became the force that controlled the power of community.

25. Ahlstrom, *A Religious History of the American People*, 218–20; and Noll, *Christianity in America*, 49.

26. See Henry F. May, *The Enlightenment in America* (Oxford and New York: Oxford University Press, 1976). Most Enlightenment thought in America was grounded in a belief in the existence of God with the belief that man's reason was sufficient for understanding all other aspects of life.

27. Edwin Scott Gausted, *The Great Awakening in New England* (New York: Harper and Brothers, 1957), 42.

28. Jonathan Edwards, *Thoughts on the Revival in New England*, in *The Works of President Edwards*, 4 vols. (New York: Robert Carter & Brothers, 1879), 3: 313.

29. Ahlstrom, *A Religious History of the American People*, 287.

30. Bonomi, *Under the Cope of Heaven*, 6.

31. Harry S. Stout, *The New England Soul: Preaching and Religious Culture in Colonial New England* (New York and Oxford: Oxford University Press, 1986), 185.

32. Bonomi, *Under the Cope of Heaven*, 14–15.

33. *Boston Gazette, or Weekly Journal*, 22 May 1750, 1.

34. David Paul Nord, "Teleology and the News: The Religious Roots of American Journalism, 1630–1730," *Journal of American History* 77 (1990): 36.

35. Paul L. Hughes and Robert F. Fries, *Crown and Parliament in Tudor-Stuart England: A Documentary Constitutional History, 1485–1714* (New York: G. P. Putnam's Sons, 1959), 333; G. M. Trevelyan, *History of England: From Utrecht to Modern Times*, 3d ed. (Garden City: Doubleday & Company, 1952), 45–46; and J. P. Kenyon, *Stuart England* (New York: Penguin Books, 1978), 243.

36. *Boston News-Letter*, 24 April 1704, 1.

37. After attempts at attaining the crown by James III failed, his son, Charles III, continued the battle to return the Stuarts to the throne of England. Their efforts failed, and the Hanoverian line, begun by the German George I in 1715, continued throughout the colonial period.

38. *American Weekly Mercury* (Philadelphia), 1 April 1725, 2.

39. Ibid., 22 April 1725, 1.

40. Ibid., 1 July 1725, 1.

41. *Boston Evening-Post*, 4 March 1745, 2.

42. Ibid.

43. *American Weekly Mercury* (Philadelphia), 19 June 1740, 2.

44. The *South-Carolina Gazette* ran numerous articles on Spanish attacks, troop build-ups, and the strengthening of fortifications surrounding Charleston and parts of Georgia during 1740. See, for example, 26 January 1740, 2; 4 April 1740, 1; 24 May 1740, 2; 1 July 1740, 2; 1 August 1740, 3; and 6 September 1740, 2.

45. *South-Carolina Gazette* (Charleston), 16 October 1740, 1.

46. *Pennsylvania Gazette* (Philadelphia), 6 June 1745, 3.

47. *Pennsylvania Journal, or Weekly Advertiser* (Philadelphia), 27 February 1750, 1.

48. *Maryland Gazette* (Annapolis), 28 February 1750, 1.

49. See, for example, *Boston Evening-Post*, 23 April 1750, 2; 9 June 1755, 2; and *New-York Evening-Post*, 9 December 1745, 2.

50. *Maryland Gazette* (Annapolis), 31 July 1755, 2 (emphasis included).

51. Many newspapers listed the number of infants baptized each week. The *Boston Gazette*, for example, published the number baptized each week through

1770. Ordinations of ministers appeared constantly throughout the period in most papers but especially in the Boston newspapers. See, for examples, *Boston Gazette,* 2 November 1730, 2; *Boston Gazette, or Weekly Advertiser,* 11 February 1755, 3; and *Boston Gazette, and Country Journal,* 3 September 1770, 3.

52. Patricia U. Bonomi and Peter R. Eisenstadt, "Church Adherence in the Eighteenth-Century British American Colonies," *William and Mary Quarterly* 39 (1982): 245–86. Bonomi, *Under the Cope of Heaven,* 220. It should be pointed out that not all scholars accept these numbers. For differing views, see Richard Hofstadter, *America at 1750: A Social Portrait* (New York: Alfred Knopf, 1972); Jon Butler, "Magic, Astrology, and the Early American Religious Heritage, 1600–1760," *American Historical Review* 84 (1979): 317–46; Jon Butler, *Awash in a Sea of Faith: Christianizing the American People* (Cambridge: Harvard University Press, 1990); David Hackett Fischer, *Albion's Seed: Four British Folkways in America* (New York and Oxford: Oxford University Press, 1989); and Roger Finke and Roger Stark, *The Churching of America, 1776–1990* (New Brunswick: Rutgers University Press, 1992).

53. *American Weekly Mercury* (Philadelphia), 16 October 1735, 2.

54. *Boston Evening-Post,* 15 December 1760, 3.

55. *American Weekly Mercury* (Philadelphia), 28 May 1730, 3; and *Virginia Gazette* (Williamsburg, Dixon and Hunter), 23 December 1775, 4.

56. *Pennsylvania Journal, or Weekly Advertiser* (Philadelphia), 19 September 1745, 3.

57. *Parker's New-York Gazette; or the Weekly Post-Boy,* 24 December 1760, 3.

58. *Story & Humprhrey's Pennsylvania Mercury; and the Universal Advertiser* (Philadelphia), 20 October 1775, 1.

59. *Pennsylvania Gazette* (Philadelphia), 16 July 1730, 1.

60. *Boston Gazette,* 13 January 1734–35, 3.

61. *Boston News-Letter,* 24 April 1704, 2.

62. *Pennsylvania Gazette* (Philadelphia), 18 September 1740, 3.

63. *Providence Gazette; and Country Journal,* 12 May 1770, 1 (emphasis included).

64. *Dunlap's Maryland Gazette; or the Baltimore General Advertiser,* 25 July 1775, 1.

65. *Constitutional Gazette* (New York), 9 September 1775, 2 (emphasis included).

66. *New-York Journal; or the General Advertiser,* 19 October 1775, 2.

67. *Boston Evening-Post,* 1 December 1735, 2.

68. *American Weekly Mercury* (Philadelphia), 22 October 1730, 1 (emphasis included).

69. *Boston News-Letter,* 19 March 1705, 1 (emphasis included).

70. *Connecticut Journal, and New-Haven Post-Boy,* 25 January 1775, 4 (emphasis included).

71. *Cape Fear Mercury* (Wilmington), 28 July 1775, 2 (emphasis included).

72. *South-Carolina Gazette* (Charleston), 12 April 1760, 1.

73. *Maryland Gazette* (Annapolis), 6 February 1755, 3.

74. *New-England Weekly Journal* (Boston), 2 November 1730, 1.

75. *Boston News-Letter,* 4 April 1720, 2.

76. *Publick Occurrences* (Boston), 25 September 1690, 1.

77. Numerous examples of beliefs in supernatural occurrences in colonial America exist. Many are discussed in Fischer, *Albion's Seed.* Fischer discusses these under the term "magic ways."

78. *Pennsylvania Gazette* (Philadelphia), 12 June 1755, 1.

79. *Publick Occurrences* (Boston), 25 September 1690, 1.

80. *Boston News-Letter,* 12 June 1704, 1.

81. *Massachusetts Spy* (Boston), 23 October 1770, 2.

82. *Boston Gazette,* 3 February 1735, 3.

83. *New-England Courant* (Boston), 3 July 1725, 2.

84. *Boston Gazette, or Weekly Journal,* 22 May 1750, 1.

85. *Boston Gazette, or Country Journal,* 24 November 1755, 1 (emphasis included).

86. Ibid., 1 December 1755, 1.

87. J. D. Douglas, ed. *New International Dictionary of the Christian Church* (Grand Rapids, Mich.: Zondervan Publishing House, 1978), s. v. "Deism," by J. W. Charley; and May, *The Enlightenment in America,* 122–23. The best example used to explain deism comes from the fourteenth century. God is portrayed as a clockmaker who creates a watch, winds it up, and then leaves it to run on its own.

88. *American Weekly Mercury* (Philadelphia), 10 September 1730, 1.

89. Ibid., 17 April 1740, 3.

90. *South-Carolina Gazette* (Charleston), 12 July 1760, 1.

91. Quoted in Harry S. Stout, *The Divine Dramatist: George Whitefield and the Rise of Modern Evangelism* (Grand Rapids: William B. Eerdmans, 1991), 286.

92. Ibid., xiii–xiv.

93. David A. Copeland, "Covering the Big Story: George Whitefield's First Preaching Tour, News Manipulation, and the Colonial Press," Paper presented at the American Journalism Historians Association annual convention, Lawrence, Kansas, 1992, 13–14. The activities of Seward on the part of Whitefield are also discussed in Frank Lambert, "'Pedlar of Divinity': George Whitefield and the Great Awakening," *Journal of American History* 77 (1990): 835; and Stout, *The Divine Dramatist,* 77.

94. The details of George Whitefield's early life and family are recorded in George Whitefield, *A Brief and General Account of the First Part of the Life of the Reverend Mr. George Whitefield from his Birth, to his Entering into Holy Orders* (Philadelphia, 1740).

95. Benjamin Franklin, *Autobiography of Benjamin Franklin,* J. A. Leo Lemay and P. M. Zall, eds. (Knoxville: University of Tennessee Press, 1981), 107.

96. Stout, *The New England Soul,* 193–194.

97. Isaiah Thomas, *The History of Printing in America* (1810, reprint, New York: Weathervane Books, 1970), 568.

98. See, for example, *South Carolina Gazette* (Charleston), 14 July 1739.

99. *Pennsylvania Gazette* (Philadelphia), 21 February 1740, 3.

100. See Copeland, "Covering the Big Story," 15–16.

101. Figures taken from the bibliographic listings in Charles Evans, *American Bibliography* (Chicago, 1904), 2: 109–326; and Roger P. Bristol, *Supplement to Charles Evans' American Bibliography* (Charlottesville: University Press of Virginia, 1970), 58–78.

102. Franklin, *Autobiography,* 105–6.

103. *Pennsylvania Gazette* (Philadelphia), 17 April 1740, 3.

104. Ibid., 23 October 1740, 2.

105. *New-England Weekly Journal* (Boston), 14 October 1740, 2.

106. Franklin, *Autobiography,* 107.

107. *Pennsylvania Gazette* (Philadelphia), 1 May 1740, 1. The numbers that were listed in newspapers for those in attendance at a Whitefield sermon could

only be estimated, and the numbers in colonial newspapers, Whitefield's *Journals,* and in the diary of Whitefield's traveling public relations man, William Seward, do not always agree. See Copeland, "Covering the Big Story," 15–17.

108. *New-York Weekly Journal,* 225 August 1740, 2.

109. *South-Carolina Gazette* (Charleston), 9 October 1740, 1.

110. *South-Carolina Gazette* (Charleston), 21 August 1740, 3.

111. *Virginia Gazette* (Williamsburg), 18 January 1740, 1.

112. "A Letter from the Rev. Mr. WHITEFIELD, at Georgia, to a Friend in London," *Pennsylvania Gazette* (Philadelphia), 10 April 1740, 1; and *New-York Gazette,* 19 May 1740, 1.

113. George Whitefield, *Journals, 1737–1741,* with an introduction by William V. Davis (Gainesville: Scholars' Facsimilies & Reprints, 1969), 404.

114. *Pennsylvania Gazette* (Philadelphia), 17 April 1740, 1. The letter was also printed and distributed throughout the colonies. Whitefield's antislavery letter is discussed in chapter 5.

115. Ibid., 1 May 1740, 3.

116. Ibid., 8 May 1740, 2.

117. Ibid.

118. *Boston Evening-Post,* 12 May 1740, 4.

119. *South-Carolina Gazette* (Charleston), 18 July 1740, 3. For a full discussion of the controversy, see J. A. Leo Lemay, *The Canon of Benjamin Franklin, 1722–1776* (Newark: University of Delaware Press, 1986), 96–102.

120. *Boston Evening-Post,* 22 September 1740, 2; *Boston Gazette* 22 September 1740, 2; *Boston News-Letter,* 25 September 1740, 2; *Boston Weekly Post-Boy,* 22 September 1740, 3; and *New-England Weekly Journal* (Boston), 23 September 1740, 2.

121. *Boston Evening-Post,* 29 September 1740, 2. The report of the tragedy also appeared in the following newspapers: *American Weekly Mercury* (Philadelphia), 9 October 1740, 2; *Boston News-Letter,* 25 September 1740, 2; *New-York Weekly Journal,* 13 October 1740, 3; *Pennsylvania Gazette* (Philadelphia), 9 October 1740, 2; and *South-Carolina Gazette* (Charleston), 6 November 1740, 3. The *Boston News-Letter*'s account of the Checkley incident was written leaving out such editorial comments as "some ignorant and disorderly persons" and that those crowding out had "no Regard" for those that were being injured. The *New-England Weekly Journal* declined to even mention the incident, and issues of the *Boston Weekly Post-Boy* are not extant for the week of September 29 through the rest of 1740.

122. Ibid.

123. *Boston Weekly News-Letter,* 2 October 1740, 1.

124. *Boston Evening-Post,* 6 October 1740, 2.

125. In his journal, Whitefield gave his account of what happened at Rev. Checkley's church. Then without any mention of sorrow, he said, "God was pleased to give me presence of mind; so that I gave notice I would immediately preach upon the common. The weather was wet, but many thousands followed into the field." Whitefield, *Journals,* 462.

126. Fleet's dislike of Whitefield was fueled, in addition to the incident in the Checkley church, by his personal aversion to ministers. Thomas, *The History of Printing in America,* 94, reports that Fleet's dislike for the clergy necessitated his emigration from England after he exhibited a display of contempt for the Church of England in 1711.

127. *Boston Evening-Post,* 8 April 1745, 2.

128. *Boston Gazette, or Weekly Journal,* 8 January 1745, 1. The *Gazette* carried negative news on Whitefield on page one as well.

129. *Boston Gazette,* 30 June 1735, 1; and 25 August 1735, 1, are but two examples.

130. *South-Carolina Gazette* (Charleston), 25 May 1745, 2. A similar letter against itinerants appeared in the *Virginia Gazette* (Williamsburg), 21 November 1745, 3.

131. *Boston Evening-Post,* 11 March 1745, 1, 2.

132. Ibid., 12 August 1745, 1.

133. *Pennsylvania Gazette* (Philadelphia), 12 September 1745, 2.

134. Many examples exist in colonial newspapers of news items concerning each of these preaching tours. Examples of news about Whitefield and his preaching tours that took place in the years of this study may be found in the following: *Connecticut Gazette* (New Haven), 19 April 1755, 3, Whitefield leaves Charleston for England; *Georgia Gazette* (Savannah), 9 May 1765, 4, Whitefield arrives in Georgia; and *South-Carolina and American General Gazette* (Charleston), 18 July 1770, 2, Whitefield preaches to the student body at Princetown.

135. *Boston Evening-Post,* 8 October 1770, 3.

136. *Connecticut Journal, and New-Haven Post-Boy,* 26 October 1770, 2.

137. Whitefield's obituary or a news story about his death appeared in the following: *Boston Gazette, and Country Journal,* 8 October 1770, 2; *Massachusetts Gazette* (Boston), 11 October 1770, 4; *Green & Russell's Boston Post-Boy & Advertiser,* 8 October 1770, 2; *Connecticut Courant* (Hartford), 9 October 1770, 2; *Connecticut Journal, and New-Haven Post-Boy,* 26 October 1770, 2; *Essex Gazette* (Salem, Mass.), 9 October 1770, 3; *New-York Journal; or the General Advertiser,* 11 October 1770, 3; *Massachusetts Spy* (Boston), 9 October 1770, 2; *New-London Gazette,* 12 October 1770, 3; *New-York Gazette; and the Weekly Mercury,* 8 October 1770, 2; *Pennsylvania Gazette* (Philadelphia), 11 October 1770, 3; *Pennsylvania Journal, or Weekly Advertiser* (Philadelphia), 11 October 1770, 3; *South-Carolina and American General Gazette* (Charleston), 23 October 1770, 2; *South-Carolina Gazette* (Charleston), 8 November 1770, 4; and *South-Carolina Gazette; and Country Journal* (Charleston), 6 November 1770, 2.

138. *Providence Gazette; and Country Journal,* 13 October 1770, 2.

139. Roger Williams, *The Bloudy Tenent of Persecution of Persecution for Cause of Conscience Discussed in a Conference between Peace and Truth* (London, 1644), 2.

140. John Milton, *Areopagitica:A Speech for the Liberty of Unlicensed Printing to the Parliament of England* (London, 1644), 134.

141. McGee, *The Godly Man in Stuart England,* 2.

142. *Boston News-Letter,* 25 August 1707, 2.

143. *New-England Courant* (Boston), 10 July 1725, 2; and *American Weekly Mercury* (Philadelphia), 22 July 1725, 3.

144. *Boston Evening-Post,* 15 December 1735, 1.

145. *Pennsylvania Chronicle, and Universal Advertiser* (Philadelphia), 19 March 1770, 1.

146. *New-York Weekly Journal,* 12 May 1740, 2.

147. Frederick A. Norwood, *The Story of American Methodism: A History of the United Methodists and Their Relations* (Nashville, Tenn.: Abingdon Press, 1974), 32.

148. *Boston Evening-Post,* 10 November 1740, 2.

149. *New-York Weekly Journal,* 31 March 1740, 4.

150. *South-Carolina Gazette* (Charleston), 13 May 1745, 2.

151. *Pennsylvania Gazette* (Philadelphia), 2 August 1750, 1; and *Maryland Gazette* (Annapolis), 22 August 1750, 3.

152. *Maryland Gazette* (Annapolis), 31 January 1765, 1.

153. *Essex Gazette* (Salem, Mass.), 6 February 1770, 2. The same news item also appeared in the *Virginia Gazette* (Williamsburg, Rind), 8 March 1770, 2.

154. *Boston Weekly News-Letter,* 6 September 1750, 2.

155. *Boston Weekly News-Letter,* 19 July 1745,3; and *Maryland Gazette* (Annapolis), 16 August 1745, 2.

156. *Pennsylvania Gazette* (Philadelphia), 30 July 1730, 2. A similar essay appeared in the *American Weekly Mercury* (Philadelphia), 25 June 1730, 1.

157. *Boston Gazette,* 17 February 1735, 2. This conversation continued in the *Gazette* through September. See the following editions: 30 June 1735, 1; 11 August 1735, 1; 25 August 1735, 1; and 15 September 1735, 1.

158. *New-York Mercury,* 12 May 1755. Similar editorial essays advocating religious separation of church and state appeared in the following editions: 31 March 1755, 1; 7 April 1755,1; 14 April 1755, 1; 21 April 1755, 1; 28 April 1755, 1; 5 May 1755, 1; 26 May 1755, 1; and 23 June 1755, 1.

159. *American Weekly Mercury* (Philadelphia), 17 July 1740, 1.

160. *Pennsylvania Gazette* (Philadelphia), 21 August 1755, 3.

161. McBeth, *The Baptist Heritage,* 255–65. A complete discussion of Baptists and religious liberty may be found in William R. Estep, *Revolution within the Revolution: The First Amendment in Historical Context, 1612–1789* (Grand Rapids, Mich: William B. Eerdmans, 1990).

162. *Providence Gazette; and Country Journal,* 11 August 1770, 3. It should be noted that Baptists' efforts to completely separate church and state relations in Massachusetts were not completely successful. In fact, it was not until 1833 that Massachusetts removed completely the concept of an established religion from its state constitution.

163. *Pennsylvania Chronicle, and Universal Advertiser* (Philadelphia), 19 March 1770, 1.

164. *Essex Journal: or, the New-Hampshire Packet* (Newbury-Port, Mass.), 18 August 1775, 2.

165. *Boston Evening-Post,* 13 October 1755, 2.

166. Ibid., 23 June 1760, 2. God's role in news of the sea is discussed in chapter 1.

167. *South-Carolina Gazette* (Charleston), 12 April 1760, 1.

168. *Newport Mercury, or the Weekly Advertiser,* 17 June 1765, 3. The role of religion and Native Americans is discussed in chapter 2.

169. See chapter 3, and Nord, "Teleology and the News," 9.

170. Samuel Walker, *Popular Justice: A History of American Criminal Justice* (New York and Oxford: Oxford University Press, 1980), 13. A discussion of crime and sin in colonial America may also be found in the section, "The Colonial Legal System," in Chapter 4.

171. *Maryland Gazette* (Annapolis), 17 May 1745, 4. Crime and its religious aspects are discussed in Chapter Four.

172. Exodus 21:24.

173. *Connecticut Journal, and New-Haven Post-Boy,* 6 July 1770, 3.

174. *Pennsylvavnia Gazette* (Philadelphia), 17 April 1740, 1. Religion in relation to slavery is discussed in chapter 5. See chapter 5, "Antislavery literature."

175. *Providence Gazette; and Country Journal,* 16 February 1765, 2; and *Bos-*

ton Evening-Post, 31 March 1755, 4. The nature of women in relation to God is central to the news of women in colonial newspapers. See chapter 6.

176. *American Weekly Mercury* (Philadelphia), 19 August 1725, 2; and *New-England Weekly Journal* (Boston), 1 January 1740, 3. See chapter 7.

CHAPTER 9. *THE CHIEF AMUSEMENT OF THIS CITY*

1. Those cities and towns were Portsmouth, New Hampshire; Boston; Salem, Massachusetts; New Haven; Hartford; Providence; New York; Philadelphia; Annapolis; Williamsburg; New Bern; Wilmington, North Carolina; Charleston; and Savannah.

2. Neither Delaware nor New Jersey had newspapers in 1770, but Philadelphia newspapers served both colonies, and New York newspapers provided a news outlet for northern New Jersey.

3. *Virginia Gazette* (Williamsburg, Purdie and Dixon), 22 January 1770, 2; *New-York Gazette: or the Weekly Post-Boy,* 16 April 1770, 4; *New-York Journal; or the General Advertiser,* 19 April 1770, 3; *New-London Gazette,* 25 May 1770, 4; and *Providence Gazette; and Country Journal,* 7 July 1770, 4.

4. *American Weekly Mercury* (Philadelphia), 23 February 1734–35, 2.

5. Ibid., 29 May 1740, 1.

6. This figure was reached by using the *American Weekly Mercury, Boston Evening-Post, New-York Gazette; or the Weekly Post-Boy, Pennsylvania Gazette,* and *South-Carolina Gazette.* The *Boston Gazette* was excluded from this tally because of the unusually high number of social items it ran in 1735. In other years, however, the *Gazette* was more in keeping with the average number listed.

7. This is the same conclusion reached by Richard D. Brown, *Knowledge Is Power: The Diffusion of Information in Early America, 1700–1865* (New York and Oxford: Oxford University Press, 1989), 41.

8. The concept that information printed in newspapers became "official" news and was consequently more accurate than information received from other sources is exactly the way that John Fleet and Thomas Fleet Jr. approached news of slave revolts in Jamaica in 1760. The brothers, who printed the *Boston Evening-Post,* accepted as factual information when they extracted it from the Jamaican newspapers. See chapter 5 and *Boston Evening-Post,* 24 November 1760, 2.

9. *Essex Journal and Merrimack Packet: Or, the Massachusetts and New-Hampshire General Advertiser* (Newbury-Port, Mass.), 1 March 1775, 4.

10. Lawrence C. Wroth, *The Colonial Printer,* 2nd. ed. (Charlottesville: University Press of Virginia, 1964), 92, estimates that in 1770 fourteen different sizes of type were available to colonial printers. Type sizes of nine (nine), eight (eight) and six point (six) were regularly used to print news in some newspapers, making it possible to print large amounts of news in a relatively small amount of space. Improvements in type quality also made it possible for printers to run more columns per page because the new, smaller types were much more legible than the type used earlier in the colonial period.

11. Newspapers used supplements to provide late-arriving news and additional advertisements. At other times, supplements were put out during the middle of a week and were often called an extraordinary.

12. Isaiah Thomas, *The History of Printing in America* (1810; reprint, New York: Weathervane Books, 1970), 434; and Sidney Kobre, *The Development of*

the Colonial Newspaper (1944; reprint, Gloucester: Peter Smith, 1960), 54. The *Universal Instructor* was not read as a part of this study.

13. The last *Boston·Chronicle* was last published on 25 June 1770.

14. Elizabeth Christine Cook, *Literary Influences in Colonial Newspapers 1704–1750* (New York: Columbia University Press, 1912), 8. Cook also says that newspapers of the first quarter of the eighteenth century contained no news (3).

15. Ibid., 2. Whether newspapers were the most important source for literature in colonial America may be argued. Newspapers did offer the fastest method of getting literary material to people.

16. *New-York Weekly Journal,* 1 January 1739–40, 4.

17. James G. Lydon, "Philadelphia's Commercial Expansion 1720–1739," *Pennsylvania Magazine of History and Biography* 91 (1967): 401–18, quoted in Ian K. Steele, *The English Atlantic: An Exploration of Communication and Community* (New York and Oxford: Oxford University Press, 1986), 301. Lydon estimates that 107 ships from Europe arrived in Philadelphia in 1724. By 1740, the number had nearly doubled to 204, holding forth the prospect for twice as much European news.

18. Richard Beale Davis, *A Colonial Southern Bookshelf: Reading in the Eighteenth Century* (Athens: University of Georgia Press, 1979), 22.

19. Calhoun Winton, "Richard Steele, Journalist—and Journalism," in *Newsletters to Newspapers: Eighteenth-Century Journalism,* eds. Donovan H. Bond and W. Reynolds McLeod (Morganton: West Virginia University, 1977), 21; and Mark Lipper, "Benjamin Franklin's 'Silence Dogood' as an Eighteenth-Century 'Censor Morum,'" in *Newsletters to Newspapers,* 73–83.

20. *Maryland Gazette* (Annapolis), 22 December 1730, 1.

21. *New-England Courant* (Boston), 25 September 1725, 1 and 2 October 1725, 1.

22. Franklin's "Busy-Body" essays have been discussed in some detail. See Anna Janney DeArmond, *Andrew Bradford: Colonial Journalist* (New York: Greenwood Press, 1969), 16–19.

23. See, for example, *New-England Courant* (Boston), 3 May 1725, 1.

24. *Providence Gazette; and Country Journal,* 5 January 1765–30 March 1765.

25. *American Weekly Mercury* (Philadelphia), 16 October 1735, 1.

26. *South-Carolina Gazette* (Charleston), 16 August 1735, 1.

27. See, Cook, *Literary Influences in Colonial Newspapers* for a thorough discussion of the works of these writers in colonial newspapers.

28. *Massachusetts Spy* (Boston), 7 August 1770, 4.

29. For a full discussion of poetry in colonial newspapers, see, David Shields, *Oracles of Empire: Poetry, Politics, and Commerce in British America* (Chicago: University of Chicago Press, 1990), and J. A. Leo Lemay, *A Calendar of American Poetry in the Colonial Newspapers and Magazines and in the Major English Magazines Through 1765* (Worcester, Mass.: American Antiquarian Society, 1972).

30. See, for example, *Connecticut Gazette; and the Universal Intelligencer* (New Haven), 6 January 1775, 4; *Maryland Journal, and the Baltimore Advertiser,* 8 November 1775, 4; *New-York Journal; or the General Advertiser,* 18 January 1770, 4; *New-London Gazette,* 9 February 1770, 4; *North Carolina Gazette* (New Bern), 16 June 1775, 5; *Pennsylvania Ledger: Or the Virginia, Maryland, Pennsylvania, & New-Jersey Weekly Advertiser* (Philadelphia), 28 January 1775, 4; *Story & Humphrey's Pennsylvania Mercury; and the Universal Advertiser* (Philadel-

phia), 14 April 1775, 4; and *Virginia Gazette* (Williamsburg, Dixon and Purdie), 5 April 1770, 4.

31. *American Weekly Mercury* (Philadelphia), 5 June 1740, 1.

32. *South-Carolina Gazette* (Charleston), 25 January 1735, 2.

33. *Virginia Gazette* (Williamsburg, Dixon and Purdie), 9 September 1775, 4.

34. *New-York Weekly Journal,* 28 January 1739–40, 4.

35. Ibid., 11 February 1739–40, 2.

36. *Pennsylvania Gazette* (Philadelphia), 1750, 2.

37. See, for example, *Boston Evening-Post,* 8 October 1770, 3; *Essex Gazette* (Salem, Mass.), 9 October 1770, 3; and *New-London Gazette,* 12 October 1770, 3.

38. *Boston Gazette,* 30 March 1730, 1.

39. *Virginia Gazette* (Williamsburg, Rind), 11 October 1770, 3.

40. *Providence Gazette; and Country Journal,* 8 December 1770, 1.

41. *Boston Evening-Post,* 2 September 1735, 2.

42. *Maryland Gazette* (Annapolis), 23 March 1775, 1.

43. *Boston Evening-Post,* 28 January 1765, 1.

44. *Weekly Rehearsal* (Boston), 16 June 1735, 2.

45. *Maryland Gazette* (Annapolis), 29 May 1755, 2.

46. *Boston Evening-Post,* 8 September 1755, 4.

47. *Boston Gazette,* 3 March 1735, 2; and *Weekly Rehearsal* (Boston), 24 March 1735, 1.

48. *Maryland Gazette* (Annapolis), 13 November 1760, 1.

49. *Boston Evening-Post,* 10 March 1760, 1.

50. *American Weekly Mercury* (Philadelphia), 2 March 1734–35, 3.

51. *Boston Weekly News-Letter,* 14 March 1745, 2; and *Pennsylvania Gazette* (Philadelphia), 4 April 1745, 1.

52. *American Weekly Mercury* (Philadelphia), 31 July 1735, 3; and *Pennsylvania Gazette* (Philadelphia), 13 November 1740, 2.

53. *Maryland Gazette* (Annapolis), 14 March 1765, 1.

54. *American Weekly Mercury* (Philadelphia), 31 July 1735, 3; *Pennsylvania Gazette* (Philadelphia), 31 July 1735, 3; *New-England Weekly Journal* (Boston), 4 August 1735, 1; and *New-York Gazette* 11 August 1735, 2.

55. *Virginia Gazette* (Williamsburg, Purdie and Dixon), 6 September 1770, 1.

56. *American Weekly Mercury* (Philadelphia), 8 April 1725, 2.

57. *Boston Weekly Post-Boy,* 13 October 1735, 3.

58. *Boston Evening-Post,* 25 June 1750, 1.

59. *Maryland Gazette* (Annapolis), 20 June 1750, 2.

60. Ibid., and *Boston Evening-Post,* 30 July 1750, 1.

61. *Boston News-Letter,* 22 July 1725, 1. The *New-England Courant* (Boston), 7 June 1725, 2, carried a similar report of the fight.

62. *Boston Evening-Post,* 14 January 1765, 2.

63. *Newport Mercury, or the Weekly Advertiser,* 6 May 1765, 3.

64. *Virginia Gazette* (Willliamsburg), 23 May 1755, 2.

65. *Boston Evening-Post,* 1 January 1750, 1.

66. Ibid.

67. Ibid.

68. *Boston Weekly News-Letter,* 24 January 1745, 3.

69. Ibid., 16 March 1750, 3–4.

70. *South-Carolina Gazette* (Charleston), 15 May 1755, 2.

71. *New-York Evening-Post,* 12 March 1750, 2; *Maryland Gazette* (Annapolis),

4 April 1750, 3; *New-York Weekly Journal,* 15 April 1750, 2; and *South-Carolina Gazette* (Charleston), 16 April 1750, 2.

72. *Georgia Gazette* (Savannah), 14 February 1765, 2.

73. *New-York Evening-Post,* 21 May 1750, 3.

74. *New-York Gazette Revived in the Weekly Post-Boy,* 21 May 1750, 1.

75. *Providence Gazette; and Country Journal,* 7 January 1775, 4.

76. See, for example, *Connecticut Gazette; and the Universal Intelligencer* (New London), 6 January 1775, 4.

77. See, for example, *Boston Weekly Post-Boy,* 25 August 1760, 3.

78. See, for example, *Maryland Journal, and the Baltimore Advertiser,* 14 June 1775, 1.

79. *Pennsylvania Gazette* (Philadelphia), 25 March 1755, 1. The number and prize list filled all of the first page of the *Gazette.*

80. *South-Carolina Gazette* (Charleston), 11 January 1734–35, 2.

81. *Pennsylvania Gazette* (Philadelphia), 24 February 1729–30, 3.

82. *American Weekly Mercury* (Philadelphia), 18 September 1735, 3.

83. *Virginia Gazette* (Williamsburg, Rind), 7 June 1770, 2.

84. *South-Carolina Gazette* (Charleston), 10 April 1755, 1.

85. *Virginia Gazette* (Williamsburg, Pinkney), 5 January 1775, 3.

86. *Maryland Gazette* (Annapolis), 19 June 1760, 3.

87. *South-Carolina Gazette* (Charleston), 15 February 1734–35, 3.

88. *Essex Journal, or, the New-Hampshire Packet* (Newbury-Port, Mass.), 8 September 1775, 3.

89. *Virginia Gazette* (Williamsburg, Pinkney), 23 March 1775, 1.

90. See, for example, ibid., 3; and *Boston Evening-Post,* 15 January 1770, 3; 5 November 1770, 3.

91. *American Weekly Mercury* (Philadelphia), 5 June 1735, 2.

92. *New-England Courant* (Boston), 18 January 1725, 2.

93. *Virginia Gazette* (Williamsburg, Dixon and Purdie), 11 November 1775, 2. The newspaper reported the death of Peyton Randolph, former president of the Continental Congress.

94. *South-Carolina Gazette* (Charleston), 30 August 1735, 2.

95. *Boston Weekly Post-Boy,* 28 January 1740, 2, carried Mrs. Bradford's obituary. *Connecticut Gazette* (New Haven), 14 April 1775, 3, stated that the printer's wife had died.

96. *Boston News-Letter,* 18 April 1720, 2.

97. *Boston Evening-Post,* 1 October 1750, 2.

98. See, chapter 6.

99. *Rivington's New-York Gazetteer; or the Connecticut, New-Jersey, Hudson's-River, and Quebec Weekly Advertiser,* 5 January 1775, 2.

100. See, for example, *American Weekly Mercury* (Philadelphia), 22 July 1725, 3; 28 May 1730, 3.

101. *New-England Weekly Journal* (Boston), 24 August 1730, 1; and *Pennsylvania Gazette* (Philadelphia), 10 September 1730, 3.

102. *Pennsylvania Gazette* (Philadelphia), 12 November 1730, 3.

103. Robb Sagendorph, *America and her Almanacs: Wit, Wisdom & Weather 1639–1970* (Boston: Little, Brown, 1970), 67.

104. Gary B. Nash, *The Urban Crucible: Social Change, Political Consciousness, and the Origins of the American Revolution* (Cambridge: Harvard University Press, 1979), 323–25.

105. See John J. McCusker and Russell R. Menard, *The Economy of British*

America 1607–1789 (Chapel Hill and London: University of North Carolina Press, 1985), 71.

106. See, for example, *American Weekly Mercury* (Philadelphia), 21 August 1740, 2; *South-Carolina Gazette* (Charleston), 22 June 1765, 3; and *Virginia Gazette* (Williamsburg, Pinkney), 12 June 1775, 3.

107. *Boston News-Letter,* 27 February 1735, 2.

108. *Connecticut Gazette* (New Haven), 21 June 1755, 2.

109. *Maryland Gazette* (Annapolis), 31 January 1760, 3.

110. *American Weekly Mercury* (Philadelphia), 30 September 1725, 2.

111. *Maryland Gazette* (Annapolis), 25 April 1750, 3.

112. *South-Carolina Gazette* (Charleston), 15 January 1750, 1–2.

113. *Connecticut Courant* (Hartford), 16 July 1770, 3.

114. *New-London Summary; or The Weekly Advertiser,* 21 November 1760, 2.

115. *Pennsylvania Gazette* (Philadelphia), 27 March 1750, 2.

116. *Maryland Gazette* (Annapolis), 5 July 1745, 1.

117. *Pennsylvania Gazette* (Philadelphia), 11 September 1735, 2.

118. *Virginia Gazette* (Williamsburg, Dixon and Purdie), 28 January 1775, 2.

119. *Boston Evening-Post,* 30 April 1750, 1.

120. *Virginia Gazette* (Williamsburg, Dixon and Purdie), 5 April 1770, 1.

121. *Maryland Gazette* (Annapolis), 24 October 1765, 2.

122. See, for example, *Boston Evening-Post,* 22 October 1750, 4; 15 December 1755, 2; and *South-Carolina Gazette* (Charleston), 20 September 1770, 2.

123. In 1735, the *American Weekly Mercury* printed fifty-eight accident reports and thirteen news items about religion. In 1740, only eleven accident reports were presented, while thirty-seven religious items, almost all of them on the controversial George Whitefield, filled the Philadelphia newspaper.

124. *Pennsylvania Gazette* (Philadelphia), 19 February 1729–30, 3.

125. *Pennsylvania Journal; and the Weekly Advertiser* (Philadelphia), 22 November 1770, 2.

126. *Weekly Rehearsal* (Boston), 28 July 1735, 2.

127. *American Weekly Mercury* (Philadelphia), 8 July 1725, 4.

128. *Boston Evening Post,* 27 January 1755, 4.

129. *New-England Weekly Journal* (Boston), 5 October 1730, 2.

130. *New-England Weekly Journal* (Boston), 10 November 1735, 4.

131. *Publick Occurrences* (Boston), 25 September 1690, 2; *Boston Evening-Post,* 28 April 1740, 2; and *Pennsylvania Gazette* (Philadelphia), 3 April 1760, 2.

132. *South-Carolina Gazette* (Charleston), 20 November 1740, 2–3; 15 November 1760, 3; and *Boston Evening-Post,* 6 February 1775, 1.

133. *American Weekly Mercury* (Philadelphia), 30 April 1730, 4; *Boston Gazette,* 11 May 1730, 2; and *Virginia Gazette* (Williamsburg, Pinkney), 12 June 1775, 2.

134. *Publick Occurrences* (Boston), 25 September 1690, 2.

135. *South-Carolina Gazette* (Charleston), 15 November 1735, 2.

136. Ibid., 20 November 1740, 2.

137. Ibid., 3.

138. Ibid., 15 November 1760, 3 (emphasis included).

139. See, for example, *Boston Evening-Post,* 12 November 1750, 1. Rhys Isaac, *The Transformation of Virginia 1740–1790* (Chapel Hill: University of North Carolina Press, 1982), 72, discusses the relative lack of furniture among Tidewater Virginia residents.

140. *Boston News-Letter,* 28 March 1720, 3.

141. *American Weekly Mercury* (Philadelphia), 3 April 1740, 3.

142. *Virginia Gazette* (Williamsburg, Dixon and Purdie), 22 February 1770, 3.

143. *Weekly Rehearsal* (Boston), 21 July 1735, 2; and *Pennsylvania Gazette* (Philadelphia), 7 August 1735, 2.

144. *American Weekly Mercury* (Philadelphia), 26 November 1730, 4.

145. *Boston Gazette,* 5 January 1730, 2.

146. See, for example, *Boston Evening-Post,* 15 December 1735, 2; 7 January 1760, 1; *Maryland Gazette* (Annapolis), 14 February 1750, 2; 28 February 1750, 2; 13 April 1775, 1.

147. *South-Carolina Gazette* (Charleston), 27 November 1740, 2.

148. *Virginia Gazette* (Williamsburg), 12 December 1746, 3.

149. *Connecticut Gazette* (New Haven), 21 June 1755, 3.

150. *American Weekly Mercury* (Philadelphia), 24 July 1735, 4.

151. *Boston Evening-Post,* 20 November 1735, 3.

152. *New-England Weekly Journal* (Boston), 14 October 1735, 2.

153. Wood cutting accidents were prominent. See, *Boston Evening-Post,* 29 December 1735, 2. Accidents where children fell into kettles of boiling liquids provided tragic and sensational elements. See, *New-York Journal; or the General Advertiser,* 8 March 1770, 2 supplement. Accidents that involved opening or cleaning wells were also fairly common in colonial newspapers. See, *Boston Weekly Post-Boy,* 4 August 1735, 4.

154. See, for example, *South-Carolina Gazette* (Charleston), 26 April 1760, 3. Tides were a part of the *Gazette*'s "Register of the Weather."

155. *Boston Evening-Post,* 8 September 1735, 2; and *New-England Weekly Journal* (Boston), 9 September 1735, 2.

156. *Pennsylvania Journal; and the Weekly Advertiser* (Philadelphia), 5 July 1770, 2.

157. *American Weekly Mercury* (Philadelphia), 16 July 1730, 2.

158. *Boston News-Letter,* 5 February 1704–5, 2.

159. *Virginia Gazette* (Williamsburg, Pinkney), 7 September 1775, 3.

160. *Connecticut Gazette* (New Haven), 21 June 1755, 2.

161. *Pennsylvania Gazette* (Philadelphia), 31 May 1750, 2.

162. *Boston Evening-Post,* 12 May 1740, 3; *American Weekly Mercury* (Philadelphia), 29 May 1740, 1; and *Pennsylvania Gazette* (Philadelphia), 29 May 1740, 2.

163. *Essex Gazette* (Salem, Mass.), 18 September 1770, 2.

164. *South-Carolina Gazette; and Country Journal* (Charleston), 22 May 1770, 2.

165. *Boston Evening-Post,* 1 July 1765, 2.

166. *Boston Evening-Post,* 24 November 1755, 4; *Boston Gazette, or Country Journal,* 24 November 1755, 1; *Boston News-Letter,* 25 June 1705, 2; 5 March 1730, 2; *Green & Russell's Boston Weekly Post-Boy & Advertiser,* 11 February 1760, 3; *Connecticut Gazette* (New Haven), 6 December 1755, 3; *Maryland Gazette* (Annapolis), 26 December 1755, 2; *Parker's New-York Gazette; or the Weekly Post-Boy,* 8 December 1755, 2; *New York Mercury,* 24 November 1760, 2; and *Pennsylvania Journal, or Weekly Advertiser* (Philadelphia), 4 December 1755, 2.

167. *Boston Gazette, or Country Journal,* 18 March 1755, 2.

168. *Boston Gazette, or Country Journal,* 24 November 1755, 1.

169. *Boston News-Letter,* 5 September 1720, 4.

170. *Boston Gazette, and Country Journal,* 11 February 1765, 1.

171. *Boston News-Letter,* 28 April 1712, 1.

172. *Massachusetts Gazette* (Boston), 5 July 1770, 3; and *Pennsylvania Gazette* (Philadelphia), 19 July 1770, 2.

173. *Connecticut Gazette* (New Haven), 22 November 1755, 4; and *Maryland Gazette* (Annapolis), 18 December 1755, 2.

174. *Parker's New-York Gazette; or the Weekly Post-Boy,* 17 March 1760, 3.

175. *Pennsylvania Gazette* (Philadelphia), 20 November 1755, 3; *Parker's New-York Gazette; or the Weekly Post-Boy,* 24 November 1755, 3; and *Connecticut Gazette* (New Haven), 29 November 1755, 3.

176. *Connecticut Gazette* (New Haven), 27 December 1755, 4.

177. *New York Mercury,* 24 November 1755, 2; *Parker's New-York Gazette; or the Weekly Post-Boy,* 24 November 1755, 3; *Pennsylvania Journal, or Weekly Advertiser* (Philadelphia), 27 November 1755, 2; and *New-England Chronicle: or the Essex Gazette* (Cambridge, Mass.), 17 April 1775, 2.

178. *Providence Gazette; and Country Journal,* 7 July 1770, 3; and *Maryland Gazette* (Annapolis), 19 July 1770, 2.

179. *Boston News-Letter,* 24 October 1720, 2.

180. *Boston Weekly News-Letter,* 24 May 1750, 1.

181. *Boston Gazette, or Weekly Journal,* 24 April 1750, 1.

182. *New-York Journal; or the General Advertiser,* 9 August 1770, 2.

183. *Pennsylvania Gazette* (Philadelphia), 7 June 1750, 2; and *Maryland Gazette* (Annapolis), 10 January 1760, 2.

184. *Pennsylvania Gazette* (Philadelphia), 5 July 1750, 2; and *Maryland Gazette* (Annapolis), 18 December 1755, 3.

185. *Parker's New-York Gazette; or the Weekly Post-Boy,* 1 December 1755, 2.

186. *Weyman's New-York Gazette,* 12 May 1760, 1.

187. *New York Mercury,* 23 June 1760, 3.

188. *South-Carolina Gazette* (Charleston), 20 September 1735, 2.

189. *Boston Gazette, or the Country Journal,* 24 November 1755, 1. See also, chapter 8.

190. *Boston Evening-Post,* 24 November 1755, 4.

191. *Maryland Gazette* (Annapolis), 10 January 1760, 3; 14 February 1760, 2.

192. *Boston Evening-Post,* 2 July 1770, 3; *New-York Gazette and Weekly Mercury,* 2 July 1770, 3; and *New-York Journal; or the General Advertiser,* 5 July 1770, 3..

193. *American Weekly Mercury* (Philadelphia), 3 April 1735, 3; and *New-England Weekly Journal* (Boston), 14 April 1735, 2.

194. *Boston Evening-Post,* 15 October 1750, 1.

195. *Newport Mercury, or the Weekly Advertiser,* 31 June 1765, 3. The incorrect dateline was not caught by the *Mercury*'s printer until after the first run, or pages one and four, had been printed. A correction, which made the proper date July 1, was placed on page two.

196. *Boston Gazette,* 20 June 1720, 1.

197. See chapter 7.

198. Frank Donovan, *The Benjamin Franklin Papers* (New York: Dodd, Mead, 1962), 86.

199. *South-Carolina Gazette* (Charleston), 31 July 1755, 3.

200. *Boston Evening-Post,* 4 June 1750, 2.

201. *Pennsylvania Gazette* (Philadelphia), 19 March 1729–30, 2.

202. *Boston News-Letter,* 13 March 1735, 1.

203. *American Weekly Mercury* (Philadelphia), 1.

204. See, for example, *Pennsylvania Gazette* (Philadelphia), 31 January 1760, 4.

205. *New-York Gazette,* 8 June 1730, 3.

206. *Maryland Gazette* (Annapolis), 24 January 1750, 1.

207. *Newport Mercury, or the Weekly Advertiser,* 25 March 1765, 2.

208. *Pennsylvania Gazette* (Philadelphia), 15 August 1765, 2.

209. See, for example, "The BANKRUPT. A Moral Tale," *Pennsylvania Ledger: Or the Virginia, Maryland, Pennsylvania, & New-Jersey Advertiser* (Philadelphia), 4 March 1775, 1.

210. *Virginia Gazette* (Williamsburg, Purdie and Dixon), 9 September 1775, 4.

211. *Virginia Gazette* (Williamsburg, Purdie and Dixon), 22 January 1770, 2; *New-York Gazette; or the Weekly Post-Boy,* 16 April 1770, 4; *New-York Journal; or the General Advertiser,* 19 April 1770, 3; *New-London Gazette,* 25 May 1770, 4; and *Providence Gazette; and Country Journal,* 7 July 1770, 4.

CONCLUSION

1. Richard D. Brown, *Knowledge Is Power: The Diffusion of Information in Early America, 1700–1865* (New York and Oxford: Oxford University Press, 1989), 39.

2. Warren B. Johnson, "The Content of Colonial Newspapers Relative to International Affairs" (Ph.D. diss., University of Washington, 1962), iii.

3. *New-York Gazette Revived in the Weekly Post-Boy,* 22 January 1750, 1.

4. *Universal Instructor in All Arts and Sciences; and the Pennsylvania Gazette* (Philadelphia), 24 December 1728, 1.

5. *Pennsylvania Gazette* (Philadelphia), 16 October 1729.

6. Frank Luther Mott, *American Journalism: A History 1690–1960,* 3d ed. (New York: Macmillan, 1962), 400, 483.

7. Jean Folkerts and Dwight L. Teeter, *Voices of a Nation: A History of the Media in the United States* (New York: Macmillan, 1989), 130; and Dan Schiller, *Objectivity and the News: The Public and the Rise of Commercial Journalism* (Philadelphia, University of Pennsylvania Press, 1981), 7.

8. Folkert and Teeters, *Voices of a Nation,* 130, refers to the insertion of "day-to-day events" as the "'new' content for the penny papers." Their assumption that the news of the Penny Press was "new" is no doubt based upon the fact that newspapers in the early national period were so very political in nature. Sidney Kobre, *The Development of American Journalism* (Dubuque, Iowa: Wm. C. Brown, 1969), 103, explains that the growth of political parties and the growth of newspapers ran parallel from the 1780s into the nineteenth century, and editors mirrored the political issues of the parties and worked hard through their newspapers to stimulate interest in that particular point of view.

9. *New York Herald,* 11 April 1836.

10. Mitchell Stephens, *A History of News: From the Drum to the Satellite* (New York: Penguin Books, 1988).

11. Johnson, "The Content of the American Colonial Newspapers Relative to International Affairs, 1704–1763, ii.

12. This figure is based upon personal review of the news content of the *Boston News-Letter,* which generally ran a full page of political news from Europe followed by up to a column more of similar news. The remaining column contained a few ads, ship news, and any other news that might have been of interest to citizens of Boston according to the *News-Letter*'s postmaster-overseer John Campbell such as the news of the activities of Native Americans, generally re-

ferred to as "the Sculking Indian Enemy" by the *News-Letter.* The *News-Letter,* of course, had no competition, and once the *Boston Gazette* and *New-England Courant* joined the newspaper scene in Boston in 1719 and 1721 respectively, the content of newspapers changed to include more variety in subject matter.

13. Sidney Kobre, *The Development of the Colonial Newspaper* (1944; reprint, Gloucester, Mass.: Peter Smith, 1960), 13.

14. Ibid., 17.

15. *Virginia Gazette* (Williamsburg), 18 January 1740, 3; *South-Carolina Gazette* (Charleston), 26 January 1740, 2; *American Weekly Mercury* (Philadelphia), 4 March 1740, 2; *New-York Weekly Journal,* 10 March 1740; and *Boston Weekly News-Letter,* 28 March 1740, 1.

16. Elizabeth Christine Cook, *Literary Influences in Colonial Newspapers 1704–1750* (New York: Columbia University Press, 1912), 3.

17. Kobre, *The Development of the Colonial Newspaper,* 17–27.

18. See, for example, Edmund S. Morgan, and Helen M. Morgan, *The Stamp Act Crisis: Prologue to Revolution* (Chapel Hill: University of North Carolina, 1953; Gary B. Nash, *The Urban Crucible. Social Change, Political Consciousness, and the Origins of the American Revolution* (Cambridge: Harvard University Press, 1979); and Arthur M. Schlesinger, *Prelude to Independence: The Newspaper War on Britain 1764–1776* (New York: Random House, 1958).

19. See, for example, Livingston Rowe Schuyler, *The Liberty of the Press in the American Colonies before the Revolution* (New York: Thomas Whittaker, 1905); Clyde A. Duniway, *The Development of Freedom of the Press in Massachusetts* (Cambridge: Harvard University Press, 1906); Lawrence H. Leder, *Liberty and Authority. Early American Political Ideology, 1689–1763* (Chicago: Quadrangle Books, 1968); Stephen Botein, "'Meer Mechanics' and an Open Press: The Business and Political Strategies of Colonial American Printers," in *Perspectives in American History* IX, eds. Donald Fleming and Bernard Bailyn (Cambridge: Harvard University Press, 1975), 127–225; Leonard Levy, *Legacy of Suppression* (Cambridge: Harvard University Press, 1960); Leonard Levy, *The Emergence of a Free Press* (New York and Oxford: Oxford University Press, 1985); and Jeffery A. Smith, *Printers and Press Freedom: The Ideology of Early American Journalism* (New York and Oxford: Oxford University Press, 1988).

20. In addition to the works named in the preceding note that discuss the trial of Zenger, see James Alexander, *A Brief Narrative of the Case and Trial of John Peter Zenger of the New York Weekly Journal;* Livingston Rutherfurd, *John Peter Zenger. His Press. His Trial and Bibliography;* Vincent Buranelli, "Peter Zenger, Editor," *American Quarterly* 7 (1955): 174–81; Vincent Buranelli, ed., *The Trial of Peter Zenger* (New York: New York University Press, 1957); Cathy Covert, "Passion Is Ye Prevailing Motive: The Feud Behind the Zenger Case," *Journalism Quarterly* 32 (1973): 3–10; Warren C. Price, "Reflections on the Trial of John Peter Zenger," *Journalism Quarterly* 32 (1955): 47–53.

21. See, for example, *Pennsylvania Gazette* (Philadelphia), 18 May 1738.

22. See, for example, *American Weekly Mercury* (Philadelphia), 24 April 1735, 2.

23. Johnson, *The Content of American Colonial Newspapers Relative to International Affairs 1704–1763,* 19; and Mott, *American Journalism,* 51.

24. *Boston Evening-Post,* 29 September 1740, 2; and *Boston News-Letter,* 25 September 1740, 3.

25. Brown, *Knowledge Is Power,* 39.

26. Anna Janney DeArmond, *Andrew Bradford, Colonial Printer* (New York: Greenwood Press, 1969), 119.

27. For a discussion of this newspaper war, see Mary Ann Yodelis, "Boston's First Major Newspaper War: A 'Great Awakening' of Freedom," *Journalism Quarterly* 51 (1974): 207–12.

28. Brown, *Knowledge Is Power,* 77.

29. *Boston Evening-Post,* 24 November 1760, 2.

30. *Connecticut Gazette* (New Haven), 16 August 1755, 3.

31. *New-York Gazette: or, the Weekly Post-Boy,* 18 August 1755, 1; and *New-York Mercury,* 18 August 1755, 3.

32. *Pennsylvania Gazette* (Philadelphia), 21 August 1755, 3; and *Pennsylvania Journal, or Weekly Advertiser* (Philadelphia), 21 August 1755, 2.

33. *Maryland Gazette* (Annapolis), 28 August 1755, 2.

34. *Boston Chronicle,* 8 March 1770, 3.

35. Historians have also attributed the demise of newspapers such as the *Boston Chronicle,* which was published by Tory sympathizer John Mein, to the politcal climate of the period. Printers and newspapers have been classified as either patriot or tory for the period by some scholars. Mein's obvious exclusion of news of local concern in 1770 may have been the result of his pro-English stance, but a comparison of the *Chronicle* with other newspapers in 1770—including other Tory newspapers—reveals that other printers were not ignoring all news of local importance in their newspapers. For discussions of the political stance of newspapers and the reaction to the tory stance, see Kobre, *The Development of Colonial Newspapers,* 114–17, 134–48; Philip Davidson, *Propaganda and the American Revolution 1763–1783* (Chapel Hill: University of North Carolina Press, 1941), 171, 249–340; Janice Potter and Robert M. Calhoon, "The Character and Coherence of the Loyalist Press," in *The Press & the American Revolution,* eds. Bernard Bailyn and John B. Hench (Boston: Northeastern University Press, 1980), 229–72; Schlesinger, *Prelude to Independence,* 219–26; and Duniway, *The Development of Freedom of Press in Massachusetts,* 131.

36. See, for example, *Pennsylvania Gazette* (Philadelphia), 31 July 1735.

37. Kobre, *Development of American Journalism,* 49.

38. Mott, *American Journalism,* 104.

39. Ibid., 59.

40. See, for example, *South-Carolina Gazette; and Country Journal* (Charleston), 6 March 1770, 3.

41. Frank Luther Mott, "The Newspaper Coverage of Lexington and Concord," in *Highlights in the History of the American Press,* eds. Edwin H. Ford and Edwin Emery (Minneapolis: University of Minnesota Press, 1954), 87–88, rightly points out that expecting the most important news to be on page one is a misperception of journalistic practices that have developed in America. Mott says that the first page was reserved for the most dignified news. It would be better to assume that the first page was reserved for news and advertisements that were available well ahead of the printing day for a newspaper. This news might be dignified or it might not, but it was news that could be set and printed earlier than the news of pages two and three. Printers could have easily switched this practice, but the logic of setting page one first with its standard nameplate probably outweighed this notion in the eighteeth century.

42. When the *Newport Mercury* put out its 1 July 1765 edition, someone forgot that the month of June had only thirty days and put the date 31 June 1765 on the newspaper. The mistake was caught, but not until the printing of the

newspaper's first side had occurred. At the top of page two, printer Samuel Hall noted the error, proving that the inside pages of newspapers were often not even set until the first pages were being printed.

43. Donald Lewis Shaw, "AT THE CROSSROADS: Change and Continuity in American Press News 1820–1860," *Journalism History* 9 (1991): 48–49.

44. John D. Stevens and Hazel Dicken Garcia, *Communication History* (Beverly Hills and London: Sage Publications, 1980), 15–32, have pointed out the mistaken assumption generally made by media historians that the linear progression of mass media has produced greater quality. Determining "better," in the case of colonial newspapers, is not the purpose of this study.

45. *Virginia Gazette* (Williamsburg, Purdie and Dixon), 22 January 1770, 2; *New-York Gazette: or the Weekly Post-Boy,* 16 April 1770, 4; *New-York Journal; or the General Advertiser,* 19 April 1770, 3; *New-London Gazette,* 25 May 1770, 4; and *Providence Gazette; and Country Journal,* 7 July 1770, 4.

APPENDIX 1. METHODOLOGY

1. Several German newspapers were published in the Philadelphia area, the first being the Philadelphia *Zeitung* in 1732 (Mott, 29). Discussions of foreign language newspapers of the colonial period may be found in Mott, and Isaiah Thomas, *The History of Printing in America* (1810; reprint, New York: Weathervane Books, 1970); and Clarence S. Brigham, *A History and Bibliography of American Newspapers, 1690–1820* (Worcester, Mass.: American Antiquarian Society, 1947), passim.

2. *Newspapers on Microfilm* (Washington: Library of Congress, 1984).

3. Thomas, *The History of Printing,* 15.

4. Brigham, *A History and Bibliography of American Newspapers, 1690–1820,* passim; and Kobre, *The Development of the Colonial Newspaper,* 96, 147–48.

5. The number of editions of colonial newspapers that was read is considered approximate because in the case of some newspapers, they did not print for every week of the year studied. In addition, some editions of newspapers are no longer extant. The seventy-four hundred editions, however, do not take into account newspapers that published multiple weekly editions, such as the *Massachusetts Spy* in 1770 or the *Pennsylvania Evening Post* in 1775.

6. Those newspapers are the *Universal Instructor,* 1728; the *Rhode Island Gazette,* 1732–33; the *Boston Independent Advertiser,* 1748–49; the *New York Independent Reflector,* 1752–53; the *New York Pacquet,* 1753; the *Occasional Reverberator* (New York), 1753; the *New York Plebean,* 1754; the *American Chronicle* (New York), 1761–62; the *Wilmington Courant* (Wilmington, Delaware), 1762; and the *Boston Censor,* 1771–1772.

7. Those newspapers not available include the *South Carolina Weekly Gazette,* 1758–64; the *Constitutional Courant* (Woodbridge, New Jersey), 1765; and the *Portsmouth Mercury and Weekly Advertiser,* 1764–65. Only three editions of the *South Carolina Weekly Gazette* are known to be extant for 1760.

8. Those newspapers are the *Albany Post-Boy,* 1772–75; and the *Virginia Gazette* (Norfolk), 1775.

9. Donald P. Warwick and Charles A. Lininger, *The Sample Survey: Theory and Practice* (New York: McGraw-Hill, 1975), 93. Warwick and Lininger demonstrate that a survey sample of five hundred produces a standard error of 4 percent.

In order to reduce the chance of error to 3 percent, one thousand samples would have to be taken, and twenty-five hundred samples would be required to reduce to error margin to 2 percent.

10. Ibid. According to Warwick and Leninger, the absolute size of the sample is more important than the proportionate size of the sample the total population. A sample of six thousand produces just as credible results as a sample population of twenty-five thousand

11. For a listing of these works, see chapter 1, note 8.

Selected Bibliography

NEWSPAPERS

American Weekly Mercury (Philadelphia), 1719–1740
Boston Chronicle, 1770–1775
Boston Evening-Post, 1735–1775
Boston Gazette, 1719–1740
Boston Gazette, or Weekly Journal, 1745–1750
Boston Gazette, and Country Journal, 1760–1775
Boston Gazette, or Country Journal, 1755
Boston Gazette, or Weekly Advertiser, 1755.
Boston News-Letter, 1704–1725
Boston Post-Boy and Advertiser, 1765
Boston Weekly News-Letter, 1730–1760
Boston Weekly Post-Boy, 1735–1755
Cape Fear Mercury (Wilmington, N.C.), 1770–1775
Connecticut Courant (Hartford), 1765–1770
Connecticut Courant, and Hartford Weekly Intelligencer, 1775
Connecticut Gazette (New Haven), 1755–1765
Connecticut Gazette; and the Universal Intelligencer (New London), 1775
Connecticut Journal, and New-Haven Post-Boy, 1770–1775
Constitutional Gazette (New York), 1775
Essex Gazette (Salem, Mass.), 1770–1775
Essex Journal and Merrimack Packet: Or, the Massachusetts and New-Hampshire General Advertiser (Newbury-Port, Mass.), 1775
Essex Journal or, the New-Hampshire Packet (Newbury-Port, Mass.), 1775
Dunlap's Maryland Gazette; or the Baltimore General Advertiser, 177.
Georgia Gazette (Savannah), 1765–1775
Green & Russell's Boston Post-Boy & Advertiser, 1760
Maryland Gazette (Annapolis, Green), 1745–1775
Maryland Gazette (Annapolis, Parks), 1730
Maryland Journal, and the Baltimore Advertiser, 1775
Massachusetts Gazette (Boston), 1765–1775
Massachusetts Gazette (And Boston News-Letter), 1765
Massachusetts Gazette, and the Boston Post-Boy and Advertiser, 1770–1775
Massachusetts Spy (Boston), 1770

362

Massachusetts Spy or Thomas's Boston Journal, 1775

Massachusetts Spy; or, American Oracle of Liberty (Worcester, Mass.), 1775

New-England Courant (Boston), 1725

New-England Chronicle: or, the Essex Gazette (Cambridge, Mass.), 1775

New-England Weekly Journal (Boston), 1730–1740

New-Hampshire Gazette (Portsmouth), 1760–1775

New-London Summary, or the Weekly Advertiser, 1760

New-London Gazette, 1765–1775

Newport Mercury, or the Weekly Advertiser, 1760–1765

New-York Chronicle, 1770

New-York Evening-Post, 1745–1750

New-York Gazette (Bradford), 1730–1740

New-York Gazette (Weyman), 1760–1765

New-York Gazette: or the Weekly Post-Boy, 1755, 1765–1770

New-York Gazette Revived in the Weekly Post-Boy, 1750

New-York Gazette; and the Weekly Mercury, 1770–1775

New-York Journal; or the General Advertiser, 1770–1775

New-York Mercury, 1755–1765

New-York Weekly Journal, 1735–1740

New-York Weekly Post-Boy, 1745

North Carolina Gazette (New Bern), 1755–1775

North-Carolina Gazette (Wilmington), 1765

North-Carolina Gazette; And Wilmington Weekly Post-Boy, 1765

North-Carolina Magazine; Or Universal Intelligence (New Bern), 1765

Norwich Packet and the Connecticut, Massachusetts, New-Hampshire, and Rhode Island Weekly Advertiser, 1775

Parker's New-York Gazette; or the Weekly Post-Boy, 1760

Pennsylvania Chronicle, and Universal Advertiser (Philadelphia), 1770

Pennsylvania Evening Post (Philadephia), 1775.

Pennsylvania Gazette (Philadelphia), 1730–1775

Pennsylvania Journal, or Weekly Advertiser (Philadelphia), 1745–1775

Pennsylvania Ledger: Or the Virginia, Maryland, Pennsylvania, & New-Jersey Advertiser (Philadelphia), 1775

Pennsylvania Mercury; and the Universal Advertiser (Philadelphia), 1775

Pennsylvania Packet, or the General Advertiser (Philadelphia), 1775

Providence Gazette; and Country Journal, 1765–1775

Publick Occurrences Both Forreign and Domestic (Boston), 1690

Rivington's New-York Gazetteer, 1775

South-Carolina and American General Gazette (Charleston), 1765–1775

South-Carolina Gazette (Charleston), 1735–1775

South-Carolina Gazette; and Country Journal (Charleston), 1765–1770

South-Carolina Gazetteer, (Charleston), 1765

Story & Humphrey's Pennsylvania Mercury; and the Universal Advertiser (Philadelphia), 1775

Virginia Gazette (Williamsburg, Dixon and Hunter), 1770.
Virginia Gazette (Williamsburg, Hunter), 1755
Virginia Gazette (Williamsburg, Parks), 1740–1750
Virginia Gazette (Williamsburg, Pinkney), 1775
Virginia Gazette (Williamsburg, Purdie), 1760, 1775
Virginia Gazette (Williamsburg, Purdie and Dixon), 1770
Virginia Gazette (Williamsburg, Rind), 1770
Virginia Gazette or Norfolk Intelligencer, 1775
Weekly Rehearsal (Boston), 1735

PRIMARY SOURCES

Baxter, Richard. *Plain Scripture Proof.* London, 1651.

Douglass, William. *A Summary, historical and political, of the first planting, progressive improvements, and present state of the British Settlements in North America.* London, 1760.

Eastburn, Robert. *A Faithful NARRATIVE of The Many Dangers and Sufferings, as well as wonderful Deliverance of ROBERT EASTBURN, during his late Captivity among the INDIANS: Together with some Remarks upon the Country of Canada, and the Religion, and Policy of its Inhabitants; tho whole intermixed with devout Reflections.* Philadelphia, 1758.

Edwards, Jonathan. *Thoughts on the Revival in New England.* In *The Works of President Edwards,* vol. 3, New York: Robert Carter & Brothers, 1879.

Esquemeling, John. *The Buccaneers of America.* 1684; reprint, London: George Allen & Unwin, 1951.

Franklin, Benjamin. *Autobiography of Benjamin Franklin.* Eds. J. A. Leo Lemay and P. M. Zall. Knoxville: University of Tennessee Press, 1981.

Hobbes, Thomas. *Leviathan, or the Matter, Forme and Power of a Commonwealth, Ecclesiastical and Civill.* 1651, reprint; Cambridge: Cambridge University Press, 1904.

Mather, Cotton. *Decennium Luctuosum. An HISTORY of Remarkable Occurrences, in the Long WAR, which NEW-ENGLAND hath had with the Indian Salvages, From the Year, 1688. To the Year, 1698.* Boston, 1699.

———. *Diary of Cotton Mather.* Ed. Worthington C. Ford. Boston: Massachusetts Historical Society, 1912.

———. *Humiliations follow'd with Deliverances, A Brief Discourse on the MATTER and METHOD, of that HUMILIATION which would be an Hopeful Symptom of our Deliverance from Calamity. Accompanied and Accommodated with A NARRATIVE, of a notable Deliverance lately Received by some English Captives, From the Hands of Cruel Indians.* Boston, 1697.

———. *Ornaments for the Daughters of Zion. Or, The Character and Happiness of a Virtuous Woman.* 1692; reprint, Delmar, N.Y.: Scholar's Facsimilies & Reprints, 1989.

Milton, John. *Areopagetica: A Speech for the Liberty of Unlicensed Printing to Parliament of England.* London, 1644.

Rowlandson, Mary. *A True HISTORY of the Captivity and Restoration of Mrs.*

MARY ROWLANDSON, a Minister's Wife in New-England. Wherein is set forth, The Cruel and Inhumane Usage she underwent amongst the Heathens, for Eleven Weeks time: And her Deliverance from Them. New-England, 1682.

Smith, John Smith. *The General Historie of Virginia, New England and the Summer Isles.* In *English Scholar's Library of Old and Modern Works,* ed. Edward Arber. New York: AMS, 1967.

Tennent, John. *Every Man his own Doctor: or, The Poor Planter's Physician.* Williamsburg, 1734.

Wesley, John. *Primitive Physick: or, an Easy and Natural METHOD of curing Most Diseases.* 12th ed. Philadelphia, 1764.

Whitefield, George. *A Brief and General Account of the First Part of the Life of the Reverend Mr. George Whitefield from his Birth, to his Entering into Holy Orders.* Philadelphia, 1740.

————. *Journals, 1737–1741.* Introduction by William V. Davis. Gainesville: Scholars' Facsimiles & Reprints, 1969.

Williams, Roger. *The Bloudy Tenent of Persecution for Cause of Conscience Discussed in a Conference between Peace and Truth.* London, 1644.

Williamson, Peter. *French and Indian Cruelty; Exemplified in the LIFE And various Vicistitudes of Fortune, of PETER WILLIAMSON, A Disbanded Soldier.* York, 1757.

BIBLIOGRAPHIES AND DOCUMENT SOURCES

American Antiquarian Society Proceedings, Vol. 23. Worcester, Mass.: American Antiquarian Society, 1913.

Brigham, Clarence S. *A History and Bibliography of American Newspapers, 1690–1820.* Worcester, Mass.: American Antiquarian Society, 1947.

Bristol, Roger P. *Supplement to Charles Evans' Bibliography.* Charlottesville: University Press of Virginia, 1970.

Cappon, Lester J., Barbara Bartz Petchenik and John Hamilton Long, eds. *Atlas of Early American History.* Princeton: Princeton University Press, 1976.

Donovan, Frank. *The Benjamin Franklin Papers.* New York: Dodd, Mead, 1962.

Evans, Charles. *American Bibliography.* Chicago, 1904.

Historical Statistics of the United States: Colonial Times to 1970. Washington, 1975.

Hughes, Paul L. and Robert F. Fries. *Crown and Parliament in Tudor-Stuart England: A Documentary Constitutional History, 1485–1714.* New York: G. P. Putnam's Sons, 1959.

Newspapers on Microfilm. Library of Congress, 1984.

SECONDARY SOURCES

Books

Adams, James Truslow. *Provincial Society 1690–1763.* New York: The Macmillan Company, 1927.

Ahlstrom, Sydney E. *A Religious History of the American People.* New Haven and London: Yale University Press, 1972.

Alexander, James. *A Brief Narrative of the Case and Trial of John Peter Zenger of the New York Weekly Journal.* Cambridge: The Belknap Press, 1963.

Andrews, Charles M. *The Colonial Period of American History: The Settlements.* New Haven: Yale University Press, 1936.

Ashburn, P. M. *The Ranks of Death: A Medical History of the Conquest of America.* New York: Coward-McCann, 1947.

Axtell, James. *Beyond 1492: Encounters in Colonial North America.* New York and Oxford: Oxford University Press, 1992.

Barck, Oscar Theodore and Hugh Talmage Lefler. *Colonial America.* New York: The Macmillan Company, 1958.

Bass, Althea. *Cherokee Messenger.* Norman: University of Oklahoma Press, 1936.

Benson, Mary Sumner. *Women in Eighteenth Century America.* New York: Columbia University, 1935.

Blake, John B. *Public Health in the Town of Boston, 1630–1822.* Cambridge: Harvard University Press, 1959.

Bonomi, Patricia U. *Under the Cope of Heaven: Religion, Society, and Politics in the Colonial Era.* New York and Oxford: Oxford University Press, 1986.

Boorstin, Daniel J. *The Americans: The Colonial Experience.* New York: Vintage Books, 1958.

Brigham, Clarence S. *Journals and Journeymen: Contributions to the History of Early American Newspapers.* Philadelphia: University of Pennsylvania Press, 1950.

Brown, Richard D. *Knowledge Is Power: The Diffusion of Information in Early America, 1700–1865.* New York and Oxford: Oxford University Press, 1989.

Buranelli, Vincent, ed. *The Trial of Peter Zenger.* New York: New York University Press, 1957.

Butler, Jon. *Awash in a Sea of Faith: Christianizing the American People.* Cambridge: Harvard University Press, 1990.

Cassedy, James H. *Medicine in America: A Short History.* Baltimore and London: Johns Hopkins University Press, 1991.

Chidester, David. *Patterns of Power: Religion and Politics in American Culture.* Englewood Cliffs, N.J.: Prentice Hall, 1988.

Coffin, Joshua. *Slave Insurrections.* New York: American Anti Slavery Society, 1860.

Cohen, Hennig. *The South Carolina Gazette.* Columbia: University of South Carolina Press, 1953.

Cook, Elizabeth Christine. *Literary Influences in Colonial Newspapers, 1704– 1750.* New York: Columbia University Press, 1912.

Cowing, Cedric B. *The Great Awakening and the American Revolution: Colonial Thought in the Eighteenth Century.* Chicago: Rand McNally, 1971.

Cremin, Lawrence A. *American Education: The Colonial Experience 1607–1783.* New York: Harper & Row, 1970.

Curtin, Philip D. *The Atlantic Slave Trade: A Census.* Madison: University of Wisconsin Press, 1969.

Dargo, George. *Roots of the Republic: A New Perspective on Early American Constitutionalism.* New York and Washington: Praeger Publishers, 1974.

Davis, Richard Beale. *A Colonial Southern Bookshelf: Readings in the Eighteenth Century.* Athens: University of Georgia Press, 1979.

Dawson, Joseph Martin. *Baptists and the American Republic.* Nashville, Tenn.: Broadman Press, 1956.

DeArmond, Anna Janney. *Andrew Bradford: Colonial Journalist.* New York: Greenwood Press, 1969.

Demos, John Putnam. *Entertaining Satan: Witchcraft and the Culture of Early New England.* New York: Oxford University Press, 1983.

Dill, William A. *Growth of Newspapers in the United States.* Lawrence: University of Kansas Press, 1928.

Dobyns, Henry F. *Their Numbers Become Thinned: Native American Population Dynamics in Eastern North America.* Knoxville: University of Tennessee Press, 1983.

Dow, Lesley. *Whales.* New York: Facts on File, 1990.

Dowd, Gregory Evans. *A Spirited Resistance: The North American Indian Struggle for Unity, 1745–1815.* Baltimore and London: The Johns Hopkins University Press, 1992.

Duniway, Clyde A. *The Development of Freedom of the Press in Massachusetts.* Cambridge: Harvard University Press, 1906.

Duffy, John. *Epidemics in Colonial America.* Baton Rouge: Louisiana State University Press, 1953.

Elkins, Stanley M. *Slavery: A Problem in American Institutional and Intellectual Life.* 3d ed. Chicago and London: University of Chicago Press, 1976.

Emery, Michael and Edwin Emery. *The Press and America: An Interpretive History of the Mass Media.* 6th ed. Englewood Cliffs, N.J.: Prentice Hall, 1988.

Estep, William R. *Revolution within a Revolution: The First Amendment in Historical Context, 1612–1789.* Grand Rapids, Mich.: William B. Eerdmans, 1990.

Evans, Sara M. *Born for Liberty: A History of Women in America.* New York: The Free Press, 1989.

Filler, Louis. *The Crusade against Slavery 1830–1860.* New York: Harper & Row, 1960.

Finke, Roger and Rodney Stark. *The Churching of America: 1776–1990.* New Brunswick: Rutgers University Press, 1992.

Fischer, David Hackett. *Albion's Seed: Four British Folkways in America.* New York and Oxford: Oxford University Press, 1989.

Folkerts, Jean and Dwight L. Teeter. *Voices of a Nation: A History of the Media in the United States.* New York: Macmillan Publishing Company, 1989.

Foner, Eric and John A. Garraty, eds. *The Reader's Companion to American History.* Boston: Houghton Mifflin, 1991.

Frank, Joseph. *The Beginnings of the English Newspaper 1620–1660.* Cambridge: Harvard University Press, 1961.

Friedman, Lawrence M. *A History of American Law.* 2d ed. New York: Simon & Shuster, 1985.

Gausted, Edwin Scott. *The Great Awakening in New England.* New York: Harper and Brothers, 1957.

Gibson, Arrell Morgan. *The American Indian: Prehistory to the Present.* Lexington, Mass.: D. C. Heath and Company, 1980.

Giesecke, Albert Anthony. *American Commercial Legislation Before 1789.* 1910; reprint, New York: Burt Franklin, 1970.

Gordon, Maurice Bear. *Æsculapius Comes to the Colonies.* Ventnor, N.J.: Ventnor Publications, 1949.

Greenberg, Douglas. *Crime and Law Enforcement in the Colony of New York, 1691–1776.* Ithaca: Cornell University Press, 1976.

Greven, Philip. *The Protestant Temperament: Patterns of Child-Rearing, Religious Experience, and the Self in Early America.* New York: Alfred A. Knopf, 1977.

Hart, Jim Allee. *The Developing Views on the News Editorial Syndrome 1500–1800.* Carbondale: Southern Illinois University Press, 1970.

Haskins, George L. *Law and Authority in Early Massachusetts.* New York: Macmillan, 1960.

Higginbotham, A. Leon. *In the Matter of Color: Race and the American Legal System.* New York: Oxford University Press, 1978.

Hoffer, Peter Charles, ed. *Early American History: Colonial Women and Domesticity.* New York and London: Garland Publishing, 1988.

Hoffer, Peter Charles. *Law and People in Colonial America.* Baltimore and London: Johns Hopkins University Press, 1992.

Hoffer, Peter C. and N. E. H. Hull. *Murdering Mothers: Infanticide in England and New England 1558–1803.* New York and London: New York University Press, 1984.

Hofstadter, Richard. *America at 1750: A Social Portrait.* New York: Alfred A. Knopf, 1972.

Hudak, Leona M. *Early American Women Printers and Publications: 1639–1820.* Metuchen, N.J.: Scarecrow Press, 1978.

Hudson, Frederic. *Journalism in the United States, from 1690–1872.* New York: Harper & Brothers, 1873.

Hull, N. E. H. *Female Felons: Women and Serious Crime in Colonial Massachusetts.* Urbana and Chicago: University of Illinois Press, 1987.

Hurd, John Codman. *The Law of Freedom and Bondage in the United States.* Boston: Little, Brown, 1858.

Isaac, Rhys. *The Transformation of Virginia 1740–1790.* Chapel Hill: University of North Carolina Press, 1982.

Jordan, Wintrop D. *White Over Black: American Attitudes Toward the Negro, 1550–1812.* Chapel Hill: University of North Carolina Press, 1968.

Kenyon, J. P. *Stuart England.* New York: Penguin Books, 1978.

Kerber, Linda. *Women of the Republic: Intellect and Ideology in Revolutionary America.* Chapel Hill: University of North Carolina Press, 1980.

Knight, Oliver A. *Following the Indian Wars: The Story of the Newspaper Correspondents Among the Indian Campaigners, 1866–1891.* Norman: University of Oklahoma Press, 1960.

Kobre, Sidney. *Development of American Journalism.* Dubuque, Iowa: Wm. C. Brown Company Publishers, 1969.

———. *The Development of the Colonial Newspaper.* 1944; reprint, Gloucester, Mass.: Peter Smith, 1960.

Kulikoff, Allan. *Tobacco and Slaves: The Development of Southern Cultures in the Chesapeake, 1680–1800.* Chapel Hill and London: The University of North Carolina Press, 1986.

Leder, Lawrence H. *Liberty and Authority. Early American Political Ideology, 1689–1763.* Chicago: Quadrangle Books, 1968.

Lee, James Melvin. *History of American Journalism.* Garden City and New York: Garden City Publishing, 1923.

Lefler, Hugh T. and Patricia Stanford. *North Carolina.* 2d ed. New York: Harcourt Brace Jovanovich, 1972.

Lemay, J. A. Leo. *A Calendar of American Poetry in the Colonial Newspapers and Magazines and in the Major English Magazines Through 1765.* Worcester, Mass.: American Antiquarian Society, 1972.

———. *The Canon of Benjamin Franklin, 1722–1776.* Newark: University of Delaware Press, 1986.

Levy, Leonard. *The Emergence of a Free Press.* New York and Oxford: Oxford University Press, 1985.

———. *Legacy of Suppression.* Cambridge: Harvard University Press, 1960.

Lockridge, Kenneth A. *Literacy in Colonial New England: An Enquiry into the Social Contest of Literacy in the Early Modern West.* New York: Norton, 1974.

Malone, Patrick M. *The Skulking Way of War: Technology and Tactics among the New England Indians.* Baltimore and London: John Hopkins University Press, 1993.

May, Henry F. *The Enlightenment in America.* New York and London: Oxford University Press, 1976.

McBeth, H. Leon. *The Baptist Heritage: Four Centuries of Baptist Witness.* Nashville, Tenn.: Broadman Press, 1987.

McCusker, John J. and Russell R. Menard. *The Economy of British America, 1607–1789.* Chapel Hill and London: University of North Carolina Press, 1985.

McGee, J. Sears. *The Godly Man in Stuart England: Anglicans, Puritans, and the Two Tables, 1620–1670.* New Haven and London: Yale University Press, 1976.

Merrell, James H. *The Indians' New World: Catawbas and Their Neighbours from European Contact through the Era of Removal.* Chapel Hill and London: University of North Carolina Press, 1989.

Miller, Perry. *The New England Mind: From Colony to Province.* Cambridge: Harvard University Press, 1953.

Morgan, Edmund S. *American Slavery, American Freedom: The Ordeal of Colonial Virginia.* New York: W. W. Norton, 1975.

Morgan, Edmund S. and Helen M. Morgan. *The Stamp Act Crisis: Prologue to Revolution.* Chapel Hill: University of North Carolina, 1953.

Morris, Richard B. *Studies in the History of American Law, with Special Reference to the 17th and 18th Centuries.* 2d ed. Philadelphia: J. M. Mitchell, 1959.

Mott, Frank Luther. *American Journalism,* 3d ed. New York: The MacMillan Company, 1962.

Murphy, James E. and Sharon M. Murphy. *Let My People Know: American Indian Journalism.* Norman: University of Oklahoma Press, 1981.

Nash, Gary B. *Forging Freedom: The Formation of Philadelphia's Black Community 1720–1840.* Cambridge and London: Harvard University Press, 1988.

————. *The Urban Crucible. Social Change, Political Consciousness, and the Origins of the American Revolution.* Cambridge: Harvard University Press, 1979.

Nettels, Curtis P. *The Roots of American Civilization.* 2d ed. New York: The Macmillan Company, 1963.

Noll, Mark A., Nathan O. Hatch, George M. Marsden, David F. Wells and John D. Woodbridge, eds. *Christianity in America.* Grand Rapids, Mich.: William B. Eerdmans, 1983.

Norton, Mary Beth. *Liberty's Daughters: The Revolutionary Experience of American Women, 1750–1800.* Boston: Little, Brown, 1980.

Norwood, Frederick A. *The Story of American Methodism: A History of the United Methodists and Their Relations.* Nashville, Tenn.: Abingdon Press, 1974.

Parramore, Thomas C. *Carolina Quest.* Englewood Cliffs, N.J.: Prentice-Hall, 1978.

Payne, George Henry. *History of Journalism in the United States.* New York: D. Appleton, 1920; reprint, Westport, Conn.: Greenwood Press, 1970.

Richardson, James. *The New York Police: From Colonial Times to 1901.* New York: Oxford University Press, 1970.

Richter, Daniel K. and James H. Merrell, eds. *Beyond the Covenant Chain: The Iroquois and Their Neighbors in Indian North America, 1600–1800.* Syracuse, N.Y.: Syracuse University Press, 1987.

Rutherfurd, Livingston. *John Peter Zenger. His Press. His Trial and Bibliography.* Gloucester, Mass.: Peter Smith, 1963.

Sagendorph, Robb. *America and her Almanacs: Wit, Wisdom & Weather 1639–1970.* Boston: Little, Brown, 1970.

Schiller, Dan. *Objectivity and the News: The Public and the Rise of Commercial Journalism.* Philadelphia: University of Pennsylvania Press, 1981.

Schlesinger, Arthur M. *Prelude to Independence: The Newspaper War on Britain 1764–1776.* New York: Random House, 1958.

Schuyler, Livingston Rowe. *The Liberty of the Press in the American Colonies before the Revolution.* New York: Thomas Whittaker, 1905.

Semonche, John E. *Religion & Constitutional Government in the United States: A Historical Overview with Sources.* Carrboro, N. C.: Signal Books, 1986.

Shepherd, James F. and Gary M. Walton. *Shipping, Maritime Trade, and the Economic Development of Colonial North America.* Cambridge: Cambridge University Press, 1972.

Sherry, Frank. *Raiders and Rebels: The Golden Age of Piracy.* New York: Hearst Marine Books, 1986.

Shields, David. *Oracles of Empire: Poetry, Politics, and Commerce in British America.* Chicago: University of Chicago Press, 1990.

Shudson, Michael. *Discovering the News. A Social History of American Newspapers.* York: Basic Books, 1978.

Shryock, Richard Harrison. *Medicine and Society in America, 1660–1860.* New York: New York University Press, 1960.

Sloan, Wm. David and Julie Hedgepeth Williams. *The Early American Press, 1690–1783.* Westport, Conn.: Greenwood Press, 1994.

Sloan, Wm. David, James G. Stovall, and James D. Startt, eds. *The Media in America: A History.* 2d ed. Scottsdale: Publishing Horizons, 1993.

Smith, Jeffery A. *Printers and Press Freedom: The Ideology of Early American Journalism.* New York and Oxford: Oxford University Press, 1988.

Steele, Ian K. *The English Atlantic 1675–1740. An Exploration of Communication and Community.* New York and Oxford: Oxford University Press, 1986.

Stephens, Mitchell. *A History of News: From the Drum to the Satellite.* New York: Penguin Books, 1988.

Stevens, John D. *Sensationalism and the New York Press.* New York: Columbia University Press, 1991.

Stevens, John D. and Hazel Dicken Garcia. *Communication History.* Beverly Hills and London: Sage Communications, 1980.

Stout, Harry S. *The Divine Dramatist: George Whitefield and the Rise of Modern Evangelism.* Grand Rapids, Mich.: William B. Eerdmans, 1991.

———. *The New England Soul: Preaching and Religious Culture in Colonial New England.* New York and Oxford: Oxford University Press, 1986.

Stowell, Marion Barber. *Early American Almanacs: The Colonial Weekday Bible.* New York: Burt Franklin, 1977.

Thomas, Isaiah. *The History of Printing in America.* 1810; reprint, New York: Weathervane Books, 1970.

Tindall, George Brown. *America.* New York and London: W. W. Norton, 1984.

Trevelyan, G. M. *History of England: From Utrecht to Modern Times.* 3d ed. Garden City, N.Y.: Doubleday & Company, 1952.

Ulrich, Laurel Thatcher. *Good Wives: Image and Reality in the Lives of Women in Northern New England 1650–1750.* New York: Alfred A. Knopf, 1982.

Urofsky, Melvin I. *A March to Liberty: A Constitutional History of the United States.* Vol. I. New York: Alfred A. Knopf, 1988.

Van Doren, Carl. *Benjamin Franklin.* New York: Viking Press, 1938.

Walker, Samuel. *Popular Justice: A History of American Criminal Justice.* New York and Oxford: Oxford University Press, 1980.

Walton, Gary M. and James F. Shepherd. *The Economic Rise of Early America.* Cambridge: Cambridge University Press, 1979.

Warwick, Donald P. and Charles A. Lininger. *The Sample Survey: Theory and Practice.* New York: McGraw-Hill, 1975.

Wells, Robert V. *Revolution in American's Lives: A Demographic Perspective on the History of Americans, Their Families, and Their Society.* Westport, Conn.: Greenwood Press, 1982.

Wood, Peter H. *Black Majority.* New York: W. W. Norton, 1974.

Wright, Louis B. *The Cultural Life of the American Colonies 1607–1763.* New York: Harper & Row, 1962.

Wroth, Lawrence. *The Colonial Printer.* Portland, Me.: The Southworth-Anthoensen Press, 1938.

Book Chapters

Bosco, Ronald A. "'Scandal, like other Virtues, is in part its own Reward': Franklin Working the Crime Beat." In *Reappraising Benjamin Franklin: A Bicenten-*

nial Perspective, ed. J. A. Leo Lamay. Newark: University of Delaware Press, 1993.

Botein, Stephen. "'Meer Mechanics' and an Open Press: The Business and Political Strategies of Colonial American Printers." In *Perspectives in American History* IX, eds. Donald Fleming and Bernard Bailyn. Cambridge: Harvard University Press, 1975.

————. "Printers and the American Revolution." In *The Press and the American Revolution,* eds. Bernard Bailyn and John B. Hench. Boston: Northeastern University Press, 1981.

Clark, D. G. and W. B. Blankenburg. "Trends in Violent Content in Selected Mass Media." In *Television and Social Behavior,* vol. I, eds. G. A. Comstock and E. A. Rubinstein. Washington, D.C.: National Institute for Mental Health, 1972.

Davis, David Brion. "The Comparative Approach to American History: Slavery." In *Slavery in the New World: A Reader in Comparative History,* eds. Laura Foner and Eugene D. Genovese. Englewood Cliffs, N.J.: Prentice-Hall, 1969.

Flaherty, David H. "Law and the Enforcement of Morals in Early America." In *Perspectives in American History* IX, eds. Donald Fleming and Bernard Bailyn. Cambridge: Harvard University Press, 1971.

Hall, David D. "Religion and Society: Problems and Reconsiderations." In *Colonial British America: Essays in the New History of the Early Modern Period,* eds. Jack P. Greene and J. R. Pole. Baltimore and London: Johns Hopkins University Press, 1984.

Harris, Marvin. "The Origin of the Descent Rule." In *Slavery in the New World: A Reader in Comparative History,* eds. Laura Foner and Eugene D. Genovese. Englewood Cliffs, N.J.: Prentice Hall, 1969.

Henry, Susan. "Ann Franklin: Rhode Island's Woman Printer." In *Newsletters to Newspapers: Eighteenth-Century Journalism,* eds. Donovan H. Bond and W. Reynolds McLeod. Morganton: West Virginia University, 1977.

Hudson, Robert V. "Non-Indigenous Influences on Benjamin Franklin's Journalism." In *Newsletters to Newspapers: Eighteenth-Century Journalism,* eds. Donovan H. Bond and W. Reynolds McLeod. Morganton: West Virginia University, 1977.

Jordan, Wintrop D. "Enslavement of Negroes in America to 1700." In *Colonial America: Essays in Politics and Social Development.* 3d ed, eds. Stanley N. Katz and John M. Murrin. New York: Alfred A. Knopf, 1983.

Lipper, Mark. "Benjamin Franklin's 'Silence Dogood' as an Eighteenth-Century 'Censor Morum.'" In *Newsletters to Newspapers: Eighteenth-Century Journalism,* eds. Donovan H. Bond and W. Reynolds McLeod. Morgantown: West Virginia University, 1977.

Mott, Frank Luther. "The Newspaper Coverage of Lexington and Concord." In *Highlights in the History of the American Press,* eds. Edwin H. Ford and Edwin Emery. Minneapolis: University of Minnesota Press, 1954.

Patterson, H. Orlando. "The General Causes of Jamaican Slave Revolts." In *Slavery in the New World,* eds. Laura Foner and Eugene D. Genovese. Englewood Cliffs, N.J.: Prentice-Hall, 1969.

Potter, Janice and Robert M. Calhoon. "The Character and Coherence of the Loyalist Press." In *The Press & the American Revolution,* eds. Bernard Bailyn and John B. Hench. Boston: Northeastern University Press, 1980.

Price, Jacob M. "The Transatlantic Economy." In *Colonial British America: Essays in the New History of the Early Modern Era,* eds. Jack P. Greene and J. R. Pole. Baltimore and London: The Johns Hopkins University Press, 1984.

Snyder, Henry L. "Newsletters in England, 1689–1715 with Special Reference to John Dyer—A Byway in the History of England." In *Newsletters to Newspapers: Eighteenth-Century Journalism,* eds. Donovan H. Bond and W. Reynolds McLeod. Morganton: West Virginia University, 1977.

Journal Articles

Allinson, Samuel, Billy G. Smith and Richard Wojtowicz, "The Precarious Freedom of Blacks in the Mid-Atlantic Region: Excerpts from the *Pennsylvania Gazette, 1728–1776,*" *The Pennsylvania Magazine of History and Biography* 113 (1989): 237–64.

Baker, Ira L. "Elizabeth Timothy: America's First Woman Publisher." *Journalism Quarterly* 54 (1977): 280–85.

Bonomi, Patricia U. and Peter R. Eisenstadt. "Church Adherence in the Eighteenth-Century British American Colonies." *William and Mary Quarterly* 39 (1982): 245–86.

Bradley, Patricia. "The *Boston Gazette* and Slavery as Revolutionary Propaganda." *Journalism & Mass Communication Quarterly* 72 (1995): 581–96.

———. "Slavery in Colonial Newspapers: The Sommerset Case." *Journalism History* 12 (Spring 1985): 2–7.

Buranelli, Vincent. "Peter Zenger, Editor." *American Quarterly* 7 (1955): 174–81.

Butler, Jon. "Magic, Astrology, and the Early American Religious Heritage, 1600–1760." *American Historical Review* 84 (1979): 317–46.

Carey, James W. "The Problem of Journalism History." *Journalism History* 1 (Spring 1974): 3–5, 27.

Cave, Alfred A. "Canaanites in a Promised Land: The American Indian and the Providential Theory of Empire." *American Indian Quarterly* 12 (Fall 1988): 277–97.

Christensen, Merton A. "Franklin on the Hemphill Trial: Deism Versus Presbyterian Orthodoxy." *William and Mary Quarterly* 10 (July 1953): 422–40.

Clark, Charles E. "The Newspapers of Provincial America." *Proceedings of the American Antiquarian Society* 100 (1990): 367–389.

Clark, Charles E. and Charles Wetherell. "The Measure of Maturity: The *Pennsylvania Gazette, 1728–1765.*" *William and Mary Quarterly* 46 (1989): 279–303.

Cott, Nancy F. "Eighteenth-Century Family and Social Life Revealed in Massachusetts Divorce Records." *Journal of Social History* 10 (1976): 20–43.

Covert, Cathy "Passion Is Ye Prevailing Motive: The Feud Behind the Zenger Case." *Journalism Quarterly* 32 (1973): 3–10.

Crane, Verner W. "Benjamin Franklin and the Stamp Act." *Transactions of the Colonial Society of Massachusetts* 32 (February 1934): 56–77.

Crosby, Alfred W. Jr. "Virgin Soil Epidemics as a Factor in the Aboriginal Depopulation in America." *William and Mary Quarterly* 33 (1976): 289–99.

Crow, Jeffery J. "Slave Rebelliousness and Social Conflict in North Carolina, 1775–1802," *William and Mary Quarterly* 37 (1980): 79–102.

Cullen, Maurice R. Jr. "The Boston Gazette: A Community Newspaper." *Journalism Quarterly* 36 (1959): 204–08.

Deyle, Steven. "'By farr the most profitable trade': Slave Trading in British Colonial North America." *Slavery & Abolition* 10 (1989): 106–25.

Dill, Bonnie Thornton. "Our Mothers' Grief: Racial Ethnic Women and the Maintenance of Families." *Journal of Family History* 13 (1988): 415–31.

Dobson, Mary J. "Mortality Gradients and Disease Exchanges: Comparisons from Old England and Colonial America." *Social History of Medicine* 2 (1989): 259–97.

Fitzroy, Herbert William Keith. "The Punishment of Crime in Provincial Pennsylvania." *Pennsylvania Magazine of History and Biography* 60 (1936): 242–69.

Fogel, Howard M. "Colonial Theocracy and a Secular Press." *Journalism Quarterly* 37 (1960): 525–32.

Francke, Warren. "An Argument in Defense of Sensationalism: Probing the Popular and Historiographical Concept." *Journalism History* 5 (1978): 70–73.

Gallop, George. "A Scientific Method for Determining Readership-Interest." *Journalism Quarterly* 7 (1930): 1–13.

Garcia, Hazel. "Of Punctilios Among the Fair Sex: Colonial American Magazines, 1741–1776." *Journalism History* 3 (1976): 48–52, 63.

Gleason, J. Philip. "A Scurrilous Colonial Election and Franklin's Reputation." *William and Mary Quarterly* 18 (January 1961): 68–84.

Greene, Lorenzo J. "The New England Negro as Seen in Advertisements for Runaway Slaves." *Journal of Negro History* 29 (1944): 125–46.

———. "Crime, Law Enforcement, and Social Control in Colonial America." *The American Journal of Legal History* 26 (1982): 293–325.

Gross, Robert A. "Printing, Politics, and the People." *Proceedings of the American Antiquarian Society* 99 (1989): 375–96.

Gunderson, Joan R. and Gwen Victor Gampel. "Married Women's Legal Status in Eighteenth-Century New York and Virginia." *William and Mary Quarterly* 39 (1982): 114–34.

Hamilton, Wynette L. "The Correlation between Societal Attitudes and Those of American Authors in the Depiction of American Indians, 1607–1860." *American Indian Quarterly* 1 (Spring 1974): 1–26.

Henry, Susan. "Colonial Woman Printer as Prototype: Toward a Model for the Study of Minorities." *Journalism History* 3 (1976): 20–24.

———. "Exception to the Female Model: Colonial Printer Mary Crouch." *Journalism Quarterly* 62 (1985): 725–33.

———. "Sarah Goddard, Gentlewoman Printer." *Journalism Quarterly* 57 (1980): 23–30.

Hester, Al, Susan Parker Humes, and Christopher Bickers. "Foreign News in Colonial North American Newspapers, 1764–1775." *Journalism Quarterly* 57 (Spring 1980): 18–22, 44.

Hiner, N. Ray. "Cotton Mather and His Female Children: Notes on the Relationship between Private Experience and Public Thought." *Journal of Psychohistory* 13 (1985): 33–49.

Johnson, Victor L. "Fair Traders and Smugglers in Philadelphia 1754–1763." *The Pennsylvania Magazine of History and Biography* 83 (1959): 125–49.

Jones, Douglas C. "Teresa Dean: Lady Correspondent Among the Sioux Indians." *Journalism Quarterly* 49 (1972): 656–62.

Kawashima, Yasuhide. "Forest Diplomats: The Role of Interpreters in the Indian-White Relations on the Early American Frontier." *American Indian Quarterly* 13 (Winter 1989): 1–14.

Ketcham, Ralph L. "Benjamin Franklin and William Smith: New Light on an Old Philadelphia Quarrel." *The Pennsylvania Magazine of History and Biography* 88 (April 1964): 142–63.

Lacourse, Richard. "An Indian Perspective—Native American Journalism: An Overview." *Journalism History* 6 (1979): 34–38.

Lambert, Frank. "'Pedlar in Divinity': George Whitefield and the Great Awakening, 1737–1745." *Journal of American History* 77 (1990): 812–37.

Lemay, J. A. Leo. "Franklin's Suppressed 'Busy-Body.'" *American Literature* 37 (November 1965): 307–11.

Lermack, Paul. "Peace Bonds and Criminal Justice in Colonial Philadelphia." *Pennsylvania Magazine of History and Biography* 100 (1976): 173–90.

Leubke, Barbara P. "Elias Boudinott, Indian Editor: Editorial Columns from the *Cherokee Phoenix.*" *Journalism History* 6 (Winter 1979): 48–51.

Malone, Henry T. "The Cherokee Phoenix: Supreme Expression of Cherokee Nationalism." *Georgia Historical Quarterly* 34 (Sept. 1950): 163–88.

Marzolf, Marion. "The Woman Journalist: Colonial Printer to City Desk." *Journalism History* 2 (1975): 24–27.

McMurtie, Douglas C. "The *Shawnee Sun:* The First Indian Language Periodical Published in the United States." *Kansas Historical Quarterly* 9 (1933): 339–42.

Meaders, Daniel E. "South Carolina Fugitives as Viewed through Local Colonial Newspapers with Emphasis on Runaway Notices." *Journal of Negro History* 60 (1975): 288–319.

Moore, Wilbert. "Slave Law and the Social Structure." *Journal of Negro History* 26 (1941): 171–202.

Murphy, Sharon. "American Indians and the Media: Neglect and Stereotype." *Journalism History* 6 (1979): 39–43.

Nelson, William E. "Emerging Notions of Modern Criminal Law in the Revolutionary Era: An Historical Perspective." *New York University Law Review* 42 (1967): 450–82.

Nichols, Roger L. "Printers' Ink and Red Skins: Western Newspapermen and the Indians." *Kansas Quarterly* 3 (Fall 1971): 82–88.

Nord, David Paul. "Teleology and the News: The Religious Roots of American Journalism, 1630–1730." *The Journal of American History* 77 (June 1990): 9–38.

Nordin, Kenneth D. "The Entertaining Press: Sensationalism in Eighteenth-Century Boston Newspapers." *Communication Research* 6 (1979): 295–320.

Norton, Mary Beth. "The Evolution of White Women's Experience in Early America." *American Historical Review* 89 (1984): 593–619.

Oldham, Ellen M. "Early Women Printers of America." *Boston Public Library Quarterly* 10 (1958): 6–26, 78–92, 141–53.

Paltsits, Victor Hugo. "New Light on 'Publick Occurrences': America's First Newspaper." *American Antiquarian Society* (April 1949): 755–88.

Parker, Peter J. "The Philadelphia Printer: A Study of an Eighteenth-Century Businessman." *Business History Review* 40 (1966): 24–46.

Preyer, Kathryn. "Penal Measures in the American Colonies: An Overview." *The American Journal of Legal History* 26 (1982): 326–52.

Price, Warren C. "Reflections on the Trial of John Peter Zenger." *Journalism Quarterly* 32 (1955): 47–53.

Reese, William S. "The First Hundred Years of Printing in British North America: Printers and Collectors." *Proceedings of the American Antiquarian Society* 99 (1989): 337–73.

Riley, Sam G. "A Note of Caution—The Indians' Own Prejudice, as Mirrored in the First Native American Newspaper." *Journalism History* 6 (1979): 44–47.

Roeber, A. G. "Authority, Law, and Custom: The Rituals of Court Day in Tidewater Virginia, 1720 to 1750," *William and Mary Quarterly* 37 (1980): 29–52.

Shaw, Donald Lewis. "AT THE CROSSROADS: Change and Continuity in American Press News 1820–1860." *Journalism History* 8 (1981): 38–50.

Shaw, Donald L. and John W. Slater. "In the Eye of the Beholder? Sensationalism in the American Press News, 1820–1860." *Journalism History* 12 (1985): 86–91.

Shiels, Richard. "The Feminization of American Congregationalism, 1730–1835." *American Quarterly* 33 (1981): 46–62.

Sloan, Wm. David. "Chaos, Polemics, and America's First Newspaper." *Journalism Quarterly* 70 (Autumn 1993): 666–81.

———. "The *New England Courant:* Voice of Anglicanism," *American Journalism* 8 (Spring-Summer 1991): 108–41.

Smith, Billy G. and Richard Wojtowicz, "The Precarious Freedom of Blacks in the Mid-Atlantic Region: Excerpts from the *Pennsylvania Gazette,* 1728–1776." *Pennsylvania Magazine of History & Biography* 113 (April 1989): 237–64.

Smith, David A. "Dependent Urbanization in Colonial America: The Case of Charleston, South Carolina." *Social Forces* 66 (September 1987): 1–28.

Smith, Jeffery A. "Impartiality and Revolutionary Ideology: Editorial Policy of the *South-Carolina Gazette,* 1732–1775." *Journal of Southern History* 49 (1983): 511–26.

Steffens, Pete. "Benjamin Franklin's Early Attack on Racism: An Essay Against a Massacre of Indians." *Journalism History* 5 (1978): 8–12.

Stephens, Mitchell. "Sensationalism and Moralizing in 16th and 17th-Century Newsbooks and News Ballads." *Journalism History* 12 (1985): 92–95.

Tannenbaum, Perry H. and Mervin D. Lynch. "Sensationalism: the Concept and Its Measurement." *Journalism Quarterly* 37 (1960): 381–92.

Towne, Susan C. "The Historical Origins of Bench Trial for Serious Crimes." *The American Journal of Legal History* 26 (1982): 123–59.

Ulrich, Laurel Thatcher. "Vertuous Women Found: New England Ministerial Literature, 1668–1735." *American Quarterly* 31 (1974): 55–78.

Vickers, Daniel. "Nantucket Whalemen in the Deep-Sea Fishery: The Changing Anatomy of an Early American Labor Force," *Journal of American History* 72 (September 1985): 277–96.

Vinoskis, Maris A. "Family Schooling in Colonial and Nineteenth-Century America." *Journal of Family History* 12 (1987): 19–37.

Walsh, Lorena S. and Russel R. Menard. "Death in the Chesapeake," *Maryland Historical Magazine* 69 (1974): 211–27.

Watson, Elmo S. "The Indian Wars and the Press, 1866–1867." *Journalism Quarterly* 20 (1943): 301–10.

Wax, Darold D. "The Image of the Negro in the *Maryland Gazette,* 1745–1775." *Journalism Quarterly* 46 (1969): 73–82, 86.

Weaver, David H. and John B. Mauro. "Newspaper Readership Patterns." *Journalism Quarterly* 55 (1978): 84–91, 134.

Wilson, C. Edward. "The Boston Inoculation Controversy: A Revisionist Interpretation." *Jounalism History* 7 (Spring 1980): 16–19, 40.

Yodelis, Mary Ann. "Boston's First Major Newspaper War: A 'Great Awakening' of Freedom." *Journalism Quarterly* 51 (1974): 207–12.

———. "Who Paid the Piper? Publishing Economics in Boston, 1763–1775." *Journalism Monographs* 38 (February 1975).

Zanger, Jules. "Crime and Punishment in Early Massachusetts." *William and Mary Quarterly* 22 (1965): 471–77.

Encyclopedia Entries

Douglas, J. D., ed. *New International Dictionary of the Christian Church.* Grand Rapids, Mich.: Zondervan Publishing House, 1978. S.v. "Deism," by J. W. Charley.

Foner, Eric and John A. Garraty, eds. *The Reader's Companion to American History.* Boston: Houghton Mifflin, 1991. S.v. "Triangular Trade."

Martin, Michael and Leonard Gelber. *Dictionary of American History.* Savage, Md.: Littlefield Adams, 1978. S.v. "Benjamin Rush."

Dissertations

Dyer, Alan Frank. "James Parker, Colonial Printer, 1715–1770." Ph.D. diss., University of Michigan, 1977.

Hewlett, Leroy. "James Rivington, Loyalist Printer, Publisher, and Bookseller of the American Revolution, 1724–1802." Ph.D. diss., University of Michigan, 1958.

Johnson, Warren B. "The Content of American Colonial Newspapers Relative to International Affairs." Ph.D. diss., University of Washington, 1962.

Kany, Robert H. "David Hall: Printing Partner of Benjamin Franklin." Ph.D. diss., Wayne State University, 1973.

Lorenz, Alfred Lawrence Jr. "Hugh Gaine: A Colonial Priniter-Editor, 1752–1783." Ph.D. diss., Southern Illinois University, 1968.

Meder, Mary Louise. "Timothy Green III, Connecticut Printer, 1737–1796: His Life and Times." Ph.D. diss., University of Michigan, 1964.

Murphy, Layton Barnes. "John Holt, Patriot Printer and Publisher." Ph.D. diss., University of Michigan, 1965.

Oller, Kathryn. "Christopher Saur, Colonial Printer: A Study of the Publications of the Press, 1738–1758." Ph.D. diss., University of Michigan, 1963.

Yarrington, Hollis Roger. "Isaiah Thomas, Printer." Ph.D. diss., University of Maryland, 1970.

Unpublished Papers

Bradley, Patricia. "Connecticut Newspapers and the Dialogue on Slavery: 1770–1776." Paper presented to the American Journalism Historians Association annual conference, St. Paul, Minnesota, 1987.

Copeland, David A. "Covering the Big Story: George Whitefield's First Preaching Tour, News Manipulation, and the Colonial Press." Paper presented at the American Journalism Historians Association annual conference, Lawrence, Kansas, 1992.

Sloan, Wm. David. "A Silence in Massachusetts: John Campbell and the Boston *News-Letter.*" Paper presented at the American Journalism Historians Association annual conference, Lawrence, Kansas, 1992.

Index